Robert Simpson Neighbors
And The Texas Frontier
1836-1859

Bust of Robert Simpson Neighbors (1815-1859) from a Daguerreotype of about 1851. Courtesy Mrs. R. S. Neighbors, Jr.

Robert Simpson Neighbors
And The Texas Frontier
1836-1859

by
Kenneth Franklin Neighbours

Published by

Waco, Texas

Bound
by
Library Binding Company
Waco, Texas

Acknowledgments

When I enrolled at Southern Methodist University in the spring of 1946, I found no entry in the card catalogue of Fondren Library for Robert S. Neighbors who was buried in my home county of Young. Since then I have been assisted by many friends in finding data.

First I am indebted to the late Mrs. Alice Atkinson (R. S., Jr.) Neighbors who made available her notes and pictures and encouraged me over the years.

Among those who read the manuscript critically were the late H. Bailey Carroll (who also instilled a love of trail tracing); Escal Duke, John N. Cravens, Sr., and Mrs. Horace Ledbetter. Mrs. Ledbetter also found what apparently remains of the diary of E. Z. Coombes for which I had wished. Chief reader was Rupert Norval Richardson whom I invited to cut ruthlessly. He cut things which he predicted would break my heart. He has also been helpful over the years. He was kind enough to correspond with me as early as my undergraduate days. He directed the thesis of Mrs. R. S. Neighbors, Jr. I am indebted to his pioneer work on the Comanche Indians which broke trail for everyone since on Indian affairs in Texas.

Along the trails I was assisted by A. W. "Buddy" Whiteley, Roy Scurlock, W. A. Springer, R. E. Lee, Sr., R. E. Lee, Jr., Earl Veal, J. N. Bennett, George Perkins, Ted Clark, Reuben Crenshaw, and his son, Reuben Dave, Henry Fletcher, Miss Elizabeth Cummings, Mr. and Mrs. Loyal Humphries, Mrs. O. L. Shipman, C. O. Froman, Jr., and especially Mrs. R. B. Durrill of Van Horne. She exchanged data, furnished a driver and vehicle, had an airplane stand by, and personally escorted me over part of the terrain in that area. I am particularly indebted to the trails historian *par excellence*, Mr. J. W. Williams who imparted lore, allowed me to tag along, and otherwise encouraged me in many ways.

Over the years I have been assisted by several generations of librarians and archivists at Southern Methodist University; the Library of The University of Texas, Eugene C. Barker,

Texas History Center, including Miss Winnie Allen, Dr. Llerena Friend, Dr. Dorman Winfrey, and Dr. Chester Kielman; The Texas State Library, Texas State Archives, beginning with Miss Harriett Smither and Mrs. Bertha Brandt through Dr. Seymour V. Connor, Mrs. Virginia Taylor, Dr. Dorman Winfrey, Dr. James Day, John Kinney and others; the National Archives; the Archivo General de la Nación; and many county archives. Others are especially noticed in footnotes.

The late Fred R. Cotten gave much valuable information and encouragement. Dr. James D. Carter gave Masonic data, as did Mr. F. A. Jenkins of Saint Albans Lodge No. 28 of Jackson, Louisiana, as well as Mr. Frank Oldham, Grand Secretary of the Grand Royal Arch Chapter of Texas.

Professor Guy B. Harrison, Jr. of Baylor University and Mr. Roger Conger of Waco were helpful in furnishing information. To these and all others I am very grateful indeed.

Prologue

Robert Simpson Neighbors came to the Republic of Texas in 1836 when he was twenty and lived less than a quarter of a century afterward, but into that brief space he crowded more activity than is ordinarily vouchsafed to most mortals until his earthly career was brought to a sudden, tragic close, and he passed to that "bourne from which no traveler returns." His activities embraced high positions of public trust in the army, the Indian service, and as a statesman. Neighbors was active in the formative period of Texas between the Revolution and the Civil War, and his course might have attracted more attention had not the space been so occupied by other luminaries.

Neighbors was prepossessing physically; his great powers were even said to amuse others. His mental powers were equal to his physical and his character was in keeping with the rest of his being. He was a true friend, loving husband and father, and kind master. His honesty and integrity were proverbial. Although he was a delightful and affable trail and camp companion, he seems never to have acquired a soubriquet, except the title of Major which he attained in the Army of the Republic of Texas and which one of his family remarked seemed to be a part of him.

The Major belonged to that small class of gentry denominated in his day as gentlemen whose simple republicanism was worn with a patrician bearing, and after whose name the courtesy title of esquire was appended. According to Colonel M. L. Crimmins, the training of the members of that class gave them the qualities and courage for leadership. The Major was a Methodist, a Mason, and a temperance leader. Clergymen noted that he was a devout Christian, yet not of the puritanical variety. Neighbors loved good music and dancing, convivial company, and on the proper occasions, such as the news of the birth of a fine son, the "cracking of a few balls of champagne" in celebration with his friends. The Major's training allowed him to mix with all classes and races of men, yet keep his proper station. He learned five languages including Indian languages and customs and was at ease in a tepee on the plains of Texas as well as in the drawing rooms of Washington. No one ever taught him to dissemble, or to compromise with what he considered justice and honor. As a consequence many storms raged around his head, and much of his career was involved in controversy.

Notwithstanding the obscurity of his boyhood, from the life of the man the conclusions may be reached that he was taught strict ethical and moral precepts; that a high sense of honor and integrity was imparted to him; and that he was given a sound education. The extent of his education is not known, but his official communications evince a fluent and forceful mastery of prose. His training fitted him for keeping careful account of large expenditures of public monies and for carrying out high missions of government. His intercourse with persons of high station indicated that he came from a background where the amenities of life were observed. His uncompromising convictions would bring him into vigorous conflict with other strong willed men.

Contents

Illustrations and Maps

Chapter I
Prisoner of Perote

The Republic of Texas to which Robert Simpson Neighbors came in 1836, in the visionary dreams of its Anglo-Saxon founders, sprawled over an immense and magnificent domain larger than any European country outside Russia. From the sandy beaches of the Gulf of Mexico on the south to Red River on the north, northwest in a long tongue of land to the forty-second parallel, and from the Sabine River on the east to the Rio Grande on the west, this great territory was drained by a network of rivers flowing southeasterly somewhat parallel to each other. The Sabine, the Neches, the Trinity, the Brazos, the Colorado, the Guadalupe, the San Antonio, the Nueces, and the Rio Grande, with all their tributaries made their way with many a bend to the waiting Gulf of Mexico. Another network on the north made a more circuitous route by the Mississippi to the Gulf: the Red, the Canadian, the Arkansas and their tributary streams.

The terrain varied from the low, flat stretches of the coastal plain to the towering peaks of the Davis and Guadalupe mountains; from the humid pine forests of East Texas to the semiarid Llano Estacado with its sea of grass. Between these extremes lay the great prairies, through which north and south ran fingers of timber known as the Lower (East) and Upper (West) Cross Timbers. Among the soils were found the sandy lands of East Texas, the black waxy dirt of the prairies, the rich alluvial deposits of the river valleys, and the tough sod of the Llano Estacado. The climate varied from the subtropical in the south to continental in the north, with subzero temperature in winter. The wide range of temperature and its sudden changes are said to give the people of Texas a high energy index, according to the late Professor Livingstone Porter.[1]

The people of Texas varied at Neighbors's arrival as much as the terrain. The preponderant Anglo-Saxons, numbering perhaps thirty thousand, with islands of the older Mexican settlements numbering three thousand among them, had

5

pushed their outposts out to a line roughly forty to fifty miles above the San Antonio Road. The outposts marking the limit of settlement stretched southwest from Nacogdoches in the east, through Fort Lacy, Fort Cook, Fort Houston, Fort Parker, Fort Milam, Tumlinson's Blockhouse, and Camp Colorado to San Antonio, and from that place southeast to Kinney's settlement on Corpus Christi Bay. The thinly settled region of Texas described roughly a long rectangle, encompassed by the hostile Mexican nation on the south and on the other sides by the many tribes of indigenous red men of doubtful friendship.

The Indians of Texas in 1836, among whom Robert S. Neighbors would spend the rest of his life, were divided roughly into two groups. In the woodlands of East Texas lived agrarian tribes, while on the plains of West Texas roamed nomadic aboriginals. Between these groups lived tribes who partook somewhat of the nature of both. A committee of the First Congress of the Republic of Texas reported the following information about the Indians of Texas. South of the San Antonio Road in the counties of Nacogdoches and Liberty lived the Coshatta, Alabama, Biluxi, and Muskogee tribes. In Nacogdoches and Shelby counties lived forty Huanies and Choctaws. In Nacogdoches County lived five hundred Kickapoos, Shawnees, Delawares, Patawatamies, and Minomminis. Above the San Antonio Road in Nacogdoches County on the waters of the Augustine, Neches, and Sabine rivers, lived about two hundred and twenty Cherokees. The tribes named above were emigrants from the United States. About two hundred and twenty-five Caddos, Ionies (Hainai), Anadarkos, and Nabadaches had lived in Nacogdoches County, but hostile whites had driven them out on the prairies. The Caddos had also emigrated from the United States.

The intermediate tribes on the prairies of central Texas were the kindred tribes of Wichitas, Keechies, Tawacanos, Wacos, and Towiash, Tawehash, or Tayovayas. These tribes had five hundred warriors, had been hostile for five years, and had captured white women and children. Farther west lived the nomadic Tonkawas, the Lipan and Mescalero Apaches. The Apaches had been pushed out of the plains by the Comanches to the mountainous region of West Texas. The Senatorial committee reported that it knew little of the true nomadic Comanches.[2] Bands of this tribe, however, roamed from Kansas to south central Texas. The Comanches by their exploits would presently give the Texans more data for their archives.

When Neighbors came to Texas in 1836 the country was in turmoil. The Anglo-Saxons, who peopled Texas under the leadership of Stephen F. Austin, along with some of the Mexican population, had fallen out with the Mexican government, and a resort to arms resulted. At the onset of the contest, the Anglo-Saxons drove the Mexican garrisons across the Rio Grande. But President Antonio Lopez de Santa Anna came in person at the head of an army which annihilated detachments of Texans at the Alamo, San Patricio, Refugio, and Goliad. Flushed with success, Santa Anna hurried after the little Texas army, which under the Fabian leadership of General Sam Houston retreated to the east. The Texans, catching the Mexican army off guard on April 21, 1836, at the San Jacinto River, disastrously defeated and captured it in eighteen minutes[3] to the cries of "Remember the Alamo!" "Remember Labardie (La Bahia)!" The captured Napoleon of the West was induced to order the other Mexican forces to retire beyond the Rio Grande and to sign a treaty recognizing the independence of Texas with the Rio Grande as the boundary.

Among the volunteers who rushed from the United States to aid their countrymen in Texas was a young Virginian, Robert Simpson Neighbors.[4] Extant records, which are incomplete, are silent on his military service during the Revolution. A half century after his death, a relative thought she remembered his saying that he was at San Jacinto.[5] The man listed on the surviving muster rolls, however, was Robert W. Neighbors.[6] Reliable authorities have stated that Robert Simpson Neighbors served in 1836 with a company of Colonel Robert M. Coleman's Regiment of Rangers on the Colorado frontier below present Austin[7] but this, too, was Robert W. Neighbors.[8] General Land Office records do not show that Robert Simpson Neighbors was granted land bounties for service in the Revolution. His land was granted under an act of January 4, 1839, which provided land to immigrants who arrived in Texas prior to November of 1841.[9] It is possible that Robert S. Neighbors served in the Texas Revolution, but the records do not show it. He left no statement of such service. As many others did, Neighbors may have arrived too late for San Jacinto.

The Neighbours family was of Huguenot origin whose French name was Voisin.[10] William Neighbours, Junior, was born in 1778 in Maryland. According to tradition he was sent back to Oxford to be educated, entered the ministry, and served for a time as a college professor in Virginia.[11] He married Miss Elizabeth Elam on July 31, 1800, in Charlotte County, Virginia, while his father was surety on his son's marriage bond.[12] William Neighbours, Junior, served in the War of 1812 and was in Baltimore in December of 1814.[13]

After the War of 1812, William Neighbours, Junior, returned to his farm on Louse Creek in the good tobacco area of Charlotte County, Virginia. To him and his wife were born at least seven children. The last child was Samuel Robertson (Robert Simpson Neighbors who dropped the u from his name), a blue eyed, fair baby boy, born on November 3, 1815, among the beautiful blue hills and valleys of Virginia,[14] and baptized into the Methodist Episcopal Church.[15]

When Robertson (Robert) was four months old, both his parents died of pneumonia.[16] William Neighbours, Junior, died intestate on April 1, 1816, and his estate "was committed to the hands of the sheriff for administration by the County Court."[17] Thomas P. Richardson, deputy sheriff, acting for Sheriff Thomas Pettus, held a sale of the household furnishings on April 25, 1816. The long list of articles sold gives a good picture of a Piedmont farm home in the early nineteenth century. Curiously, the sale was in pounds and shillings at that late date. Each child received a modest sum when the estate was finally settled in 1820.

Grandfather William Neighbours, Senior, having died shortly after his son, the older children were placed at various times under the guardianship of Morris Hamner, George Percivell and Charles Rainne. It was Charles Renne or Rainne who sued in the name of Nancy Neighbours to settle the family estate. From time to time the Charlotte County court authorized payments to various claimants for articles or care furnished the children. William and John died. Asa was bound out as an apprentice to one of his mother's relatives, Thomas Elam, until released by the court.[18] Nancy married Christopher Ash, of County Cork, Ireland, on March 12, 1821.[19] At the sale of her father's estate she had bought a pine chest, no doubt to keep her linens in. Mary married Lee Hughes. Asa Neighbours was still in Charlotte County, Virginia, as late as 1833[20], and had married firstly Rebeccah G. Green on January 3, 1831, and secondly, Mary Million on March 2, 1835. It is known that part of the family moved to Kentucky and then to Turkey Hill and Belleville, Illinois. A half century after his death, a relative thought she remembered that Robert remained in Virginia until he was nineteen.

The Charlotte County court placed the baby, Samuel Robertson (Robert Simpson) under the guardianship of Samuel

Hamner, a well to do, slave holding planter, who seemed to have provided well for him from the small portion of the family estate and doubtless from his own means as well. Among other things Hamner was paid accounts from the estate for the schooling of his ward to a Mr. Middleton for one year and a Mr. Jackson for nine months. Nothing else is known about the boyhood of Samuel Robertson or whether some future guardian changed his name to Robert Simpson Neighbors.[21] Fire destroyed a great bulk of records which might have thrown light on his early life. The remainder of his private records was placed in the Texas Memorial Museum in Austin.[22]

When Robert appeared in Texas as a young man of twenty, he had the characteristics of his family. A contemporary noted that he stood six feet two and was ruggedly built.[23] His picture showed his shoulders broad and square while his chin was strong and firm. His visage appeared solemn and determined, but good humor must have shown often there for there are references to his affable manners and fund of good stories. The blue eyes of the Neighbours clan were his. His hair color is unknown but some of his descendants had red hair.

In 1836 Robert came to Texas from Louisiana,[24] possibly in the company of other volunteers. Sometime later he returned to Louisiana where he found employment as a clerk in Jackson, West Feliciana Parish.

While living in Jackson, Neighbors petitioned to join St. Albans Lodge No. 28, of the Free and Accepted Masons. A committee consisting of A. M. Dunn, J. Rist, and J. E. L. Pegram reported favorably on the applicant. Neighbors was initiated on August 8, 1838; passed to the Fellow Craft degree on August 25, 1838; and was raised to the Master Mason degree on September 14, 1838.[25] To the day of his untimely death Neighbors remained an active and faithful member of the Masonic Fraternity.

Neighbors, after he moved to Houston, Texas, attended a called meeting of Holland Lodge No. 1 on October 12, 1838, where he was recorded in the minutes as a visitor from St. Albans Lodge No. 28, of Jackson, Louisiana. Among those present were Charles Mason, Secretary *pro tempore*, William G. Cooke, Worshipful Master *pro tempore*, Edwin Moreland, and J. G. Welschmeyer. These men would presently occupy high places in the government and armed forces of the Republic of Texas, and Neighbors would be associated with them. Neighbors was present at another called meeting of Holland Lodge No. 1 on October 25, 1838.[26]

9

Houston, the capitol of Texas in 1838, was already showing the enterprise that made it a metropolis in the twentieth century. According to John James Audubon, Houston in 1838 consisted of about 800 houses, some framed, but mostly unfinished log cabins. There were a few hotel accommodations, but most people lived in tents largely concealed in the tall weeds. The inhabitants, of many nationalities, protected their trousers from the foot deep mud by tucking them in their boot legs. On visiting President Sam Houston, Audubon found him busy examining papers.

> I was puzzled to understand how he could be so indifferent to his surroundings, the floor covered so deep in mud it could not be seen; papers and books were piled on two tables, and save a few chairs, there was no other furniture in the house. . .[27]

Neighbors took employment in Houston as a clerk in a mercantile establishment. Cornelius C. Cox, the fourteen-year-old brother-in-law of General Sidney Sherman, was placed in the same firm to further his education. Late in life Cox still remembered the kindness of young Neighbors who in this tent city took him to his own lodging. The accommodations, though only a loft over a building separate from the store, were better than the tents most had. Even so Neighbors could only offer his young companion a few blankets on the floor. After a night of warfare with the army of fleas which ubiquitously infested the city, the young mens' bodies were flecked and their clothes bloody. Houston was swarming with rats almost as large as prairie dogs, young Cox thought, which ran and squealed the live long night. Between fear of losing a nose or toe to the rats and fighting fleas, the young men got little sleep. Neighbors and Cox took their meals at a hotel near the bayou where onions supplied the lack of fresh vegetables. Years afterward Cox could remember the smell of onions which he and Neighbors met at every turn in Houston.[28]

On January 30, 1839, Robert Simpson Neighbors was commissioned a first lieutenant in the First Regiment of Infantry of the Army of the Republic of Texas.[29] It might be conjectured that Neighbors had had previous military education or experience but all efforts to determine this have been futile. It might be speculated that his acquaintance with persons of high station through his interest in Masonry had recommended him to a place of trust. Neighbors was sent to Fort Travis at the east end of Galveston Island, where he was soon made commanding officer of the post. The fort was a star redoubt armed

10

with fifteen guns, twelve and twenty-four pounders which fired "canister grape and round shot with sabots fixed for ammunition red hot shot from its furnace." Near the Texan fort were the remains of the fortifications of Jean Lafitte, marked only by a few hillocks of sand and mud. Treasure hunters had hastened the passing into oblivion. The wreck of his luxurious mahogany ship was also fast disappearing, as firewood for the Texan soldiers.

After a checkered career since San Jacinto, prospects seemed brighter for the Army. In 1840 it consisted of the field and general staffs, fifteen companies of infantry, and five companies of cavalry amounting to about five hundred men. Among the officers and enlisted men were individuals with whom Neighbors would be associated in other capacities for the rest of his life.

Among the military activities of the period were the expulsion of the Cherokees from East Texas; the massacre of Comanches at the Council House in San Antonio; the Plum Creek fight; and Colonel John H. Moore's two fights on the Colorado. Neighbors was assigned quartermaster and commissary duties after September 5, 1839. He served mostly in San Antonio, but was ordered from time to time to carry out assignments at other places such as Austin, Houston and Galveston. After June 6, 1840, his superiors addressed him by the title of major. His commendations by his superiors were always of the highest order.

Early in his career, Neighbors evinced his use of blunt speech in dealing with what appeared to be improprieties—a characteristic that would arouse strong feeling in other strong willed men. This is demonstrated in a bit of explosive correspondence between Major Neighbors and Lieutenant Colonel Adam Glendennin. The tiff was set off by the following peremptory note from Neighbors to Glendennin at Camp Cooke:

Sir:

There has been complaints made to this department of depredations committed by the soldiers, in cutting the corn from Col Karns Labor—You will take measures to find who the depredators are, and punish them for the same.

If prompt measures are not taken by the officers to prevent depredations on the citizens the officers will be held strictly responsibile for all depredations committed.

By order of the Quarter Master Genl.

Smarting from the cut, Glendennin fired back:

Sir:

I return you a copy of the document sent me this morning, with a demand that it be handed to Col. Cook Qr Master Genl. that he may know with what respect his emanuensis addresses his orders to officers of the same service. I presume *Sir* you must have been under the impression that the officers at this post were in partnership with the Soldiers in these depredations.[29a]

Neighbor's duties were not always routine nor pleasant. He once bought for the Army 500 pounds of corn from Alonzo B. Sweitzer near Austin.[30] When Major Neighbors appeared for the corn, Sweitzer told him that it could not be taken until the government paid him for another claim. The Major replied that as the corn had been paid for, he should certainly take it and directed his men to load the wagons. Sweitzer, prominent and irascible, assured Major Neighbors that the corn would be taken from him before he reached Austin. According to Randolph B. Marcy,

The major comprehended the import of the threat, and told the man he should encamp at a certain spring, where he could be found until nine o'clock on the following morning, and that he should be ready to receive any propositions he might have to make. He knew the man to be of desperate character, and anticipated trouble with him. He therefore, on the following morning, cleaned, recharged, and recapped his rifle, and awaited the issue.

Several heavily armed men rode up with Sweitzer who ensconced himself behind an unoccupied hut and fired several ineffective pistol shots at Major Neighbors. The officer's rifle missed fire twice, whereupon he coolly and deliberately pricked some powder in the cone and recapped while Sweitzer continued to fire. Neighbors fired at last, shooting his assailant through the brain, "and he fell dead in his tracks," in the words of Friend Marcy.

The men who accompanied Sweitzer had taken no part in the fight and congratulated the Major on ridding the neighborhood of a bad character. Captain Benjamin Hill was authority for the statement that Sweitzer was a "d--d mean man" and in the wrong when Neighbors killed him in the line of duty as quartermaster.[31]

The Value of the whole regular military establishment had long been questioned by the public generally, if an editorial

12

in the *Telegraph and Texas Register* was any gauge of public opinion. The editor deprecated the widespread lack of appreciation of the preparations to defend the country which he then detailed and averred that to break up these arrangements now "would not be economy but prodigality."

Such vigorous defense of the army did not save it and the navy from the ax of Congress which voted to disband the regular army establishment. Whereupon Secretary of War and Navy Branch T. Archer wrote with regret to Colonel William G. Cooke to proceed to demobilize.

In accordance with Archer's orders that all property be turned over to the quartermasters, Neighbors was retained in the service for the time being. William L. Cazneau, commissary general, wrote him:

> You are authorized and required to take charge of all public property where it can be identified—that in possession of Capt Hays, the Secretary of War authorized him to retain untill his return from the Rio Grande—
>
> It is absolutely necessay that Six or Seven thousand pounds of dried Beef should be delivered in this place by the 15th of May. You will make your contracts accordingly, on the best terms, the price is high, but the Beef must be delivered, without fail—& in packs of 100 lbs.—for which the Cost will promptly be paid on delivery.[32]

The order for seven thousand pounds of beef was no doubt in preparation for the Texan Santa Fe Expedition. This was a visionary project of President M. B. Lamar, who wished to make good the claims of Texas to her western boundary on the Rio Grande and to obtain for Texas the benefits of the Santa Fe trade.

The Major's connection with the Texan Santa Fe Expedition seems to have been mostly as quartermaster in gathering herds of livestock for the expedition. References occur to his paying of men for herding and branding of horses and beeves at such widely scattered places as Wells Bend of the Colorado, Camp Walnut Creek, and the camp on Little River. The government had several livestock brands: T.A., A.T., or composite T and A, all of which stood for Texas Army; T.C. for Texas Cavalry, and the lone star.

On June 20, 1841, the Texan Santa Fe Expedition consisting of the commissioners, William G. Cooke, Richard F. Brenham, and José Antonio Navarro, and four companies of troops under Hugh McLeod, left Camp Cazneau on Brushy Creek north of Austin for its destination, Santa Fe, "Texas." Major Neighbors little knew when he said farewell to his comrades in arms that he and they, after varying vicissitudes, would ere long be incarcerated in dungeons in Mexico.

With the army disbanded, Major Neighbors's records as quartermaster have few entries thereafter. He seems to have spent some time during the remainder of the summer and part of the fall in San Antonio, but his duties seem mostly to have been in Austin, where the records show he was furnished funds for fuel and quarters. He continued to receive the allowance for two servants and four horses. No doubt in Austin he attended the Masonic meetings of Austin Lodge No. 12, whose minutes are not extant.

President Lamar, on December 11, 1841, by and with the consent of the Senate, commissioned Neighbors a captain and quartermaster "in the service of the Republic of Texas," retroactive to July 15, 1840, effective during the pleasure of the President, for the time being.[33]

Two days later a new President, General Sam Houston, took office on December 13, 1841, for the second time. Congress proved as parsimonious as Houston's first. Expenses were pared to the bone. Salaries were cut and every official possible eliminated from the payroll. Neighbors seems to have drawn his last pay on December 20, 1841.[34]

About this time the country was disquieted by rumors of the disaster of the Texan Santa Fe Expedition which had been launched with such bright hopes. Then came confirmation from Commissioner William G. Cooke himself. Unexpected difficulties which beset the expedition led to its division still far from its goal. Thereafter treachery of one of its members and the deceit and guile of Mexican officials led to the piecemeal surrender of the dismembered parts of the expedition. Immediately upon surrender, the terms of capitulation, which among other things called for the expedition to be allowed to march back to Texas, were violated, and its members marched toward prison in the heart of Mexico, under conditions of needless brutality.

In a flurry of proclamations and conflicting orders the wily Old Sam joined in the popular reaction while seeking to control the situation. When he ordered General Alexander Somervell to take charge of the volunteers that had gathered at Bexar under Vice President Edward Burleson, with Major Neighbors serving as quartermaster, the troops refused to receive Somervell. When Burleson offered a second time to turn over the command to Somervell, he declined, since he did not wish to

14

subject himself to the mortification of a refusal to obey his orders. Whereupon Burleson from the Alamo ordered the army disbanded, and the return of impressed property to Major Neighbors.

Neigbors served six weeks as quartermaster with Burleson, and after the troops were disbanded with the privilege of enlisting under Somervell, Neighbors enlisted as a first lieutenant in Captain Lewis P. Cooke's Company of Mounted Gunmen, and served until April 27, 1842. As Captain Cooke was furloughed the day that Neighbors joined the company, Neighbors became the commanding officer for his period of service.[35]

After Neighbors enlisted in Captain John Coffee Hays's Company of Mounted Gunmen about August 15, 1842,[36] rumors became so strong that an invasion force was approaching San Antonio that Captain Hays took five of his men on a scout for the enemy. The Americans at San Antonio considered evacuating the town, but Hays asked them to remain until he sent back some word. Neighbors was left on duty in Bexar, it is supposed, to be present at the Fourth, or Western District Court, which had opened under Judge Anderson Hutchinson. Many previous courts had been broken up by Mexicans and Indians.

After Captain Hays's departure, a mass meeting was held at which a committee of Mexican citizens offered to determine whether the invaders were a regular force or bandits. A Mexican who accompanied the commissioners returned about nightfall with the information that he had approached near enough to the enemy camp to determine that there were about one hundred horses, when the commissioners asked him to return to town with that observation.[37] Since it seemed likely that the marauders were banditti, preparations were made for the defense of the town. One hundred Texas Mexicans organized themselves into a company under Salvador Flores. Seventy-five American Texans organized themselves into a company under Chauncey Johnson,[38] with Neighbors serving as first sergeant of this company.[39] The company slept on its arms at Sam Maverick's place on the corner of the public square.

About daylight on the morning of September 15, 1842, Neighbors and the other defenders were awakened by the report of a cannon, and prepared to receive the enemy. Presently music was heard, but a dense fog prevented sight of the foe. When it lifted enough for the Texans to see moving legs half way across the square, they opened fire. The Texas Mexican company under Flores fired also, but shortly thereafter,

15

José Antonio Menchaca, Texas veteran of San Jacinto, who was with the Texans, "cried out that the d----d Mexican friends had retreated." As the enemy advanced, his infantry and artillery fired at Maverick's corner. Another volley from Neighbors and his comrades threw the enemy column into disorder, causing it to retreat to the other side of the military square. The fog lifted enough for Neighbors and his friends to discern that they were contending against a large body of Mexican regular troops. Advancing under a white flag, Colonel José María Carrasco informed the Texans that they were fighting against 1,600 men under General Adrian Woll, whose terms were to surrender within ten minutes, or to be cut to pieces. The Texans sent Sam Maverick and W. E. Jones as commissioners to explain that they had supposed they were contending against robbers and to request that they be permitted to retire from the town under arms. Upon the requests being refused, the Texans decided to surrender upon the condition that their lives be spared; their property, except their arms, be respected; and that they be treated humanely, not as prisoners of war, but as gentlemen. Neighbors and his fellow Texans, numbering fifty-six, including Antonio Menchaca, were marched to the court house where they delivered up their arms and were placed under guard.[40] Neighbors, listed as quartermaster general,[41] gave up his rifle, a pair of holster pistols, and his pistol belt.[42] The Mexican loss was ten or twelve killed, twenty-three mortally wounded, and two crippled for life. James L. Trueheart, one of the Texan defenders, remarked tersely that the loss of the Americans was one dog and one hen.[43]

Four of the captured Texans, including Menchaca, were released. While Woll remained behind for further exploits, at sunset on September 15, 1842, the remaining fifty-two Texans including Neighbors, Judge Hutchinson and the entire court, were headed under guard for the Rio Grande.

In the camp on the Hondo, a good natured lawyer among the prisoners arose and suggested to Judge Hutchinson that since the entire personnel of the interrupted trial were present—judge, lawyers, principals, witnesses, and peace officers—that the sheriff be ordered to call the court to order and proceed from the point where they had been so rudely interrupted. The judge could not see even grim humor in the jest, and so far as the record goes, the case of Shields Booker vs. San Antonio was never resumed.[44]

Neighbors, along with his comrades, had his horse and saddle taken from him.[45] A few were supplied inferior horses, but

16

most walked. The men requested Woll to permit J. R. Cunningham, an attorney, to remain until he recovered somewhat from
a fever. Woll refused and Cunningham died on the Leona.
Neighbors and the other captives reached the Rio Grande on
September 22, 1842, where they bathed in the river, a source of
much pleasure after the long march.

Meanwhile Colonel Mathew Caldwell, a Santa Fe prisoner,
defeated Woll on the Salado near the rancho of Major
Neighbors. When fifty-three men from LaGrange under Captain Nicholas Mosby Dawson attempted to join Caldwell, Woll
raked them with artillery on the prairie, slaughtered thirty-
eight in cold blood after they surrendered, and marched the
mangled survivors to join Neighbors with the Bexar prisoners.
Later Samuel Walker, Thomas Jefferson Green, William A. A.
(Big Foot) Wallace, and the survivors of the retaliatory attack
on Mier swelled the ranks of prisoners with Neighbors. Their
ranks had been decimated by the drawing of black beans at
the well known episode at Salado.

While Neighbors and the other Bexar prisoners were at
San Fernando, Mexico, Woll arrived with the Dawson prisoners
including Edward T. Manton, but they were not allowed to
see each other for some time. Instead of being released here
as the Bexar prisoners had been led to expect, Neighbors and
his comrades were marched to prison in Mexico. The former
Santa Fe prisoners among the Bexar group were left to be
shot by Santa Anna's orders, but were saved by Woll's intercession. As Neighbors and his fellow captives wended their weary
way southward, their treatment varied with the change of
guards.

Neighbors and his comrades made long, weary marches by
day, followed by incarceration in indifferent quarters at night.
Once the place of rest was a granary; another time, a sheep
fold; another, bloody rocks where beeves had been slaughtered;
occasionally, an inn. Sometimes the Mexican rabble in towns
cursed Neighbors and the other captives; more often compas-
sion was expressed by kind words and deeds. At one point of
the journey, however, the prisoners were observed by a collection of runaway Texan slaves in a cornfield. One tall negro
man stretched himself to his full height, and cried, "Oh, white
man, you are catching hell now!"[46]

The journey southward carried Neighbors and his comrades
through barren, desolate country at times; at others, through
fertile, well cultivated lands, or well stocked haciendas. Mon-
clova was reached on October, 16, 1842; Saltillo on October

23; San Luis Potosi on November 23; the snow crowned peaks of Popocatepetl and Ixtaccihuatal were seen on December 13; Mexico City was sighted from San Juan Tihuacan on December 14; and Puebla was reached on December 17.

Neighbors and the other captives were ashamed to describe the shabby indifference of American citizens to their plight; but foreign subjects, especially Germans, were uniformly solicitous of the welfare of their fellow countrymen among the prisoners. Neighbors and the other prisoners at Puebla found a champion in a British subject. Sam Maverick noted in his diary that as they left Puebla under heavy guard on December 19, an Englishman followed them through the dense crowd. Maverick wrote:

> The brave old Englishman went out a mile or two cursing our guard and walking in our ranks, giving cigars etc. At last the officers tried to get rid of him. He drew his pistol and rushed upon them telling them of Waterloo, etc. and offering to fight them all: "I can whip six of you, carajos, etc." "Negroes imprisoning white men."

On December 22, 1842, Neighbors and the other weary prisoners reached the dread fortress of San Carlos de Perote, built by the Spaniards in 1773, in a barren valley high in the mountains between Puebla and Vera Cruz. This cold, dismal stronghold was to be the prison of Neighbors and his fellow captives for upwards of two years.

Neighbors and the Bexar prisoners were chained in pairs and incarcerated in two long, narrow cells on the east side of the castle. The cells were twenty feet wide by seventy feet long. The only light came from a small grate over the door which opened into the court and from a loop hole four by twelve inches which pierced the eight feet thick walls to the outside. In this dreary prison, Neighbors and his comrades passed Christmas of 1842, separated from friends and loved ones and suffering the anguish of imprisonment.

On January 4, 1843, Neighbors and the others were ordered out to work. They talked of refusing, but exercise in the open air was preferable to idleness in the cold cells. Neighbors and company, however, did not hurt themselves working. They were put to carrying sand into the castle, but sharp rocks plied furtively to the bottoms of the sacks made holes from which more sand streamed onto the ground than was carried into the castle. The captors were baffled by the sudden proclivity of the sacks to spring leaks. Hand barrels and carts were then provided for hauling the sand, but these were sabotaged also.[47] The principal occupation of Neighbors and companions soon became that of annoying their captors.

Every morning Neighbors and five of his comrades, including Big Foot Wallace, were hitched to a cart and escorted to the city market to procure supplies for the day. The "off lead" man of this six-man team seemed unable to resist the temptation of playing a practical joke upon the simple minded guards.

> As an instance, one morning, while they were being driven into the market, they were passing the stall of a very old Mexican woman, whose peculiarly fantastic costume, and shriveled, haggard countenance gave her more the appearance of a fiend than a human being. As soon as the *off leader* caught a glimpse of this hideous old woman, he cast a wink back at his comrades, and, suddenly raising his head and snorting like a horse, started off in a trot, sheering around her, and gradually turning his head in imitation of a horse who shuns a suspicious-looking object.[48]

The whole team bolted and ran a mile before the astonished guard could head them off. To the officer's indignant inquiry, the leaders claimed that they were frightened at the sight of the horrible looking old woman. When asked if he were not frightened, too, the officer slapped his breast and explained graniloquently that he was a soldier. On the return trip when the team showed signs of fright, the officer ordered two of his men to take the leaders "by the heads" and lead them circuitously around the old hag. Neighbors and his friends heard the officer tell his superiors upon his return to Perote that the Texans were not so brave after all.

Food for Neighbors and fellow captives was wretched. Twenty-five cents a day was allowed for each man by the Mexican government, but most of this went into the pockets of the corrupt governor of the castle. Occasionally a miserable, old cow was butchered. When the captives protested a snake bitten cow being butchered, the captain of the guard, José María Diaz de Guzman, replied, "Well, I'll not give you the snake bitten part." The captives had their revenge by caricaturing the captain upon the walls of their cells. One cartoon showed Guzman fishing up bowels from a kettle upon a fork, saying, "These are very good guts, Texians." The other officers laughed immoderately at the joke, but "Guts", as the Texans dubbed the captain because of his protruding paunch, almost exploded with ire.

According to Edward T. Manton, they ate all they could get and wished for more.

> Our breakfast consists of a piece of bread about the size of one of your biscuits, at dinner two pieces, a saucer of boiled potatoes and the broth with onions and red pepper in it with another sauce of rice, at night a saucer of beans and then comes on lock up hour until morning. We then have liberty of the yard during the day which enables those who have money to live quite well, there being a store inside where bread and other things can be bought; fruit is very cheap—12 oranges for 6 cents.[49]

With the unquenchable spirits of free souls, Neighbors and his friends celebrated Texan Independence Day of March 2, 1843, in prison. Thomas Jefferson Green spent has last dubloon to provide refreshments. Hen's eggs, ass's milk, *vino mescal*, and other dainties went to mix a potent eggnog. As the night wore on, the Texans became more and more uproarous and made the walls of the castle ring with song and shout. The guard threatened to fire upon them, and was told to shoot and be d---d. The alarmed captain hurried with his protruding paunch preceding him to learn the cause of the riot and was told that the captives were celebrating one of their saint's days. As the Texans did not interfere with his mode of worship, it was hoped that he would not interfere with theirs. "*Bueno, senior*," he replied and was about leaving when the Texans winked at William James Trimble to perform his star act.

> Trimble could mimic the look of an owl, and twist his head, and whoop, far better than the most eloquent owl upon the great Mississippi. This poor fellow, thus having the wink at the time that the guards came up, squared himself, rolled his eyes entirely over in the sockets, twisted his head "clean around" on his shoulders, and gave a whoop that beat the best of owls.
>
> Our burly captain turned round, frowned, and then hesitated whether to be mad or pleased, whether to laugh or swear, and, after a moment's hesitation, with a vacant look, he burst forth in an exclamation, 'Tecolote,' and moved on. The universal roar of laughter from our companions hurried him forward. '*Tecolote*', in native Mexican means 'screech-owl,' and thus poor Trimble carried the soubriquet to his grave.[50]

At Castle Perote Neighbors and his comrades found being chained to another person most disagreeable. The captives resorted to several methods of ridding themselves of their chains while in their cells. One was to bribe the smith to put lead rivets in the manacles, which could be removed at night. Another method was to pound the link of chain with a cannon ball upon a rock until the link came in two. When leaving the cell, the break in the chain was held in the hand to escape detection. When prison officials approached the cells, all hands sprang for their chains. The governor of the castle was told that it would take a smith for every Texan to keep them in irons. Santa Anna personally scolded a smith for dereliction. The poor smith protested that the best and largest irons were put on the Texans, but when the smith's head was turned, he said, the Texans laid their irons aside and did "just so" at him. According to Green,

> What the poor smith meant by "just so", in which he suited the action to the word, was the "you-can't-come-it-Judge" motion—a la Kendall. This motion is performed in the following scientific manner, to wit: place the extreme end of the thumb on the tip of your nose; then lock the little finger of your left hand into the thumb of your right, and with the four digits of the said right, give a quivering motion, as if you were performing upon the piano variations to the *Battle of Prague*; give a comical wink, and pronounce the talismanic words, *"You can't come it Judge,"* and you have it. This is what the Mexicans cannot comprehend, and you see them frequently practising it at one another with as imperfect a knowledge of its meaning as a Texian has of the *rationale* of animal magnetism.

One skilled Texan built a violin to whose music the prisoners danced to get exercise in their cells at night. He brought the instrument back to Texas where it is on display in the Texas State Archives.

According to Edward T. Manton, a daily chore was killing lice. He wrote:

> We are as lousy as we can be, make it a regular business every day to pull off our shirts and kill them; while I write my companion [Nathaniel W. Faison] to whom I am chained to is setting by me lousing himself. My clothes are so rotten and threadbare that they will hardly under go the operation of getting off and on.

On one occasion one of Neighbor's fellow captives, Isaac Allen imbibed too freely and strutting before the quarters of the governor of the castle, sang out at the top of his voice, "Viva la Texas!!", wrote Green.

> The old governor came out in the greatest rage, and sent for 'Guts' to know what that *land robber* meant by insulting

21

him in that manner; and threatened 'Guts,' severely on
account of his getting brandy. Old 'Guts,' full of wind and
wrath, brought out his guard at a charge bayonet, and rushed
Ike off to the solitary calaboose.

'Now,' says Guts to Ike, 'you bloody robber! I will keep you
here until you rot, unless you tell me where you got your
brandy from.'

'Well,' says Ike, 'I got it from you.'

'You audacious rascal!' says Guts, 'how dare you say so?
Don't you know it is false?'

Yes,' says Ike, 'I know it is false, Guts, but I will tell the
governor I got it from you; he knows how far you will go
for a *medio*, and will believe me; and I will swear it, too,
on the largest cross upon the Bible.'

'Not,' says Guts, 'upon the holy cross?' his eyes dilating
with horror at Ike's heresy and fear of the governor.

'Yes,' says Ike, 'I'll be____if I don't Guts: and, what is more,
the governor will give you____for selling me the aguardiente.'

Guzman swelled with anger, then thought of the governor and
cried, "Go out of here' I'll not have anything to do with such
a heretic."

On July 2, 1843, sixteen of Neighbors's fellow captives
escaped during the night from Castle Perote through a tunnel
they had drilled laboriously through the eight feet walls.
Thomas Jefferson Green and others made their way stealthily
to Vera Cruz and took ship to Texas via New Orleans.

Gloom and despair settled deep upon the remaining prisoners. The long confinement, poor food, vermin and unhealth-
ful, cold quarters took their toll of the health of the captives.
The miseries and the needless brutality of their guards, some
of whom were felons, did not cut as deep wounds in the spirits
of the Texan captives as did the selfish conduct of those of
their own fellows who assumed an air of superiority. This bale-
ful spirit exhibited itself in the form of some whom Manton
called Stars assuming aristocratic airs and segregating themselves in a small room from their fellows. When the good people
of Vera Cruz sent clothing to the Texans, L. Colquhoun, to
whom the articles were sent, allowed the occupants of the small
room to have first choice. Many of the others only got cast-off
rags of the first group.[51] Many of Neighbors's comrades were
seized with "jail fever" from which they became delirious and
violent. Some died while tied to their beds in the infirmary.
Severe headaches, high fever, and violent pain wracked the
bodies of the victims, then they lapsed into a coma lasting
for days. While the sick were helpless, they were robbed of

their scanty apparel and effects by the unscrupulous among their captors. Scarcely a day passed without a death.

Neighbors and the other captives, however, were not entirely forgotten. The American and British ministers, General Waddy Thompson and R. Packenham, cooperated in trying to alleviate the privations and sufferings of the Texans and from time to time obtained the release of small numbers. As a courtesy to his departure, Thompson obtained from Santa Anna the release of the remaining Bexar and Dawson prisoners on March 23, 1844. Neighbors and his thirty comrades set out next day for Vera Cruz. On the way they had an interview with Santa Anna at *hacienda de enero* where he supplied them with passports. At Vera Cruz United States Vice Consul L. L. Hargous personally advanced money to the destitute Texans and showed them many kindnesses. Neighbors and comrades went aboard the United States Brig *Bainbridge* where General Waddy Thompson awaited them. General Thompson further provided for the Texans from his own purse and extended them many courtesies.

Neighbors arrived at New Orleans on Friday April 12, 1844, where General Thompson was saluted with fifteen guns. Neighbors and his comrades created excitement wherever they went and were obliged to repeat many tales and answer many questions. They were provided with clothing, provisions, and other necessities by western visitors in the city. Citizens of New Orleans by public subscription raised $500.00 for the Texans, who after filling their most pressing needs, sent the remaining $300.00 to their Mier comrades still in Castle Perote. The *Telegraph and Texas Register* thought, "This noble act deserved to be recorded in enduring letters on the pages of Texian story." When Neighbors and twenty-three others arrived at Galveston on the *Neptune*, they were greeted with great enthusiasm and were treated as guests of the city. Houston was no less demonstrative when the former captives arrived there.

Neighbors again took up his residence in Houston where he resumed his place in the social life of the city. The minutes of Holland Lodge, No. 1, indicate that he attended from May of 1844 through January of 1845.

After some months Neighbors went into the hotel business. As the proprietor of the Mansion House, advertised as inferior to none in the South, he had the pleasure of entertaining some of the Mier prisoners who had been released recently from

Perote. Before January 8, 1845, the Major had ceased to operate the Mansion House.

After giving up the hotel business in Houston, he took up his residence in Washington-on-the-Brazos where President Houston had moved the seat of government. Neighbors at once associated himself with his Masonic brethren.

Once again Neighbors entered the public service of the Republic of Texas. On February 12, 1845, Thomas G. Western, superintendent of Indian affairs, handed Neighbors a commission from President Anson Jones to serve as agent to the Lipan and Tonkawa Indians.

The first phase of Neighbors's life in Texas, the military, had closed. Experiences fully as colorful and fascinating were in the offing.

Chapter II
The Red Man's Brother

The framework of policy in which Neighbors would work for years in the Indian service was laid at Houston's second inauguration. When President Sam Houston came to office on December 13, 1841, he sent out his agents to work with the Indians and to induce them to walk the white path of peace. The agrarian tribes were gathered at Bird's Fort on the Trinity, east of present Fort Worth, where a treaty of peace was signed on September 29, 1843. A year from that day President Houston himself met the same Indians, along with the southern Comanches, at the council grounds on Tehuacana Creek near Torrey Brothers Trading House, and concluded a peace treaty. An integral part of Houston's peace policy was the establishment of government licensed trading houses on the frontier where the Indians might come to trade for fair prices. This encouraged the Indians to fill their needs by trade rather than by plunder. The agrarian tribes agreed also not to come below the line of posts, but the Comanches would agree to no boundary.[1]

On Monday, December 9, 1844, President Sam Houston surrendered the reins of government to Anson Jones, the last President of Texas. When on February 12, 1845, Superintendent of Indian Affairs Thomas G. Western handed Neighbors his commission signed by Anson Jones, President, as agent to the Lipans and Tonkawas, Western instructed Neighbors to proceed to Bastrop, which seems to have been the designated headquarters of Neighbors. There he was to learn the whereabouts of the Tonkawas, assemble them for a talk, and remove them from the settlements to a location on the San Marcos River. He was to take the Tonkawas to the trading house occasionally and see that strict justice was done to them.[2] The Tonkawas had once been stronger and had ranged over Central Texas, but disease, poverty, and war with the Spaniards and the powerful Comanches had reduced the Tonkawas to a pitiable state indeed. The aggressions of the white man were pushing the

25

Tonkawas farther and farther out on the prairie in the path of the Comanches, thus grinding them between the upper and nether mill stones. The Lipans were a band of the Apache tribe which had been master of the plains until the contest with the Comanches.

Western's instructions to Neighbors thus initiated a new policy in Indian affairs. Hitherto, the Indian agencies had been residential. The agents located at fixed points such as trading posts where they ministered to the partly agrarian tribes. With Neighbors, Western initiated an itinerant agency or field system. The Indian bureau was under the department of war. Thus Neighbors was serving again under his old superior, William G. Cooke, now secretary of war and marine. Neighbors had done business as quartermaster of the Army of the Republic of Texas with merchant Thomas G. Western, now superintendent of Indian affairs.

Western was soon pleased with the progress of the Tonkawas under Neighbors's supervision. Western ordered the agent to arrest one Pennington, an illicit trader who had led the Delawares into the settlements to trade, while representing himself as their agent. Western instructed Neighbors to keep the Delawares out of the settlements until their own agent, Benjamin Sloat, could come for them.

> These refractory spirits must be subdued and the sooner you begin the less trouble you will have with them. While you treat them with kindness, be firm, you have the strong arm of the Law to sustain you with the military to support you if Necessary.[3]

A month later Western wrote Sloat that, "The notorious 'Pennington' as I am informed by Agent Neighbors is no more, he *died* on the Guadalupe, as he says." Neighbors sent Delaware Bob and his band wending their way eastward to Agent Sloat at his agency at the council grounds at the Falls of the Brazos. Major Neighbors had not allowed Pennington and the Delawares to trade a single article in Bastrop.

After being with the Tonkawas long enough to gain their confidence, Major Neighbors discovered the basis of their superstitious aversion to farming. Using all his persuasive powers, Neighbors, at the peril of his life, got the chief to allow him to secrete himself in the lodge where the most sacred rite celebrating the origin of the tribe was held. Soon about fifty warriors dressed as wolves entered and after sniffing around over the ground, to the astonishment of the agent, dug up a live Tonkawa (previously interred for the performance). A council of sage old wolves was called.

The Tonkawa addressed them as follows: 'You have taken me from the spirit land where I was contented and happy, and brought me into this world where I am a stranger, and I know not what I shall do for subsistence and clothing. It is better you should place me back where you found me, otherwise I shall freeze or starve.'

After mature deliberation the council declined returning him to the earth, and advised him to gain a livelihood as the wolves did; to go out into the wilderness, and rob, kill, and steal wherever opportunity presented. They then placed a bow and arrows in his hands, and told him with these he must furnish himself with food and clothing; that he could wander about from place to place like the wolves, but that he must never build a house or cultivate the soil; that if he did he would surely die.

This injunction, the chief informed the major had always been strictly adhered to by the Tonkawas.[4]

When not actually fighting the Tonkawas, the Comanches treated them in a most insolent and domineering manner. While Neighbors was with the Tonkawas, a band of forty Comanche warriors led by Old Owl rode into camp. At the chief's lodge, the Comanches demanded "in a most abrupt and dictatorial manner" that their horses be cared for and supper prepared, as they proposed to spend the night. The orders were obeyed with alacrity, and forty of the best looking Tonkawa maidens were assigned to entertain the guests.

Neighbors used the opportunity to establish friendly relations with the Comanches, explaining his functions as agent, and expressing the desire of the government for peace, especially with the Comanches. The chief replied that the whites were great rascals, but he liked the Major and especially his coat. The Major understanding the import of the compliment, made him a present of it. Others expressed their admiration for portions of his clothing, until Neighbors stood forth in only his shirt. The Major laughed heartily at their grotesque appearance as they strutted about with portions of his recently acquired wardrobe upon their tawny figures. The Comanches were so pleased with his generosity that they proposed to adopt him into their tribe and to take him along on a horse stealing raid among the Mexicans. Neighbors went along hoping to prevent depredations. The party came to the rancho of an old Mexican where Neighbors applied for beef, telling the Mexican that he would be paid by the government. The Mexican, who refused to comply unless paid in advance, was apprised by Old Owl that unless two beeves were forthcoming within half an hour, the rancho would be burned and all the beeves taken. Needless to say the beeves were produced forthwith. Neighbors soon tired of the safari and took his leave.[5]

In what was probably his last report to Superintendent Thomas G. Western before Texas ended its national existence and united with the United States, Agent Robert S. Neighbors summed up the progress of the Lipans and Tonkawas. The two tribes were occupying vacant lands between the San Marcos and San Antonio rivers. The Tonkawas had made great improvement under Western's instructions to Neighbors. Compared with their former state, the Tonkawas were in a happy and thriving condition. He had largely overcome their prejudice against farming, and they were anxious to be located on land that they could call their own, where they might be instructed on the vocation of farming. The Lipans were also anxious to be settled, but in the meantime, they would plant corn again at their own town on the Cibolo. The Major recommended that both tribes be settled on land and taught the arts of civilization. In view of the coming change of government with annexation, Neighbors urged that the matter be expedited. Neighbors never lost sight of the objective until he had carried it out, although it would eventually cost him his life. Both tribes had been asked to attend the council at Comanche Peak where the United States Commissioners Pierce M. Butler and M. G. Lewis wished to meet all the Indians of Texas.[6]

Shortly thereafter, on February 18, 1846, Superintendent Thomas G. Western made his final report to Secretary of War and Marine William G. Cooke in whose department the Bureau of Indian Affairs was placed. On the day that the Republic of Texas was no more, February 19, 1846, President Anson Jones, the last President of Texas, signed the last voucher of Thomas G. Western, superintendent of Indian affairs. With that act there passed from sight the man who had achieved so much in the interest of the Indians in Texas. Many exacting experiences awaited Neighbors in the Indian service after annexation.

Neighbors became involved in making the first United States treaty with Texas Indians after Texas entered the Union. In the fall of 1845, Pierce M. Butler and M. G. Lewis were authorized to make an expedition into Texas to try to bring its Indians into treaty relation with the United States. The belligerent attitude of Mexico made it imperative that peace be maintained along the Indian frontier. Butler failed to get a military escort from General Matthew Arbuckle at Fort Gibson, but was able to enlist the services of prominent members of the Five Civilized Tribes.[7]

Butler's party entered Texas by way of Coffee's Fort, or trading house at Preston on Red River, near present Denison, and proceeded southward to the council grounds near Torrey's Trading House on Tehuacana Creek, arriving in February of 1846. The party was joined by the Texas agents, R. S. Neighbors, L. H. Williams, and John F. Torrey. Neighbors had with him the Tonkawa Indians, and Jim Shaw, the noted Delaware scout and interpreter.

Neighbors and the other former agents of the Republic of Texas were in an anomalous situation. The government which had commissioned them had ceased to exist. Butler retained the services of Neighbors and the other Texas agents for the time being.

The expedition set out for Comanche Peak, six miles southwest of present Granbury in present Hood County, and runners were sent to find the Comanches who were in no hurry to sit in council. Comanche Peak is only thirteen hundred feet above sea level, but from its summit one can see as far as the eye will allow. To the discerning eye, Comanche Peak can be identified at least as far as fifty miles.

Butler and Lewis decided not to hold a general council at Comanche Peak, but to use it as a point from which to contact the various tribes so that a time and place could be agreed upon for a grand council. Parties of various tribes dropped by to look in upon the commissioners and to sample their food. With a number of Lipans and eighteen Tonkawas, Neighbors arrived at the peak on February 17, 1846, with "warriors and women armed with lance, bow and quiver, red painted, flags dragging the ground."[8] The Comanches had been shy of coming into council since the Council House massacre in 1840. They declined all overtures to meet the United States commissioners until Senator Sam Houston sent Neighbors with the ring and casket, the symbols which Houston had told the Comanches would indicate the lawful authority of anyone representing himself as an agent of the government.

The Comanche chief, Buffalo Hump, with two hundred Comanches came to Comanche Peak at the end of February. Butler held his first conference with them on March 5, 1846, at which the chiefs, evincing much tact and caution, indicated that Barnard's Trading House near present Waco would be a suitable meeting place, set the time as the next new moon, which would put the meeting in early May, and departed on the night of March 9, 1846, much pleased with the presents they had received.

Neighbors was present for the council at the mouth of Tehuacana Creek on the Brazos below present Waco. At the conclusion of the council, a treaty was signed on May 15, 1846, by the United States commissioners and the chiefs of the Comanches, Ionies, Anadarkos, Caddos, Lipans, Tonkawas, Keechies, Tawacanos, Wichitas, and Wacos. The treaty was witnessed by Robert S. Neighbors, Hugh Rose, John H. Rollins, Thomas I. Smith, E. Morehouse, Louie Sanchez, John Connor, and Jim Shaw.

According to the terms of the treaty, which was to guide Neighbors throughout his career, the United States might license traders to go among the Indians; the Indians must give up all white and negro prisoners; the whites must give up all Indian prisoners; felons of either race must be tried by law; horse stealing by either race must be stopped; trading houses might be located upon the borders of the Indian country at the discretion of the President; peace must be maintained; those guilty of introducing ardent spirits among the Indians must be punished according to the laws of the United States; and the President might send blacksmiths, teachers, and preachers among the Indians, who were to protect them. The amount of presents to be given the Indians that fall was left blank in the treaty. The Senate filled in the sum of ten thousand dollars.[9] Sam Houston charged upon the floor of the United States Senate that while Butler was ill, Lewis persuaded the Indians to mark a blank piece of paper, which Lewis filled in later to suit himself. Houston charged that the amount promised orally to the Indians was an annuity of $14,000.[10]

Neighbors was selected to accompany a delegation of the most important chiefs to visit Washington and other points in the east to impress upon the Indians the power and resources of the United States and to acquaint them with the operations of the national government. Among the chiefs were Old Owl and Santa Anna of the Comanches and José María of·the Anadarkos. The party arrived at Washington, D.C., about June 25, 1846. Lewis and Neighbors stayed at the Globe Hotel, while quarters were found for the Indians in the suburbs where they would have more room and be less annoyed by the crowds. Illness delayed Butler's arrival in Washington until July.

The Indians grew restless especially after some of them fell sick. Neighbors started back to Texas with the Indians about July 26, 1846; reached Nachitoches, Louisiana, on August 13; Fort Jessup, Louisiana, on August 25; and Torrey's Trading House on August 30, 1846. After Neighbors gave the chiefs the horses they had ridden, they scattered in haste to their tepees on the prairies.

Butler and Lewis had promised the Indians that their annuity would be given them at the council grounds on Tehuacana Creek in the fall. In accordance with Commissioner W. Medill's instructions, Major Neighbors met the Indians of Texas at the Council Springs.

The Indian delegation, in its exuberance over the trip to Washington and the promises of presents, invited friends from far and near to come and receive them. Nearly 3,000 Indians appeared at Torrey's Trading House at the appointed time. Congress adjourned, however, without appropriating the money, and Neighbors was given the onerous chore of telling the Indians of the default of the government. The disappointed chiefs told Torrey that, as he was a white man, he would be held responsible for the promises of the white man's government. Unless the promised presents arrived within a given period, the goods would be taken from his establishment in reprisal. An express was sent to Senator Houston, who authorized the Torreys to issue goods to Indians in the amount of $10,000. When the Indians returned, they were met by Neighbors, J. C. Neil, T. I. Smith, and L. H. Williams, were given their presents, and then departed to the prairies in fine spirits. Congress later appropriated funds to pay for the gifts.[11]

When war between the United States and Mexico broke out over the Texas boundary, Governor J. Pinckney Henderson took command of the troops requisitioned by General Zachary Taylor to serve under his command in Mexico and relinquished the authority of his office as required by the Texas constitution to Lieutenant Governor A. C. Horton. Acting Governor Horton wrote President James K. Polk that Texas besides troops to defend its frontier needed a United States Indian agent:

> I beg leave, in conclusion, to recommend to your Excellency Robert S. Neighbors Esq. for the office of Indian Agent. He has great experience in the Duties of this Office, an intimate personal acquaintance with the various tribes, and possesses their confidence in every respect. I have no hesitation in saying that a more suitable person could not be found.[12]

Major Neighbors made his headquarters as Indian agent at what the Indian bureau of the old Republic of Texas had designated as Post No. 2, located at Torrey's Trading House. This trading house was one of a series authorized by the Republic of Texas under the Treaty of Bird's Fort. The trading houses served as headquarters for the Indian agents, as military intelligence posts, and as outlets for the peltries taken by the Indians. It was intended that these trading houses should enable the Indians to provide for their needs legitimately instead of by the war path. The Indians came to exchange peltries for cutlery, cloth, powder and lead, hoes, axes, trinkets, and other objects. The trading houses served as centers for assembling the tribes for councils with the government. There was usually an abundance of grass, fuel, and an established transportation and commissary system which made the trading houses useful for council purposes. When the Indians came to trade, the Indian agents used the opportunity to obtain intelligence of the condition and movements of the various tribes.

Neighbors remained in the Indian service under the direction of the governor, apparently in the service of the state. Early in January of 1847, he brought Governor Henderson, who had resumed office, information from Torrey's Trading House that bands of Apache Indians had intruded into Texas from west of the Rio Grande. These intruders had scattered along the headwaters of the Colorado River, whence Governor Henderson wanted them evicted, lest they set up a claim to territory. Henderson sent Neighbors to inform the intruders that they must leave the state. At the same time, Henderson recommended to Secretary of War W. L. Marcy that Major Neighbors be continued in the service of the government as Neighbors, Henderson said, could do much to keep the Indians quiet.

> The various tribes in Texas know him well and have more confidence in him than they would have in a Stranger. I would also suggest the propriety of giving him power to employ Jim Shaw the Indian before referred to. He speaks the languages of most of the Indian Tribes in the State and is known to them all.[13]

While on this mission, Neighbors visited the new German colony above San Antonio on the waters of the Guadalupe and Pedernales. This colony had been planted under the auspices of the *Verein zum Schutze deutscher Einwanderer in Texas*, or Society for the Protection of German Emigrants to Texas, variously called the *Mainzer Verein* or *Adelsverein* organized between April 12, 1842, and March 24, 1844. Under the leadership of such men as His Highness, the Prince Carl von Solms-Braunfels and Ottfried Hans, Freiherr von Meusebach, lands on the frontier of Texas had been purchased and settlements established.[14] Neighbors found the leaders of the colony preparing to complete their land surveys, which would expire if not completed before September 1, 1847. These lands were in the Fisher-Miller grant, which was a part of the hunting grounds of the Comanches. The German leaders "were under the impression that a force would be necessary and had commenced organizing the German colonists into companies to force the surveys."

When Governor Henderson learned that the Germans were preparing to enter the Comanche range with a military force, he feared that a general Indian war might ensue while the United States was engaged in the Mexican War. The governor requested Major Neighbors to hasten to dissuade Ottfried Hans [John O.], Freiherr von Meusebach, the director, from the venture. If this could not be accomplished, Henderson wished the Major to assist Meusebach in making an agreement with the Comanches.

On arriving at Fredericksburg on February 5, 1847, Neighbors found that Meusebach and 40 well armed men had departed ten days before, and in keeping with Henderson's orders, set out to overtake him. Doctor Ferdinand von Roemer, a German geologist and naturalist of note who asked permission to join Agent Neighbors, arrived at Neighbors's camp, four miles northwest of Fredericksburg on February 6, 1847. The Indian agent was accompanied by Jim Shaw and two pack mule drivers, one a young white man and the other a Shawnee.[15]

Jim Shaw, or Bear Head, as his Delaware name meant, was described in 1854 by William Parker, who said:

> He was the finest specimen of the Indian I saw during the trip, about fifty years old, full six feet six in height, as straight as an arrow, with a sinewy, muscular frame, large head, high cheek bones, wide mouth, and eye like an eagle—his countenance indicative of the true friend and dangerous enemy.

Major Neighbors and his companions proceeded rapidly after Meusebach through the bleak countryside. Neighbors and his party crossed the clear, rapid Llano and proceeded to the San Sabá. There in a valley on February 10, 1847, according to Roemer, Meusebach's party was found peacefully encamped in its covered wagons and tents near Ketumee's Comanche camp of tepees.

When Neighbors informed Meusebach of Governor Henderson's message, Meusebach felt that the Americans might be a little jealous of the Germans and declared that he thought the danger had been overdrawn. Then Meusebach invited Neighbors to remain with him and assist in negotiating with the Comanches.

On the following day, the Comanche head men held a council with Meusebach, who was assisted by Major Neighbors, while Jim Shaw acted as interpreter. This camp was only a small band of the southern or Penateka Comanches, and none of the principal chiefs was present. After stating his peaceful intentions, Meusebach expressed a desire to continue up the San Sabá to the old Spanish fort, the Presidio de San Louis de las Amarillas, and upon his return, to hold a council with the principal chiefs, Santa Anna, Mope-choco-pe, and Buffalo Hump. The terrain became so rough that Meusebach sent the wagons and most of his men back to Fredericksburg, while Meusebach and Neighbors continued with a party of seventeen mounted men. On February 18, 1847, as Neighbors and his companions were travelling through the prairie, the party suddenly saw through the mesquite trees the walls of the old Spanish fort looming up in front of them, at present Menard. On the advice of Jim Shaw, Neighbors and his companions remained at the fort site a day drying meat, as it was known that their improvident Comanche hosts could not feed them. On the return journey, Neighbors, with the sharp eyes of the frontiersman, bee lined a bee tree which was robbed of enough honey to supplement the ration of dried meat, but enough was left to carry the bees through the winter, as was the custom of the settlers.

On February 28, 1847, the party observed the main Comanche camp in a valley about twenty-five miles from the mouth of the San Sabá. A herald met the party and conducted it to a camping site, where Neighbors and Meusebach were visited by the three principal chiefs, Mope-choco-pe, Buffalo Hump, and Santa Anna. Santa Anna had recently made a trip to Washington, D. C. with the Major, which, it was expected, would incline Santa Anna to be conciliatory.

At the council next morning, Neighbors heard Meusebach offer one thousand Spanish dollars for the right to establish a settlement on the Llano, and the right to survey the land north of that river, especially the valley of the San Sabá. After a consultation of the chiefs, Mope-choco-pe stated that an answer would be given the next day.

At the council next day, the cautious, distrustful Comanches accepted Meusebach's proposals, after having discussed them from all angles. After the council Meusebach entertained the chiefs with a meal of venison and rice. That night Neighbors and his companions were entertained with a farewell but weird serenade, which Roemer said sounded more like a charivari and consisted of monotonous chanting to the sound of a drum.

On the return trip south to Fredericksburg, Neighbors and Meusebach were overtaken by Santa Anna with his wives and other Comanches. When the Comanches saw that the party's days of affluence were over, one of them brought in a wild horse from the hunt, which most of the white men found palatable. The return trip to Fredericksburg was made without event and ended March 7, 1847.

In a communication to Commissioner W. Medill, Major Neighbors summed up the eventful expedition into the Comanche territory in the following two cryptic sentences:

> For your information, I here state—That Gov. Henderson, apprehending serious difficulty with the Comanches about the 1st of Feby last, from the introduction of settlers and the surveying of that section of Country granted to a German Company, by the late Replic of Texas in 1841-2. Whilst at war with the Comanche Tribe (a part of said Grant being now inhabited by the Comanches), The Said Company was compeled to complete their Surveys by 1st Sept. next or forfeit their claims, they were under the impression that a force would be necessary, and had commenced organizing the German Colonists into companies to force their Surveys—Gov. Henderson solicited my interference. I immediately met the Comanches, and succeeded in forming the preliminaries of a friendly arrangement which is to be carried into effect the 1st of May.

The last sentence puzzled Rudolph Leopold Biesele and Irene Marschall King who dwell upon the role of Meusebach which certainly should be recognized in the final treaty making. Biesele assured me, however, that he was sure that he had not given Neighbors sufficient credit. Meusebach thought that the Americans might be a little jealous of the Germans. It may be the other way around. Rupert Norval Richardson and others acknowledged the accomplishments of Neighbors. Neighbors himself buried the episode in two cryptic sentences in a long report while Roemer wrote thirty-eight printed pages. As for Neighbors's statement about the formation of German military companies, Biesele describes their formation by

Solms and their use by Meusebach. F. Shubert had already entered the Comanche country with an armed force while Biesele stated that Meusebach had with him a mounted company of well armed men. Neighbors had one interpreter and two pack mule drivers.

Having agreed with the chiefs at the council to meet them at the formal treaty conference,[16] Major Neighbors returned to Fredericksburg in May of 1847 with the trader and Indian agent, John Torrey, Jim Shaw, and John Connor, Delaware scouts and interpreters, for the drawing up and signing of the treaty between the Comanches and the Germans. According to the treaty, they agreed to visit each other's settlements on the Llano; and the Germans were to be allowed to survey the land as far as the Concho, or to the Colorado if Meusebach saw fit. In consideration of these concessions, Meusebach agreed to pay one thousand dollars in money and to supply the Comanches while in Fredericksburg for the treaty making, which it was estimated would amount to another thousand dollars. Among those signing the treaty were J. O. Meusebach, R. S. Neighbors, F. Schubert, J. Torrey, Jim Shaw, John Connor, Santa Anna, Buffalo Hump, Old Owl, and Ketumse.[17] The treaty was signed on May 9, 1847.

On April 13, 1847, Major Neighbors had received a communication dated on March 20, 1847, from United States Commissioner of Indian Affairs W. Medill which stated that the Major had been appointed United States special Indian agent for Texas.[18] The fact that a special agency was created, that the appointment was made by the secretary of war instead of by the President and confirmed by the Senate, and that the appointment was for a year only, indicated that the United States had formulated no permanent policy for the Indians of Texas.

During the spring of 1847, Agent Neighbors received a directive from Henry R. Schoolcraft of the Bureau of Indian Affairs requesting information about the Indians. Congress had passed an act on March 3, 1847, authorizing a study of the Indians of the United States. Neighbors called upon David G. Burnet, first President of the Republic of Texas for information. Neighbors himself wrote a good sketch of the Comanches in the limited time that he could devote to the matter. The Major's report was styled by the editors as, "The Na-u-ni, or Comanches of Texas; Their Traits and Beliefs, and Their Divisions and Intertribal Relations," and was published in Schoolcraft's work called, *The History, Condition and Prospects of the Indian Tribes of the United States.* In his report Neighbors described the Comanches, their country, customs, religion, language, and many other matters. Neighbors's report is still of interest to scholars.[19]

Neighbors set out on his tour of the prairies, and arrived on May 22, 1847, at the principal village of the Comanches, which he said was about one hundred miles north of Austin. The head chiefs, Pah-hah-yuca, Mope-choco-pe, and Pochanaquahiep, and the principal men were present in the village. The head chief, presumably Pah-hah-yuca, met Neighbors some distance from the village and gave him a cordial reception. In the course of the council next day, Neighbors read and explained the Butler and Lewis treaty as it had come mangled from the Senate. Strong feeling arose when the chiefs learned that the Senate had stricken out Articles III and V. Article III forbade white men to enter the Indian country, while Article V gave the tribes the right to send delegations to Washington when their interest required it.

Major Neighbors arrived on May 30, 1847, at the village of the Caddos, Ionies, and Anadarkos situated on the Brazos forty-five miles from Torrey's Trading House. This distance by trail would indicate José María's village sixteen miles west of present Hillsboro. Neighbors found the Indians well satisfied and friendly, cultivating large fields of corn and apparently in a prosperous condition. The village consisted of about one hundred and fifty houses built of wood and covered with grass. Before visiting the Wacos, Wichitas, Tawacanos, and Keechies, who had been committing depredations, Major Neighbors applied to Captain Marshall Saxe Howe for an escort of Rangers, which was denied. The agent then engaged six Delawares and obtained from José María six Anadarkos under the second chief, Powiash or Towiash. José María himself would have gone but for a painful fall from his horse.

With this small band of friendly Indians, Neighbors arrived on June 10, 1847, at the village of the hostile bands. This was Keechi village on the left bank of the Brazos ten miles west of present Graford in Palo Pinto County. There Neighbors assembled the chiefs, boldly demanded the stolen horses, and threatened the chiefs in the strongest terms, if they did not comply with his request. At the council which followed, the Indians agreed to deliver up the stolen horses in accordance with the treaty of 1846. Fifty-three head of stolen horses were recovered, and the Wichita chief promised to send to the village on the Wichita River for the remainder of the animals. Towiash and John Connor ably assisted Major Neighbors who had confidence in the durability of the present friendly relations, but expressed greater confidence in the proposed line of military posts on the frontier to keep the Indians in check.

Because of financial difficulties, the Germans were not prompt in paying the Comanches the money promised in their treaty. The Major was said to be much displeased with the default, according to F. Schubert, one of the leaders.[20] When four surveyors were killed on the Llano, the Germans concluded that the Comanches did the crime in retaliation for the delay in paying them. The surveyors were working under Robert Hays, the brother of Colonel John Coffee Hays. From San Antonio Colonel Hays offered Major Neighbors every aid in his power to arrest the murderers.[21]

Major Neighbors, who was on his way to the Indian country when he received Hays' letter on July 16, 1847, reached the scene of hostilities to find that the Comanches had fled with all their possessions in the direction of the "Grand Prairie" to the north. The Major followed the trail two hundred fifty miles above the settlements before turning back on the assurance of Jim Shaw and the Delawares that it was imprudent to follow the Comanches farther. The agent reiterated his recent warning to his department that trouble would ensue unless the boundary question were settled to the satisfaction of the Comanches. Neighbors called upon the governor of Texas for aid in keeping the surveyors out of the Comanche land, but was told that there was nothing the governor could do legally.[22]

Agent Neighbors, determined to find the Comanches to settle the difficulty, set out from Austin to Torrey's Trading House on August 10, 1847. There were several branches of Torrey's Trading House. One was at New Braunfels; one on the North Bosque; another at the Falls of the Brazos about five miles below Marlin; and one on Tehuacana Creek. Butler and Lewis referred to the post as being at the mouth of Tehuacana Creek on the Brazos which is south of Waco, while later research has located it about eight miles south east of Waco at the mouth of Trading House Creek, a tributary of Tehuacana Creek. The company of Torrey and Brothers consisted of John F., David and Thomas Torrey.

Neighbors continued his journey to the Comanche country on August 20, 1847, and arrived three days later at the village of the Caddos, Ionies, and Anadarkos. This was either at the

38

later site of Fort Graham, or José María's later village below Kimball's Bend in Bosque County. The Indians were friendly but suffering from the drought which had caused a crop failure. Large quantities of liquor had been introduced among them. At the Keechi village on the Brazos about one hundred seventy-five miles above Torrey's, or about ten miles west of present Graford, Neighbors found the Pawnees, Caddos, Ionies, Keechies, Wacos, Tawacanos, and Wichitas assembled "for the purpose of holding a grand medicine dance, which was in full operation at the time of my arrival, and continued for four days afterwards." Major Neighbors found the Indians indigenous to the region in a flourishing condition since they had fine crops of "corn, beans, pumpkins, melons, &c." The Indians received the Major and his party in a friendly manner, furnished them provisions, and invited them to the dance. The Indians manifested every desire to abide by the agreement which had been made with Agent Neighbors in June.

Heavy rains detained Major Neighbors at the Keechi village several days. On September 2, 1847, Old Owl, whom the Major designated as the second chief of the Comanches, arrived at the village with several chiefs and a large party. (It was the custom of the Comanches to visit the agrarian tribes at harvest time and eat them out of house and home.) From the Comanches Neighbors learned that the cause of the Comanches' flight was in part the trouble with the Germans over the surveying of land, as Neighbors thought. The flight was induced mostly, however, by the intrigue of Mexicans in San Antonio. Major Neighbors held a council of all the Indians at the Keechi village on September 6, 1847, and announced that the presents intended for them at the coming council had arrived and would be distributed on September 25, 1847, the next full moon. The announcement was hailed with general satsifaction. The Major learned that Buffalo Hump had gone on a raid into Mexico about the first of August and was still absent with from six to eight hundred warriors.

While Neighbors was at the Keechi village, a party of six white and Indian traders arrived from "east of Red river," with forty gallons of whiskey and a quantity of powder and lead to trade to the Texas Indians. The agent had no force with which to arrest the rascals, but caused them to flee with their contraband by threatening to induce the Indians to confiscate the goods and put the traders to death. On his return route to Austin, Neighbors encountered a party of Cherokees, with six kegs containing thirty gallons of whiskey, who were on their way to trade at the Caddo and Ioni village. The agent seized the liquor and destroyed it. Neighbors reminded the Indian commissioner that he had no definite instructions for dealing with the liquor traffic, and added:

In the absence of all law regulating intercourse with our wild bands, and the serious difficulties attending the introduction or ardent spirits into their country, I shall be compelled, for self-preservation and the protection of our frontier settlers, to deal with the traders in the most summary manner. Not wishing to do so, until full notice was given to all concerned, I have, thus far, confined myself to the destruction of the spirits, and warning the offenders of the consequence of the second offence.[23]

Indian affairs in Texas were singular. Texas at annexation kept its public lands. No right of the Indians to land in Texas was recognized beyond that of tenants at will. The laws of the Republic of Texas regulating intercourse with the Indians were inoperative, and those of the United States were never extended to Texas. This anomalous situation brought on an undesirable impasse of several years duration, while the United States government by its inaction tried to force Texas to provide lands for the Indians. Professing to believe that Indian hostilities in Texas were caused by the state's failure to provide land for the Indians, the United States authorities assumed a dilatory and lackadaisical attitude toward depredations in Texas, it seemed to Texans, and not without basis.

The problem of jurisdiction became acute when white men insisted upon intruding into Indian country. Neighbors submitted the question to Governor J. Pickney Henderson who tried to revive the intercourse laws of the Republic of Texas and declared

the laws of the late 'Republic of Texas' regulating intercourse with the Indians to be in force, and designated a temporary line about thirty miles above our highest settlements as a point 'above which no white person should be allowed to go unless for legal purpose.'[24]

The line designated by Henderson in 1847 pleased neither whites nor Indians. Neighbors had Ranger officers to evict several white men from land the Indians had been cultivating, but was finally told by Captain S. P. Ross that Colonel Peter Hansbrough Bell, the commanding officer, forbade Ross to interfere with the intruders. Old Owl's wrath also was stirred by the unilateral line.[25]

40

The Indians assembled at Torrey's Trading House, as Neighbors had directed them to do, on September 25, 1847. On September 28, 1847, Neighbors distributed presents to an estimated 2,200 Indians of the Comanches, Ionies, Caddos, Anadarkos, Wacos, Keechies, Wichitas, Tawacanos, Tonkawas, and bands of Delawares, Shawnees, and Cherokees resident in Texas, and some few Biluxies, Kickapoos, and Pawnee Mohaws. Considerable numbers of citizens were present as well as Lieutenant Colonel P. H. Bell. Sixty chiefs were present, including Pah-hah-yuca, Mope-choco-pe, and Santa Anna. Buffalo Hump was still absent in Mexico with a large body of warriors. The day before the council, at which the presents were distributed, Neighbors assembled the chiefs to whom he read and explained the Butler and Lewis treaty. The agent avoided as much as possible any questions of land and boundaries, but assured the chiefs that the government would settle the matter in good time to their entire satisfaction.

Neighbors made his itinerary among his charges as unwearyingly as a Methodist circuit rider, encouraging, chiding, or rebuking as the circumstances warranted. Neighbors made repeated efforts to recover Cynthia Ann Parker, captured by the Comanches in May of 1836, at Parkers Fort, near present Groesbeck. The friendly chiefs promised many times to deliver her up, but never did so. Cynthia Ann was thought to be with the Tenawish band of Comanches with whom the southern Comanches had but little contact. Neighbors said:

> I have used all the means in my power during the past summer to induce those Indians to bring her in, by offering large rewards, but am assured by the friendly Comanche Chiefs that I would have to use force to induce the party that has her to give her up. She is now about 18 years of age. It would be an act of humanity, if the Department could restore her to her friends, all other white persons have either died or been set at liberty with the above exception. She is the only one I can hear of among the 'Prairie Tribes.'[26]

When Neighbors set out again to find the Comanches on January 31, 1848, his itinerary took him far out on the prairies and far up the Brazos to present Baylor County. Old Owl, who had sent for Neighbors, met him about fifteen miles from camp and received him in the most friendly manner. As it was late, Old Owl spent the night with Neighbors on the prairie in order to guide him to camp next morning and to protect him from the Comanche bands that had declared themselves hostile.

The hostile bands were the Tenawish, Noconas, and a small portion of the Penatekas over whom Old Owl had no control. On returning from a recent raid on Mexico, these bands heard from the Lipans that the Comanches were at war with the Texans, Old Owl explained, and attacked a Ranger camp of Captain J. S. Sutton. The horses these bands stole were taken from them by the chiefs at the main camp, so that the animals could be turned over to government officials. The renegades threatened to steal horses until the chiefs tired of returning them. On the next raid, the Rangers killed two Comanches. Then the brother of one of the slain killed a man and his wife near San Antonio in retaliation. Old Owl warned Neighbors to be on guard when he reached the Comanche camp, as a Tenawish chief, brother of a Ranger victim, wished to kill Neighbors and his companion, John McLennan, the Major's interpreter. "Bosque John" was captured when six years of age by the Keechies and became a warrior and expert horse thief. After his recovery, he became a valuable interpreter and well-to-do farmer. He was the nephew of Neill McLennan for whom the county is named.[27]

Major Neighbors, along with John McLennan, Jim Shaw, and Old Owl arrived on February 14, 1848, at the main Comanche camp on Lewis Creek, locally called Plants Creek, which empties into the Brazos at present Seymour in Baylor County. Neighbors found in the camp about two hundred and fifty Comanche lodges, fifty Tonkawa lodges, and ten Wichita lodges. The Penateka chiefs were present and warmly welcomed Neighbors, while the Tonkawas expressed the intention to defend Neighbors to the death. The great chief Pah-hah-yuca, head chief of the Tenawish and Noconas, arrived in the evening, bringing with him the hostile Tenawish, Nocona, and Kotsoteka chiefs, in order to put an end to hostilities. Each chief was gravely presented to Neighbors with the customary ceremony. That night Old Owl made a feast in his lodge, as he said he wished Neighbors and the estranged chiefs to eat and be friends just as the Major and the Hois or Penatekas were friends. Then the chiefs and Neighbors made speeches. The speeches of the old chiefs were doubtless more polished, but the young Tenawish chief's speech was quite effective.[28] Neighbors said that as the evening wore on, he

> found them to be a very jovial set, and the evening was spent in eating and smoking, and the discussion of the usual themes among the prairie bands, viz: 'war and women,' finding myself in the end, upon a good understanding with them.[29]

At a council next morning, the chiefs professed a desire for peace, but pleaded their inability to prevent their warriors from stealing horses occasionally, and suggested that nothing more be said about stolen horses. Neighbors refused to entertain this proposition, and warned the chiefs they would be held to strict accountability until the stolen horses were returned. Until such restitution was made, the Comanches would be considered hostile if they approached the settlements. Old Owl later returned part of the horses. After taking leave of the Comanches, Major Neighbors came back by the settlements of the small agrarian tribes on the Brazos.

Major Neighbors found all the tribes on his itinerary disturbed by rumors set afloat by Kickapoos and Seminoles. These United States Indians, under the instigation of the Seminole Wildcat (Coacoochee) and Alligator, spread rumors that the whites intended to drive the Indians out of Texas. The wily Wildcat had on foot a project to found an Indian colony in Mexico, and was preparing the way for recruits. The Kickapoos always fled upon the approach of Major Neighbors, although the Texas Indians pressed them to stay. The Major arrived back at Torrey's Trading House on March 1, 1848. He had been gone thirty days on his itinerary, and had visited every tribe in Texas except the Lipans on the Rio Grande. Everywhere the Indians assured him of their friendly intentions.[30]

Major Neighbors made a journey to Austin in early April of 1848. When he arrived on April 10, he learned that the Lipans wished him to visit their camp on the headwaters of the Guadalupe. About one hundred miles above Austin, however, the Major fell in with the principal chief of the Lipans, Chiquito, who stated that he was on his way to Torrey's Trading House to assure Neighbors of continued peaceful intentions. The agent said he talked with the Lipans at great length about their long absence from council and the doubtful position they had occupied. Chiquito stated that after Captain Bezaleel W. Armstrong attacked the Lipans last August, they had joined the Apaches on the Pecos, and were afraid to approach the white settlements until Neighbors's assurance of friendship reached them through friendly Indians. Since the Lipans were disposed to peace, and had committed no act of aggression, he accompanied them to Torrey's where he made them presents.

The agent, in view of the many attacks upon the Indians by the Rangers, deemed it proper to require an escort which Lieutenant Colonel P. H. Bell furnished for him to visit the

Wichitas. Neighbors took with him Captain Shapley Prince Ross and some thirty Rangers. In present Palo Pinto County, Neighbors visited the camp of Had-a-bar's band of Caddos, who had been located at that point on the Brazos for twenty-one years. This village, still known as Caddo Village in the twentieth century, was at the mouth of Caddo Creek on the right bank of the Brazos opposite from the Keechi village in the northwestern corner of present Palo Pinto County.[31] The Wichitas and Tawacanos, who lived north of the Caddos, were visited next. Then Neighbors set out to visit the Wacos who lived on the other side of the Brazos at a distance of about eight miles, at the mouth of Waco Creek, in what is still known as Waco Bend of the Brazos in the southeastern corner of present Young County.[32] The river had gone into high flood and was impassable. When the rations were exhausted and some of the Rangers grumbled at the diet of watermelons and roasting ears, Neighbors directed Ross to send the men home. Twenty-five were sent back in charge of Alpheus D. Neal.[33]

In about a week the Brazos fell, and Neighbors ordered the party to accompany him across the river to vist White Feather, Chief of the Wacos, who gave a Masonic sign as he approached, much to Captain Ross's astonishment. White Feather came forward to meet the white men a short distance from his village, and invited them into a large circular wigwam of grass. Captain Ross, D. C. Sullivan, and Fred Kirke went in with their arms on. When White Feather observed this fact, he remarked that it was unusual for armed men to enter a council room. When Neighbors's interpreter, L. H. Williams, interpreted White Feather's comment, Ross replied that the party came to fight, not to treat. Things looked squally when warriors filed into the council room with their bows strung under their blankets, and occupied the platforms around the inside edge of the wigwam which were used at night for beds. Jim Shaw expected trouble and protested, "Maj. Neighbors, the government of the United States pays me $500 a year to interpret, and not to fight."[34]

Neighbors proceeded to accuse the Wacos of horse stealing. Ah-ha-dot asked whether the Major supposed that people accustomed to stealing all their lives could be broken of the habit all at once. Ah-ha-dot averred that reconstruction must be done little by little. The stolen horses had been gathered up and that was all he could do, the chief stated. Accordingly, eighteen horses were delivered up to the agent after the council.

When the talk ended, White Feather invited Neighbors's party to a feast. The Indian who acted as master of ceremonies plunged a long, sharp stick into the kettle and brought up corn meal dumplings.

> He would carefully lick off any thick, watery substance adhering to the viand, and then make a deposit in the wooden bowl. Len. Williams had the bad manners to express a hope that, the sergeant would not lick his dumpling, but he reckoned without his host: the sergeant was equally polite to all.

While the feast was in progress, a white man made his appearance in the festive circle. Neighbors asked his name, residence, and business. The man replied that his name was Miller, that he was from the Indian territory, and that he had come to trade with the Indians. "Trade what?" asked the Major. "Whisky," replied Miller. Neighbors closed the colloquy by observing tersely that:

> 'You know it is against the law to sell whisky to Indians. It is my duty to visit your camp, and ascertain whether you have whisky. I shall be there in the morning, and if I find things as you say, I shall hang you.' The visit was made, and Miller was missing.

Farther down the country near present Weatherford, Neighbors came upon a party of four Cherokees with five or six kegs of whisky for trade with the Texas Indians for horses. The Major assured the Cherokees the traffic was illegal and dangerous to the people of Texas. When Neighbors ordered the "busthead" poured on the ground, Ross saw one of the Cherokees inspecting his gun and knew he meant to fight. Ross, Sullivan, and Kirke closed in on the Cherokees, pistols in hand, while others spilled the liquor on the ground.

On the next trip, Major Neighbors, taking Captain Ross and fifty troops, penetrated via Fort Graham to a point Neighbors estimated to be three hundred miles west of Torrey's Trading House. Neighbors, learning from Old Owl that Santa Anna and Buffalo Hump were near Double Mountain Fork of the Brazos, resolved to visit them, as some of their men had been responsible for stealing horses from the Ranger companies of Captain Samuel Highsmith and Captain H. E. McCulloch for which the Lipans and others had been unjustly blamed. Old Owl accompanied Neighbors on the journey. At Hubbard's Creek, in present Stephens County, Ketumse, a war captain in Santa Anna's band, was encountered on October 8, 1848. Ketumse joined Neighbors on the trip to Santa Anna's camp.

At the Comanche village or camp, on the Clear Fork of the Brazos, Neighbors was well received by Santa Anna and the other chiefs. The Major inquired about the clashes between the Comanches and the troops. The chief who led the warriors most of the time was pointed out, and Neighbors directed his question to him. Kar-wa-be-bo-we-bit, or Can-See-Nothing, replied that it was the fault of the troops. The Comanches, he said, had made peace with the whites, but not with Mexico. The white troops were stationed on the Comanche war trails, and attacked the Comanches without provocation, the chief said.

Can-See-Nothing was a signatory of the Butler and Lewis treaty of 1846. He readily admitted that it was he, and not the Lipans, as had been alleged, who stole the horses from Captain William G. Crump's company, but he declined to give them up, as he said he had lost horses in the skirmishes. Buffalo Hump also declined to cease raiding in Mexico, for he said one of the Mexican captains had one of his daughters and refused to give her up. Neighbors said he endeavored with only parital success to persuade the Comanches to avoid the country between the Rio Grande and San Antonio. The chiefs did promise to visit the military stations in peace first and ask for permission to pass.

Since the Comanches admitted to Neighbors that they had been responsible for the difficulties between the whites and Lipans, Santa Anna agreed to meet with Neighbors and a delegation of Lipans in San Antonio in order to rectify the misunderstanding between the Lipans and Crump's company of Rangers. The facts in the case were these: Can-See-Nothing brought the horses stolen from Crump's company to the Lipan camp. Chiquito protested that the Rangers would follow the trail to his camp and attack his people. Can-See-Nothing replied that he did not care, as the Lipans acted as guides and scouts for the troops, when they attacked the Comanche camps. The Rangers trailed the stolen horses to Chiquito's camp, and attacked the Lipans without trying to talk with them. Chiquito said that if he had been given the opportunity, he would have joined the Rangers in the purusit of Can-See-Nothing.

According to Santa Anna's promise to Major Neighbors, a small party of Comanches met him in San Antonio, but the Lipans did not appear. Neighbors then sent his interpreter, Jack Harry, a Delaware, with a few Comanches to the Lipan camp to invite the Lipan chiefs to meet Neighbors at Torrey's Trading House.

Chiquito at Torrey's stated to Neighbors that he came to make peace. Chiquito then explained that the hostility of the Lipans had been caused by the attack upon them by the Rangers of Lietenant H. M. C. Brown who followed Can-See-Nothing's trail to the Lipan camp. Thirty Lipans were killed, and two hundred of their horses were taken. Chiquito and his people fled to the Rio Puerco, or the Pecos, and retaliated upon the Texans. Chiquito recalled that the last man he killed had saddle-bags and probably lived on York's Creek in DeWitt County. Neighbors and Ross recognized the victim as Captain John York. Neighbors charged, "that was not the last; you killed a man near where I live, and cut him all to pieces." Chiquito vigorously denied this accusation. Chiquito blamed the Tonkawas, two of whom, he said, were seen with a leg tied to each saddle. Chiquito denied that his people were cannibals, and agreed to face the Tonkawas in the matter.

When Neighbors and Major Ripley A. Arnold, United States Army, assembled the Tonkawas, Chief Placido appealed to his people to confess, if any were guilty of the crime. Two warriors arose and confessed, but pleaded in extenuation that the man killed was not a white man but a bearded one, a German. Neighbors was unable to prevail upon Arnold to arrest the culprits. Instead Arnold made Placido and Campo responsible for the production of the bodies of the malefactors when requisitioned. If they were not forthcoming, Placido and Campo would be taken instead, Arnold declared. The chiefs protested that they had no place to confine the men, while Arnold had a guard house. Arnold was adamant. Placido and Campo concluded that safety lay in flight, and at the same time stole twenty-one horses from the neighborhood. The chiefs wandered from tribe to tribe, but no one would receive them. After some months the chiefs gave themselves up. No punishment was meted out to them, as no blame was attached to them.

In February parties of the small agrarian tribes visited Neighbors at Torrey's Trading House. These Indians wanted Neighbors to tell them where to settle for the year, and he advised them to settle on the Brazos near Comanche Peak in De Cordova's Bend. The Major expected the settlement to have concentrated at it the Caddos, Ionies, Anadarkos, Wacos, Keechies, Tawacanos, Cherokees, Creeks, Shawnees, and Delawares. At Neighbors's suggestion, George Barnard, who had bought out Torrey, agreed to establish a branch of the trading house at the settlement, just below De Cordovas Bend

47

on the left bank of the Brazos, and began making preparations to move.[35]

According to some sources, Neighbors was supposed to have accompanied Colonel John Coffee Hays on his expedition to Chihuahua, which took place between August and December of 1848.[36] It has been shown, however, that Neighbors was on the Texas frontier transacting Indian affairs during the period in question.

On December 26, 1848, Major General William Jenkins Worth, said to have been the most brilliant general of the Mexican War, landed at Galveston to take command of the Department of Texas.[37] The next day Worth wrote Commissioner of Indian Affairs W. Medill that among the official papers left by his predecessor, none attracted his attention more than those relating to Indian affairs.

> I cannot discover that my predecessor has taken any action on the several reports of Major Neighbors, acting Indian Agent & Lt Col Bell, recently commanding the Texas Rangers on the frontier, and the orders of the dept of War thereon: but enough appears to satisfy my mind that an agent is indispensably necessary to preserve the quiet of the border, who shall faithfully represent the General Government in its civil capacity, and from a careful examination of his correspondence, I feel strongly that Major Neighbors is precisely the man for the place—I beg your prompt consideration in this matter, and if you agree with me, in the estimate of the Major's fitness to endeavor to secure his appointment. I have not the slightest knowledge of him other than what is derived from his correspondence, from which I infer that he is intelligent, humane & firm.[38]

Major General Worth and Major Neighbors found in each other kindred spirits, who quickly established the happiest concert of action. Before Worth made any disposition of the forces which were to operate against the Indians, he consulted Neighbors. Worth consulted him also in locating troop stations where they could best aid the Indian agents. All matters relating to Indian affairs were freely discussed between the two officials, whose cooperation was facilitated by the fact that Indian affairs at that time were administered by the war department. To aid him in his policy making, Worth had Neighbors report from time to time on the state of Indian affairs in Texas. For example, in late winter of 1849, Worth requested Neighbors to give him a census of the Indians in Texas.

From frequent inquiry among the Indians, Neighbors estimated there were 20,000 Comanches with 4,000 warriors; 1,500 Kiowas with 300 warriors; 500 Lipans with 100 warriors; 1,400 Caddos, Ionies, and Anadarkos with 280 warriors; 300 Keechies with 60 warriors; 1,000 Wichitas, Wacos and Tawacanos with 200 warriors; 650 Tonkawas with 130 warriors; 650 Delawares and Shawnees with 130 warriors; 50 Creeks with 10 warriors; 25 Cherokees with 5 warriors; making a total of 29,575 souls with an estimated 5,915 warriors.

General Worth acting on orders from Washington, D.C., to open communication to the West, also requested Neighbors to explore a wagon route to El Paso through "a section of country hitherto deemed impassable." Secretary of War William L. Marcy, for whom Fort Marcy in New Mexico was named, ordered General Worth to have examined the country between San Antonio and Santa Fe for a road and to establish a fort in the vicinity of El Paso.[39]

This mission led Neighbors into exploits which marked him as one of the trail blazers of West Texas.

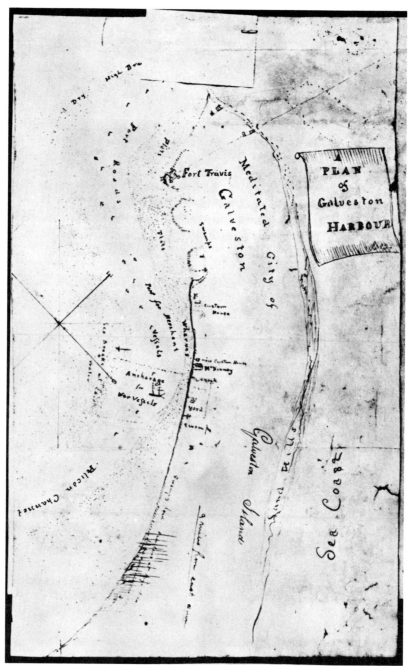

Plan of Galveston Island showing Fort Travis. Texas State Archives.

Presidio or Fuerte San Carlos de Perote built by the Spaniards
to guard the Royal Road between Veracruz and Mexico City.
Built in 1773.

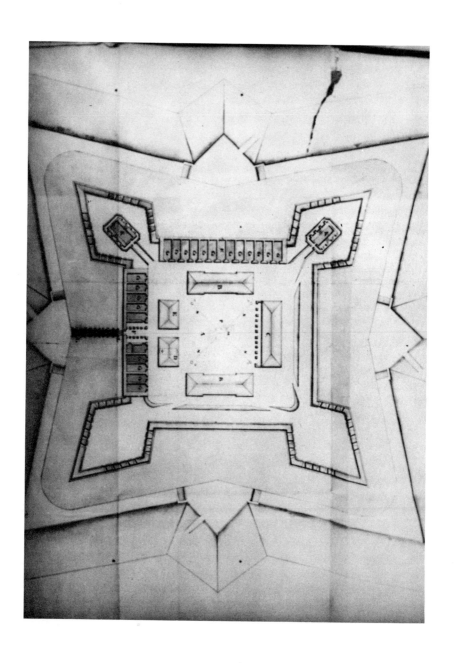

Plan of Fuerte San Carlos de Perote. Archivo General de la
Nacíon.

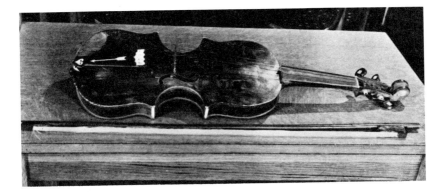

Violin made at Perote by Mier prisoner, Henry Journeay. Presented to the Texas State Archives, Texas State Library, by his son. Courtesy Mrs. R. S. Neighbors, Jr.

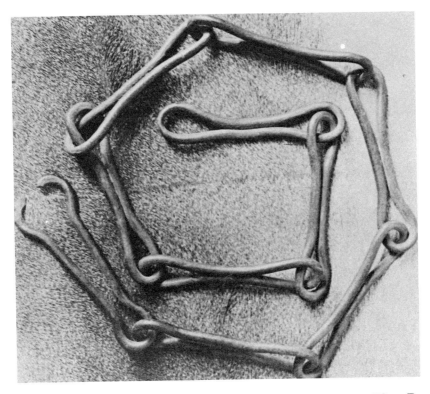

Chains worn by Samuel Maverick at Perote. Courtesy, Mrs. R. S. Neighbors, Jr. through the Library of the University of Texas, Archives Division.

Edward T. Manton, 1820-1893, Dawson Company, Perote prisoner. Courtesy William A. Cooper, his great grandson.

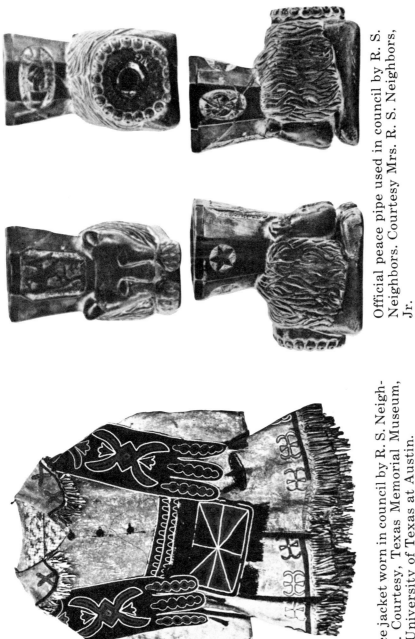

Official peace pipe used in council by R. S. Neighbors. Courtesy Mrs. R. S. Neighbors, Jr.

Peace jacket worn in council by R. S. Neighbors. Courtesy, Texas Memorial Museum, the University of Texas at Austin.

Comanche Peak. Hood County.

56

Indian artifacts Major Neighbors brought his children. Background, Ross Simpson Neighbors, Senior, the son he never saw. Courtesy Arthur Donaldson.

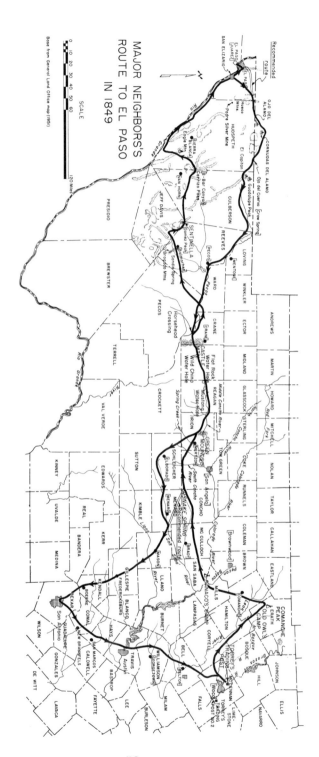

Map of Major R. S. Neighbors's route to El Paso in 1849.

58

Padre Silver Mine, Hueco Mountains.

Carrizo Pass, Beach and Diablo Mountains.

Castle Gap on line of Upton and Crane Counties

Brogado Mountain, Balmorhea, where Major R. S. Neighbors
camped at the Spanish outpost near the spring.

Sierra del Alamo, present New Mexico, point on 1849 route.

Cornudos del Alamo, present New Mexico, point on 1849 route.

El Capitan, 8,078', point on 1849 route.

Robert S. Neighbors and his wife Elizabeth Ann about 1851.
Courtesy, Mrs. R. S. Neighbors, Jr.

George Barnard. Courtesy, Fort Belknap Archives, Inc., gift of Burl Barnard.

Part of meteorite given by Major R. S. Neighbors to the state of Texas. Texas Memorial Museum, the University of Texas at Austin. Courtesy, Mrs. R. S. Neighbors, Jr.

Chief José Maria of the Anadarkos. The National Hall of Fame for Famous American Indians, Anadarko, Oklahoma. Nominated for the honor by the author.

Wichita work arbor, Indian City, Anadarko, Oklahoma. Foreground Mrs. Rose (Dan) Hunt.

Wichita Indian Medicine Lodge under construction in 1955 at Indian City Anadarko, Oklahoma. Construction supervised by Dan Hunt who lived in one as a boy in Kansas.

Chapter III
The Trail Blazer

The successful opening of a wagon road to El Paso in 1849 by Neighbors was the culmination of a long-felt desire on the part of Texans, going back as far as the Texan Santa Fe Expedition of 1841, to make contact with the lands along the upper Rio Grande and beyond. The latest manifestation of this desire had been the expedition of Colonel John Coffee Hays the previous year, 1848, which wound up in Chihuahua.[1] The acquisition of the Mexican Cession led the general government to desire communication with the West Coast, and the Sutter's Mill incident aroused a nation-wide, indeed international, desire to open up communication with the new El Dorado. Newspapers of the time were filled with projects for connecting the Mississippi valley with California by land, and other routes were proposed by sea and across the isthmus of Darien. Texas newspapers during the winter of 1848-1849 carried notices of expeditions organizing in Texas to get an early start to California in the spring.

Besides Neighbors's expedition, Worth sent Lieutenant William Henry Chase Whiting along a more southerly route from San Antonio to El Paso. Whiting with fifteen men left San Antonio on February 12, 1849. The purpose of the military was to open communication between the Gulf and West coasts.[2] Neighbors's interest in making the expedition stemmed from the considerations that, "In addition to the necessity of acquiring correct knowledge of the country, it is important that, the Indians through whose hunting grounds the trains for El Paso must pass, should be advised of the movements and intentions of our troops."

It was no easy matter to open communications with El Paso. The Spaniards had traversed the region at various times but failed to maintain regular communications. When going from San Antonio to Santa Fe, a long circuitous route was ordinarily taken far to the south, then to the north, thus avoiding the Great Plains. The Texans also had failed to open a route. The

Texan Santa Fe Expedition ended in disaster in 1841. When Colonel Hays tried to reach El Paso, in 1848, his guide became lost, and after suffering many hardships, Hays's party reached Presidio del Norte, Chihuahua, and turned back. The early death of some of Hays's men, including Captain Samuel Highsmith, was later attributed to the privations suffered on the trip, and Hays himself suffered from rheumatism thereafter. A Doctor Wham who went insane and "rode off in a fury" one night, was lost in the black ravines, near the Rio Grande. In the Davis Mountains before he reached Fort Leaton, Whiting was threatened with annihilation by Gomez, the fierce Apache chief. According to newspaper reports, a government wagon train, which left by another route after Neighbors started, broke down and was expected to take months to reach El Paso.

Neighbors left San Antonio, passed through Austin, where Doctor John S. Ford indicated his desire to join him, and proceeded to Barnard's and Torrey's Trading House where Neighbors spent several days making preparations for the journey.[3] Neighbors selected the following men to accompany him: John S. Ford, Daniel C. Sullivan, Alpheus D. Neal, white men, and four Indians, John Harry, a Delaware, Joe Ellis and Tom Coshatee, Shawnees, and Patrick Goin, a Choctaw, who were placed by Neighbors under the direction of James Shaw, Delaware.[4] Sullivan and Neal had been in Ross's troops who went with Neighbors on previous missions.[5] Ford said Sullivan was what people call a "character."

> He was of medium height, compactly built, and weighed about 135 pounds. His hair was white, likewise his eye-brows and eyes. The latter were in constant motion, as if under the influence of a current of galvanism, yet they produced no unpleasant impression upon the beholder. His countenance was pleasant, his impulses generous, his intercourse with fellowmen gave evidence of manliness and frankness. He was insensible to the feeling of fear; brave to a fault—a kind and accommodating friend, and a bitter and dangerous enemy. He had an inseparable companion, Alpheus D. Neal, of about the same height, but more robust. He had all the manly qualities of his friend.[6]

Sullivan, when a mere lad, had been taken prisoner at Mier, but had proved to be a difficult prisoner in Mexico. When given tools to work, he threw them into a water closet; when he was placed in a kitchen, the cooks fled with broken heads; after being placed on probation with a kind-hearted old priest, he was brought back for being incorrigible. After his release he joined Captain Shapley Prince Ross's command of Texas Rangers, and took up his practical joking there. When members of the command from farther east found him apparently eating buckeyes, Sullivan blandly explained that they were "Spanish chestnuts."

> You can find plenty of them down on the branch." His were too precious to be given away. The "Chestnuts" were gathered and eaten; and there was a grand cascading, and a terrible swearing, heard in that camp for hours.[7]

John S. Ford was persuaded to join Neighbors by citizens of Austin who wished their city connected with El Paso. Ford, who was then editor of the *Texas Democrat* of Austin, had distinguished himself as a Texas Ranger in the Mexican War and was to gain further distinction fighting the Comanches and in the Confederate service. Ford and Neighbors were closely associated at various periods after the El Paso expedition.

The arrival of some Comanches delayed Neighbors's departure. The Comanches had come to Torrey's Trading House to trade their buffalo robes, deer skins, and artifacts for provisions, clothing, and cutlery. Neighbors engaged Buffalo Hump as guide to El Paso. Chief Buffalo Hump's raids in Mexico made him well acquainted with the intervening region.

The experience of Colonel Hays's expedition had indicated that a route from San Antonio to El Paso by way of the "large bend" of the Rio Grande was unsatisfactory, and that the way by the San Sabá was preferable. The initial part of the route selected by Neighbors lay above the San Sabá and Concho rivers to the Horsehead Crossing of the Pecos. Neighbors's party left the North Bosque Settlement on March 23, 1849, which could have been Torrey's Trading House founded in 1842 mentioned by Ford.

One morning Buffalo Hump awoke the camp with a medicine song. Ford said,

> It stirred up recollections of boyhood—the calling of hogs—the plaintive notes of a solitary bull frog—the bellowing of a small bull, and all that sort of noises. Anon the awful melody of the sonorous gong was reproduced; the next moment the mornful howl of a hungry wolf saluted the ear, which gradually softened into something like the gobble of a turkey. It might have been a choice asortment [sic] of Comanche airs gotten up to amuse and do honor to the Supervising Agent, but it failed to solace his white companions. The performance commenced

about an hour before daylight and did little to soothe the slumbers of the morning.[8]

According to Noah Smithwick, who lived among the Comanches for a time, the first brave who awoke always broke forth with a matin lay. He said:

Although it was customary for the first fellow who woke in the morning to announce the fact in song, the act seemed rather a spontaneous outpouring akin to that of the feathered songsters than a religious rite; the song itself resembling the láy of the birds in that it was wordless save for the syllables, ha ah ha, which furnished the vehicle on which the carol rode forth to the world; the performance ending in a keen yell.[9]

Old Owl led Neighbors's expedition into Owl's camp on the headwaters of the Leon on the fourth day. Information on the route from the North Bosque to Old Owl's camp and from thence to Spring Creek is too laconic to trace in detail. Ford indicated the site was on the headwaters of the Leon which he further identified as a creek, possibly Armstrong Creek east of present De Leon.

About forty or fifty children who were in the creek bathing ran for the wigwams crying "pav-o-ti-vo, pav-o-ti-vo"—white man, white man—as loud as they could. The white men camped near the Indians, and both satisfied a mutual curiosity by visiting each other's camps. One old crone was estimated to have seen a hundred summers, "and scolded like other old feminines."[10]

Ford wore long boots *a la Napoleon*.

He found that a snake will recoil when anything is descending upon it suddenly. A nimble person may jump with both feet on a snake, and leap off instanter, and not be bitten. It is a dangerous and foolhardy thing to do, yet he did it to the great astonishment of the Comanches. We reached the "Cross Timbers." The Indians found a large diamond rattlesnake; and waited for the snakeman. He came up. There was the reptile in a huge coil, his head about three feet from the ground; eyes brilliant and scintillating with anger. His rattles were sounding the alarm of danger, and seemed to be capable of being heard at the distance of a hundred yards. The spots on his body were diamond shaped, and of a bright yellow color. He was about ten foot long. A more beautiful serpent is seldom seen, and one more able to inflict a fatal sting. The writer was cautioned by Jim Shaw: "Don't go any nearer, that snake can bite a man a little further than his length —about ten feet. He can strike you on your mule. He jumps as

71

he strikes." These snakes were reputed to be remarkably active, and very strong. The force exerted in delivering a blow or bite was sufficient to move the whole body. The snakeman gazed at the serpent for a few minutes; rode away, and has not jumped on, even a garter snake, from that day to this blessed moment.[11]

Indian affairs detained Neighbors in camp for several days. Buffalo Hump was allowed sufficient time to arrange his affairs for leaving. Neighbors travelled from Old Owl's camp "south of west, and rather down the country," in the direction of Spring Creek on the Colorado. After Old Owl separated from the group, Neighbors marched leisurely toward the southwest with Buffalo Hump's band.

As the cavalcade moved along, the Comanche children "beat the thickets for rabbits, birds, and rattlesnakes." When a snake was found, shouts rent the air, the children encircled it, and fired arrows into it until life was gone. Then cries of triumph would go up, and the young warriors would gallop to the front to announce the victory. The women would whip up the pack mules, the excitement would spread through the whole band, and even the whites would yell lustily.[12]

Lost in the world of nature with nature's children, it was easy for the white men to feel the lure of the primitive way of life.

> To roam amid the unchanging scenes of Nature, where the foot of civilized man never trod before, perhaps; to view the work[s] of God in their primeval grandeur, and to realise that you constitute a part of these, conspire to produce a bouyancy of spirits, pleasant sensations, a rapture earth seldom affords to men. These are the charms which allure the woodsman to a life apart from other men.

But a civilized man must catch himself before surrendering completely to the siren voice of the wild.

> The picture above is the bright side of savage life. Turn to the other; ignorance of God and the world, hunger, thirst, cold; filth; the deprivation of the comforts, the amenities, and social pleasures of civilised life, and then choose for yourself. If savagery is right civilization is wrong. There can be no middle ground.[13]

The peace and quiet were suddenly shattered one day by a squaw riding by at full speed, followed by a brave who gave her rousing whacks with a gun stick. Neal reported that it was the result of Sullivan's deviltry. In response to the desire of the squaws to learn more about white men, Sullivan had been delivering them a lecture. "The warrior came along, discovered that his wife constituted one of Sullivan's audience, and the row commenced." That night Jim Shaw returned from Buffalo Hump's wigwam a badly scared Indian. Shaw thought the party might all be killed before morning. He blamed the whole trouble on Sullivan, and "lectured and swore at him considerably."

The names of Nabors Creek and Jim Shaw Creek in close proximity in Mills County may mark part of the itinerary. On April 2, 1849, Sanaco's camp on the Colorado was reached. His camp was near the mouth of Spring Creek, which is about twelve miles as the crow flies above the confluence of the San Sabá and Colorado rivers. This was the site of the battle where the Comanches defeated Colonel John H. Moore in 1839. Besides the band of Sanaco at the camp, Yellow Wolf's band was present, as well as a part of Buffalo Hump's. The camp was so large Ford estimated the number of Indians at ten thousand.

At Sanaco's camp the wrath of Rip Ford[14] was kindled by the sight of a mutilated captive white woman. She had sandy, red hair and blue eyes, and her cheeks were marred by long scars put there by the slash of a knife—as a sign of bereavement. "Her face seemed the personification of despair. It filled the beholder with the idea of unutterable woe." Jim Shaw warned Ford not to speak to the captive as it might cost him his life. Ford felt enraged that the white woman had been captured and forced to become the wife of a savage.

> Not only his wife, his menial, his slave. To be the humble servitor of his whims and caprices; to be punished for a seeming disposition to disobey his behests—to be beaten, lassoed, and pulled through prickly pears, with a rope around the middle, and filled full of thorns to gratify the vengeance of one possessing less pity than a brute.[15]

Ford shut out the harrowing thoughts for the moment, but in his Memoirs said that:

> The writer has since that period done some rather rough Indian fighting. When leading a charge against the red men, the woman with auburn hair, slashed cheeks, and countenance of extreme sorrow, has appeared to lead him. She was before his mind's eye, and he struck for her and for vengeance.[16]

Unexpected opposition to the expedition arose at Sanaco's camp. Sanaco had been told by Major Collinson R. Gates at Fort Martin Scott that the general government planned to open a road through the Comanche range, that settlements would be made on the Concho and other points, and that "a railroad would in a short while be constructed from the coast of Texas to Chihuahua." When the head men heard this, they opposed the making of an expedition through their territory. Buffalo Hump as a result of this development and other arguments, returned part of his pay as guide, and declined to accompany the party farther. After three days of negotiations, Major Neighbors was finally able to persuade the chiefs to allow Guadalupe, the captain of one of the bands, to accompany him as guide. But the Major said he "exhausted every art of persuasion, and succeeded more by appealing to their cupidity than otherwise." Guadalupe was accompanied by his married sister and her female companion.

Sullivan had by this time established a reputation among the Indians for being insane and not responsible for his acts.

> He took advantage of the supposition, and was seldom out of devilment. He stuck pins in warriors, and made them cut capers very unsuaual for braves to perform. He notified the Indian public that he would give a performance, free of charge, and invited a general attendance. He had a good audience. He played the buzzard—performing feats imitative of those customary to that melancholy bird, in near proximity to a dead horse. He next illustrated the antics of a lizard. He went off on all-fours at a brisk gait, ensconced himself behind a log. He would peep over the log, and drop out of sight in the twinkling of an eye. The sight of his contorted face, and his white eyes, as they danced in his head, produced shouts of laughter. Anything more ludicrous has seldom been witnessed. He sang a lisping song—"Miss Julia was very peculiar"—was the chorus, if memory serves. The Comanches did not understand a word, yet they applauded, and laughed immoderately. One young warrior laughed himself almost into convulsions. His friends carried him off, fearing he would make himself sick. To use the worn out phrase of the day, the performance was a complete success![7]

On the fifth day of April, 1849, Neighbors left Sanaco's camp, struck and proceeded up Brady's Creek. Here Neal was lost to the party. He pursued a deer, and was unable to find the expedition again, although the Major remained in camp a whole day to wait for him. Neal later made his way back to the settlements. On Brady's Creek Neighbors made camp near a war party of Comanches on their way to raid Mexico. "They spent most of the night singing and yelling."

Upon reaching Snake Spring,[18] a head tributary of Brady's Creek, about three miles southwest of present Eden, Neighbors struck west in the direction of the main Concho, A-hope Ho-Nope, or Blue River, as the Indians called it. The head spring of what Neighbors designated as the main Concho, presently known as the Middle Concho, was reached on April 12, 1849. The Major reported that the surface of the country from Brady's Creek to the head of the Concho was gently undulating, and had an abundant supply of water, timber, and grass. After leaving the Concho, the old Connelley trail to Chihuahua was followed for a short distance.[19]

Seven miles southeast of present Crane, on the line between Upton and Crane counties, Neighbors reached Castle Mountain, so named because the immense boulders on it resembled castles. The pass through the mountain was almost on a level with the tableland to the east. In a *Week pah*, as the Comanches called a gap with water in it, a strange Comanche warrior was encountered. When Guadalupe came up, the two Comanche warriors knew each other and made camp together.

The camp was on the main war trail from the Comanche range to Chihuahua. The warrior and his squaw were on their way home with plunder, animals, and a Mexican slave. When Tall Tree told the brave that the expedition was short of rations, he "generously slaughtered a fat mule." Mule meat was found to be almost as palatable as beef, and the feast was enjoyed with much gusto. Next day the last piece of bacon was eaten, and hunger faced the expedition.

Neighbors reached the banks of the Pecos on the morning of April 17, 1849, and made camp that day on the left (east) bank of Horsehead Crossing, about fifteen miles above present Girvin in Survey No. 44, Block 9, H & G N Survey.[19a] Ford said,

The Horse-head crossing of the Pecos was so named on account of the large number of skeletons of horse heads lying on both sides of the river. The Indian explanation was simple and plausible. The crossing being on the main trail to and from Chihuahua was a favorite camping place, both going and coming. The first waterhole south-west of the crossing was sixty miles distant. Indians returning from Mexico, with stolen horses, would drive them hard to reach water. The loose animals, on reaching the Pecos, would plunge into the stream to quench their thirst, and drink until they became sick, and would die soon.

Neighbors reported that the surface of the divide between the Concho and the Pecos was covered with white sand and gravel, admirably adapted for a wagon road. The Major

75

ascended the Pecos twenty-eight miles, crossed over, and after travelling forty-eight miles in a southwesterly direction, came to the Toyah River, which he said rose in the Pah-cut Mountain, now called the Davis Mountains. He reported that the route from the Pecos was over smooth valleys suitable for the passage of any wheeled vehicle. The Toyah was a "swift stream about 40 feet wide, 18 inches deep, and affording sufficient water power to move any sort of machinery."

Neighbors made camp on the Toyah, in the vicinity of present Balmorhea at present Brogada, near what was said to have been an old Spanish military station, the outline of whose ruins may still be seen. Near by was an immense boulder of red stone three hundred feet high, the end point of the Brogada Mountains, close to which Sandia Spring, came pouring forth.[20] Corn had been planted not far off by Mescaleros.

While camped here Sullivan and Guadalupe almost came to mortal blows. Ford said:

> For several days our guide and Sullivan had been cross to each other. Sullivan persisted in dubbing the great Comanche war captain "Blunk," which incensed him, and got him laughed at. We were satisfied a company of emigrants had been there ahead of us. They were evidently moving without a guide, and at random. That day we picked up a poor horse, which had been broken down and abandoned. We managed to get him to camp, and we decided to kill and eat him. Horse flesh is considered a delicacy by the Comanches. Tall Tree roasted a bountiful [feast]—enough to feed about ten hungry men. He announced his intention to "come mucho"—eat a great deal. He ordered Sullivan to bring water from the spring about ten feet off. A large sized row commenced then and there. Sullivan gesticulated, and swore in English, Spanish, Soc, and a sprinkling of Caddo. Tall Tree called down anathemas upon Sullivan in pure Comanche, bad Spanish and English, besides in tongues unknown to all of us. The quarrel progressed until a resort to arms was purposed, when Maj. Neighbors and others interfered. The muss did not take off the keen edge of Tall Tree's appetite. He stowed away meat enough to feed a family of buzzards.[21]

Rip Ford could not eat the horse meat. "It tasted like a sweaty saddle-blanket smells at the end of a day's ride. The liver had an offensive smell, but by holding his nose he forced down some of that strong scented viand."[22]

The next morning the party struck Mescalero Springs at the base of the Davis Mountains and eighteen miles southwest (S.70W.) from the camp on the Toyah. This could have been either the Casey Spring on Casey Draw, or the head spring of the left branch of Cherry Canyon both of which were owned by Mrs. Velma Casey Roundtree in 1962. "Here there was once a Spanish post. There are peach trees in the vicinity. The mountain affords timber: Pine, Oak, Cherry, &c., were seen at different places."[23] Neighbors then turned the northern end of Pahcut or Davis Mountains around Sentinella, present Gomez Peak. A valley led toward Puerto Carriso, visible as a gap between Beach and Diablo mountains more than fifty miles in the distance.

Camp that night was at Jo Ellis's Water Hole (named for one of the Indians in the party) about twenty miles southwest of Sentinella.[24] Near camp was a small hill, "at the base of which cropped out a beautiful stone—white, with red streaks running through it. Someone afterwards decided it to be porphyry, *quien sabe?*" Here hunger led Neighbors's party to eat the cabbage-like mescal heads, which were supposed to be cooked by placing the mescal in a hole in the ground, and allowing a slow fire to burn over them. Someone must have allowed the fire to go out during the night, as next morning the half-raw mescal made the men apprehensive of colic.[25]

Neighbors was in what frontiersmen called starving man's luck. No Indians could be found from whom to procure food. The party resorted to eating stalks of the maguey plant roasted.

> The taste was not savory by any means. A man would sally out of camp, and return bringing a load of green stalks.—Sullivan said it reminded him of 'feeding horses on green corn stalks.' In addition we had a cup of coffee, and a quart of mush made of pinoli—pen-no-le the meal of parched corn, and divided into thirteen parts. No one contracted gout.[26]

Neighbors reached the Carrizo Mountains north of present Van Horn on April 24, 1849, and made his way through Carrizo Pass or Dead Man's Pass, called by the Mexicans, Fresno, between Baylor, Beach, Diablo, and Carrizo mountains. Carrizo Pass, Puerto Carrizo, which leads into present B Bar Canyon is full of reddish stone, is "rough and scraggy," and at that season had an abundance of wood and water.[27] The expedition emerged into a valley west of Van Horn. Ford said,

> The Puerto de la Cola del Aguila—'Eagle Spring' now called—was visible to our right. The writer [Ford] called the attention of Maj. Neighbors to it and suggested the propriety of going through it. [The 'puerto' is an optical illusion seen from the east side and is not actually a pass.]The Major [very

properly] thought it better to follow the guide. He was leading us directly toward a mountain [Eagle Mountain Range]. We began ascending ridges. The sides were not far from perpendicular; the tops were only a few yards across—it was up and down—the evolutions of Barry Cornwall's 'Stormy Petrel' was a small thing by the side of ours. We slept without watter—and had nothing to eat. To make the matter worse the writer fell sick—the green stalks were too much for him.[28]

The next morning the terrain of Eagle Mountain became "rougher, more rocky, and the ridges were precipitous." After a turn more to the south, Neighbors and his men emerged into an open valley. About a mile from the Rio Grande, a "trail was reached with shod horse tracks on it." This was the trail of Whiting whose return route left the valley of the Rio Grande at this point. The two expeditions missed each other here by only two or three days, since Whiting started back from El Paso on April 19, 1849.[29] The Rio Grande was reached, at a point below the mouth of Quitman Arroyo near present Guerra School.

A council was held at which it was decided to send ahead two men, mounted on the best mules, who would try to reach a settlement and send back aid to the rest of the expedition. Neighbors and Sullivan rode ahead, and reached Presidio San Elizario on April 29, 1849. Five miles from San Elizario the rear echelon met a Mexican with supplies sent back by Neighbors.

At San Elizario the inhabitants treated the party kindly and after resting a day or two, a few of the party accompanied Neighbors to El Paso [Juarez] on May 2, 1849. El Paso meant Paso del Norte on the Mexican side, for the Texas town of El Paso did not develop until later. Although Whiting had left San Antonio forty days before Neighbors left the North Bosque Settlement, Whiting had reached Ponce's ranch, opposite El Paso del Norte, on April 12, 1849, only twenty days before Neighbors. This demonstrated the superiority of the upper route of Neighbors.

On the American side of the Rio Grande, an American woman known as the Great Western kept a hotel. Rip Ford said she was tall, large, and well made. "She had the reputation of being something of the roughest fighter on the Rio Grande; and was approached in a polite, if not humble manner by all of us—the writer in particular," Ford admitted. The Great Western, a devotee of General Taylor, had followed the general from Florida to Mexico. When a man came running back to the Great

78

Western's establishment from the battle of Buena Vista and cried breathlessly that Taylor was whipped, the Great Western floored the prophet of doom with a blow between the eyes, as she bawled, "You damned son of a bitch, there ain't Mexicans enough in Mexico to whip old Taylor."[30]

Neighbors reported the part of the route from Cola del Aguila [Eagle Mountain] to El Paso, a hundred miles along the Rio Grande, to be unsuited for a wagon road. The route had too many ravines, gullies, and sand hills. At El Paso Neighbors learned of a route previously used by the Mexican army from El Paso to the Pecos, which was well watered and suitable for a wagon road. He returned to San Elizario to procure supplies, and hire Señor Alvino Zambrano[31] to guide him to the Pecos.

The expedition left San Elizario on May 6, 1849, and returned by way of the Heuco Tanks, thence over the present Texas-New Mexico line by the Ojo del Alamo, the Tanks of Cornudos del Alamo, and back into Texas by the Ojo del Cuervo or Crow Spring,[32] and the Guadalupe Mountains to the Pecos River. A halt had been made at the Hueco Tanks, the largest of which was situated in a cave and contained about fifty thousand gallons of water. The surrounding valley was a natural fortress easily defended and often used by Mexicans and Indians. The Ojo del Alamo, twenty-four miles from Hueco Tanks, was a cluster of eight springs on the north side of the Sierra del Alamo. Ten miles farther was the Cornudas del Alamo, a small mountain about seven hundred feet high composed of huge red granite boulders in whose fissures water could be obtained. Neighbors and friends travelled twenty miles to the Ojo del Cuervo, a large spring of cool fresh water bursting forth on the plain. The Great Salt Plains lay to the right as the party proceeded east to the Guadalupe Mountains. The little cavalcade wound around the base of El Capitan, and up the side of the canyon as does the twentieth century highway to Carlsbad, New Mexico. From the Guadalupe Mountains to the Pecos the route of Neighbors lay over a high tableland. The soil consisted of sand and gravel but was firm. The terrain had scattered mounds and hills, but these stood far enough apart to offer no impediment to travel. Ford waxed poetic to depict:

Bold running streams of pure, clear water, whose banks are fringed with trees and shrubbery, presenting the varied appearance of pool, riffle, and lake—now creeping through reeds, grass, and flowers, and anon tumbling from a ledge of rocks, giving to circumscribed spots, scenery of wild and singular beauty, water the slope from the Sierra Guadalupe to the Pecos.

No incident of interest was noted until the Pecos was reached, except the killing and eating of a panther. Panther meat was not palatable. "It had a peculiar fresh taste, very difficult to get rid of."

Neighbors reported that the route followed from El Paso to the Pecos was admirably adapted to a wagon road, and that only two places required any labor. A few stones needed to be removed from Hueco Pass, and some leveling was needed at the base of the Guadalupe Mountains, though this could be avoided by going a little farther south around the mountains. Neighbors reported that the right bank of the Pecos was more suited than the left for a road. He said he was confirmed in this opinion by the fact that the Indians and Mexicans had used that side. "On the Eastern bank there are more hills and large lakes:—and all great bends are on that side—therefore I consider the Western bank preferable."

As Major Neighbors rode along a bend in the Pecos, Jim Shaw excitedly reported that all the Indians in the world were just ahead, bathing in the river. Under the circumstances Neighbors decided the only safe course was a bold one and rode dashing into the camp making friendly signs and salutations. The bathers, who were members of the emigrant train of Isaac H. Duval, thinking themselves invaded in turn by Indians, scrambled out of the water, grabbed their rifles, and, naked and wet, aimed them at Neighbors. According to young Benjamin Butler Harris, when Duval's party discovered their error, the late bathers shamefacedly dropped their rifles and hastily pulled on their clothes to greet the visitor. Duval was one of the two secretaries at the making of the United States treaty with the Indians of Texas in 1846.

Harris is authority for the statement found no where else that with Neighbors's party were the Comanche chief, Santa Anna, and some Mescálero Apaches with their chiefs. Harris and Patrick Goin, the dark skinned Choctaw member of Neighbors's party, came close to mortal blows when Goin invited himself to Harris's mess for breakfast. Harris mistook him for a negro and ordered him to wait. Major Neighbors interfered, explained Goin's race, hands were shaken, and the breakfast finished amicably.[33]

Of Horsehead Crossing of the Pecos, Neighbors said: "The

banks are low, bottom firm and hard, and the water more shallow than at any point touched by the road, yet the depth is too great for fording, and a good ferry boat will be requisite."

From the Pecos onward Neighbors furnished guides to emigrant trains. A member of his party, named Johnson, a Corralitos merchant and member of Whiting's party who had been discharged at Ponces' Ranch on April 18, 1849, became the guide for Duval's party. Farther along the trail, John Harry was engaged by Captain B. O. Tong, of Seguin, who had forty-five wagons in his train. Neighbors met Captain John Murchison, of La Grange, with forty wagons on May 24. Captain Murchison stated:

> We are indebted to Major Neighbors and Dr. Ford for our success; had we not have met them and procured a guide to pilot us, we would have been as badly lost as any others .... Eternity itself can only tell the great good that Neighbors and Ford have done for the human family in reviewing and describing this road. It is now one of the best roads I ever saw in all my life . . . .

Captain Thomas Smith's company from Houston was met on May 27, near Good Spring Creek. Neighbors's friend Cornelius C. Cox was in the company. The P. F. Smith Association was found encamped fifteen miles below the old Spanish fort on the San Sabá on May 29, 1849. Sam Whiting, a former editor of Austin and an acquaintance of Neighbors, was with the P. F. Smith group. Neighbors had bought supplies from Whiting while serving as quartermaster in the Army of the Republic of Texas. Sullivan became the guide for the P. F. Smith train.

Major Neighbors had returned along his outgoing route from the Pecos to Green Mounds, probably present Lopez Peaks, slightly southwest of present San Angelo. Here he diverged from his recommended route to try the emigrant trail to Fredericksburg. He did not endorse the diversion because it was too far south, too rough and rocky, and not well watered in summer. Neighbors's expedition reached Fredericksburg on May 31, 1849, and San Antonio on June 2, 1849, eight days after Whiting, who started forty days before Major Neighbors. Neighbors's outward journey to El Paso had taken twenty-three days of actual travelling time; the return trip, twenty-two. Neighbor's return was saddened by the news of the death of General Worth who fell a victim of cholera on May 17, 1849.

Neighbors reported to Brevet Brigadier General William Selby Harney, Worth's successor, that his return route from

El Paso was well suited for a wagon road. Major Neighbors said:

> There is no portion of the route I cannot represent as possessing an adequate supply of water at all seasons except it be from the head of the Cincho [Concho] to the Pecos a distance of 60 miles, and there are four water holes known to be upon it with water enough for all purposes; should these fail in the hot summer months, the difficulty can be easily obviated by sinking wells in the valley of the wild China Water hole, and the pass of the Castle Mountain, at which points water can be reached within a few feet of the surface.

Major Neighbors called attention to the strategic location of the route. He pointed out that it was readily accessible to the Gulf Coast, and that, "Thoroughfares from middle, Eastern and Northern Texas to California, must connect with it at Fredericksburg or some other point on the Colorado." Along with his report, Neighbors sent a map showing his outgoing and return routes. The map apparently was forwarded to the War Department by General Harney, but cannot be located at present.

The Major commended the services of James Shaw and Captain Guadalupe. Of Rip Ford, Neighbors said, "In Dr. John S. Ford I found an energetic and able assistant, the services rendered by him were important to the successful termination of the expedition. I cheerfully recommend him to your favorable notice."

The report of Major Neighbors covered eight pages. Its contents were full and adequate for all practical purposes, but the language was terse and succinct. Not a word was said of the fatigue, the cold, the heat, the thirst, and the hunger suffered on the expedition. To his superior in the Indian Bureau, Neighbors summed up the achievements of the expedition in one sentence amid his regular report.

> I have the honor to notify you of the return of myself and party to this place after an absence of three months in the prairies, which time was occupied in a successful exploration of the country between the Pecos and Rio Grande rivers, by order of Major. Genl Worth; and by which the practicability of a wagon route through that country is fully established, and a section of country hitherto deemed impassable, opened to the emigrants.

Harney ordered Lieutenant Colonel Joseph E. Johnston to send out surveying parties along both Whiting's and

Neighbors's routes. Lieutenant Francis T. Bryan made a survey of Neighbors's return route, and reported favorably on it. The way became known as the Upper Route and was soon in frequent use by emigrants and the military. In August of 1849, alone, over four thousand emigrants had gathered in El Paso. The Southern Overland Mail later followed the route from the Concho to El Paso. Modern highways and railroads approximate both the outgoing and returning routes of Neighbors. Neighbors and Ford estimated the distance from Austin to El Paso to be 598 miles. Modern road maps give the same mileage. Neighbors made his calculations from the distance travelled in a day by a mule—"four miles to the hour in going out, and three and one-third in coming in."

Ford made a detailed report of the expedition in a letter to the *Texas Democrat*. From Ford's notes Robert Creuzbar made an excellent map of the route which was published for the aid of emigrants. Ford thought the expedition of Neighbors had other far-reaching effects.

> Previous to the expedition of Lieut. Whiting, and Maj. Neighbors, the country between San Antonio and El Paso was esteemed almost a desert. The public was now placed in possession of proofs to the reverse. At the next meeting of the Texas legislature Major Neighbors was sent to El Paso, as the Agent of the State. He organized the country of El Paso, and proceeded to Santa Fe. President Taylor claimed that, the territory belonged to the United States, and issued a proclamation and designated 'one Robert S. Neighbors' as a trespasser, etc. The contest between the General Government and the State of Texas concerning the ownership of this territory became a political question, and engendered bad blood. Mr. Clay introduced a bill known as 'The Compromise Measure,' which became a law and probably prevented serious trouble to the people of the United States. The sale of a part of New Mexico to the United States for ten millions of dollars furnished Texas the means to settle her revolutionary debt, and she did so. It is no strain upon truth to assume that, the expedition of Maj. Neighbors was a factor in these important events. It certainly precipitated action in the matter.

Shortly after his return, the Corpus Christi *Star* reported that Neighbors was involved in a serious affray at San Antonio where a Mr. Young for reasons not now known, attacked Neighbors with a stick, whereupon Neighbors drew his pistol and "shot Young in the hip inflicting a serious and it is thought mortal wound." A search of other contemporary records has failed to throw further light on the incident.

Upon his return from El Paso, Agent Neighbors found orders awaiting him to report to Washington to assist in working out a satisfactory Indian policy for Texas. Neighbors had given the problem much thought during his long service, and had a definite program to present. His five proposals called for the general government to extinguish the Indian title to as much land as the state needed for immediate use; to acquire from Texas sufficient land for permanent settlement of the Texas Indians; to extend the intercourse laws of the United States to the Indians of Texas; to establish a general agency with at least three sub-agents and interpreters to reside among the Indians; and to establish the necessary military posts in the Indian country to assist the agents in carrying out all laws and treaties. Along with this program, the Major envisioned the government's extending such services as carpentry, blacksmithing, agricultural instruction for adults, academic education for the children, and the supplying of cattle, tools, seeds, and utensils until the Indians became self-sustaining.[34]

After Major Neighbors arrived in Washington, he learned that he had been superseded in the Indian service by John H. Rollins.[35] Since the commissioner stated that Neighbors's service had been satisfactory, it must be concluded that the spoils system had removed a Democrat to make room for a Whig.[36] Public opinion did not favor Neighbors's replacement. The *Texas State Gazette* commented that:

> Major Robert S. Neighbors has been superseded in the Indian Agency for Texas, by the appointment of J. H. Rollins, a citizen of Mississippi! What may be the peculiar qualifications of the new agent, that should have induced the Government to import him into this State from another, we know not. In our judgment, it was not an easy matter to find a man anywhere whose qualifications for this service, are comparable to those of Maj. Neighbors. Long experience, activity, courage and knowledge of the character of the prairie Indians, and of their haunts and hunting grounds, we look upon as very necessary aids to a successful discharge of the duties of this important agency. We think no good will result from the change. It is true that Indian difficulties have for some time existed on our frontier, but they have arisen more from a want of the necessary military force and competent subagents along the line, than from any remissness or misconduct of the gentleman to whom the whole duty of controlling the

Indians has been entrusted. A just and considerate government would have given us more than one agent for our thousand miles of frontier, exposed at all points to the incursions of numerous bands of roving Indians.

Senator Sam Houston did not approve of the change. On the floor of the United States Senate, Houston later championed Neighbors:

> I will say that many of the evils growing up on the frontier of Texas have been owing to the appointment of agents disqualified in many respects, as I believe, for the discharge of the duties that would devolve upon them, in maintaining the peace of Texas, and vindicating the rights of its citizens. So long as the agent was continued who occupied that position at the time when the predecessor of the present individual who fills the Executive chair came into power, peace was maintained on our borders. That agent [Neighbors] was a man who had been accustomed to frontier life—a man familiar with the Indians and with their habits—a man who would traverse the prairies with them. He was the individual who discovered the first route to El Paso from the settlements of Texas, where water and grass could be obtained. He remained their guardian—associated with them. He controlled them, regulated their bad passions, and led them in the paths of peace and quietness. Then our frontier had safety and protection. He was removed—not for cause, but to place an individual there who was sinking under a consumption, and unable to perform any duty. He never went amongst the Indians. If they came to where he was, he was incapable of transacting any business with them, and finally, under the influence of disease, he passed off. He was a man unacquainted with the habits of the Indians—unacquainted with the means of controlling them.

Rupert Norval Richardson, the Comanche chronicler, said of Neighbors's service during this period:

> Even if Robert S. Neighbors had never rendered any other public service, he merits the gratitude of Texas for his work in restraining the Comanche warriors during this period, and credit is due also to the worthy old chiefs, Pah-hah-yo-ko, Old Owl, and Santa Anna . . . .

When Neighbors visited Sam Houston in Huntsville on the return from Washington, Houston asked him to convey to General Memucan Hunt, Houston's "highest consideration and regards, and most respectful salutations and compliments," but also his regret that Hunt had voted against "the democratic party at the last election." Hunt and confederates, including Anson Jones, seized the opportunity as a vehicle upon which to launch a bitter attack upon Houston and to include Neighbors incidentally in the diatribe. When Major Neighbors saw Hunt's letter in the *Texas State Gazette*, he wrote the editor refuting the charges.[37]

Neighbors continued in public service, but his next exciting mission was for the state of Texas.

Chapter IV
The Commissioner

The success of Major Neighbors in opening communications with the upper Rio Grande region, and his first-hand knowledge of the country and its inhabitants, made him a likely agent for Texas to send to claim the region. On January 3, 1850, Governor Peter Hansbrough Bell nominated Neighbors, his old associate since the days of the Army of the Republic of Texas, as the commissioner to organize the western counties of Texas along the upper Rio Grande, and respectfully asked the advice and consent of the Senate. A joint resolution was passed by the legislature to pay the commissioner's salary in advance.[1] But to travel hundreds of miles across a wilderness, much of it a desolate waste inhabited by aboriginals, to win the allegiance and cooperation of alien people long prejudiced against Texas, and to wrest the region from the maw of the United States, Neighbors was advanced the total salary of $550, without one cent for an expense account.

Thus Major Neighbors was thrown into the cauldron of the dispute over the Texas boundary which engaged national attention for such a long period, led to threats of civil war and secession, and was not finally settled until the so-called Compromise of 1850. The background of the problem went back to the earliest days of the Republic of Texas.

The treaty of Velasco with President Antonio Lopez de Santa Anna of Mexico recognized the Rio Grande as the boundary of Texas, while the first session of the Congress of the Republic of Texas on December 19, 1836, claimed the same boundary.

Other events, however, compromised the claim of Texas to the region. During the Mexican War, in the absence of the civil authority of Texas in the upper Rio Grande region, Secretary of War W. L. Marcy had ordered Colonel S. W. Kearny to set up a temporary civil government under the direction of the military, which had remained in power.

During the Mexican War, the Texas legislature took steps to secure the lower Rio Grande region by creating the counties of Nueces, Webb, Starr, and Cameron. Ex-President Mirabeau B. Lamar, while a captain of Texas forces stationed in the region, initiated county organization, and the Texan proceedings thus far were confirmed by the terms of the treaty of Guadalupe Hidlago.

The Texas legislature then took steps to secure the upper Rio Grande at its session early in 1848. Santa Fe County and the Eleventh Judicial District, coextensive with the remaining region in question, were created. The same law made it the duty of the governor to call upon the President to order military officers at Santa Fe to co-operate with Texas officials, and to put down any resistance to the laws of Texas. Governor George T. Wood notified President James K. Polk of the action of the legislature. Secretary of War Marcy ordered the commanding officer at Santa Fe not to interfere with any government established by Texas in the region, but to aid and sustain any officials sent by Texas.

Major Neighbors was not the first agent to attempt organization of the region. On October 6, 1848, Governor Wood notified President Polk that the Honorable Spruce M. Baird of Nacogdoches had been appointed judge and James W. Webb, district attorney, of the Eleventh Judicial District. Webb never went and Baird, thanks to the opposition of the military junta in Santa Fe, was unsuccessful and returned to Texas.

It was evident from the treatment accorded Judge Baird in Santa Fe that Major Neighbors had not fallen into a bed of roses. The statute under which he was to act called for the organization of the counties of Presidio, El Paso, Worth, and Santa Fe, all carved from the former huge county of Santa Fe. Neighbors decided to organize El Paso County first. He left Austin for El Paso on January 8, 1850. Neighbors's pack mules broke down on the way, forcing him to abandon copies of Texas laws which he brought with him. By the time he reached San Elizario, his animals were in need of provender, and Major William S. Henry, commanding the garrison at that place, kindly supplied eighty quarts of corn. For this Good Samaritan deed, so out of keeping with the designs of the national administration, Major Henry would be pursued with vindictive malice by his superiors. While Neighbors was on his way to El Paso, Congress was whipped to a state of white fury over the issue of the Texas boundary.

Charles C. Mills wrote from Washington to Governor Bell that:

The House of Representatives is not yet organized. It is a crisis in our affairs, and what it will result in, God only knows. There is but little disposition on the part of the southern members to bear with northern encroachment ahy longer and there is evidently a determination on the part of many of them, to engage in no legislation, until the question is settled, and if the present Congress does not settle it: I am of opinion that the South will never meet the North again in general Council. Texas having so recently come into the union, should not be foremost to dissolve it; but I trust she will not waver, when the crisis shall come.

Senator Thomas J. Rusk wrote Governor Bell of the hostile acts of Taylor against the claims of Texas; that Henry Clay had introduced a series of resolutions against the South and especially repudiated the Texas boundary. Rusk took issue with Clay at once and was determined to oppose him adding:

There is much excitement here, and God knows how it will all end. I hope for the best, and trust that while our State stands firm in the maintenance of her rights, violent expressions, which neither advance the cause, nor the character of the State, will be as much as possible avoided. Our interests will certainly be advanced by a prudent, and might be retarded by an opposite course.

Commissioner Neighbors reached San Elizario, El Paso County, about February 3, 1850. The commissioner published the governor's proclamation explaining the history of Texan claims to the region and called upon the citizens to assist him in organizing the county. These were the same people who had received Major Neighbors so hospitably the previous year when he had connected their region with the East by a practical road. Some of the settlements in the county were San Elizario, Senecu, Socorro, Ysleta, Ponce's Ranch, Franklin, Magoffinsville, San Diego, and Doña Ana. The residents presently cooperated wholeheartedly with Neighbors in organizing the county of El Paso. On February 23, 1850, Commissioner Neighbors at Franklin took the earliest opportunity to notify Colonel John Munroe at Santa Fe of his arrival to extend the civil jurisdiction of Texas over a region of which Munroe was military governor. The commissioner found no opposition and had issued writs of election for El Paso County which "extends for sixty miles below El Paso to twenty miles above San Diego and due east from each point to the Pecos River." The Texas agent announced his intention of coming to Santa Fe next, after celebrating the election in El Paso County.[2]

Concerning the election of officials in El Paso County, Neighbors wrote a friend in San Antonio:

89

I have no doubt you will be pleased to learn that I have been successful in organizing this county [El Paso]. The election went off in fine style, on the 4th day of March, and at several of the precincts, especially at this town [Doña Ana, forty-eight miles above El Paso on the Rio Grande, now in New Mexico], we had splendid balls in honor of the extension of civil law. This is a fine country, and has some five thousand inhabitants. The county gave seven hundred and sixty votes, all of which were for Austin [as the state capitol for twenty years], except three for Huntsville, and one for San Antonio, and will poll over one thousand votes at the next election.[3]

Governor Bell commended the commissioner highly on his mission to El Paso, saying:

Upon his arrival in the County of El Paso, he took the necessary measures for its immediate organization, and by his prudence, zeal, and activity, he succeeded to the fullest extent of our expectations. Within the space of a few weeks, he affected with a people heretofore unaccustomed to our Government and laws and strongly imbued with prejudices against us as a race, a full recognition of the rights and of their relations in the performance of all the obligations of good citizens. The complete and perfect returns of the organization of that country [sic] made by him to the State Department, afford the best evidence of the ability with which the organization was conducted, and it is adverted to now for the purpose of shewing the capacity of the Commissioner for the performance of the duties assigned him, and that the want of entire success in executing the act referred to above is in no wise to be ascribed to any deficiency on his part.

When Judge Baird heard of the success of Major Neighbors in El Paso County, upon the advice of District Attorney Webb, Baird withdrew his resignation. When Governor Bell inquired his intentions, the judge wrote that he was camped west of San Antonio with a caravan of traders and emigrants on his way to El Paso and Santa Fe.

Major Neighbors wrote Governor Bell from Doña Ana that he had little hope of success in Santa Fe. He was hampered by lack of funds, but thought that if he had sufficient means to employ persons to "bring matters forward at the Towns where Elections would be held, our laws could be extended peaceably over that Territory." The Texan emissary remarked that he had not been given one dime as a contigent fund, and that the enormous prices for subsistence in the region had already exhausted the full amount of his salary. He found himself poorly sustained in what he considered more important than money—proper pledges to the inhabitants in regard to their land titles. Richard Howard and others from San Antonio had already located on the lands of others. On his own initiative, Neighbors pledged the faith of the state that no more lands could be located until the claims of the actual settlers were investigated and hoped that he would be sustained in the pledge. A document with the state seal guaranteeing such a pledge, he thought, could carry all the territory.

The Texas agent thought that Colonel Munroe's order forbidding opposition on the part of the military to Neighbors' mission also meant that he was to have no cooperation. The agent thought the military orders for the area were kept secret so that the state would not know the circumstances under which it would have to act. It was apparent that he would need a military escort to accompany him from point to point. Bell had asked for a military escort for Neighbors, but the legislature had failed to provide one. The commissioner thought the organization of Worth County would depend upon the organization of Santa Fe County, as the Worth County area was under the same influences. He would be unable to organize Presidio County without an escort because the Indians in the region were hostile to the whites there. The few whites were employed by Benjamin Leaton, who Commissioner Neighbors said was suspected of having murdered David Torrey and his party, who had been sent to treat with the Apaches. United States troops in the region were insufficient for coping with the Indians. Most of the troops were infantry. The one company of dragoons under the command of Major Enoch Steen at Doña Ana was not enough, thought Neighbors. Of Major Steen, Neighbors said:

> The Maj is a gallant officer, and a perfect Gentleman; He is a perfect Texan in principle, and the strongest advocate of our claims I have found in this territory. He declares openly, that he would resign his commission and take up arms to defend the Texas claim to this Territory, and has by his own means neutralized one of the Presses in Santa Fe.

Commissioner Neighbors notified Colonel Munroe of his intention to proceed to Santa Fe to organize the county and called upon Monroe for assistance. When the commissioner arrived in Santa Fe, however, Munroe had issued orders for the military forces to maintain neutrality and stated to Major Neighbors that he could not assist in any way the advancement of the cause of Texas. Of the interview, Neighbors reported:

In my conversation with Col Munroe, I asked the plain question, 'Are you willing to acknowledge the Jurisdiction of Texas, if I hold Elections, and qualify the officers elected?'

His answer was, 'I am not prepared to answer that question. I have no right under my orders to abolish the present Government. The Judges and other officers are Commissioned by the United States.'

During the Conversation, in alluding to the probability of the executive of the State extending Jurisdiction over this Territory by proclamation, and enforce the Laws by a military force, he says, 'That would be the proper course for Texas to pursue, there would in that case be no opposition.'

The main opposition came from Judge Joab Houghton, one of the judges of the superior court under the military government. Before Commissioner Neighbors arrived in Santa Fe, Houghton circulated a proclamation in Spanish calling upon the inhabitants neither to respect nor obey the acts of the Texas commissioner. The disgruntled judge called upon the people to stay away from the polls in any election called by Commissioner Neighbors and admonished them to resist his efforts to organize Santa Fe County. Houghton asserted that if his suggestions were obeyed, the mission of the new commissioner would be as futile as that of Judge Baird the past year. Houghton held out the hope that the delegate sent to Congress would accomplish his mission of establishing a territorial government.

Judge Houghton threatened to imprison anyone attempting to establish the authority of Texas over the region. He and his clique controlled the only press in the territory, the *New Mexican*,[4] and Commissioner Neighbors stated that nothing contrary to their wishes could be printed, hence the people, who had received the commissioner courteously, were misinformed about Texas claims. In fact, Neighbors declared:

The Civil Jurisdiction of the Territory is fully in the hands of these individuals, viz. Judge Houghton as chief Justice—a bitter, unprincipled, and vindictive Whig,[5] and two Mexican district Judges, Ortiso and [Beaubien]. They are all then bitterly opposed to Texas, or the extension of the Jurisdiction of Texas. They have the reputation amongst the intelligent portion of the American Community of being corrupt in every sense of the word, and the fear of investigation into their past Conduct is one reason they have for being opposed to a change. They control the whole Mexican population.

They give an order to a prefect, a prefect to an Alcalde—an alcalde to an alguazil, and those that oppose these measures suffer the penalty. . . . This is the party that opposes the claim of Texas, and fills even the Halls of Congress with their resolutions passed at public meetings, a party that completely and absolutely controls the whole Mexican population above the 'Jornada del Muerto' and are so void of principle, that they would induce the Pueblo Indians to commence Hositility or resort to any other measures whatever that would keep them in power.[7]

Major Neighbors decided against attempting to organize Santa Fe County at that time. Although he estimated that two-thirds of the American population of the area favored the Texas claim, this group was in the minority under the junta that existed, and Neighbors feared that the two groups would become embroiled if he held elections and installed officials.

While Commissioner Neighbors was in Santa Fe, Colonel George A. McCall, the last of the agents sent by the president, arrived with President Taylor's instructions for the military officers to advance the interests of the "people" in organizing a state government. Accordingly, an assembly of personnel of the military government posing as the "people" petitioned the commanding officer to issue a proclamation calling a convention to form a state government. Neighbors called upon Colonel Munroe and confronted him with documents disclosing the hands of President Taylor and Judge Houghton behind the movement. One was a letter to the editor of the *New Mexican* which said that the latest mail brought an urgent request that a state government be formed in order to preserve the Union from destruction over the slavery question. "ONE OF YOUR PARTY," the editor's correspondent, urged that the requested action be taken. Among the documents were Spanish translations of the President's orders to Thomas Butler King and McCall to foment a state movement, the President's message to Congress of February 21, 1850, Clay's proposals in Congress, an announcement of the failure of the territorial movement, and the circular calling the assembly mentioned above whose list of signatures was headed by Judge Houghton's.

Neighbors entered a vigorous protest both to the commanding officer and to the people. He pointed out that this action violated the third section of the fourth article of the United States Constitution, the second section of the joint resolution for the annexation of Texas, the preamble of the Texas Constitution, and the joint resolution for the admission of Texas into the Union on December 29, 1845.[8] Senator Sam Houston had imformation from a source which he considered reliable that the twenty-three persons advocating a state government for New Mexico were without exception government employees and government contractors who were speculators as well, and in one case a peculator.[9]

When Colonel Munroe issued a call for a state convention, Secretary of State Daniel Webster, after Taylor's death, admitted to Governor Bell that this and Munroe's other actions were in obedience to orders from President Taylor.[10] Yet when the United States Senate had fallen upon Taylor and demanded that he state whether he had issued any orders to the military officers at Santa Fe to hold possession against the authority of Texas, or in any way embarrass or prevent the exercise of the jurisdiction of Texas over that country, Taylor made the astonishing reply that "no such orders had been given," and purported to send all the relevant orders. It must have galled the President to have a mere Texas agent frustrate his deep laid plans of state. It was an interesting coincidence that both Taylor and Neighbors were from Virginia and had been residents of West Feliciana Parish, Louisiana, but there is no evidence that they knew each other there. Nevertheless, the President was vexed enough to call Neighbors a trespasser and to declare to the Senate that:

> I have now to state that information has been recently received, that a certain Robert S. Neighbours, styling himself commissioner of the State of Texas, has proceeded to Santa Fe, with a view of organizing counties in that district under the authority of Texas. While I have no power to decide the question of boundary, and no desire to interfere with it as a question of title, I have to observe that the possession of the territory into which it appears that Mr. Neighbors has thus gone was actually acquired by the United States from Mexico, and has since been held by the United States, and in my opinion ought so to remain until the question of boundary shall have been determined by some competent authority. Meanwhile, I think there is no reason for seriously apprehending that Texas will practically interfere with the possession of the United States.

Senator Houston took umbrage that President Taylor should call Major Neighbors "a self-styled agent of Texas," and should state that he had no serious apprehension that Texas would interfere with the arrangements at Santa Fe. Houston approved the report that three thousand Texas troops had been called out to suppress the rebellion at Santa Fe. Throughout his running speech of several days, Houston ably defended the claim of Texas to the region. Taylor's biographer points out that Houston was answered by Allen A. Hall, editor of the *Republic*.[12]

The *Northern Standard*, its able Charles DeMorse in Washington watching events at first hand, upon hearing of Taylor's stand said that, "We have never yet had confidence in General Taylor, either as to honesty or capacity . . . . Since his inauguration his policy toward this State has been mean and picayunish, but this last brick is the unkindest cut of all."[13] The conclusion seems inescapable that Taylor had been guilty of guile in his New Mexico designs.

After the New Mexico military junta initiated the movement for a state government, Major Neighbors decided to remain in Santa Fe only long enough to urge the claims of Texas. Neighbors intended by protest and every way possible to "delay action on the part of the masses in favor of a State Government." While there he intended to gather information on forage and supplies for the Texas troops expected to be sent. He planned to return by way of El Paso and hoped to arrive in Austin by the time the governor was prepared to move with troops.[14] Neighbors's previous decision not to attempt to hold elections seems to have been sound.

When Judge Baird later proclaimed the first Monday in August as election day, the appointed time passed without a solitary effort being made to proceed with the elections. The holding of the Texas elections was no doubt discouraged by the same force which prevented the holding of elections under the proposed state constitution for New Mexico. Colonel Munroe forbade the proposed state elections and disposed his troops to prevent them. Although he was silent on the Texas elections, Munroe announced his determination to maintain the military government of which he was the head.

An observer in Santa Fe, James S. Calhoun, United States Indian Agent, thought it ironical that the same force which encouraged the movement for a state government in New Mexico prevented its initiation. Calhoun thought the people of New Mexico were opposed to the clique under the military government whose operations were "arbitrary, partial, and unjust."[15] Ralph Emerson Twitchell declared that Munroe ignored the direct orders of the secretary of war and continued the military government until the later establishment of a territorial government by Congress.[16]

The ominous connotations of the return of Major Neighbors to Austin led the *Northern Standard* to aver that the "Federal

95

administration entertains towards Texas a most unchristian hatred, and is willing to trample upon every consideration, not only of right, but of common decency to do her wrong. Our Whig principles and attachments would incline us to think otherwise, were the thing possible—but it is not possible." Whig principles or no, the paper could not resist taking a whack at Old Zack:

And whatever may be the result, the people of Texas are bound to remember Zachary Taylor. When told of the massacre of their fellow citizens, he sneeringly impugns their veracity, and imputes their complaints to mercenary motives. Without the sanction of law he endeavors to abridge their constitutional limits; and, by every act which can define a tyrant, he manifests the unfathomable hate with which their adverse vote in 1848 has inspired him. That citizen of Texas who can fail to reciprocate the President's affectionate interest may be a good 'Taylor-Whig' but a poor apology for a Texan.[17]

According to the *Northern Standard*, the arrival of Major Neighbors in Austin on June 3, 1850, and the dissemination of his report to the newspapers by Governor Bell occasioned great excitement and mass meetings over the state. Chief Justice John Hemphill presided over the public meeting in Austin where resolutions were adopted which requested the governor to demand that the United States renounce all civil jurisdiction over the western region of Texas, and called upon the governor to put down the insurrection in Santa Fe by force. At LaGrange Judge Andrew Rabb[18] presided over a meeting at the courthouse on June 29, 1850, where a resolution was adopted which stated that whereas the report of R. S. Neighbors had furnished undoubted evidence of efforts in the county of Santa Fe to organize a state government to deprive Texas of a portion of its territory, time for words had passed, and the governor was urged to put down the insurrection by force. The sixth resolution took an even graver turn. It resolved:

That we regard a dissolution of the union as the greatest calamity which could befall not only the people of the U. S. but all mankind but if a conflict must come between the different sections of the Union on account of the violation of Constitutional rights, Texas will be found with the *south*—and that she will not yield one inch of her territory unless she does so, upon conditions which are honorable to herself and to those whose interest it is her duty to maintain.[19]

Another mammoth meeting in July at San Jacinto expressed similar resolutions.[20]

A great many leaders throughout Texas and the South wrote Governor Bell volunteering to raise troops to put down the insurrection at Santa Fe, and to resist the usurpation of the United States.[21] Governor Bell called a special session of the legislature, and even before its assembly, issued commissions to leaders to raise troops for Santa Fe.

When the legislature assembled on August 12, 1850, Governor Bell sent that body a message the next day, which one member of the legislature admired for its dignified, determined, and patriotic tone.[22] Stating that the report of Robert S. Neighbors was the reason for calling the session during the great heat of summer, Bell reviewed the terms of the act under which Neighbors was sent to organize the western counties, commended his commissioner highly for his success in El Paso County, and attributed the failure in Santa Fe to the opposition of the military and the President of the United States. Bell reviewed his futile efforts to communicate with Taylor and declared that the time for forbearance and moderation had passed. The rights of Texas must be maintained, Bell declared, "at all hazards and to the last extremity." He therefore asked for two regiments of mounted troops to put down the insurrection in Santa Fe, declaring that if this course brought the state in conflict with those who unlawfully exercised authority in Santa Fe, none would regret it more than he. He felt assured that, "Texas would stand exonerated before the world, even should that conflict shake to its very center the most glorious confederacy upon which the sun has ever shone.[22]

> Those who now deny our claim, would continue to do so, were it placed before them in characters written with a sunbeam. It stands in the way of the attainment of their darling object in respect to slavery, and to deny it affords the only pretext which can be found for avoiding the stipulations of the compact under which Texas became a member of the Confederacy. Public faith is to be sacrificed at the shrine of an unhallowed fanaticism, and in the councils of the country, the constitution itself should be made to yield to a morbid philanthropy originating and existing only in the heated imaginations of partizan zealots.[23]

The reading of the governor's message to the legislature was interrupted frequently by enthusiastic bursts of applause, and a joint select committee was raised to which was referred that part of the message dealing with Santa Fe. One of the first things done by the committee on the evening of August 15, 1850, was the adoption of the following unanimous resolution: "Resolved, That Texas will maintain the integrity of her Territory at all hazards and to the last extremity." That night nothing could be heard in Austin but the deafening roar of cannon which shook the violet crowned hills of the Colorado to their foundations, according to one member of the legislature.

A member of the legislature, probably A. J. Titus of Red River County, remarked that:

> Major Neighbors is here, and his views and opinions will have considerable weight and influence upon the action of the Legislature. Those who know him best, have the utmost confidence in his sound judgment and experience, and as there is nothing with him paramount to Texas and her interests, as his untiring energy in the performance (so far as he could) of the very difficult and hazardous mission from which he has recently returned, has so fully proven, whatever opinion he may advocate is certainly entitled to, and will no doubt receive, mature consideration.[24]

Commissioner Neighbors's expenses on his mission to organize the western counties far exceeded his salary. On August 18, 1850, Governor Bell recommended and the legislature, on August 28, 1850, approved an act to reimburse the commissioner in the amount of $1,256.51.

The extreme to which vindictiveness was carried against anyone favoring the Texas cause was shown in the shabby treatment of an army officer who had dared to show Major Neighbors a common courtesy. While Neighbors was at San Elizario, Major William S. Henry, as stated above, furnished the Texan commissioner eighty quarts of corn for his animals. For this hospitable act, Henry was court-martialed, fined ten dollars to pay for the corn, reprimanded, suspended from rank and command for six calendar months, and deprived of his pay. Upon the recommendation of several members of the court, Major Henry's suspension and loss of pay were remitted. The *Texas State Gazette* asked:

> Can the history of the world furnish a similar example of meanness in those composing the military arm of a nation's defense. If so, we have yet to hear of it.

When Millard Fillmore, who succeeded to the presidency after the death of President Taylor, heard of the movement in Texas to send troops to Santa Fe, Fillmore threatened to call out the militia, the army, and the navy to uphold the military government, and sent reinforcements to the region. The issue was finally settled, not by force, but by the Compromise

Measures of 1850. Senators Houston and Rusk on the floor of the Senate made masterly defenses of the Texas claim, while David S. Kaufman and Volney E. Howard did yeoman service for Texas in the House. Houston took occasion to praise highly his young friend, Major Neighbors. Speaking on June 13, 1850, after the Major's success in El Paso, but probably before hearing of the turn of events in Santa Fe, Houston said:

> She [Texas] sent her commissioner, a single individual, unguarded—not a corporal's guard with him—and the people of New Mexico have acquiesced in the authority of Texas, conveyed by that single individual.

On Wednesday, July 3, 1850, Senator Houston discussed the character of Neighbors more extensively.

> The commissioner sent by Texas to Santa Fe was a gentleman of manly and sterling qualities. How did he demean himself? In a manner becoming the character which he bore, and the interesting mission which he had to execute. He was respected by all, and his mission promised to be successful; and no doubt it would have been so, had not the military power been employed to resist him. That power, united with a clique (to whose character I shall directly advert, in order to show who they are, and what they are; how they got there, and what they are doing there, and what they intend to do, and their object in the formation of a State Government), to defeat the object of the commissioner.
>
> Yes, sir; this commissioner deported himself as an officer of his Government, as a soldier who had passed through Indian trails, endured hardships, borne fatigues, and undergone privations within the territory to which he was then commissioned. He was only zealous to maintain the honor, and uphold the rights of his own State; he was worthy of his position, and most worthily did he conduct himself.

In the final compromise in Congress, Texas was to be paid ten million dollars for its territory outside of a line beginning at the 100th meridian, running west along latitude 36° 30', the Missouri Compromise line, to the 103rd meridian, thence south to the 32nd parallel, thence west to the Rio Grande. The western line was not surveyed accurately, hence the Texas boundary is three miles west of the 103rd meridian.

The most reasoned appraisal of the settlement was given by William Campbell Binkley, who said:

> The boundary thus agreed upon was far enough west to conciliate the Texans; far enough east to satisfy the advocates of the New Mexican rights; while the sum offered to Texas was almost the exact amount needed to cancel her public

debt. Each of the three interested parties had gained its fundamental aims, and therefore the settlement made would seem to present the nearest possible approach to the establishment of justice for all.[25]

Neighbors must be given some credit for the state's holding as much territory as it did. His expedition to lay out a road to El Paso in 1849 opened communications with that region, and made it possible for him to organize a county there the next year. He was responsible to some extent also for the state's being able to make good its claim to the rest of the region, and for the state's being able to sell it for enough money to pay the public debt of the Republic of Texas. Yet, unfortunately, not a county in that vast region bears his name.

Neighbors's next venture was in the railroad business. While the legislature was in session in the early fall of 1850, it passed an act to incorporate the San Antonio and Mexican Gulf Railroad, in which the Major was a stockholder. Other stockholders were S. A. Maverick, J. O. Meusebach, I. A. Paschal, and Volney E. Howard.

The act provided that the railroad should run between Lavaca and San Antonio. The railroad company in which Neighbors was interested eventually acquired the entire right-of-way from San Antonio to the Gulf. Construction continued over a period of several years, and the company claimed its grants of public lands. The railroad was sold in 1859, to I. A. Paschal, one of the original stockholders, for $51,000.

In the meantime Neighbors had established a ranch on Salado Creek in Bexar County where Henry K. Judd, the United States census taker on November 8, 1850, still listed Neighbors as Indian agent, and found him keeping bachelor's hall. In his household were his fourteen year old Mexican ward, Ignacio Serna, whom he had rescued from the Comanches in 1847 and whom he reared and educated; another fourteen year old boy, Emil F. Wurzbach, born in Germany[26]; two laborers, A. H. Wallhouse of Pennsylvania, and Frederick Snider [Friedrich Schneider] of Germany. To the Major's undoubted delight and comfort, nearby lived his sister Mary, her husband Lee Hughes, farmer, and his laborer James Romines of Arkansas.

Neighbors put an end to keeping bachelor's hall when he took time out in the summer of 1851 to marry a young lady of Seguin. Details of the courtship are lacking, but it must have been a whirlwind affair. Seguin was a town of several hundred people, and may have been a favorite courting place of young gentlemen serving on the frontier, as John Coffee

Hays also met his bride there. On July 15, 1851, Robert Simpson Neighbors married Miss Elizabeth Ann Mays at her home near Seguin. The service was performed by the Reverend Doctor James W. Hollansbee of the Methodist Episcopal Church, South.[27]

The groom was thirty-six, while his bride was eighteen. A daguerreotype shows Neighbors to have been a robust, handsome man, towering over his frail, young bride. The newly wedded made their home on his stock farm on the Salado then six miles from San Antonio,[28] now part of the city. Since Neighbors had been reared as an orphan, and had spent years in the military and Indian services, the quiet of his own home must have been wonderful, indeed. The Major became a general favorite among his wife's people. He seems never to have been given a soubriquet by his family or friends, but was referred to as the Major, a title which seemed to be a part of him, his sister-in-law said. Apparently the young couple spent a great deal of the time with the wife's people near Seguin, since the first three children were baptized in the Methodist Episcopal Church, South, of Seguin,[29] a church of several hundred people by 1851. When the Major went to Austin in the fall of 1851 to take his seat in the legislature, he took his young bride with him.

Chapter V
The Solon

In the spring of 1851, Neighbors had decided to enter politics. *The Texas State Gazette* carried an announcement that:

Maj. Robert S. Neighbors is a candidate for Representative in Bexar and Medina counties. His circular appears in the last [San Antonio] *Ledger*, and is an admirable document—clear and explicit, and radically sound on the subject of our public debt. The State needs just such men as Maj. Neighbors in the next Legislature—of sound practical views, and the firmness to adhere to, and carry them out under all circumstances.[1]

The Major and Sam Maverick were elected to represent the Bexar and Medina District in the legislature. Neighbors was present for the organization of the House on November 3, 1851. The Honorable Thomas H. Duval, secretary of state, took the chair, and with the assistance of John W. Hampton, former clerk of the House, proceeded to organize that body. Sixty-one members, including the Major, took the oath, and a·roll call having indicated a quorum present, the next business was the election of a speaker. A spirited contest came on between David C. Dickson, the Major's brother Mason, and Hardin R. Runnels of Cass and Bowie counties. Ballot after ballot was taken before, late in the evening Dickson was elected, with the support of Neighbors, by a vote of thirty to twenty-seven. On the motion of B. F. Tankersly, a committee of Neighbors and Tankersly was appointed to wait upon Dickson, inform him of his election, and conduct him to his seat.

After having been conducted to the Chair by Neighbors and Tankersly, Dickson arose and made a short but fitting address to the House. Among the problems to be decided by the body, Speaker Dickson said, was the settlement of the heavy public debt of the Republic of Texas. This must have been of particular interest to Neighbors since he had played a large role in providing the means for paying this debt, and since the Republic of Texas owed him for past service. On the motion of Neighbors, Sam Maverick, his colleague from Bexar and Perote prisoner, came forward, presented his credentials, took the oath, and found his seat. On the motion of Runnels, the House adjourned.[2]

On the next day, Tuesday, November 4, 1851, Speaker Dickson appointed Major Neighbors teller in place of H. P. Bee. The Major was put on the committee on contingent expenses with Messrs. W. C. Edwards, James N. Scott, James Hooker, and Sam Maverick. Neighbors was also put on the committee on Indian affairs with B. M. Browder, J. W. Throckmorton, Ben F. Neal, and A. J. Titus. On the motion of Neighbors, E. H. Tarrant was added to the committee. The committee, on the motion of Neighbors, was authorized to act and to report in conjunction with the committee on Indian affairs of the Senate, headed by the Major's old associate, John S. Ford. A large De Cordova map of Texas was furnished the committee by the House.

On November 10, 1851, Major Neighbors submitted to the House the petition of Thomas Sevala, free man of color, who prayed permission to remain in the state, and the petition was referred to the Judiciary Committee. It was represented that Sevala, or Cevallas, had been a resident of Texas since 1835, had fought and had been wounded at the battle of Salado in 1842, and had demeaned himself as a quiet, good citizen. The committee reported that contrary to its feelings and the policy of the state, it recommended the passage of the bill.

The hall of the House on November 17, 1851, was the scene of a railroad convention at which the delegates from Bexar were Neighbors, Maverick, and O. Evans, stockholders in the San Antonio and Mexican Gulf Railroad. All persons friendly to railroad improvements were requested to participate in the deliberations. At the gathering of the convention on November 27, 1851, a resolution was passed requesting the legislature to set aside three million dollars as an internal improvement fund, and other resolutions recommended the encouragement of railroads by government loans and land script.

During the course of the session, Neighbors voted for such measures as the building of a new capitol, the establishing of a penitentiary, the repair of Austin's portrait, married women's rights, the incorporation of Austin College, the pay of presidential electors, the moving of the bones of the men of the Dawson massacre to LaGrange, the paying of six hundred dollars to Jim Shaw for the ransom of a Mrs. Tidwell and three children from the Comanches, and against the division of Texas at the Brazos into two states.

A bill was proposed to validate in El Paso and Presidio counties land grants made prior to March 2, 1836. No doubt this was to keep the pledge Commissioner Neighbors made to the citizens of that region when on his mission to organize those counties.

Major Neighbors had been interested for many years in settling the Indians of Texas on land where they could be taught to subsist by farming and to leave the scalps of the white settlers in place. A bill by Neighbors to withhold from location all land north of lattitude 33° 30' as a region where the general government might locate the Indians of Texas was not acted upon, but a joint resolution by Neighbors and his opposite number of the Senate, John S. "Rip" Ford, his old associate, to authorize the governor to negotiate with the United States an arrangement to settle the Indians in northern Texas passed the last day of the session. The resolution read:

> Resolved by the Legislature of the State of Texas, That the Governor be authorized to conduct negotiations with the Executive authority of the United States concerning an Indian territory in the northern part of the State for the use of Indians who were of the State according to its present limits at the date of annexation, and also concerning other bounds for some small tribes; and that in such negotiations the following particulars be observed: First—the sovereignty, domain and contracts of the State shall be respected. Second —private rights shall be regarded, so that if interfered with, just compensation shall be made therefor. Third—the terms that may be stipulated shall be subject to ratification or rejection by the Legislature.[3]

Pryor Lea wrote his brother Luke Lea, United States commissioner of Indian affairs, that the passage of the resolution was extremely difficult because of the Texan prejudice against Indians.[4] This resolution was the basis upon which Neighbors was later able to settle the Indians of Texas on reservations.

As time approached for the House to adjourn *sine die*, Neighbors offered the following resolution, which was adopted unanimously:

> *Resolved*. That the thanks of the House be tendered to the Hon. D. C. Dickson, for the distinguished ability and impartiality with which he has presided over the House, and for his courteous and gentlemanly bearing towards its members during the present session of the Legislature; . . .

Speaker Dickson acknowledged the resolution, and thanked the members for their kindness during the session. The House adjourned *sine die* at seven p.m. on February 16, 1852.[5]

In the meantime the Democracy of Texas had endorsed as presidential electors, Robert S. Neighbors, Guy M. Bryan, Lemuel D. Evans, and George W. Smyth. It was a period of transition when the alchemy of sectionalism was dissolving party lines because of abolitionist agitation. When Judge W. D. Ochiltree, a staunch Whig, heard of the election of the four Democratic electors, he declared that Major Neighbors was the only sound Democrat in the lot. Ochiltree designated as Taylor Whigs two of the candidates and attached the free soil label to Evans. The *Telegraph and Texas Register* stated that Major Neighbors was elected to the Democratic National Convention in Baltimore, but the Major was not listed among the eleven delegates at the Baltimore convention which met in June of 1852.

The home of Neighbors and his wife was brightened by the birth of their first child, Mary Beatrice, on August 10, 1852. The proud parents had the baby daughter christened in the Methodist Episcopal Church, South, of Seguin.

Neighbors was active in local Democratic rallies during 1852. On September 24, 1852, the Democrats of Gonzales County assembled at the courthouse in Gonzales, for the purpose of getting out the vote at the general election. Wiley V. Collins was called to the chair, and A. Jones was elected secretary of the meeting.

> The democratic Elector, Maj. R. S. Neighbors, then addressed the meeting in a zealous and sensible manner, and moved that the Circular of the Democratic State Central Committee be then read, after which the meeting proceeded to the appointment of a county committee.

The Whigs nominated their last great general, Winfield Scott. After a spirited campaign, the Democratic electoral candidates in Texas triumphed, and the electoral college met in Austin to cast ballots for the President of the United States. Major Neighbors arrived in Austin early in December and took lodging at the Swisher House, which is said to have been about where the Woolworth Store was later located at 600 Congress Avenue.[6] The Major cast his ballot in the electoral college for the successful candidate for the presidency of the United States, Franklin Pierce.

Representative Neighbors and the other solons were called to a special session of the legislature early in 1853. One of the measures recommended by Governor Bell at the last session was the employment of a state force to protect the frontier from Indian depredations. Neighbors, as a member of the committee on Indian affairs, presented a joint resolution to authorize the governor to afford protection to the frontier, but the resolution failed of passage on the last day of the regular session. In the late spring and early summer of 1852, reports of widespread depredations in the lower coastal region and all along the Rio Grande valley, led the governor to commission Captains G. K. Lewis, H. Clay Davis, and Owen Shaw to raise three companies to operate in the affected region for six months.

The legislature, in answer to Governor Bell's call, convened in Austin on January 18, 1853, and received the governor's message. Governor Bell reviewed the neglect of the legislature to provide money for defense at the last session, and spoke of his embarrassment when depredations broke out in the Rio Grand valley. Bell stated that such troops as Smith sent to the area were not adapted to the needs of the service, hence Bell called out volunteers whose services he reviewed. Bell exonerated Fillmore, but excoriated Secretary of War C. M. Conrad.

Major Neighbors was not present on the day set for the legislature to convene, nor was a quorum present. A quorum, including Neighbors, was present next day and business began. Many matters besides pay for the volunteers came before the legislature. On January 15, 1853, a joint session of the legislature elected Sam Houston, with Neighbors's affirmative vote, to the office of United States Senator. The Major's bill to set aside definite lands for the Indians came up again, but was lost in the final attempt at passage. On January 29, 1853, a bill by E. H. Tarrant was approved to appropriate $91,246.92 to pay the expenses of the three state companies. A joint resolution on February 7, 1853, called upon the governor to ask the United States government to reimburse the state for its expenditures on the volunteers.

During the special session, Speaker Dickson appointed Major Neighbors to the committee on military affairs, and appointed him chairman of the committee on internal improvements. The Major introduced a bill on January 12, 1853, which provided for state encouragement of internal improvement. He supported another bill which was passed to authorize the governor to have the Bexar archives translated, which contained a treasure house of information. Major Neighbors and others recommended P. L. Buqurr as a competent person to translate the Bexar archives. The legislature adopted a slave code also.

During the special session, the bill brought over from the regular session to pay Jim Shaw, Neighbors's old Indian guide, for ransoming Mrs. Tidwell and three children was passed. On Feburary 5, 1854, Neighbors introduced a bill to grant his old interpreter and scout, John Connor, a league of land, which could not be alienated, for the use of Connor and his family. The rules were suspended and the bill passed on the third reading in the House, was passed by the Senate, and approved by Governor Bell on February 7, 1853. Antonio Menchaca, one of the Bexar defenders in 1842, was granted a league of land.[7]

On February 3, 1853, a motion introduced by Major Neighbors was passed which provided for a committee to inform the governor that the House would adjourn *sine die* on Monday, February 7, 1853. As chairman of the committee on Monday, February 7, 1853, Major Neighbors waited upon the governor and informed him as directed. "His Excellency returned answer that he had no further communication to make to the Legislature," and at eight p.m., Neighbors offered a resolution which was unanimously adopted to tender the thanks of the House to Speaker Dickson for the manner in which he had discharged his duties. On the motion of Guy M. Bryan of Brazoria, the House adjourned *sine die*.

About the same time, Major Neighbors was engaged by the Texas Emigration and Land Company to locate and survey lands in Peters' Colony. The Major, with his equipment, passed through Austin early in April of 1853, on his way to West Texas. The *Texas State Gazette* observed that, "We think the company very fortunate in securing the service of so competent and worthy a gentleman as Maj. Neighbors for this difficult duty, and we hope he will do much towards adjusting in a satisfactory manner the land matters of this colony." Surveying and soldiering had been complementary vocations since George Washington's time. Other early Texans such as John Coffee Hays had combined the two.

Surveyor Neighbors, with a party of Delaware and Shawnee Indians, proceeded toward the region of the upper Brazos. Neighbors first surveyed the connecting line from Pecan Bayou to Fort Belknap, a distance of seventy-eight miles. This Pecan Bayou flows through Callahan, Coleman, Brown, and Mills counties to empty into the Colorado River. He was furnished with field notes for only five surveys previously made in the region. He was embarrassed in his work, he said, because the irregularity of the previous surveys prevented his connecting with them.

107

State law forbade the location of more than three hundred twenty acres in one body along the front of a navigable stream. Neighbors found that the Peters' Colony certificates had been made in two surveys of three hundred twenty acres each, and that claimants had located these certificates side by side along the Brazos which gave each such claimant a frontage of six hundred forty acres, or a mile in length. He asked the land commissioner, Stephen Crosby, whether such surveys were permissible. Another peculiar kind of survey ran for a mile near the river, but left a narrow lane between it and the river. The company's surveyor said he had not surveyed over any of these particular surveys, but wanted to know about their legality as soon as possible. There was one kind of survey which he expressed his intention not to respect. This type took up as much as 2,000 acres for a claim of 640 acres by running across the bend "of a River so as to touch at each point." Neighbors observed that he thought he had found the finest body of good farming land that he had seen in Texas, and thought it a pity that the land had been tied up so long.

With the return of the Democratic Party to power under President Franklin Pierce in 1853, Senators Sam Houston, Thomas J. Rusk, and the Texas delegation in Congress pressed for the appointment again of Major Neighbors as Indian agent for Texas. Senator Rusk wrote Robert McClelland, secretary of the department of the interior, to which Indian affairs had been moved from the War Department:

> Maj. Robert S. Neighbors who was recommended as one of the agents is a gentleman of energy and large experience with the Indians and much might be expected from his exertions if made in time and before any acts of hostility are committed . . . . Maj. Neighbors is a gentleman in whom you may place full confidence and should be placed in full control of the affairs in relation to the Indians in Texas & much should be entrusted to his discretion. I hope his appointment as well as instructions may be sent out early and I would be glad to have a copy sent to me at Nacagdoches as I desire to communicate with him previous to his going among the Indians.

Commissioner of Indian Affairs George W. Maypenny, on May 9, 1853, notified Senator Rusk and Neighbors that he had received the appointment of supervising agent of the Indian service in Texas. Neighbors replaced Agent Horace Capron and was given the duties of supervising agent previously excerscised by George T. Howard, who was retained in the service. The unfounded statement that Neighbors had maneuvered politically to get the appointment[8] is contradicted by his own statement that he neither sought nor solicited the position.[9]

Major Neighbors had won the approbation of his fellow Texans serving the civil government of the state. He again had the opportunity to try out his plans to solve the Indian problem of Texas, which had been interrupted by the elevation of Zachary Taylor to the presidency of the United States in 1849.

Chapter VI
Supervising Indian Agent for Texas

When Robert Simpson Neighbors returned to the United States Indian service in Texas in 1853 as supervising agent for the whole state, he found conditions had deteriorated during the Whig interregnum. Houston stated that,

> On the advent of the new [Taylor] Administration he [Neighbors] was removed, and men incompetent, both physically and mentally, were placed in charge of the Indians. The consequence was, that the Indians had not a friend to travel with them; one who had been associated with them in their hunts, and who had explored the route from Fredericksburg to El Paso, where the engineers had failed to establish a particular route for carrying conveniences of every kind.[1]

One of the first problems to confront Neighbors was the recent removal from Texas of intruding Indians from the United States. The commissioner of Indian affairs had entrusted the removal to Neighbors's predecessor, George T. Howard who did not report officially how many Indians he removed. When the commissioner ordered Neighbors to investigate, he found that eighty was about the number of Indians including fifty Delawares and Shawnees along with thirty Quapaws and others. Rupert N. Richardson very properly termed Howard's efforts at removal a fiasco.[2]

Major Neighbors, who was appointed to office on May 9, 1853, was ordered to begin active duty on August 6. George W. Hill, secretary of war and marine when Neighbors was in the Texas army, replaced Agent Jesse Stemm. Neighbors assigned Hill the small agrarian tribes on the upper Brazos where Neighbors had settled them in 1849; assigned Howard to the Lipans, Mescaleros, and Tonkawas in southwest Texas; while Neighbors took the Comanches and others on the central frontier in order to exercise with greater facility his duties as supervising agent.[3] The Comanches had declined markedly since Neighbors left them in 1849. Cholera, smallpox, veneral diseases, and now whiskey had taken their toll.

110

Hill found the remnant tribes on the upper Brazos discouraged and perplexed. The whites had forced them to abandon field after field, often before they could harvest their crops. The Indians, Hill thought, had little encouragement to undertake the hardship of clearing new land of the tough, heavy, prairie sod. The Ionies and Anadarkos near Comanche Peak made only enough corn to last about four months. These tribes and the Caddos had been pushed from East Texas by the whites. The Caddos near the junction of the Clear Fork with the Salt Fork of the Brazos made so little corn that most of it was consumed in roasting ears. The Caddo chief was dead, and the young men had taken to whiskey. Game was scarce for all the Indians. The Wacos, Keechies, and Tawacanos were absent, probably north of Red River. Agent Hill declared to Neighbors that if the government's present policy, or lack of policy, rather, continued, the Indians must always be subsidized, or else starve, or steal. Hill advocated providing farming land for the Indians.[4]

In his first report to the commissioner after being sworn into office, Neighbors reviewed the condition of all the Indians of Texas, the historic policy of Texas of regarding Indians as tenants at will, and proposed policies for the general government's enactment. The Major spoke of the destitute condition of the Indians of Texas, the damage done them by United States intruding Indians who destroyed game, introduced whiskey among them, and destroyed settlers' crops by starting prairie fires. He advocated the removal of these intruding Indians, of whom he branded the Kickapoos the worst offenders.[5]

The policy which Agent Neighbors advocated most strongly for the solution of the Texas Indian problem was that which he had advocated before his removal in 1849—the acquisition of farming land for the Indians where they might have permanent homes. The agent stated that the status of the Indians had been reviewed thoroughly by the Congress of the Republic of Texas in 1840 and 1841, when it had been found that at no time had Old Spain or Mexico granted land to any Indians in Texas. Texas had followed the policy of Old Spain in regarding the Indians as tenants at will, and Neighbors had little hope that the state would take any action to give the Indians land unless prompted by the general government. He stated that the subject of land for the Indians had engaged his attention for some years past, and reviewed his efforts in the last legislature. Neighbors's present recommendation was that a part of the appropriation for the Indian service in Texas be applied to the purchase of land for the Indians of Texas. No

111

better place for the Comanches could be found than upon the prairies which they considered their own home, he said, while the small agrarian tribes could be located upon the upper Brazos where they had resided some years. The Tonkawas who had been driven from place to place were at present upon the Colorado, and the Lipans were on the headwaters of the Nueces. Neighbors thought that land should be purchased for these Indians near the military stations in southwest Texas. He also pointed out that the anomalous status of the Indians of Texas, where the intercourse laws of the United States had not been extended, made it imperative that the supervising agent have a large amount of discretion in exercising his functions.

At the outset of his administration of Indian affairs in Texas, Major Neighbors was embarrassed by the lack of instructions to govern his actions as supervising agent. The commissioner instructed Neighbors to call for the instructions that had been given Howard, but Howard demurred, saying that the orders had been mislaid and could not be found. Neighbors requested that the commissioner give him definite and explicit orders, for he said:

> There appears to be some doubt resting on the mind of Special Agent Howard in regard to the duties of a Supervising Agent. He appears to think that the only duty required of me in that capacity is—to assign each agent to his district, designate the tribes over which he shall have control—assign him his portion of the appropriation for disbursements—and to forward the reports of the agents to the Department. It appears to me that if this is the whole duty expected of me, the Department may as well dispense with a Supervising Agent.

Major Neighbors went on to say that it would be impossible to carry out his duties and to obtain concert of action among the agents unless the other agents reported to the supervising agent instead of directly to Washington. The fact that he was given the makeshift title of supervising agent and the pay of the other special agents instead of the title and pay of a superintendent indicated that the general government had adopted no policy.

Neighbors decided to visit the Comanches who were assembled on the headwaters of the Colorado. On August 16, 1853, he left San Antonio for Fort Chadbourne, where he arrived on August 24, 1853. In the neighborhood he found the whole southern band of Comanches under their principal chiefs, Sanaco, Buffalo Hump, Ketumse, Yellow Wolf, and others, with whom he spent ten days counseling. Since the department had not indicated a policy for the Texas Indians after seven years,

Neighbors stated that the consultation was of a general character in which all topics of interest to the Comanches were discussed.

In the spring of 1854, Major Neighbors learned of the shocking murder of former Agent Jesse Stemm and his companion, William Lepperman, by Kickapoos four miles from Fort Belknap. Brevet Major H. W. Merrill informed Neighbors that Lieutenant A. D. Tree was in pursuit. Neighbors and Merrill offered a reward of $500 for delivery of the murderers for trial. When Lieutenant Tree arrived, he found that the Kickapoo tribe had held a council at which the execution of the criminals was decreed. One was killed by his nephew; the other by his brother. Tree recovered all the stolen property.

Major Neighbors then learned that a party of Tonkawas, the Till Eulenspiegels of the Indian race, had gone on a stealing spree. In the Bosque valley, twelve Tonkawas entered the home of Canute Canutson, a Norwegian, on Neil's Creek in Bosque County, while the man of the house was absent. The women of the household fled with their money, while the Tonks cut open the beds and carried away valuables and utensils. After committing other thefts, the Tonks went by José María's village in De Cordova's Bend on the Brazos River, three miles north of the present settlement of Fort Spunky, where they stole forty horses and headed for the Colorado. The Tonkawas stole from the wrong party in this instance. José María, the redoubtable old warrior, with his men overtook the whole raiding party, which had rendezvoused at the mouth of the San Sabá on the Colorado, where José María's men killed one, wounded another, and took the rest prisoners. The culprits confessed to the depredations on the Middle Bosque, and José María recovered all the plunder except two of his horses, whose restoration was promised.[6]

Noah Smithwick and his neighbors in Burnet County notified Governor E. M. Pease that horses had been stolen from the Dancer and Bedford farms on Long Creek and complained that scarcely a day passed without news of depredations. These petitioners and those on the Bosque each asked that a company of Rangers be raised in their areas. When Pease notified Major Neighbors of the Tonkawa forays on the Bosque, the agent replied that the Tonkawas were in the agency of Special Agent Howard, but that he himself would proceed "at once to the Camp of the Tonks and investigate their proceedings with a Company of Mounted Rifles—and shall take measures to prevent a repetition of like occurrences."

Pease also received notices of depredations in Comal County, on the Leona, Sabinal, and Rio Seco which were attributed to the Tonkawas and Lipans.

Major Neighbors arrived at Fort Inge on April 7, 1854, where he assembled the tribe of Tonkawas and investigated the matter. The Major found that as Pease had reported, the raiding party had consisted of twelve Tonkawas, two of whom were killed. Nine were pointed out by the chief upon Neighbors's demand and delivered over to the military at Fort Inge. The culprits acknowledged having committed the offenses, but Neighbors was able to recover only the two horses which he said belonged to the Ionies. These were no doubt José María's horses. Neighbors apparently had not learned that José María had chastised the Tonks and had taken their plunder. The supervising agent wrote the governor that his instructions did not point out the manner of proceeding after Indians were turned over to the agent by their chiefs. By the treaty of 1846, however, the culprits were to be turned over to the civil authorities for punishment, and the agent urged the governor to requisition them quickly as the sons of the principal chiefs were leaders of the party. The agent also informed the governor that the Lipans, who were then supposed to have murdered the Forrester family, were in San Fernando, Mexico, where large bodies of Indians were congregating in a threatening manner.

Pease replied that he had notified the citizens affected of the jailing of the Tonks, that he was ready to requisition the Tonks when proper warrants were issued for their arrest by the officers of the county in which the offenses were committed. Pease confided to Neighbors that he did not think the Indians could be convicted even if delivered to the civil authorities. Identification would be well nigh impossible, and the courts would likely regard the confessions as made under duress.

Neighbors found that Agent Howard had confined Chiquito, the Lipan chief, and his men in the guard house at Fort Inge. Evidence seemed to exonerate them, so Neighbors had them released, except Castro's family. These were held until Castro should explain his desertion of Howard's scouting party at the time of the Forrester murders, and his subsequent flight to Mexico.

On May 3, 1854, Major Neighbors preferred charges against Agent Howard for dereliction of duty. Reports from white settlers and Indians on the frontier claimed that Howard's neglect of his duties had led to difficulties. Neighbors's own investiga-

114

tion convinced him that Howard's neglect and mismanagement had been responsible for the objectionable conduct of the Tonkawas and Lipan Apaches. In the extensive correspondence over a period of months regarding the matter, Neighbors wished to make it clear that,

I have not been governed in the least degree by any personal ill will or prejudice toward Agent Howard but by a desire to execute faithfully the important trusts confided by your department.[7]

Howard on his part resorted to personalities in his correspondence with the commissioner, procured various certificates to try to prove his innocence, and tried to construe his duties to make himself independent of Neighbors's supervision.

In the meantime Major Neighbors had received Acting Commissioner C. Mix's letter of September 6, 1854, stating that the Major would be retained as supervising agent and disburser of funds for the Indian service in Texas. The Major returned answer that:

In reply to your letter of the 6th I would state that the decision of the Department is satisfactory, both to Special Agent Howard as well as myself—In a personal interview had with him since the date of that decision, he has expressed himself as perfectly satisfied and has assured me that hereafter there will be full concert of action between us:—and our former misunderstanding is at an end.

Agent Howard appeared to agree but added: "Our duties are so well defined and so entirely independent of each other."

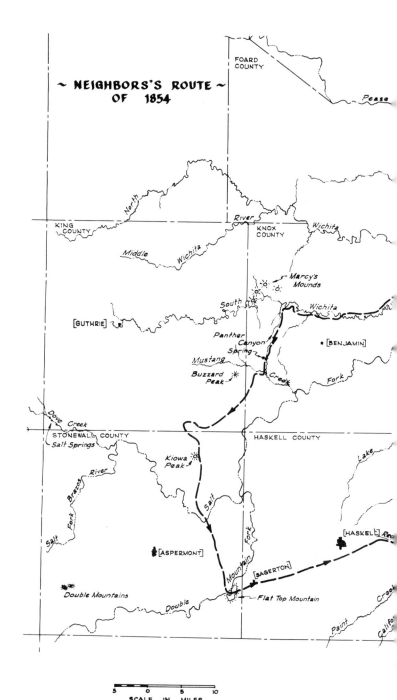

~ NEIGHBORS'S ROUTE ~
OF 1854

FOARD
COUNTY

Pease

KING
COUNTY

North River

KNOX
COUNTY

Wichita

Middle

Wichita

Marcy's
Mounds

South

Wichita

[GUTHRIE]

Panther
Canyon
Spring

Mustang

[BENJAMIN]

Buzzard
Peak

Creek

Fork

Dove Creek

STONEWALL COUNTY

Salt Springs

HASKELL COUNTY

Lake

Kiowa
Peak

River

Brazos

Salt

Fork

Salt

Salt

Fork

[HASKELL]

[ASPERMONT]

Mountain

[SAGERTON]

Double Mountains

Double

Flat Top Mountain

Paint

Creek

Califo

5   0   5   10
SCALE IN MILES

COMPILED BY KENNETH F. NEIGHBOURS

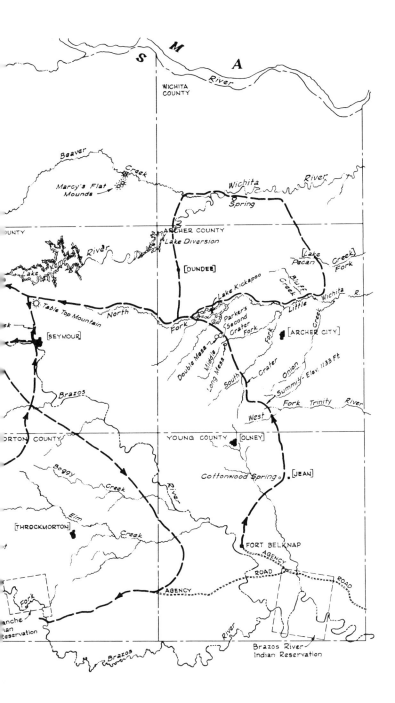

Map of route of Exploration of 1854.

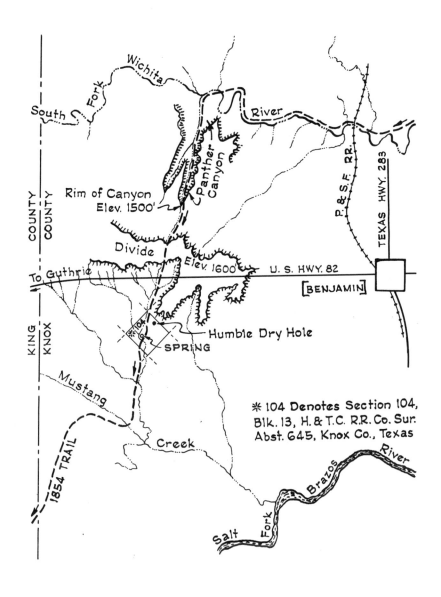

Western Section of Marcy-Neighbors Trail of 1854.

Cottonwood Spring on Preston Road. One mile west of Jean, Young County.

Dripping Spring at Smelter Tank on McFaddin Ranch, west of Benjamin. Point on 1854 route.

Kiowa Peak in Stonewall County. Point on 1854 route.

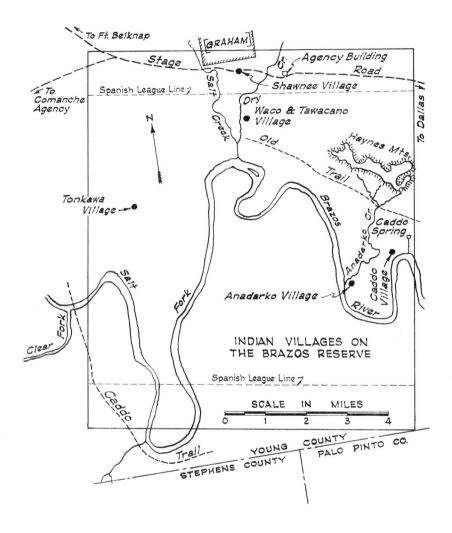

Map of Indian Villages on the Brazos Indian Reservation, Young County, Texas.

121

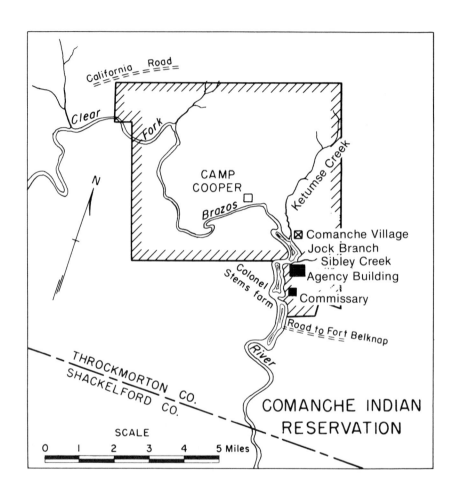

Map of Comanche Indian Reservation, Throckmorton County, Texas.

Wichita Grass Houses, Indian City, Anadarko, Oklahoma, 1959.

Authentic and original Wichita Grass House in the Fort Sill area about 1885-1890. Courtesy J. Dale Terry.

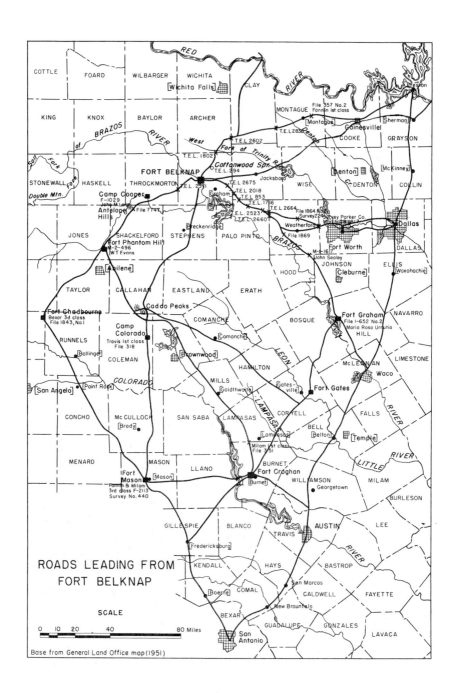

Map of roads leading from Fort Belknap.

Restored Commissary, Fort Belknap.

Original Powder Magazine, Fort Belknap.

Fort Belknap.

Restored Commissary, Fort Belknap.

MAJOR
ROBERT SIMPSON
NEIGHBORS

As Indian Agent, forceful peacemaker and humanist Maj. Neighbors had more influence over Texas Indians than any other man of his era came to Texas in 1836.

He served as Quartermaster in Texas Army 1839-1841. While on Texas Ranger duty in San Antonio 1842 he was taken as a prisoner of war to Mexico by Gen. Adrian Woll and spent 18 months in Perote Prison.

Began his service to the Indians in 1845 as agent for Lipan Apache and Tonkawa tribes. He used field system of control visiting Indian homes learning a Red Man's way of life, improving living conditions helping them to trade. He ably defended their rights. Was counselor and friend and sought new homes for them never faltering in commitment to their safety.

As a Texas Commissioner in 1850 he organized El Paso County. He was also a state representative, 1851-1852 and a presidential elector 1852.

Major Neighbors later became the supervising agent for all of the Indians in Texas. Frontier civilians and soldiers failed to support his Indian policies. Many became hostile. On Sept. 14, 1859, he was murdered by a white man as he was returning after safely removing all reservation Indians from Texas. He was buried in Belknap Cemetery (½ mi. E. of town).

(1967)

(Marker on grounds of Fort Belknap. Powder magazine (original) and Cox grape arbor in background).

Texas State Marker honoring R. S. Neighbors at Fort Belknap.

127

TONKAWA SCOUTS

By the time of the Civil War 1861-1865 Texans knew the horrors of Indian warfare. Hostile tribes made a business of stealing horses, cattle, women and children. The paths they followed in the "Bright Comanche moons" were marked by fires and ruin.

The Tonkawa tribe by contrast sought friendship with Texans. They became valued allies in the Civil War scouting against hostile Indians and watching for signs of federal invasion. Old Texas Indian fighters who once had fought Tonkawas along with others in wartime asked for Tonkawa Scouts along the frontier defense line from Red River to the Rio Grande. Commanders valued them so much they fed them at personal expense when necessary to obtain their help. A few Tonkawa Scouts were more useful than two or three companies of regular soldiers. They could stalk enemies better than blood hounds.

They paid for their Confederate loyalty on October 25, 1862 near present Anadarko, Oklahoma. Hostile Indians attacked the Tonkawa camp killing 137 men, women and children out of 300. When later their Chief Castile requested a tribal home in Texas, they were located at Fort Griffin where they remained until 1884 and then were removed to Oklahoma.

(Marker on the grounds of Fort Belknap)

Texas State Marker honoring Tonkawa Scouts at Fort Belknap.

Original Corn House, Fort Belknap.

Building housing the Fort Belknap Archives, Inc. built in
1973-1974 of original Fort Stones hauled back from Ghost Town
of Newcastle. Rebuilt on site of original infantry quarters.

SITE OF
COTTONWOOD SPRING

19th Century Oasis around a lone Cottonwood tree and a good spring. Wagon ruts from heavy traffic attracted here are still visible on hill to the southwest. In 1849 Capt. Randolph B. Marcy U. S. Army camped with his soldiers at this spring as they mapped a gold seekers road to California. Capt. Marcy was to return as escort (1851) for Col. W. G. Belknap en route to establish Fort Belknap (15 mi. SW) and with Maj. Robert S. Neighbors (1854), exploring for Indian Reservation sites. Maj. Enoch Steen of the 2nd U. S. Dragoons was here in 1855 platting a route to Fort Riley, Kan. The Leach Wagon Train camped here in 1857 while opening the Butterfield Overland mail route along the Preston Road to Red River. Riding to the north of Red River to fight wild Comanche raiders two expeditions camped here in 1858: Capt. John S. ("Rip") Ford with Rangers in April; Maj. Earl Van Dorn with U. S. Cavalry in the fall. Maj. Neighbors in Aug. 1859, escorting Texas Indians to Reservations in present Oklahoma, found the spring dry.

Water returned, however, cattlemen used the spring for generations until in mid-20th century the water table dropped permanently and the cottonwood died.

(1974)

Texas State Marker at Cottonwood Spring. Dedicated March 23, 1975. Belknap's initials were W. G. not W. F.

BRAZOS RIVER
INDIAN RESERVATION

In February 1854 the Texas Legislature designated 12 Spanish leagues (or 53,136 acres) of land to be maintained as Indian Reservations by the Federal Government. In August 1854 Major Robert S. Neighbors United States Supervising Indian Agent and Captain Randolph B. Marcy of the United States Amy made surveys in both Spanish and American measurements. American dimensions were platted totaling 69,120 acres. In the 8 League tract here in Young County on either side of the Brazos River —were placed tribes of Anadarko, Caddo, Tehuacana, Tonkawa, Waco and others. Together with splinter groups of the Cherokee, Choctaws, Delaware, Shawnees and some other remnants. The southern Comanches had their 4 League Reservation about 45 miles to the west.

Under the guidance of United States agents, the Indians on the Brazos River Reservation made much progress in agriculture, stock raising and other arts of civilization. Drouth and other adversities however led to closing of the reservation.

Emptied in 1859 when the Indians were removed to vicinity of present Anadarko, Oklahoma lands of the Reservation reverted to the state and were opened to the pre-emption of Texas Citizens in 1873.

(1970)

Texas State Marker for Brazos River Indian Reservation. Graham, Texas

131

Chapter VII
The Explorer

After laboring since 1845, when he was Indian agent for the Republic of Texas to procure a home for the Indians, Major Neighbors was finally joined by a powerful champion of the cause, whose closely reasoned arguments could not be answered but in the affirmative. On September 19, 1853, Jefferson Davis, secretary of war of the United States, wrote to Governor Peter Hansbrough Bell, urging the establishing of reservations as a solution to the defense of the frontier.[1]

When the legislature met in the fall of 1853, Governor Bell, having in mind Neighbors's joint legislative resolution of February 16, 1852, reviewed the recommendations of Secretary of War Davis and of Supervising Agent Neighbors for locating the Indians on lands of their own.[2]

The legislature responded favorable, and on February 6, 1854, Major Neighbors, who was in Austin urging the passage of the bill, forwarded Commissioner Manypenny a copy of a law passed that day by the Texas legislature which granted twelve leagues of land to the United States for the use of the Texas Indians. As the Indians were destitute, the agent urged the commissioner to make haste, and recommended that the person selected to locate the land consult the commanding general of the district whose cooperation would be necessary.

The governor forwarded Secretary of War Davis a copy of the reserve law which he remarked was passed in accordance with the recommendations of Major Neighbors, the United States supervising agent for Texas Indians, and urged the general government to act quickly in selecting the lands as the public domain of Texas was being rapidly located by individuals.

Commissioner Manypenny notified Major Neighbors on April 16, 1854, that he and Captain Randolph Barnes Marcy had been selected to locate the lands for the Indian reserves. The agent replied that he would proceed as soon as possible on the mission.

Major Neighbors left San Antonio on June 1, 1854, and was absent until September 4, 1854. The Major took with him his faithful Delaware guide and interpreter, John Connor; two other Delawares, John Jacobs, and John Jacobs, Junior; a Sawnee,[3] probably Jack Hunter, and possibly Jim Shaw.[4] Major Neighbors and Captain Marcy planned to rendezvous at Fort Belknap, which is on the upper Brazos about three miles south of present Newcastle. Major Neighbors went by way of the villages of the small tribes on the Brazos where he held consultations with the head men in order to explain the intention of the government. The Major arrived at Fort Belknap on or before June 29, 1854, to await Captain Marcy.

Two men better qualified for the mission could not have been found for both were superb frontiersmen. Major Neighbors's qualifications for the mission are too familiar to require comment. Captain Marcy, who graduated from the United States Military Academy at West Point in 1832, spent most of his life on the frontier. In 1849 he escorted a train of emigrants from Fort Smith, Arkansas, to Santa Fe, and on his return explored a new route across Texas from Doña Ana to Fort Smith. He commanded the escort of General William Goldsmith Belknap in 1851, while Belknap selected sites for military posts in Texas, including the one that bore his name. The next year Marcy explored the headwaters of the Canadian and Red rivers. Marcy and Neighbors became fast friends, and Marcy cherished the memory of "friend Neighbors" long after the Major's untimely death. Marcy served in the United States Army during the Civil War and as a brigadier general served on the Texas frontier after the war.

Captain Marcy procured supplies, transportation, and an escort of forty men from Fort Smith and Fort Washita, proceeded to Fort Belknap, where he joined Major Neighbors with his Indian guides on July 12, 1854. Neighbors and Marcy held a council with the small tribes on the Brazos: The Ionies, the Anadarkos, the Caddos, and the Wacos. José María, Anadarko chief and head chief of the small tribes, indicated that his people wished to be located on the Brazos near where they were below Fort Belknap for protection. Heretofore, José María said, they had been robbed of everything by the plains Indians and at times by the whites. The whites did, however, leave enough for the Indians to subsist on. If they must die at the hands of either, they preferred to enter the happy hunting grounds with full bellies, hence their request to be located below Fort

Belknap. They were assured that their wishes would be complied with if no more suitable place were found on the Big Wichita or farther up the Brazos. Marcy and Neighbors examined the General Land Office maps of Texas and were disappointed to find that most of the land with water and timber had been claimed by citizens.

The two leaders left Fort Belknap on July 15, 1854, and proceeded northeasterly fourteen miles on the road to Preston as far as the Cottonwood Spring, eight and four-tenths miles southeast of present Olney and one mile west of present Jean, where Marcy had instructed his escort and train to await his return. The ruts of the old Preston Road may still be traced in the second half of the twentieth century as they came over the rise to the south and down to the spring which is at the base of a rocky ledge about ten feet high.[5] William B. Parker, a friend who accompanied Marcy, observed that night in his journal that:

> Major Neighbours was a fine looking man, in the full vigour of manhood, about six feet two inches in height, with a countenance indicative of great firmness and decision of character. He was the Indian Agent for Texas, and joined the expedition to assist in the explorations and locations, a service which his great experience and judgment peculiarly fitted him for.

The next morning, July 16, 1854, the expedition proceeded along a line of march slightly west of north through rolling country covered with buffalo grass and mesquite timber. Neighbors and Marcy encamped that night at a head spring of one of the branches of the West Trinity six miles east of present Olney. The end of the day found Neighbors and his party feasting on a fat buck killed by John Jacobs, one of Neighbors's Delaware hunters.

> The Major, an old campaigner, whose mouth had been watering for a taste of the juicy buck, immediately gave orders to one of the Indian corps, and soon the smoking ribs invited us to a feast which needed no Appician appetite to enjoy.

Parker stated that their course continued northwest on July 17.

> In a short time the scene changed, and we were amidst the first bold scenery we had yet encountered. Long ranges of precipitous bluffs [six miles slightly northeast of present Olney] bounded the horizon, looking like so many barriers to our future progress. These bluffs were of igneous formations, and afforded a fine field for the geologist.
> In many places large slabs of sandstone were poised upon pencils of red clay, looking like a miniature Stone Henge,

134

or the ruins of the Pantheon, the whole presenting a singular feature in the landscape.

Parker's notes on the grasses and other vegetation provide clues that are of assistance in the second half of the twentieth century in restoring range grasses. The party crossed the West Fork of the Trinity, nooned, and crossed a ravine over a bridge the men made of gum elastic timber.

The end of the day found Neighbors and party camped at the head of what Marcy's account called a branch of the Little Wichita, but which Parker's account and Marcy's map correctly called the West Trinity. The next morning on July 18, 1854, the expedition turned due west toward the six conical mounds that lie scattered in crescent formation between present Olney and Archer City. The leaders turned somewhat southward to miss the numerous branches of the Little Wichita, but found this would veer them too far off course. At a point about six miles northeast of present Olney on land now owned by Mr. Joy M. "Hap" Graham, Neighbors and Marcy found themselves on the summit level of three streams: The Trinity, the Brazos, and the Little Wichita.[6]

A most beautiful panorama opened out to the view of the members of the expedition. Marcy, letting enthusiasm get the better of his judgment, waxed almost poetical—certainly ecstatic—as he exclaimed in his journal:

On our left, in the distance, could be seen the lofty cliffs bordering the Brazos, while in front of us, towards the sources of the Little Witchita, were numerous conical mounds, whose regular and symmetrical outlines were exhibited with remarkable truth and distinctness upon a ground of transparent blue sky. On our right several tributaries of the Little Witchita, embellished with light fringes of trees, flowed in graceful sinuosities among green flowering meadows, through a basin of surpassing beauty and loveliness as far to the east as the eye could reach; all contributing enticing features to the romantic scenery, and producing a most pleasing effect upon the senses.[7]

Parker thought the party passed through the crater of an ancient volcano extinct before the flood as indicated by the scoriae covering the ground, among which were fossils. The explorers nooned under a live oak, the first which the party had seen on the route from the Belknap-Preston Road. After travelling one mile that afternoon, camp was made in deference to the rough terrain. Here Parker gathered seed of what he called mesquite grass which he said had a "long head upon it like oats, yields two crops during the year, is very hardy and good alike for pasture or fodder." (This sounds more like side oats grama.) He proposed to introduce it in the North.

Before proceeding further with the narrative, it should be said that the present counties between Fort Worth and New Mexico were not then organized, and the frontier settlements had not penetrated much farther than the line of forts through Fort Worth, Fort Gates, Fort Graham, and those to the south. The expedition pursued a circuitous itinerary, however, through the present counties of Young, Archer, Wichita, Baylor, Knox, King, Stonewall, Haskell, and Throckmorton. In the eastern counties of this block, the best lands had been claimed by citizens, while the western counties were too arid and the water too impregnated with gypsum and salt, to be suitable for the reserves. The leaders did not know this, however, as Marcy pronounced much of the territory covered "terra incognita."

The route of the expedition was well documented. There remains the joint report of Marcy and Neighbors; Marcy's report to the war department; and Parker's published journal. The accounts of Marcy and Parker sparkle with scintillating descriptions of the country and lively references to the characters and incidents of the journey, leaving in the mind of one who pores over the records an imagery as clear and sparkling as cut crystal.[8]

The explorers continued to pursue a northwesterly course on July 19, 1854, which led across several branches of the Little Wichita that had to be bridged, and led past the semi-circle of conical mounds, including Double Mesa eight miles southwest of present Archer City. The territory was fertile but was almost treeless. Marcy with great insight remarked that

In previous communications to the War Department, I have spoken of the great deficiency of building timber, where I have travelled west of the "Cross Timbers," It may be added here, that the same facts are observed in this section, and although mesquite is found sufficient for fuel, yet there is a great scarcity of timber, suitable for building purposes. There are, however, many quarries of stone, which might answer as a substitute.

If this country is ever densely populated by agriculturalists, a new era in husbandry must be instituted. Nature seems to demand this. Instead of clearing up timbered lands for the plough, as in the eastern states, it will be necessary to cultivate timber; indeed this has already been commenced in some western prairies with successful results.

136

Parker made frequent references to the killing of rattle-snakes. These were found more frequently in valleys and timbered areas. John Connor explained that fires destroyed the snakes on the prairies. Major Neighbors was particularly active in dispatching rattlesnakes. He killed one seven feet long with eleven rattles, and next day:

> The largest rattlesnake yet killed was added, by the Major's unerring six shooter, to our collection—eight feet long and eleven rattles. Wagon shot a buck antelope, the first we had in camp. They resemble the goat more than the deer, and the flesh also tastes more like goat's flesh.

The explorers, after travelling an unrecorded distance that morning, camped at noon by a spring tributary of Kickapoo Creek at the summit of a hill, near, Parker said, another crater covered with scoriae. This was near Double Mesa[9] about eight and four-tenths miles southwest of Archer City on the Megargel highway, according to Mr. John Kay, the scholar geologist of Wichita Falls. Parker noted a new species of cactus, growing like a tree. Eight miles of travel brought the expedition to a broad lowland valley through which ran what was stated to be the main trunk of the Little Wichita, whose banks were about ten feet high and were skirted by elm and cottonwood. The uncorrected elevation was 1500 feet above sea level. This stream is presently known as the North Fork of the Little Wichita, whose water was so salty and bitter it gave the horses cramps. Bivouac was made that night on its banks. The explorers remained in camp next day making preparations for the two leaders to scout toward Red River, while the escort remained behind. Parker remarked:

> We were sorry to lose the Major, even for a short season; since he joined our mess, we had received much valuable information and entertainment from his vivid and thrilling descriptions of frontier life in Texas, since its first settlement, with which he was identified.
>
> A plain, practical man, of sound judgment, great energy and common sense, he spoke, 'to the manor born,' no hearsay, but all of which he saw, and part of which he was. An intercourse of fourteen years with the wild Indian tribes, gave him a fund of information and insight into their habits, wants, and the best means of treating with them—invaluable to him in his official capacity, and deeply interesting to the ethnologist and tourist.
>
> The Major had been a state prisoner twenty-two months in the Castle of Perote, during the Texas revolution, and was a fine specimen of a frontier man in the prime of life. His cooperation effected the best results for the expedition.

On July 21, 1854, the two leaders with three others and the Delaware scouts, struck out along the Little Wichita in an easterly direction, leaving the escort behind with orders to move the train towards the headwaters of the Little Wichita. After travelling about fifteen serpentine miles along the North Fork of the Little Wichita, the two leaders discovered Bluff Creek which joined North Fork from the north. Camp was made at the junction of the two streams. Here the spirits of the explorers were gladdened by the robbing of a bee colony in a gigantic, old cottonwood tree.

On July 22, 1854, the party travelled east along the Little Wichita for an estimated thirteen miles. It should be remarked that the explorers had an odometer strapped in a leather case to a wheel of the ambulance which measured the distance quite accurately for the train and escort. The leaders estimated distances travelled by the mounted party by the speed of the animals.

Neighbors and Marcy turned north roughly parallel to the route followed by Highway No. 281, and, after five miles, crossed a tributary of the Little Wichita, now called Lake Creek, a stream which they called Pecan Fork, whose water stood in pools at that season, but, being free from salts was palatable. There was more timber, especially pecan, on this branch than on the others but none on the prairies. The two leaders proceeded over a very elevated prairie in a slightly northwesterly direction seven miles to the crest of the ridge between the Little and Big Wichita rivers. After travelling eight miles down a smooth grade, the party dined in a hackberry grove at the entrance to the valley of the Big Wichita whose banks were struck within three miles, near the mouth of Antelope Creek. After ascending four miles, the explorers camped at a cold spring of water which burst forth from the bank near the river on the Robert Scott Survey No. 1-1123.[10] The Earl Van Dorn Road later crossed here, as shown by the survey of the land just mentioned. The precious, cold water was doubly welcome after the tiring day's ride through the fierce, summer heat. The Delawares estimated the distance from the mouth of the river to be twenty-five miles.

On July 23, 1854, the party reluctantly left the cold spring and proceeded up the Big Wichita about four miles to its confluence with a stream which the leaders named Beaver Creek because of the evidence of that animal. The stream has continued to bear that name.[11] The party proceeded up Beaver Creek an estimated twelve miles and camped for noon. On his map Marcy showed a series of flat mounds in Wilbarger County towards the headwaters of Beaver Creek about ten miles southwest of present Electra although the expedition did not go that far. That evening Neighbors and Marcy travelled slightly southwesterly to the Big Wichita where camp was made on the north bank in a ravine near some pools of fresh water. On July 24, 1854, the two leaders struck south to rendezvous at noon with the escort and train which had proceeded northwesterly in a leisurely fashion and had gone into camp only an hour before.

The escort welcomed Neighbors and the returning party particularly because part of the honey from the old cottonwood had been brought back, as well as some grey grouse. Doctor George Getz Shumard had found "a new and beautiful species of lily, of a brilliant purple, the petal black and cone-shaped. As the Major had never met with it before, we called it the *Comanche Lily*."

Specimens of the soap plant were also found and the seed obtained. This plant grows like the palm, and the Mexicans use the roots for manufacturing a very fine soap. We had a fair opportunity of testing the worth of this soap, as the Major had brought a supply with him from home when he joined our camp. It has a very soothing effect upon the skin when suffering from the attacks of insects, or irritation from sunburn, etc. For ordinary purposes it is as good as the best.[12]

Early on the morning of July 25, 1854, the expedition headed west along the Little Wichita towards its headwaters. Good progress was made as the animals were in fine fettle. After proceeding about twelve miles, camp was made on the south bank near some pools of muddy water. Travel that day had been through the valley of the North Fork of the Little Wichita along its south bank west of present Lake Kickapoo, north of present Megargel in Archer County, and into present Baylor County. The course, as observed by the present writer, was through a broad, desolate valley of barren breaks studded with leaden-hued shrubs such as the chaparral, while the blue clay banks exposed on the hill sides are dotted with large sandstone slabs scattered at random, some of which erosion has left perched Stonehenge style on pedestals of clay soil. On July 26, the explorers travelled west along the high, level prairie west of present Mabelle in Baylor County which forms the divide between the Big Wichita and the Brazos, the party having left behind the headwaters of the Little Wichita early in the day. Parker left his impressions of the divide.

This is a big narrow ridge of land, very barren and entirely without water. Water is found on either side, but in spite of the most earnest search none could be found until late in the afternoon, when the Major, always active and on the alert, who had been scouring the country around, found tolerable water both in quantity and quality in a ravine at the foot of a rough and sterile declivity, more than a half mile from any good camping ground.

The condition of the animals made it imperative to camp. Some of the oxen lay down in the yoke, and all were panting and lolling their tongues as a sign of exhaustion. The party bivouaced on the high bluff overlooking the Big Wichita north of present Seymour in Baylor County. The Brazos could be seen at an estimated distance of about twelve miles south of the bivouac, and the Little Wichita was not far behind on the trail. Parker remarked that it sounded strange that the members of the expedition and the animals suffered for water within sight of three large streams, but he explained that these were so impregnated with minerals that the water was unfit for drinking except in dire emergencies and then only with serious after-effects. This is still true in the second half of the twentieth century. Deep trails are pointed out where cattle walk up grade three miles or more from Lake Kemp on the Big Wichita to drink from surface tanks. Animals will not drink the river waters unless forced by long thirst.[13]

During the day the expedition had passed a prominent mound, upon the highest elevation of the dividing ridge, which from its peculiar outline made it a landmark. At its base were found rich specimens of blue carbonate of copper and near by a vein of rich iron ore fifteen feet thick.[14] This mound is presently known as Table Top Mountain which is six miles north of Seymour and about two miles south of the shores of Lake Kemp. Copper ore may still be found at its base.[15] The dwarf red cedar mentioned by Marcy as first appearing at this point are also still evident, which further identifies the site. Table Top Mountain is between Gray and Brushy creeks.

The Delawares, having reported that no sufficient water supply could be found for a distance of twenty-five miles, made it advisable to leave the train and escort behind. Accordingly the next morning a suitable place for a camp was found about ten miles south of the Big Wichita on a small tributary of the Brazos where there was a sufficiency of water, grass and fuel for the train. The proposed camp site, according to Marcy's map, appears to have been on Lewis Creek (called Plants Creek locally) which empties into the Brazos at the west edge of present Seymour. According to Marcy, Neighbors recognized the spot as the scene of his visit to Old Owl's camp and his narrow escape from the hostile bands previously related.[16]

On the morning of July 29, 1854, Marcy gave orders to Lieutenant N. B. Pearce to move the camp of the train and escort to the selected site on Lewis Creek. Then Marcy, Neighbors, Parker, and Shumard, together with five Indians and four soldiers set out on horseback to explore the headwaters of the Big Wichita and the Brazos. Their route through buffalo grass and mesquite timber led west for ten miles along the crest of the lofty cliffs bordering the Big Wichita, then reaching the desolate breaks and white dwarf cedar, they descended the tortuous banks of the dry bed of the stream. Only holes of brackish water were found in its course, or when a little running water was found, it was bitter and soon disappeared in the sand. Bivouac that night was made on top of the bluff where forage was found for the horses. While members of the party were bathing in the clear, salt waters of the river, shouts from the Indians and crackling sounds proclaimed a fire on the plateau. The bathers hurried *sans culotte* (nude) to the scene where the bivouac was found in flames, which were finally beaten out with blankets and cloths. The Indians lost considerable property, but the other baggage was saved. Except for this incident, Parker declared this was

> the most charming night of our trip, cool and free from insects, with a sky above as clear as sky could be, and countless meteors coursing their way over the Heavens, principally from the northeast.
>
> The twilight in this country is remarkable, prolonging the evening until a very late hour, and when the sky is perfectly clear, lingering on the verge of day-break. On this night it was singularly so, and at no time between sunset and dawn, was it dark enough to obscure an object at one hundred paces distant. We made, this day, a march of forty miles.

After crossing the line of present Knox County, the explorers took the South Fork of the Big Wichita because they mentioned the cedar growth and gypsum formation, while the North Fork has vegetation of shinnery or stunted oaks and sandy soil.[17] The explorers entered the region of gypsum water, and by July 30, 1854, some of them were suffering from diarrhea and cramps in the bowels, while all felt more or less uncomfortable. The party camped at a spring of icy cold, but bitter water.

141

On the morning of July 31, 1854, the expedition left its salt water bivouac at six o'clock, and after proceeding ten miles up the river came where it divided into three prongs, eight miles northwest of Benjamin. Marcy with his gift for descriptive prose gave his impressions of the region.

Taking the principal one of these [Panther Canyon] we followed it up for several miles through the lofty bluffs bounding the valley, until we reached its source upon the plateau above. We found ourselves here about two hundred and fifty feet above the bed of the stream, and, on turning towards the valley from whence we had just emerged, a most beautiful and extensive picture greeted our eyes. The different confluents of the Wichita dividing out as they neared their sources into numerous ramifications, all of which we were enabled from our lofty observatory to trace in their tortuous meanderings to the very heads, and beyond these could be discerned the dim outline of a range of mountains, which stretched away to the south towards the Brazos. All united in forming a landscape pleasing to the eye; but this is the only feature in the country which has left an agreeable impression on my memory, and I bade adieu to its desolate and inhospitable borders without the least feeling of regret, for it is, in almost every respect, the most uninteresting and forbidding land I have ever visited. A barren and parsimonious soil affording little but weeds and coarse unwholesome grass, with an intermixture of cacti of most uncomely and grotesque shapes, studded with a formidable armour of thorns which defies the approach of man or beast, added to the fact already alluded to, of the scarcity of wood or good water, would seem to render it probable that this section was not designated by the Creator for occupation, and I question if the next century will see it populated by civilized man. Even the Indians shun this country, and there were no evidences of their camps along the valley; so that the bears (which are numerous here) are left in undisturbed possession.[18]

George Getz Shumard, the geologist described the same terrain thusly:

The Wichita river takes its origin in a system of high bluffs (the borders of the Llano Estacado) which at the head of the river forms a regular semicircle or horseshoe, and from which are sent out a number of small streams, converging at a distance of two or three miles from the main river—which from its source to its mouth, runs through high bluff banks, composed mostly of red clay and gypsum, through extensive beds of which all of them flow.[19]

The area thus described was in present Knox County about seven miles directly northwest of Benjamin on the rim of

Panther Canyon on the Fant Estate. Marcy's grim prophecy was not quite borne out, but the region is only sparsely inhabited in the second half of the twentieth century. Marcy was actually about forty-five miles directly east of the source of the South Fork of the Big Wichita which arises in eastern Dickens County. After travelling south six miles through mesquite groves, the explorers rejoiced to find a miniature spring of fresh water "dripping slowly out from under a rock near the crest of the ridge dividing the waters of the Wichita from those of the Brazos." This afforded welcome relief after the intense suffering from thirst and gypsum water. This spring is at Smelter Tank on McFaddin Ranch. An extensive plain of coarse thin grass was traversed south of the spring which further identifies the region as in the vicinity of Benjamin in Knox County where the coarse tabosa grass is found.[20]

The march southwestward was parallel to a chain of mountains on the right about fifteen miles away. Marcy's "mountains" were a range of hills, about seventeen miles west of present Benjamin, which stretch away toward the south. The march led directly toward the large, perfectly conical Kiowa Peak. Others in the range, such as present Buzzard Peak, were truncated and irregular. An estimated twelve miles brought the explorers to a branch of the Brazos, now called Little Croton Creek, which Marcy said was fifty feet wide and two feet deep with a rapid current flowing over a bed of quicksand. The water was bitter and unpalatable as usual. Bivouac was pitched on the banks of this stream, about ten or twelve miles northwest of present Knox City.

The explorers travelled in a direction slightly southwesterly toward the conical peak (Kiowa Peak) on August 1, 1854. After an estimated twelve miles, another branch of the Brazos, North Croton Creek in southeastern King County, was struck, which spread out over a broad bed of loose sand in which most of the water disappeared. Marcy and Neighbors ascended this branch a few miles and struck a tributary of an entirely different character.

> It was shut in by high, abrupt clay banks, the water clear, deep, and covered with water grasses, very much like one of our northern spring brooks, and I felt the utmost confidence that we should find the water fresh, but it proved to be, if possible, worse than that in the other branches.[21]

This branch of the Brazos, which was thirty yards wide and from two to fifteen feet deep, ran through a valley about two miles wide. No trees grew upon its banks, but it was literally

143

alive with catfish and buffalo fish. The party dined upon some of the fish cooked by Major Neighbors, who was held in high esteem as a cuisiniere by the camp. The explorers gave the stream the name, Cat Fish Fork, but it is known as Pen Branch.[22] It is a popular fishing place where catfish, bass, and buffalo fish are still plentiful. The stream is enclosed in a deep canyon, and the clear water is filled with water grasses, as Marcy observed, with runners a yard long.[23] Eight miles below Pen Branch the Round Mountain or Kiowa Peak in northeastern Stonewall County was passed. Parker described the peak as a bell-shaped mound of alternate terraces of gray limestone (which was actually gypsum). After travelling five miles below Kiowa Peak, the explorers pitched bivouac in the mountains beside two pools of water.

One of the soldiers became violently ill from the effects of the water. The trooper suffered from cramps in his bowels and from diarrhea and could keep in the saddle only with great difficulty. Later analysis showed the water contained sulphate of lime, sulphate of magnesia, sulphate of soda, chloride of sodium, and hydrosulphuric acid. This was quite enough to make a man sick. So many of the men, both white and Indian, took sick that what Parker designated as the gentlemen[24] of the expedition took over the guard mount. For two days intensive fires had been seen far to the east, which the Delawares said indicated a large war party of northern Comanches on the way to plunder and ravish Mexico. During the night the gentlemen on guard observed that the horses showed unusual wariness and restlessness. It was later learned from Ketumse that a band of two hundred and fifty northern Comanches, Kiowas, Arapahoes, Cheyennes, and Sioux bound for Mexico hovered around the expedition for two days, but

> finding but thirteen in our party, they hesitated to attack us, feeling sure that a *large command* must be in the neighborhood, as they could not believe that so small a force of white men would venture so far into their fastnesses, unless supported at short distance by a large party—so that the order of things was reversed, in our case, and in our weaknesses, we found our immunity from annihilation.

The journey on the morning of August 2, 1854, led through rugged, mountainous terrain for several miles. Members of the expedition climbed to the peak of a high eminence from which they could observe the country for miles.

> The principal trunk of the Brazos, which was about two miles to the south, could be traced in its course through the moun-

tains to the west, to its very source, and beyond this, after passing a plain of several miles in extent, could be seen another group of mountains much more elevated than those we are now traversing. They seem to be about forty miles distant, and present much the appearance of some of the most elevated spurs in the Wichita range, and fully as elevated.

The outline of the crest of this group is more deeply serrated and irregular, and the apices of the peaks more acute than those of the range we are now standing upon, having every appearance of upheaval and volcanic origin. If this conclusion is correct, they are probably composed of primitive rocks, and from their geographical position and the direction of the group, both of which are nearly in direct line connecting the two primitive ranges of the Guadalupe and Witchita, it has occurred to me that this might be an intermediate outcrop of the same continuous chain. I was surprised to find these lofty mountains at the sources of the Brazos, as I had before supposed the entire face of the country lying between the Pecos and Red rivers to be one continuous and unbroken plain, and that the Brazos, like the Red and Colorado rivers, had its origin in the table lands of the Llano Estacado. On facing to the east, and looking back over the country we had been traversing, it seemed to be an almost perfectly smooth and level surface, without a hill or valley, through which we could trace the several tributaries of the Brazos, as they flowed on in graceful curves, until they finally united in one common receptacle, generally known as the main or "salt fork." This we followed with our eyes for many miles, when it gradually disappeared in the murky atmosphere in the distance.

After feasting our eyes for some time upon this rare and magnificent scenery, we reluctantly turned our steps down the mountain, and rode forward to the river.[25]

Marcy's observation post was described by Parker as a dazzling white bluff of gypsum standing seven hundred feet above the plain. Parker, with keen perception, noted that to the right or west appeared two conical peaks at what he thought was the source of the Brazos. The twin peaks looked like two dim clouds in the distance. This was Double Mountain, in Stonewall County, thirteen miles southwest of present Aspermont.[26]

Shumard further noted that

Beyond the mountain appeared a line of high bluffs (the Llano Estacado) which in the distance looked like clouds floating upon the horizon.[27]

After descending the gypsum bluff, which is about eight miles directly northeast of present Aspermont,[28] Marcy and

145

Neighbors travelled south about two miles to the Salt Fork of the Brazos which is about forty yards wide at that point. The water was extremely saline to the taste, and the Comanches later related that the stream passed through a plain of salt, above which the water was palatable. The field of salt is one hundred and twenty acres in extent in the southwestern corner of King County, four miles southwest of Hayrick Mountain on W. A. Springer's land. The site is actually on Dove Creek, a tributary of Salt Fork of the Brazos. Salt springs bubbling up built tall cones which were a source of salt for the Indians.[29]

Ten miles south of the Salt Fork of the Brazos a pool of fresh water was found and camp was made. Captain Marcy was eager to explore the mountains beyond the supposed head of the Brazos, but Major Neighbors was unwilling to proceed farther. He, as well as the others, had suffered from the bad water, and one trooper was almost too ill to keep to his saddle. It was obvious also that the region was unsuitable for Indian reservations. Marcy contented himself with viewing the region from afar, and marking the courses of the streams from compass observations.

> The next morning we directed our course towards the eastern extremity of a low mountain, nearly south from our last camp, which I recognized as the same I had seen in 1849, from the point where the Dōna Ana road strikes a stream which has heretofore been known as the double mountain fork of the Brazos. My Delaware guide [Black Beaver] upon that occasion correctly informed me that this mountain was near the south fork of the Brazos.[30] [Actually Double Mountain Fork]

The low mountain, presently called Flat Top Mountain, is in southeastern Stonewall County about three miles southwest of present Sagerton. The location of the salt plain rules out possible landmarks upstream.

After crossing Double Mountain Fork, the explorers ascended Flat Top Mountain on the Swenson Ranch, which has something of the appearance of a gingerbread figurine dropped on the plain by the Double Mountain Fork whose course it diverts north to join Salt Fork.[31] From the top of the mountain, the explorers noted that to the east stretched a continuous mesquite flat, while to the west appeared the peaks at what Marcy thought to be the head of the Brazos, which actually arises in New Mexico. Marcy sketched in his journal the outline of twin peaks in the distant west which he failed to recognize as Double Mountain and named it Mount

Cooper on his map. Double Mountain is only twenty-four miles west of Flat Top Mountain, but its twenty-three hundred feet peaks appear only as a blue haze on the distant horizon, dim, mysterious, and crouching sphinxlike. After travelling six miles on top of Flat Top Mountain, the explorers plunged their mounts off the precipitate bluff on the east side.

Travelling until 10:00 p.m., the explorers camped at a pool of despicable water from which was prepared a cup of salt coffee, which with a "venison steak, cooked by friend Neighbors in his best style (which 'by the bye,' would not bring discredit upon a professional cuisinere), we managed to make a supper," Marcy remarked. After travelling eighteen miles, they made camp on present Red Creek (dubbed Panther Creek) which debouches into North Paint Creek three miles south of Irby on Highway Number 380. North Paint Creek flows into Paint Creek five miles northeast of Paint Creek Reservoir Dam on Stamford Lake. Next morning Neighbors and his party turned left northeasterly up North Paint Creek (dubbed Spring Creek), which they ascended twelve miles. After passing present Atchison Draw in northeast Haskell County, the explorers came upon a chain of seven lakes of clear, sweet water on present J. R. Coody Ranch. The lakes, the longest of which is about three hundred yards in extent, are retained in the bed of North Paint Creek by ledges of limestone.[32]

> Here we nooned, dining off some of the delicious catfish, cooked in the Major's best style, whose kindness, in this respect, throughout our dreary journey, can never fade from our memories.[33]

Neighbors passed the sources of North Paint Creek near present Highway Number 380, and after travelling fifteen more miles over mesquite uplands, made camp at the head spring of one of the branches of Miller Creek at present Swenson Ranch headquarters. Fifteen miles farther along on August 6, the explorers crossed present Miller Creek, a broad, clear stream, a tributary of the Brazos, ten miles south of Seymour. The stream flowed over a flat rock bottom, and so was dubbed Flat Rock Creek. The joints in the limestone strata in the area are so regular and closely fitted as to suggest their being placed by masons. Captain Marcy decided to move to this point the main camp which had been left on Lewis Creek on July 29, 1854. Parker observed:

> Here for the first time I saw fish shot from horseback. Whilst the Major's horse was drinking, an enormous catfish made his appearance, and lay still long enough to receive a bullet

147

from his famous revolver, which had done such good service in ridding us of rattlesnakes during our trip.

The Salt Fork of the Brazos was struck ten miles north of Flat Rock (Miller) Creek, and after ascending five miles, the hearts of the wayworn explorers were gladdened by the sight of the encampment of the escort and train which had been moved from Lewis Creek to the springs on the streamlet which empties into the Brazos two miles east of present Red Springs in Baylor County.[34] The camp was in a beautiful valley surrounded by high bluffs where Marcy said,

> We joined our comrades, and after the privations we had necessarily been subjected to during our excursion, enjoyed exceedingly the few luxuries our remaining stores afforded.

The next day the camp was removed to Miller Creek about ten miles southwest of Seymour and remained there until the morning of August 9, 1854, when Neighbors and the explorers journeyed southeast twelve miles to a small tributary of the Brazos where camp was made. The next day's travel brought them to a large creek (Boggy Creek) where, while encamped, quite a sensation was created by the approach of several strangers. They proved to be Ketumse, a Comanche chief, and two of his wives. He had received Major Neighbors's message to meet him in council.

"Ke-tum-e-see, was a fine-looking man, about fifty years old, full six feet high, with a dark red bronze complexion."[35] He wore an old straw hat and cotton shirt, while his horse's bridle was ornamented with fifty dollars worth of silver. One of his wives had a costly silver girdle, but otherwise the women were quite squalid.

Ketumse assured Marcy and Neighbors of his friendship and the willingness of his band to colonize on farm land. He stated that other Comanche chiefs had expressed the same willingness, but he correctly doubted their sincerity.

Continuing the march southeast on August 11, 1854, the explorers came to a large stream of running water in eastern Throckmorton County, Elm Creek, which had to be bridged, and crossed on the morning of August 12. About seven miles east of present Throckmorton they crossed the Doña Ana road laid off by Marcy in 1849. The next day they intersected the Fort Belknap-Fort Chadbourne road about ten miles southeast of present Throckmorton and followed it west to the Clear Fork of the Brazos. Upon ascending the right or west bank, the newcomers to the region were astonished to see extensive fields of corn and oats. This was the farm of the late Indian

Agent Jesse Stemm.[36] The party camped one-half mile below the farm at a spring on the Clear Fork eleven miles west of present Woodson.

Two emmissaries of Chief Sanaco, who claimed supremacy over the southern Comanches or Penatekas, arrived and announced his imminent approach. The emissaries caused some merriment among the troops, since they appeared riding almost nude but with skin umbrellas hoisted overhead. The uninhibited native sons of the plains dressed (or undressed) to suite the climate, while the white men dressed as their ancestors had in northern climes and suffered from heat in consequence. Troopers would never tolerate an umbrella in their midst.[37]

Sanaco with several sub-chiefs and a chief of the middle Comanches arrived on August 18, 1854. Sanaco had already sent word by his emissaries not to put any reliance in Ketumse as he did not speak for all the Comanches. Sanaco was said to be prepossessing in appearance, being about five feet eight inches in height, not stout, "but his frame firmly knit, very dark complexion, with a countenance mild but decided," Parker wrote.

Captain Marcy had an ox killed for the Comanches, which the women prepared in various ways, principally by jerking. The entrails, after being drawn through the coals, were devoured immediately, reeking with excrement. The chiefs ate with the officers, and while observing great decorum, stopped not until everything was consumed.

At a council on the night of August 20, 1854, Captain Marcy told the chiefs of the intentions of the government and remarked on the progress that other tribes had made after adopting the reservation plan. He stipulated the benefits the government would bestow on the Indians, but indicated firmly at the same time that they must give up their marauding life. When pressed to the point, Sanaco declared:

> You come into our country and select a small patch of ground, around which you run a line, and tell us the President will make us a present of this to live upon, when every body knows that the whole of this entire country, from the Red River to the Colorado, is now, and always has been, ours from time immemorial. I suppose, however, if the President tells us to confine ourselves to these narrow limits, we shall be forced to do so, whether we desire it or not.

The joint report of Marcy and Neighbors said that many of the chiefs and Comanches seemed willing to try the reservation experiment and expressed a desire to have their reservation located on the Clear Fork in the vicinity of the council site which was one of their wintering places. Major Neighbors gave them presents, at which they expressed their pleasure. In a few days the Comanches left for the prairies very much satisfied. Ketumse lingered to beg food, but when refused by the commissary, he left in a black mood. Knowing ones thought he might return for revenge.

Marcy and Neighbors selected a site for the Comanche reservation of four leagues (23,040 acres) on the Clear Fork between the Doña Ana or California and Fort Belknap roads in present Throckmorton county in the area desired by the Comanches. A reservation of four leagues was selected for the small agrarian tribes on the north side of the Brazos just below the junction of the Clear Fork in present Young County. The pure water of the Clear Fork so modified the water of the Salt Fork that animals would drink it readily. Another reservation of four leagues contiguous to the Brazos reservation was surveyed south of the river for the Indians of West Texas. Major Neighbors doubted that they would accept it, and suggested that one on the Toyah west of the Pecos be selected for them. Parker wrote,

> Major Neighbors returned to his home near San Antonio, and took with him Conner, the two Jacobs, and Jack Hunter, the Shawnee. We parted with the Major with regret, his fund of anecdotes of Indian life and customs, and his great experience on the frontier, imparted with so much affability and enthusiasm had wiled away many an hour in camp and on the march, and we missed him very much.

Major Neighbors arrived in San Antonio from Fort Belknap on September 4, 1854, and reported that Marcy was far along with the survey of the reserves. Their joint report of the explorations and the surveys of the reservations were sent to the commissioner of Indian affairs and to Governor Pease, whom Neighbors requested to record these on the General Land Office maps so that citizens would not locate upon them. Marcy wrote the governor that he had surveyed each reserve in both Spanish and American measurements. The Texas law did not specify which measurement to use so Marcy said he presumed the standard United States measurement was intended and that he was sustained by the secretary of war. Governor Pease, a Connecticut Yankee, remarked to Neighbors that if Marcy had not been ignorant of Texas law, he would have known that unless specified, league meant Spanish league. Pease, expected, however, that the legislature would approve the

American league survey,[38] and noted that he would enter the surveys on the General Land Office map.

The reserves were selected and surveyed, but much work remained to carry out Major Neighbors's long cherished dream. The department of the interior had yet to approve of the steps taken and provide funds for the costly removal of the Indians to the reserves. In the meantime the regular affairs of the Indian service in Texas went on.

Chapter VIII
The Colonizer

While the agents marked time waiting for the department to approve the removal of the Indians to the reserves, Major Neighbors and the other agents made their annual reports. The Major reported that the status of the Comanches had not changed since his last annual report, and observed that his recommendations on that occasion still held.[1]

Agent Hill reported from Fort Belknap that the Ioni, Anadarko, and Caddo tribes, numbering about 500 souls, were anxious to be settled on their lands on the reservation. Agent Howard's tribes had behaved themselves well that year and had rendered good service to the United States troops on the frontier in the capacity of trailers, spies, and scouts. His Indians numbered about fourteen hundred souls, he said, and were in the vicinity of Fort Clarke awaiting the will of the government on removing them to the reservation.

Another daughter was born on October 8, 1854, to Neighbors and his wife. They had her christened Frances Elizabeth Ritchey Neighbors in the Methodist Episcopal Church, South, of Seguin. She died on December 1, 1854.[2]

Neighbors left San Antonio on November 10, 1854, to make one of his frequent tours of the prairies. He arrived at Fort Chadbourne on November 17 where he found a small party of Comanches. Thence he proceeded in company with Agent Hill to Fort Belknap where they found the whole southern band of Comanches numbering about 1200 souls. In haste Major Neighbors reported to Governor Pease the apprehensions of Major Enoch Steen, commanding Fort Belknap, that troops assembling at Fort Chadbourne for a campaign under Captain W. J. Newton "will make no distinction between hostile and friendly Indians." Steen and citizens were afraid this would bring on a general Indian war. Neighbors requested the governor to ask General P. F. Smith to suspend hostilities against the friendly Indians until the government could colonize them. Major Neighbors remarked to Commissioner Manypenny that

It is certainly strange that one Department of the Government should employ agents to make peace, select lands for permanent settlements, and induce large bodies of Indians to hold themselves in readiness for settling down, and another should assemble troops in the same neighborhood to make war on the same Indians, without directing any concert of action between the Indian Agents and military for the protection of the friendly Indians.

The agent estimated that it would cost millions of dollars to carry on a border war: at least $50,000 per head for the three thousand Indians on the borders of Texas. Major Neighbors drew upon his past experience in the Army of the Republic of Texas to declare with prescience that:

> From 1838 to 1842 the Republic of Texas attempted to carry on a war of extermination against our border Indians; she had all the appliances necessary for successful warfare and a part of the time one thousand men in the field, and leaders who were in every way experienced in Indian warfare; the result was a perfect failure, and after exhausting all her resources, she had to resort to the peace policy, and the General Government has had it in her power ever since the date of annexation, to settle our Indians down peaceably—and it is altogether for the want of an established policy and proper management that we are at the present day troubled with Indian depredations; and so long as the Department listens to the newspaper reports of the day, and to men who wish to make capital out of the Indian depredations in our State, and fail to establish a policy, for the government of the Texas Indians founded in justice and liberality, she may expect a recurrence of the same troubles.

In January of 1855, Major Neighbors, preparing to leave for Washington, gave Agent Howard special instructions to guide him during his absence. Agent Howard should go to Fort Chadbourne and cooperate with Captain Newton, Second Dragoons, in a campaign against the middle and northern Comanches. Howard was to be certain that the southern Comanches and small tribes assembled on the Brazos near Fort Belknap were not molested. Agent Howard failed to carry out this mission, as will be seen.

On January 25, 1855, Commissioner Manypenny notified Secretary of Interior McClelland that Supervising Agent Neighbors had arrived in Washington to confer on the business of settling the Indians on the reserves. The commissioner recommended the acceptance of the reserves as selected and agreed with the agent's views on the hostile action of the military. Secretary McClelland acknowledged the receipt of the agent's letters to Manypenny, approved the survey of the reserves, and the agent's proposed policies, while sending to the war department the report of Neighbors on the military's intention to attack the Indians.

Presently Major Neighbors reported to the commissioner that Agent Howard had failed to carry out his orders of January 8, 1855, and that the military had scattered almost the entire southern band of Comanches. Neighbors forwarded Howard's letter of explanation that he failed to go because he had no escort.

The scattering of the Indians occurred on this wise. On January 3, 1855, Major E. Steen went from Fort Belknap to the Comanche camp on the Clear Fork to recover five of E. N. Smith's mules. The chiefs recovered the mules readily and supplied one of their own for one missing. The chiefs were friendly and awaited the opportunity to settle on the reserve. They offered the services of guides and any other service their people could perform. When within twenty-five miles of Belknap, Steen was overtaken by Ketumse who reported that John Lyendecker, a German trader, from the vicinity of Fort Chadbourne, had sent word by two Indians to Sanaco and Buffalo Hump that a strong force would in two or three days proceed from Fort Chadbourne to exterminate the southern Comanches, and that Steen had received similar orders. The bands of Sanaco and Buffalo Hump fled precipitately to fastnesses far to the north, leaving their baggage and provisions. Since the Council House massacre of their chiefs, the Comanches scattered like a covey of quail at the slightest hint of hostile action. Ketumse did not credit the report and intended to follow Major Neighbors's instructions.[3]

Hill who had gone, in obedience to Neighbors's orders, to personally contact the military expedition in an unsuccessful effort to prevent the debacle, suggested to Neighbors:

> I hope you will at once urge upon the Deptnt. of Interior the importance of sufficient concert of action, between that & the Deptnt. of War, to guard against attacks upon Indians, among whom·the Agents sleep and travel, & whose minds they are instructed to prepare for permanent settlement, under guarantees from the Govtnt. of the United States, through legitimate channels, & this without notice to such Agents. If such use of my labors with these people cannot be prevented, I would be pleased to know it. (Another copy

of the same letter reads): If such use is to be made of my labors with these people and secret attacks be made upon them, I would be pleased to know it.

Major Neighbors wrote Commissioner Manypenny that: I have also to inform you that the military expedition against the Comanches has returned without having overtaken the Indians. It is reported a perfect failure, as there has been no engagement, no blood spilled; it is hoped that confidence will soon be restored through the Agents, and the Indians be induced to settle down.

Captain Newton C. Givens about this time also started his career, in which he later made quite a stir, of trying to undermine the Indian service. Major Steen gave Givens orders to pursue a party of marauders who had stolen some animals on the Clear Fork. Instead of pursuing the trail of the raiders, Givens went to the camp of the southern Comanches, which Steen supposed Givens found abandoned after Sanaco's flight. Steen declared that Givens had no evidence against the southern Comanches and expressed his dissatisfaction with the way the scout terminated. He thought Givens should have followed the trail and punished the actual thieves. Givens made a curious report on November 6, 1854, that a party of southern Comanches committed depredations between Fort Belknap and the reservation, that he had followed and detected the guilty, "but for certain reasons had not arrested them."

In compliance with the orders of Major Neighbors, Agent Howard collected the Tonkawas, numbering two hundred and fifty, in the Nueces valley, but because of the orders of P. F. Smith, Howard was unable to encamp the Tonkawas near Fort Inge. As the supervising agent had directed, Agent Howard made his estimate of requirements for the removal and the route to be travelled. Then Agent Howard exceeded his superior's orders and made a contract for supplying the Indians from the time they left the Leona until their arrival at Fredericksburg. The contract was with Howard's protege and retainer, Robert W. Keyworth. The exceeding of Major Neighbors's orders by Agent Howard apparently did not suit Neighbors. In any event, Major Neighbors acknowledged Agent Howard's report of March 23, 1855, and drew up counter instructions for him in terms of which there could be no mistaking.

Notwithstanding the efforts of Major Neighbors, the plan to move the Tonkawas miscarried. As Agent Howard reported himself unwell, therefore, Neighbors proceeded to Fort Inge alone to supervise the moving of the Tonks. Neighbors arrived on April 5, 1855, and found that three days previously a man by the name of Saunders had collected eighteen armed men for the purpose of robbing the Tonkawas of their ponies. The Tonks learned the object of the white men, sent the Tonkawa women and children into the mountains, and prepared for defense. The whites, frightened by the stand of the Tonks, withdrew without firing a shot, but threatened to return with a larger force. The Tonks took alarm and fled precipitately to the mountains where Major Neighbors was unable to find them. He then ordered the wagons back to San Antonio and expressed his intention to start the wagons to the reservations with supplies in a few days. The Major averred that,

> This disgraceful proceeding occurred in the immediate vicinity of Fort Inge where a company of United States troops are stationed. The officers knew that the Indians had been assembled for the purpose of being removed to their future home on the Brazos river, and by a mere expression of opinion might have prevented it. This shows the absolute necessity of giving the Indians protection and of establishing concert of action between the officers of the respective services.

Agent Howard alone could explain why the Indians were left in an unprotected state, said Neighbors, and he expressed the opinion that had an agent been on the ground to attend to the wants of the Indians and to protect them, the failure could not possibly have occurred. Major Neighbors declared that the officers at the fort had always furnished the agent an escort when called upon and that an investigation would show a great lack of efficiency on the part of Agent Howard, if nothing worse.

> I have no hesitation in stating that this state of affairs has been produced by a reckless disregard of the duties of his office on the part of Special Agent Howard. He has since my return from Washington, failed in the execution of every trust reposed in him by me, and has disobeyed my instructions or evaded their execution in such a manner as to render plans under your instructions of 2d Feby entirely unsuccessful. He has thrown every obstacle in my way in the removal of the Indians in his district by causing unnecessary delay. And is justly chargeable with the expense attending the failure in the removal of the Tonkahuas.

Then Major Neighbors asked to be relieved of any further responsibility for Howard's acts:

> Having lost all confidence in him I am unwilling to again take the responsibility of assigning him to duty or to risk

the execution of any of the important trust confided to me in his hands, as nothing but disaster and unnecessary delays and failures has attended everything in relation to Indians in connection with him. I hope therefore and respectfully request that you will assign Special Agent Howard to such duties as you may think proper provided they have no connection with those assigned me. To any farther connection between us as Indian Agent, I must strongly protest.

There were no Indians in Howard's district, the Major stated. The Lipans and Mescaleros were in Mexico. Major Neighbors feared the Tonkawas had followed the same example, had become hostile, and would commit serious depredations on the western frontier. He declared finally that, "I would much prefer that the Special Agent would retire on his salary and have nothing to do with the Indians, as I should not then be embarrassed with failures in the measures I am endeavoring to carry out."

Agent Howard had already tendered his resignation to the department on April 2, 1855, to become effective on June 30, 1855, but he did not notify Major Neighbors until April 27, 1855. Howard stated that he had "been in a measure forced from the service by the personal hostility of Maj. Neighbors.

In writing to Commissioner Manypenny of Agent Howard's resignation, Major Neighbors remarked,

I notified you that I should not again assign him to any further duty; he had been confined to his room by sickness [rheumatism] for some days past; he has been unwilling to proceed to the Indian reservation.

Neighbors refused to approve Howard's accounts because of their irregular nature. Howard eventually went over Neighbors's head to the President of the United States to no avail. The accounts were not approved until they met Neighbors's specifications and one objectionable claim was withdrawn.

In preparation for colonizing the Indians, Major Neighbors, at Fort Belknap on March 1, 1854, made a contract with Charles E. Barnard to furnish 100,000 pounds of beef monthly to the reservations from March 1, 1855, until such time as the contract was annulled by the Major. He found about eight hundred Caddos, Ionies, Wacos, Tawacanos, and others near Fort Belknap ready to settle on the reserve. The Major instructed Agent Hill to assign the tribes to their locations, to start them farming, and to begin the construction of agency buildings. After finding that only 180 Comanches under Ketumsé remained after the flight, Major Neighbors located Ketumse temporarily on the Brazos Reserve with the small tribes.

According to Major Neighbors's instructions, Agent Hill by March 31, 1855, ahd assembled seven hundred thirty-four Indians on the Brazos reserve. These were portions of the Waco, Caddo, Anadarko, Tawacano, Bidais, and Comanche tribes. Agent Hill placed the Caddos near the east line of the reserve on the north bank of the Brazos River; the Anadarkos, one and one-half miles west of the Caddos on the north bank of the same river; and Chief Acaquash with the Wacos and Tawacanos were placed together about five miles from the Caddos and about one mile north of the Brazos and east of Salt Creek at the present junction of the Bunger Road. Agent Hill did not mention the Ionies specifically, but they had settled on the reserve voluntarily the previous fall and had always been closely identified with the Anadarkos. Agent Hill remarked that there was a plentiful supply of good water at the locations, such timber as the country afforded, and the best river bottom land for farming purposes in the country.[4] A portion of the reserve was hilly and heavily timbered. Haynes Mountain lay between the Brazos and the northeast corner of the reserve. The Comanches were located temporarily with the small tribes, but the guests declined to assist with the farming. They preferred to wait until settled on their own reserve to start farming. In the meantime, they proposed to observe how it was done.

Agent Hill said he had selected a suitable place for the erection of agency buildings about two and one-half miles from the Brazos River and one and one-half miles east of Salt Creek. The location was about six hundred yards south of the north line of the reserve, Hill added, and was on the Hugh F. Young survey about three miles southeast of the present town of Graham. Agent Hill reported plenty of good water at the location and that other conveniences were fair. The agent had closed no contract for buildings but had notified a bidder of the acceptance of his proposal.[5]

The first agency buildings may have been at the ancient ruins six-tenths of a mile west of the north spring on the Hugh F. Young survey. These ruins consist of the foundation stones of a double log cabin with a dog run in between and the ruins of a smaller building that served as the office. Later other buildings were built east of the south spring on the Hugh F. Young survey. These were probably the school, laborers' cabins, and sutler's store buildings. The stage road from Fort

Belknap to Dallas ran by the south spring as shown on the General Land Office map of 1859 of Young County.

Word finally came from Sanaco's stampeded band. Agent Hill's runners had not returned, but two of Sanaco's people on April 2, 1855, reported that when Sanaco's people fled the prior January, they took refuge in some cedar mountains on one of the branches of Red River. Sanaco's people had thought Ketumse's band was exterminated until two runaway Mexicans reached them in February. The Indians reported that a war with the Osages had cut the Comanches off from the buffalo. Many Noconas and Tenawish had been killed, including some of their principal men. Smallpox had also broken out among the northern bands.

Major Neighbors on May 31, 1855, found five hundred fifty-seven Indians on the Brazos reserve. The Comanches under Ketumse, numbering two hundred twenty-six, had proved too quarrelsome and were sent wending their way to their reserve on the Clear Fork, with barely enough beef to sustain themselves for the quarter. Agent Hill expected considerable numbers of Indians to arrive by the beginning of the next quarter—250 Tonkawas, 150 Wacos and Tawacanos, and 50 Caddos. Two hundred ninety-five acres had been planted in corn at government expense, while the Indians themselves had prepared and planted about one hundred acres. The weather was very dry, but the Indians had applied themselves beyond Hill's most sanguine expectations. Attention to Indian affairs for the last two years had caused him to neglect his private affairs, he said, and he asked Major Neighbors for sixty days leave of absence, which the Major granted.

Major Neighbors for a time was left alone to handle Indian affairs in Texas. Agent Howard's resignation became effective on June 30, 1855, while he had performed no service since his notice of resignation in April. Agent Hill was on leave and had also tendered his resignation to become effective on June 30, 1855. Major Neighbors urged the department to appoint new agents speedily as he could not carry out the colonization policy satisfactorily alone. John R. Baylor of LaGrange, a member of the last legislature, was appointed to replace former Agent Howard, and was instructed by the commissioner to report to Neighbors at San Antonio for instructions. Baylor was informed that all of his correspondence with the department would be conducted through Major Neighbors.

Major Neighbors arrived at Fort Belknap on May 20, 1855, and reported to Commissioner Manypenny that he would re-

159

main with the Indians as much thereafter as was necessary. Undoubtedly Neighbors felt profound satisfaction in finally implementing his plans of mamy years to colonize the Indians. He reported to the commissioner that the Indians were making progress in farming, building shanties, and fencing their fields. Fencing was a laborious task since the fences were made of wooden rails. The Tonkawas, 150 strong were on the Llano by June 22, and were expected in a few days,[6] while parties of Wacos, Tawacanos, and Ionies were on Red River near the mouth of the Big Wichita stricken with the smallpox. Neighbors instructed the Indians to wait until they were well before proceeding to the reservation. There were 249 Comanches on their reserve on the Clear Fork, and those stampeded by P. F. Smith's campaign were expected soon. Neighbors asked for instructions for preserving order, dealing with intruders, and for protecting the Indian settlers, in view of the fact that the intercourse laws of the United States were never extended to Texas. He expected the colonization policy to succeed in spite of the opposition of some army officers on the frontier.

Besides this opposition, Neighbors was also troubled by unauthorized trading in the vicinity of the reserves. When he ordered Conrad Neuhaus, proprietor of a trading post, saloon, and billard hall in Belknap, to cease and desist from trading with the Indians, Neuhaus's partner advised him to comply as he said Neighbors "is able to brake us up if he takes his head towards it."[7]

Referring to the efforts of Major Neighbors to colonize the Indians, Senator Houston declared on the floor of the Senate:

Some time since the present agent in Texas was ordered to lay off a section of country in that State for the use of the Indians. He did so. He said to the fierce Comanches, 'Come here, my brothers, and settle down.' They have done so. The Indians to whom I before alluded, who were driven off by the former agent, after robbing them of their horses, upon the assurances given at the return of the present worthy and intelligent agent, faithful to his trust, came back in perfect confidence, and set themselves to building their houses to shelter their women, old men, and children, while the warriors went out to kill game. There they are. The southern Comanches went within the border, and said, 'Let us settle'; but they were immediately told, through the influence of the army, I suppose, that they must not settle there. I saw, not long since, a letter from a most intelligent gentleman, who said that the officer at Fort Belknap, with three companies of rangers, and two of regulars, was daily expecting to make a descent on the poor Indians who had been settled there by the Agent [Steen was incorrectly suspected of the debacle], under pledges of the Government, which promised them that they should have a country where they should throw away the arts of the wild and the red man, and become domestic, agricultural, and civilized in their pursuits. They have acquiesced to that policy of the Government, but are in constant dread lest the military gentleman in command of the fort, in order to gain laurels and acquire glory, and do honor to his profession, may make a descent with the regulars and volunteers, or rangers, upon the poor Indians. If intelligence of such descent should arrive, I should not be surprised. I shall be distressed, to be sure; but it will only be one of a thousand distresses which I have felt at the wrongs inflicted on the Indians.

Learning that his old associate, Shapley Prince Ross, had applied for an appointment as Indian agent, Major Neighbors endorsed him highly, saying to the commissioner of Indian Affairs:

I learn that Capt. S. P. Ross of Waco, Texas, has applied for an appointment as one of the Special Indian Agents of Texas. I have known Capt. Ross intimately since 1846, and have frequently acted in concert with him in connection with Indian matters during Mr. Polks administration. I have found him at all times competent and trusty in the discharge of his duties, and wherever he has been brought in contact with the Indians he has never failed to gain their confidence and respect. The Capt. is an old and tried democrat, and I can think of no one that will apply for an appointment as Special Agent of Texas so capable and worthy as Capt. S. P. Ross. If you can obtain his appointment in place of Special Agent Hill, resigned, you will confer a great benefit upon the service in Texas and to myself as the Supervising Agent.

Ford said Neighbors brought Ross's commission from Washington. When Captain Ross expressed his appreciation for Hill's aid in securing the appointment, Hill is said to have replied, according to John S. Ford,

You owe nothing to me. The Indians through their chiefs procured your appointment. They spoke of a tall man living on the Brazos, who had fought them 4 years and treated them well. He is brave, and brave men are not mean.

Major Neighbors learned of an interesting incident involving Ross, not long after Captain Ross assumed office. Jim Shaw told him that a Tawacano wished to speak with him in private. In his office Ford said, Agent Ross was confronted by a large Indian,

His first salutation was "get up." Ross arose. The next expression was "you killed my brother." Ross felt like a man who needs a revolver and a bowie knife. "He was the only brother I had; the bravest man on the frontier. Now I want you to be my brother. If you consent I will do all you tell me—go when you ask me, and stay as long as you like." He produced a large mesquite thorn; raised the skin and muscle of his left side, over his heart; ran the thorn through the flesh; and cut out the thorn with his knife. He held up the bloody token, and called on the Great Spirit to witness his sincerity in adopting R. as his brother. Ross recognized him as the brother of Big Foot. To the credit of the red man he complied faithfully with his promise.

The department was slow in acting on the resignation of Agent Hill, who reported again for duty at the Brazos Agency on July 31, 1855, where he was relieved by Ross on September 1, 1855. Hill died soon after his resignation.

The Texas Reserve Indians were not immune to raids from their brethren in the Indian Territory or from other areas in the West. Agent Ross reported to Supervising Agent Neighbors that when five Tenawish Comanches stole horses from the Brazos Reserve, a party of twelve Delawares and a Caddo went in pursuit. Across Red River the Delawares met ten northern Indians who informed them that war had been declared upon all Texans, both red and white. The two groups camped within thirty steps of each other that night. About midnight a proposal was made to the Delawares to gamble. As daybreak approached, the northern Indians suddenly attacked the Delawares but were slaughtered for their pains. Stealthily while they gambled, the Delawares had nearly cut in two the bow strings of their foes. Two of the enemy were allowed to escape to carry the news of the disaster to their tribe. Various possessions of murdered white people were found among the plunder taken from the marauders. Agent Baylor wrote to Major Neighbors that "the Captain commanding the party killed was a Yamparico and had a black Cloth Coat an undershirt and Dagaureotype with him and on his shield was some twenty white scalps mostly white Woman's Hair. I have his shield."

Major Neighbors went to San Antonio to buy equipment for the Indians on the reservation and while there wrote Commissioner Manypenny of raids on the southwestern frontier by Lipans and Seminoles from Mexico. The Major stated that the Mexican government had given these Indians asylum, that the Mexican officials in Piedras Negras informed him last spring that agents had been appointed to these Indians and that he would not be permitted to hold intercourse with them.

John R. Baylor presented himself to Major Neighbors at the Brazos Agency on September 14, 1855, and was assigned to the Comanches on their reserve on the Clear Fork. Apparently the Baylor and Neighbors families were acquainted socially in San Antonio. Baylor's sister Fan wrote him that she expected to see Major Neighbors while he was in the city. Fan said her mother was in terror because Baylor was to handle the money for his agency, and implored him to request Major Neighbors to obtain a small iron safe.[8] According to Baylor's family, the Major quickly formed a high estimate of his sub-agent's ability to handle Indians. In December Fan wrote Baylor that,

> Mother says you will be as popular among the Indians as our dear Father was: they all loved him and trusted him. Maj. Neighbors says he will resign in a year and that you may be Superintendent. He says you have a tact in managing the Indians that he never saw in any one else.

Agent Baylor had assured his sister that his duties would be light so she thought Baylor would have time to pursue some mining and prospecting in the San Sabá region. She said that if Baylor found a copper mine and a "little silver ready to sell it will be a nice *nest egg*."[9] Baylor expressed the wish that every Baylor die a millionaire.

Agent Ross's quarterly report to Neighbors on December 31, 1855, showed that the Indians had worked their crops communally, but some had individual holdings of livestock, especially horses. During the last quarter the Indians had built fifteen comfortable log houses, and a number were then under construction, besides the large number of large, circular grass houses completed. The Indians had planted eight hundred peach trees presented to them by the late Agent Hill, and then were engaged in fencing their lands. Agent Ross had issued one wagon to each tribe, besides plows and tools. The Indians took special care of the stock cattle and perfect harmony prevailed among the tribes.

Perusing Agent Baylor's report, Neighbors found that there were four hundred and fifty Comanches on the reserve on January 1, 1856, and that he expected more. Sanaco had come in and declared himself ready to settle his band. He brought eleven horses stolen by his men and declared that in the future he would observe the treaty and keep the peace. The Comanches were reported pleased with the prospects of farm-

163

ing and tended their cattle day and night. Baylor reported that the reserve was protected from the northern Indians by four companies of cavalry; expressed the opinion that it would take time to civilize the Comanches; but even if they were never civilized, he declared that it would be cheaper to feed them than to fight them.

The organization of the Indian service in Texas then consisted of a supervising agent, resident agents on each reserve, interpreters, farmers, laborers, sutlers, carpenters, contractors for corn, beef, and supplies, and at a later date, teachers, and a missionary. At times surgeons were employed to treat the Indians. The sutler for both agencies was Charles E. Barnard, who had John Shirley as his agent on the Comanche Reserve. The farmers were employees who instructed the Indians in agriculture, supervised the day laborers, and exercised some supervision over the Indians in whose area they lived.

The complement of buildings at the Brazos Agency came to include a double log house used as the agent's dwelling; a single log house used as an office; a single log house used as a commissary store; a double log house in which the laborers were housed; a school house; a blacksmith shop; the interpreters' house; a privy; a spring house; and two houses for the laborers at the villages, one at the Caddo and one at the Waco. There is no indication of the type of joints used in constructing the log houses. Besides the log houses built from time to time by the Indians, there were thirty-eight dome shaped, grass thatched native houses built at the Anadarko village; thirty-five at the Caddo; twenty-three at the Tawacano; sixty-one at the Tonkawa; twenty-six at the Waco, besides two log cabins; and seven grass houses at the Shawnee village. José María and Jim Shaw built themselves log houses. The agency buildings at the Comanche Reserve consisted of about eleven drop log cabins, including the agent's house, commissary store, laborers' house, and school. Only Chief Ketumse built himself a panel log house, while the tribal members continued to live in tents.

With the Indians of Texas colonized on the reservations at last, with a full complement of agents, and with the Second Regiment of Cavalry and its brilliant galaxy of Southern officers arriving in Texas to cooperate with the Indian service, two years of comparative peace and progress were vouchsafed the project of which Major Neighbors had dreamed so long. These were the halcyon days of the reservations.

164

Chapter IX
The Indefatigable Agent

With the coming of the United States Second Regiment of Cavalry under the command of an old Texan, Colonel Albert Sidney Johnston, and with a staff of intelligent Southern officers such as Lieutenant Colonel R. E. Lee, Lieutenant Colonel W. J. Hardee, and Major George H. Thomas, Major Neighbors for a period received about the only semblance of cooperation from the military that he got at any time during the experiment of colonization.

The Second Regiment of Cavalry was an elite body. Secretary of War Jefferson Davis threw such a galaxy of brilliant officers into the regiment that he was accused afterward of anticipating the Civil War. Seventeen generals of the Civil War were from this regiment. Twelve of these served in the Confederate armies. Twenty-five of the officers were graduates of the United States Military Academy at West Point. Seventeen of them were from Southern states. Not only were they from the South, but it was said that they were the best representatives from that section.[1] Besides R. E. Lee and Albert Sidney Johnston, some of those who became Confederate generals were William J. Hardee, Earl Van Dorn, E. Kirby Smith, N. G. Evans, Charles W. Field, John B. Hood, William P. Chambliss, and Charles W. Phifer. Union generals from the regiment were George H. Thomas, I. N. Palmer, George Stoneman, R. W. Johnson, and Kenner Garrard.[2]

The men of each troop were selected from each of eight different states, while one troop was selected from many states. The companies sent to Camp Cooper on the Comanche reserve were from Alabama, Missouri, Kentucky, and Ohio, each company from a separate state. Even the horses of each company were carefully chosen of one color, being grays, sorrels, bays, and roans.

Jefferson Davis played a crucial role in having the reservations established as a solution to the Indian problem in Texas, and hence to the military problem. Douglas Southall Freeman thought there could be no doubt but that Davis had a special purpose in sending the Second Cavalry to Texas and in sending R. E. Lee, an officer of intelligence, to Camp Cooper on the Comanche Reserve.[3] Lee did not arrive until the following spring, but the colorful regiment with Albert Sidney Johnston in command reached Fort Belknap on December 27, 1855. Two squadrons were assigned to Camp Cooper to assist Agent John R. Baylor, while Johnston proceeded with the rest of the regiment to Fort Mason, via Fort Chadbourne.[4]

At this crucial period, Agent John R. Baylor absented himself without leave from the reserve. Sanaco and his band who had recently come to the reserve were troop-shy. In January of 1855, P. F. Smith's hostile campaign had sent Sanaco flying to the cedar mountains of Red River, just when Neighbors was preparing to move the Indians to the reserves. With the advance of the two squadrons of cavalry toward Camp Cooper on December 31, 1855, special efforts were needed to prevent the Comanches from stampeding again. Instead, Baylor left conflicting requests with John Shirley, assistant sutler to Charles Barnard, raised doubts in Ketumse's mind about prices, and promised to bring a cheaper trader to the agency. Shirley remarked:

> I am informed that he [Baylor] is at present interested in the behalf of DeWitt & Wolfe, San Antonio, and with his *sham military influence* & popularity, together with exciting the Indians he is vain enough to believe that he can carry out his aim. He has made no settlement here for the beef or goods that he received.

Agent Ross was good enough to go to the Comanche Agency for four days to reassure the Comanches.

Baylor arrived at his home in Fayetteville, Texas, on January 16, 1856, and wrote Major Neighbors explaining his absence without leave. Baylor said he received letters from home urging his immediate return. Baylor's wife was pregnant and expecting to be confined on March 5, 1856.[5]

Neighbors reported to the commissioner that a small party of Comanches had left during Baylor's absence and submitted letters including Baylor's personal ones, as the "best vindication that I can submit for his continued absence." Neighbors thought Baylor would attend to his duties more closely after he moved his family to the reserve.

Major Neighbors had been in Austin and San Antonio since December 18, 1855, attending to the duties of his supervising

166

agency. The legislature was in session, and it seems the Major was working for legislation for the benefit of the Indian service in Texas. He reported to the commissioner on January 23, 1856, that he would start for the frontier via Austin on January 25, 1856. On that date, however, a baby boy, christened Robert Barnard Neighbors, the first son and third child of the Major and his wife, was born in the home of his grandparents near Seguin. The boy was given the name of Robert, while his middle name was for his father's friend, George Barnard. The baby boy was christened in the Methodist Episcopal Church, South, in Seguin.[6]

From Austin on February 4, 1856, Neighbors wrote his wife at her parents' home near Seguin:

My dear Wife

Contrary to my expectations I have been detained here till now. I leave this place for Belknap tomorrow. My mule gave out and got so lame that I have been compelled to Buy a horse—and as I had the opportunity concluded to send him back to your Pa to remain until I return. You will please My Dear, ask your Pa to have my mule taken care of and kept in good order until I return. I have no news. Mr. Bee has promised to call and see you. He will tell you all the news about Austin.

My Sweet Wife I should like above all things to be with you and my Son and Daughter. I have never felt it such a hardship, before to leave you, and shall certainly hurry back as soon as possible, as one embrace from you would be worth more than wealth or honour. Kiss [the] children and give my best love to your mother and the family.

Hoping that I shall soon hear from you and that yourself and the children will remain in good health,

I am as ever
Your Devoted Husband
Robt S. Neighbors

P.S. I sent the mule by Ben's [his brother-in-law] servant [or slave] who will bring it over to your Pa's.[7]

While in Austin Major Neighbors sent the commissioner copies of two laws passed by the legislature. One authorized the extension of the United States intercourse laws over the Texas Indians, especially the prohibition of the sale of ardent spirits to them, and the other created a reservation of five leagues west of the Pecos for the Lipan and Mescalero Apaches who roamed around the Davis and the Guadalupe mountains. Neighbors suggested that funds be made available for him to visit these Indians and that $30,000 be appropriated to move them to the new reserve. No doubt Major Neighbors had been instrumental in getting these laws passed during his stay in Austin.

Bad weather delayed Neighbors several days in Austin, but he arrived at the Brazos Agency on February 16, 1856, where he found affairs in good condition. On the Brazos Reserve, farming came to a standstill because of the inclement weather. One ox died from the cold, and all were in bad shape, while one yoke strayed away. The government farmers assisted the Indians in building huts and fencing land during the cold spell.

The Major set out through the inclement weather for the Comanche Agency where he arrived about February 26, 1856, and remained eight days. Baylor still had not returned, but Neighbors had a letter from him stating that he was on the way. The Indians were quiet, but were suffering much from the severe cold. A five-inch snow fell on March 1, 1856, and the weather was still cold a week later. Major Neighbors reported to the commissioner that the Comanches were suffering greatly from venereal diseases, and asked permission to expend funds for medical services, as the Indians wished it very much. Major Neighbors returned to the Brazos Agency on March 5, 1856, where Baylor arrived on March 10, 1856.

By May 1, 1856, Neighbors's Indian flock had been added to by Buffalo Hump (Pochanaquahiep) and forty-three starving Comanches. Chief Iron Sides (Pah-hah-yuca) of the Tenawish came in and made an unfulfilled agreement to bring in his people. Agent Baylor invited the other northern chiefs who had suffered much in the winter. The agent expressed the opinion that another expedition against the northern Comanches would cause more to come in. This was the time to attack, Baylor declared, for soon the Indians would steal enough horses to remount. There were five hundred seven souls among the Comanches on the Upper Reserve, according to Agent Baylor's census. The weather was so dry on the Comanche Reserve that the corn had not come up.

Major Neighbors learned that an agreement had been drawn up by the chiefs on the Brazos or Lower Reserve for their mutual benefit and for the government of their people.

A *sine qua non* to the success of the colonization policy as Major Neighbors pointed out at its inception, was the support of the frontier settlers. Neighbors's policies were discussed in a quaint letter written to Commissioner Manypenny by

'Thomas Lambshead from Clear Fork of the Brazos May 1, 1856, in which he endorsed Neighbors and the agents highly.[8]

Mexican captives among the Comanches were a matter of concern to Major Neighbors. Since there were still nearly twenty Mexican captives on the reserve, the Major wanted the department's orders for their disposition. At present he had not the means to subsist them and send them away, but he suggested that the captives be redeemed. The treaty of 1846 forbade the Comanches to acquire more. On May 14, 1856, he instructed Agent Baylor to purchase Tito Rivera, a Mexican boy twelve years of age. The boy had first attracted the Major's attention two years previously by writing several letters for Sanaco as his amanuensis.[9]

Military support of the colonization program was never constant. At times concert was close and cordial; at others, capricious. Even R. E. Lee thought the government's Indian experiment was ill-advised. When Chief Ketumse paid a ceremonial call upon Lee after his arrival, the perfect gentleman of the South spoke rudely to him and declared that he would meet him as a friend if possible but as an enemy if necessary. The chief left perplexed at this curt reception. Lee expressed the opinion to his wife that the hostile northern Comanches were not worth the trouble they caused man and horse. The drawing rooms of Stratford Hall and Arlington had not fitted a gentleman of the Tidewater for the realities of the frontier. If Lee, the flower of Southern chivalry, entertained such uncharitable feelings toward the Indians, what was to be expected of officers of lesser backgrounds?

Nevertheless, when Lieutenant Colonel R. E. Lee reached his command at Camp Cooper in the spring of 1856, he quickly established the closest concert with his fellow Virginian, Major R. S. Neighbors. The Major apprised Lee of the movements of hostile Indians and furnished the best scouts to accompany army expeditions. Colonel Lee in turn sent detachments upon the Major's request to confine the Indians on the reservations while the expeditions were searching for hostile Indians. The colonel also helped the Major redeem captives from among the Comanches and to return them to their homes in Mexico. Only a few examples of the correspondence of Lee and Neighbors are extant so that some of their collaboration must be reconstructed by inference. On May 22, 1856, Colonel Lee wrote Major Neighbors from Camp Cooper,

> I am very sorry to have missed you. Upon hearing of your return, I waited at the Agency some minutes for your Arrival,

169

but as you did not make your appearance, I thought I should find you at Camp. I also regret to learn that you return to the lower Agency tomorrow. There were several things I wished to talk to you about.

As regards the U. S. horses on Elm Creek, which you propose moving by means of the Indians, I am willing to pay the price named @ $20. apiece, for their deliverance here in good Condition. Unless *delivered* as I explained to you before, I Cannot pay anything.

If you Can get reliable men to undertake it please make the arrangement.

Wishing you a pleasant journey

I remain very truly yours

R. E. Lee

P.S. I hope my men behaved themselves well & did all you required.

R. E. Lee[11]

Major Neighbors wrote next day from the Brazos Agency requesting Colonel Lee to send him a company of the Second Cavalry to the Lower Reservation for the purpose of restraining the Indians to the limits of the reserve, apparently in preparation for an expedition against hostile Indians. Colonel Lee replied,

I recd. by yesterdays mail an order from the HdQrs Dept. of Texas concerning a Genl Court Martial at this place on the 1st Prox°—on which is placed all the Compn. Officers of the Command but one. You will see therefore it will be impossible for me to Comply with your Request, until after the adjurnment [sic] of the Court. Should the desired expedition then in your opinion be necessary, It will give me pleasure to direct it. Our forage is furnished by Contract at this place. We have no means of purchasing it, & we shall be able to transport but a limited supply for the expedition. We shall therefore have to rely upon you to supply the troops with such corn as they may require.

I am very respt your obt servt

R. E. Lee Lt Col

Lt Col 2 Cavly[12]

Three days later Colonel Lee received Special Order No. 64 from P. F. Smith in San Antonio directing the colonel to lead an expedition against the Tenawish, Noconas, and Sanaco's band of southern Comanches who had been plundering the settlements. Colonel Lee was instructed to take two companies from Camp Cooper, two from Fort Mason and to rendezvous in the vicinity of Fort Chadbourne. Smith admonished Lee to act in concert with Major Neighbors in order to harmonize the policies of the war and interior departments.[13] From the tenor of these instructions apparently P. F. Smith had learned something from the Sanaco debacle the year before.

The occasion for Major Neighbors's requisition of troops from Colonel Lee was no doubt the fact that Captain Seth Eastman, the artist, of Fort Chadbourne had sent Major Neighbors word that two express riders were killed between the fort and San Antonio. Neighbors replied that any Indians found off the reservations were to be treated as hostile. On June 8, 1856, Captain Eastman reported that on the day before between five and six o'clock, a party of Comanches consisting of twenty men and some squaws came into the fort. When a demand was made for the surrender of the party, the Comanches prepared to fight. In the ensuing struggle, seven Indians were killed, while the others were wounded and escaped on their horses.

Lively preparations were set afoot at Camp Cooper for the lark of an expedition against the Indians on the plains of Texas. Before Colonel Lee left, he rode down to the Comanche Agency to see Major Neighbors who "received him courteously." Neighbors told Lee where Indian camp sites were to be found, the routes by which to reach them, and furnished Lee the services of Jim Shaw and a detachment of Delaware trailers. "After the conference Lee rode back to Camp Cooper with deep respect for Neighbors, for he not only knew well the habits and problems of both the wild and sedentary Indians, but was alert and progressive."[14] Agent Ross sent fifteen trusty men under Jim Shaw who proceeded on June 12, to join Lee at the appointed rendezvous near Fort Chadbourne.[15] During the expedition, only the Reserve Indians killed two wild Comanches and captured a woman.

Major Neighbors, always on the alert for means to speed the development of Texas, about the first of June of 1856, sent Governor Pease a specimen of stone coal from Fort Belknap. More than a half century later mines were opened there, a railroad was built to transport the coal to market, and the town of Newcastle grew in the coal fields three miles north of Fort Belknap. The mines were abandoned when the discovery of petroleum in the area and labor trouble rendered them unprofitable.[16] Hence, the railroad was abandoned in 1954. Major Neighbors also sent Governor Pease something else of interest.

I have also found and send down by same conveyance the Metereoric Stone or Iron that I spoke to you about. It is a beautiful specimen—and weighs about 500 lbs. I landed it at Clear Fork and have had no opportunity of getting its correct dimentions—as yet. I shall be in Austin during the next month and wish to consult you about what disposition to make of It. It is a regular meteor and no mistake, and is as heavy as the same sized peice of Lead.

Neighbors later brought the meteor to San Antonio, whence it was moved to the capitol building in Austin, and although the building burned, the meteor was unharmed. It is at present in the Texas Memorial Museum, Austin, Texas.

At the end of June of 1856, Neighbors found that melons, pumpkins, peas, beans, and other vegetables had been planted in the corn rows on the Comanche Reserve. Baylor expected to plant fruit trees next year in an effort to make the Comanches' home agreeable to them so they would stay on it. He had given Ketumse permission to move the Indian camp temporarily to Six Mile Creek to save the crops. The Comanches were pulling melons the size of hen's eggs and were giving "the roasting ears fits." Ketumse put a guard around the field, but the Comanches pulled the fences down and rode in by the dozens to pull corn ears.

Baylor thought the move to Six Mile Creek would be a recreation for the Indians. Chief Iron Sides (Pah-hah-yuca) was said to be near but afraid to come in after the Fort Chadbourne killing. (According to Rip Ford, Ross said Iron Sides and Pah-hah-yuca was one and the same man.)

At the Brazos Reserve where Neighbors took charge of Agent Ross's duties while he attended court in McLennan County, the Major found there had been several new arrivals among the Wacos and Tawacanos. The Indians on the Brazos Reserve had worked well, although they had to plant the third time on account of the grasshoppers. The grasshoppers all went north during the month of May in three distinct migrations on May 10, May 16, and May 20. Neighbors observed that, "The light of the sun was partially obscured by the immense numbers of these insects."

Neighbors and the agents were well pleased with the progress of the Indians, but fortunately a competent outsider, Middleton Tate Johnson, also gave his appraisal of their progress. Johnson, who spent several months in the vicinity of the reservations, was a frontiersman of long standing and had served in the Texas armed forces on the frontier. He found that the Indians had made decided improvement and were in far better condition than any he had seen in Texas. The Indians apparently were contented and well pleased with settled life, were rapidly becoming semi-civilized, and were divesting themselves of their nomadic habits and restless disposition. They were sleek and fat, while those on the Lower Reserve were beginning to dress in the white man's costume and to adopt his customs. Those on the Lower or Brazos Reserve were erecting log buildings, were putting several hundred acres under cultivation, and were engaging in stock raising, as well as farming. The work among the Comanches was done, Johnson said, mostly by squaws and Mexican captives, while the braves hunted and fished.[17]

Colonel J. K. F. Mansfield, inspecting the Department of Texas in the summer of 1856, was at Camp Cooper and Fort Belknap from July 31 to August 6. After commending the agents and progress of the Indians, Colonel Mansfield stated that:

Major R. S. Neighbors is the principal Indian Agent for Texas, and is a Gentleman extremely well qualified from his experience in, and knowledge of the Indian character, to manage them. The Indians have confidence in him and he has great command over them. These Indians have been supplied through him with all the necessary farming utensils and a wagon, and a five yoke team of oxen to each tribe, with an American to teach them to cultivate the soil, and a smith and armorer allowed them for repairs, and 300 head of cows and calves have been distributed among them. They have established their own police and prohibited spiritous liquors.[18]

The Dallas *Herald* thought that if the colonizing policy succeeded, too much praise could not be awarded to Major Neighbors, the tireless agent, "under whose auspices the policy had been inaugurated." The paper then reviewed the Major's long efforts to colonize the Indians, and continued, "We now see the astonishing results. Major Neighbors, more than any other living man, has the confidence and respect of the Indians. His influence with them has undoubtedly contributed much to this result."

When some protested the legality of the prohibition joint resolution, Major Neighbors countered by having the legislature pass a law instead, which extended the United States intercourse laws relating to alcohol within ten miles of the reservation. The Major sent a copy of the law to Manypenny

173

and requested to know whether this authorized him to proceed against those who violated it. The constitutionality of the prohibition law was upheld by the United States District Attorney for the Western District Richard B. Hubbard, the future governor of Texas. The treaty of 1846 also provided for prohibition.

During the month of July, Major Neighbors learned of a marauding band from the Comanche camp outside the reserve which came to woe. Captain Eastman reported that four Comanche youths had come into the whiskey shop at Fort Chadbourne and asked to be sent back to the reserve. The boys said they went out mustanging with a big Comanche who died on the excursion, after which they lost their horses. The boys came in on foot armed with their bows and arrows. Eastman sent them in a wagon with an escort to Agent Baylor with a request to be informed whether the boys' story was true. Eastman added that he expected Major Neighbors in a few days at Fort Chadbourne.

When Major Neighbors opened his dispatches in San Antonio, he found that Baylor put the boys in the guard house for a week when they arrived. Then he turned the boys over to Ketumse with instructions to whip them and shave their heads. The boys, who had gone off with Comanche Sam,[19] had attacked some white men who were in swimming. Though nude, the white men whipped the Indians, killed Comanche Sam, a Mexican boy and another Comanche man, then took all the horses of the party. Agent Baylor asked Major Neighbors for instructions in dealing with such renegades who went out from the reservation to kill white people and steal. The agent said, "I can't allow these rascals to stay here and make arrows and fatten themselves and then leave and depredate on our frontier. I am determined to stop it and want your advice how to prevent [it]." His allowing the Comanches to camp away from the reserve doubtless contributed to the outbreak.

Baylor's allowing the Comanches to camp off the Reserve led to other difficulty. Buffalo Hump and Ketumse led seventy-five warriors on to the Brazos Reserve for a confrontation with the agrarian tribes over their furnishing scouts and guides for the military. Chief José María cowed the Comanches with his readiness to fight, and Agent Ross assured them the Caddos would kill any marauding Indians regardless of who or where they were. The Comanches had pledged to do the same, Ross reminded them.

Major Neighbors expressed the opinion to Commissioner Manypenny that the Comanche hostile visit to the Lower

174

Reserve was the result of Agent Baylor's allowing them to camp outside the reserve, and stated that he had instructed Baylor to return the Comanches to their reserve at once. The Comanches had expressed a longing for Neighbors at San Antonio to come to see them, but Baylor thought there was no great necessity for it.

They think it no trouble for you to ride up and see them any time they want to talk. They are doing as well as usual. And I think with you that they must learn to give you up and depend on some one else.

The confidence which Major Neighbors's policy of colonizing the Indians had inspired in white settlers is shown in the fact that by 1856 the white settlements had flowed around the Brazos Reservation and had grown to such an extent that the legislature created the counties of Erath, Parker, Jack, Palo Pinto, Wise, and Young.

That summer Young County was organized by the election of county officers, and the selection of a county seat. Peter Harmonson was elected chief justice; Patrick Murphy, sheriff; William Burkett, county and district clerk; and the county seat was placed at Belknap. James H. Swindells was selected to survey and to lay off the town. The townsite was laid off one-half mile east of the fort.

Major Neighbors spent some time in his home in San Antonio, where his wife, Elizabeth Ann, his young daughter, Mary Beatrice, and his baby, Robert Barnard, six months old, awaited him. Their home was then on present Soledad Street, within a half-block of present Wolf and Marx Department Store. Next door to the Major's home was the Methodist Episcopal Church, South, to which the family belonged, as stated, and which is called Travis Park Methodist Church at its present site where it was moved.

While Major Neighbors was in San Antonio, he was prompted, he said, by "the certainty of death and the uncertainty of life" to make his last will and testament, in which he bequeathed his estate to his wife and children. The Major's wife and James Vance were made the executors without bond of the Neighbors's estate at the Major's death. Joseph Ulrich and S. G. Newton were witnesses.

Major Neighbors arrived back at the Brazos Agency on September 5, 1856. Toward the end of September, he made a trip to Dallas to open bids for supplying 182,000 pounds of flour to the Reserve Indians. The editor of the Dallas *Herald* declared that it was highly gratifying to meet "our indefatigable Indian

175

Agent, Major Robert S. Neighbors, in town." The Major gave the editor a resume of conditions on the reserves and spoke of the successful outcome of the colonizing policy. The editor concluded his remarks about the visit by touching upon the attribute of Major Neighbors which commended him to his fellow citizens: his integrity.

> We regret to learn from Major Neighbors that he has determined to resign his agency during the ensuing winter and spring. He has retained it for the last four years at a pecuniary sacrifice. His salary is altogether inadequate to the onerous duties of his appointment. The retirement of Major Neighbors will be a misfortune for the northern frontier. His place cannot be supplied. He originated and has carried into successful practice the 'feeding policy' in Texas; he has the entire confidence of the Indians, and exercises an unbounded influence over them. He has faithfully applied the appropriation made by the government to the benefit of the Indians; and by his economical management and disbursement of them, has saved thousands of dollars to the government. The best evidence of his strict integrity is that he will leave this arduous service, in which thousands of dollars pass through his hands, poorer than he entered upon it.

In his annual report to the commissioner, Neighbors stated that there had been an increase of four hundred thirty-four Indian settlers on the reservations. Major Neighbors felt confident that great improvement had been made in the condition of the Indians, thus showing "that the present policy in regard to the Indians of Texas has been as successful as its most sanguine advocates claimed for it, and demonstrating the fact that it is practicable to settle down and civilize the wildest of our Indian tribes."

In response to the query of his friend, the Reverend John W. Phillips of San Antonio, presiding elder in the Methodist Episcopal Church, South, concerning the condition of the Indians on the reservations and the advisability of sending a missionary, the Major had answered that as the Indians spoke many languages, he suggested that they be taught English which some already knew. By the treaty of 1846, Neighbors said, the Indians were bound to receive and to protect a missionary, but that he would not approve a mission without a school. The present colonization policy depended upon the rising generation, said the agent, and the youth needed instruction in agriculture. He promised to present the matter of a mission and a school to the general government. The Major asked for

$5,000 for missions and schools at the Brazos and Comanche agencies. He concluded with the statement that:

The progress made by our Indians since my last annual report, and the satisfactory condition in which I find them at this date, is mainly attributable to the efficient services rendered by special agents Ross and Baylor; they have been constantly at their posts, and the efficient manner in which they have discharged their duties entitles them to the full confidence of the general government as well as our frontier citizens.

Baylor in his annual report to Major Neighbors concluded that,

I feel confident that the Indians now here, and those bands belonging to them who are expected, will keep the treaty they have made, and abandon the roving life they have heretofore led.

One comparatively peaceful year for the reserves had slipped by. Major Neighbors's dream of colonizing the Indians seemed to be materializing before his eyes. The Indians were making astonishing progress in establishing homes and mastering the arts of agriculture. The agents were constant and diligent in their duties. Only Agent Baylor seemed unable to prevent young Reserve Comanche braves from joining their marauding northern brethren. Nevertheless, the white settlers approved and sustained the colonizing policy, and Colonel Albert Sidney Johnston, with his Second Cavalry, gave his unstinted support.

Chapter X
That Distinguished Individual

The year of 1857 was a successful one for Major Neighbors's colonization program, but not so peaceful as the year of 1856. The reservation policy so far had had the support of the white populace. A hint of dissatisfaction was registered in January of 1857.

B. E. Tarver, a member of the Fourth Legislature with Major Neighbors, wrote Governor Pease a forceful letter on the problem. The informant said he had just returned from the northern portion of the state, an area as large as Ohio but given up to savages. The former state legislator, averring that the United States had failed to protect Texas, further detailed atrocities at the hands of savages which had gone unavenged by the United States government. In addition he said Jack Hunter, an Indian scout who had served Major Neighbors in former days, had been killed in the service of the United States Army within a day's ride of Fort Belknap; twelve or fifteen valuable horses had been taken from Marlin's Ranch, eight miles below Fort Belknap; and two teamsters had been killed and scalped twenty-five miles from the fort, at the West Fork of the Trinity on the road to Gainesville.

John Forbes wrote Governor Hardin R. Runnels that raiders had killed and stolen in the counties of Bosque, Palo Pinto, Erath, and Comanche, on Resley Creek and the South Bosque, who Forbes averred, were trailed toward the reserves.

In October of 1856, Major Neighbors had announced to the commissioner his intention of going to Washington to make a final settlement of his accounts in preparation for his resignation at the end of the present administration. The records are silent on the date of the departure of the Major and his wife Elizabeth Ann who accompanied him. After his departure, however, citizens in the vicinity of the reservations sent a petition dated January 20, 1857, at Fort Belknap, bearing witness to the faithful performance of duty by Major Neighbors and praying his continuance in office.[1]

On March 19, 1857, while Major Neighbors was present in Washington, Commissioner Manypenny approved several of the Major,s cherished projects. The commissioner approved the Major's plan for a school for the Indian children and instructed him to have a suitable building erected, employ a teacher, and work out the other details at his discretion. The commissioner instructed the agent to reclaim all the captives among the reserve Indians without ransom, if possible, so that the traffic would be discouraged. Commissioner Manypenny agreed to the establishment of a new reservation west of the Chickasaws in the Indian Territory east of the North Fork of Red River on the same footing as those in Texas. The commissioner saw no objection to the new reservation's being placed under the Texas superintendency, but no Texas Indians were to be put upon it as that would violate the agreement the commissioner had made with the Choctaws and Chickasaws. When the new agent qualified himself under a recent law, the matter would be taken up again, the commissioner stated.

While Major Neighbors was in Washington, Senator Rusk obtained an increase in salary of the supervising agent that would make it equal the salaries [$2,000.00] of the superintendents of other agencies. Texas was still a temporary agency, however, and the Major's title remained that of supervising agent. In the nation's capital, Major Neighbors and his wife stayed at the Kirkewood Hotel, and received an invitation from President-Elect James Buchanan to the inaugural ball. Details of the trip of Neighbors and his wife to Washington are tantalizingly lacking. One little memento remains, however. This is Elizabeth Ann's plainly but exquisitely inscribed personal card, which read, "Mrs. R. S. Neighbors—Texas."[2] The couple returned to Texas by way of Belleville, Illinois, where they visited the Major's sister Mary Hughes, his brother Asa and their families. The Major was said to have made many friends during his short sojourn in Illinois. The couple arrived in San Antonio before April 22, 1857, while Major Neighbors arrived at the Brazos Agency on April 27, 1857, and commented that the cold and frost had retarded the wheat and corn of the Indians.

On Neighbors's orders, Agent Baylor with troops destroyed barrels of whiskey, wine, and other beverages within the extended reservation zone. When the owner sued Baylor, Neighbors asked permission from the commissioner to employ an attorney to defend Baylor, while paying for the cost out

179

of the appropriation for Indian purposes. The department gave its approval.

Supervising Agent Neighbors learned that there had been more excitement on the Comanche Reserve. Someone disguised as an Indian had shot at Lieutenant Herman Biggs in his bed at Camp Cooper. After Agent Baylor was notified, he, with a few Indians and soldiers, started in search of the trail of the assailant. While looking for the trail, the path of the searching party led through the Indian camp, which stampeded the women and children, who did not come back until later in the night.

Toshahua was accused of killing a soldier near Fort Chadbourne, but the agent declared that Toshahua was on the reserve at the time of the killing. Soldiers at Camp Cooper on the reservation also accused the Indians of killing a soldier, but Baylor said the man was beastly drunk and probably killed himself. The Indians were accused of everything by everybody, which kept them in a state of alarm, he added. Ketumse had been absent "looking up his stock" ever since corn planting started, and Baylor declared that he would be unable to get the chief back except by force. In fact, Agent Baylor had lost the control and the confidence so far of the Indians that Ketumse had even ceased to speak to him.

Supervising Agent Neighbors was concerned that Agent Baylor's reports continued to reflect the demoralized state of his Indians and his inability to control them. The Indians refused to plant their crops unless Baylor gave them presents. The agent said he told them they should have no presents until their fields were worked. The Indians still showed little interest in their work, and he had to give them more liberal presents for fear they would leave the reserve. The agent hoped Major Neighbors would allow the amount expended beyond the original estimate. Baylor related that the Comanches then planted a part of their fields, and he hoped they would soon plant the rest.

A few days later Baylor wrote his sister that:

> I have not yet got my leave.[3] But when Neighbors comes he will bring it I think. I have heard nothing from him, but expect him in a few days. My Indians are all quiet and at work and I could leave as well as not if I had permission. *I will come if possible* you may rely on that. I am extremely anxious to see you before you leave Texas. As I dont know when I will ever visit the settlements again, while I remain in office. I am waiting to know whether I am to be 'rotated'

out or not, if not, I am safe for four years more, and can then afford to quit. I can have in that time a stock Ranch that will support a family. I will know when Neighbors comes all about it, and I am anxious to see him.[4]

In Washington on March 14, 1857, Commissioner Manypenny had informed Major Neighbors that Baylor had been removed as special agent, and that Matthew Leeper had been appointed in his place. Major Neighbors was instructed to inform Baylor that he had been superseded and to turn over all government property and money. The commissioner notified Leeper of his appointment, in a letter dated March 14, 1856. Whether this was a mistake or whether the commissioner had actually considered appointing Leeper to replace Baylor the year before when Baylor's agency was thrown into confusion by his absence without leave can only be conjectured.

Commissioner Manypenny did not state the reason for Baylor's dismissal. There was some question about Baylor's accounts, according to the records. Major Neighbors returned Baylor's final accounts to him for correction and then submitted "them with Mr. Baylor's explanations for the action of your Department." At a later period when Baylor charged Major Neighbors and the other agents with having "a good time of it" on government money, Major Neighbors declared that:

J. R. Baylor was considered, I have no doubt, a good judge, because he was dismissed from service by the general government for 'having a good time of it' during the eighteen months that he was in service. This his own accounts will show whenever any one chooses to investigate.

Baylor's accounts were still suspended as late as July 6, 1859, long after his dismissal, when Baylor again communicated with the department in an effort to get them settled.[7] Baylor later gave as the reason for his dismissal his alleged championing of the white settlers against the depredations of the Indians.[8]

Colonel Matthew Leeper appeared at the Brazos Agency on May 14, 1857, and filed his bond with Major Neighbors, who instructed him to proceed at once to the Comanche Reserve to relieve Agent Baylor of his duties. Leeper reported to Neighbors on June 1, 1857, that there were three hundred eighty-seven Comanche colonists and seven Mexican captives on the reserve. The women outnumbered the men 176 to 70. Agent Leeper observed that the Indians' crops looked very well in spite of the cold, frost, and dry weather. There had

181

been a fine rain recently, however, and Leeper expected good crops of corn and melons. The wheat crop was short because of the dry weather earlier, but the harvest was to begin in a few days. Leeper thought the Comanches had made more progress toward civilization than any other Indians in the same length of time. This indicates Baylor had made some accomplishments during his tenure.

Major Neighbors, in reply to a query from Agent Leeper as to the duties, scope, and authority of an Indian agent, enumerated Leeper's duties, which provided an insight into the activities of the Indian service. It was Leeper's duty to enforce the treaty stipulations and to protect the Indians from both wild Indians and white men, while seeing that justice was done to all parties. Leeper was to maintain an effective police of the reserve in concert with the military, Neighbors said, especially enforcing the liquor prohibition laws; to supervise the employees of the government, to encourage the Indians in farming and in stock-raising; to take stolen property from the Indians, if any were discovered, and to return it to the owners; to arrest any offenders and to turn them over to the state civil officials, since all crimes on the reserve were punishable by state law; to sustain the head chief in his authority; to reconcile differences among the Indians, and to continue to pay Chief Ketumse $30.00 a month from the funds for presents so that Ketumse could devote his time to his duties as chief and give up hunting; to disburse the government funds for his salary, the salary of the interpreter, and for presents for the Indians; and to report regularly upon his actions and the conditions on the reserve. To each soul on the reservation the agent was to issue a ration of two pounds of beef, three-fourths of a pound of flour or corn, and four quarts of salt for each one hundred rations. The ration was to be reduced as the Indians increased their production of food. Leeper was to use his discretion in minor matters not covered by his instructions, but to consult the Major on major decisions.

In the midst of reports of fair prospects of success for the Major's colonization policy he received news which eventually sealed the doom of himself and the Texas reservations. Commissioner J. W. Denver notified Neighbors that the new reservation in the Wichita Mountains would not be under the Texas superintendency, but under the southern. Denver and the secretary of interior agreed that Major Neighbors should have charge of the new reservation, but the agent of the Choctaws and Chickasaws, Douglas H. Cooper, objected. The southern

Comanches, Wichitas, and other nomadic tribes would be placed upon the reservation, which would be under the jurisdiction of Superintendent Elias Rector, with whom Neighbors was to cooperate in establishing the reservation.

When Major Neighbors received Denver's letter, he expressed his disappointment, as the change was contrary to the wishes of the Texas delegation in Congress and the wishes of the commanding general and officers of the Texas department. It had been expected that the new reserve would be the means of ridding Texas of raids and of making the El Paso Road safe. The Major declared that since most of the southern Comanches would be on the new reserve, the Texas Comanche Reserve should be abandoned and the Comanches on it united with the main band.

A year later Senator Sam Houston was still trying to get the new agency placed under the jurisdiction of Major Neighbors.

Houston said:

> Major Neighbors, anterior to the annexation of Texas, had been an agent for years; he had traveled with the Indians; he was the first explorer that ever found a route directly from the settlements of Texas to El Paso. By traveling with the Indians and associating with them after he was appointed agent, he had their confidence, and they took him where he found water and grass and everything necessary, and he went on comfortably to El Paso by a direct route, which our engineers failed in finding. The access now is easy, with everything necessary for the facilities of travel. For years before annexation we had no bloodshed on our frontier . . . .

Senator Rusk gave his approval also for placing the new agency under Major Neighbors's superintendency, and the secretary of interior and commissioner of Indian affairs concurred as well, to no avail.

While Major Neighbors was in San Antonio, his friend and champion, Senator Sam Houston, made a speech in the city in his campaign for governor of Texas. The election of Hardin R. Runnels instead of Houston meant that Major Neighbors would not have Houston's powerful support in the governor's chair when the Major made the fight of his life. Runnels had never seen eye to eye with Major Neighbors on Indian policy and did not give the Indian colonization program the necessary support.

In September of 1857, Neighbors and the other agents gave their annual reports. The Major reported that the Brazos

183

Reservation Indians had made 8,000 bushels of corn and 1,560 bushels of wheat, besides "a very large supply of beans, peas, pumpkins, melons &c., ample for their subsistence during the next year." He reported that there were settled on the Brazos reservation 1,014 souls, an increase of 66 settlers since the last annual report. There were 424 souls on the Comanche Reserve, a decrease of 133 since the previous year's report. Neighbors said he could not make the same favorable report for the Comanches that he had made for the Brazos Indians, largely because of the bad influence of the Comanches not on the reservation whose war trails ran nearby. The wild northern Comanches tolled warriors from the reservation to join them in making raids on Mexico and the Texas frontier settlements. He declared he could see but little difference between the condition of the Comanches then and at the time of his last annual report. He added with some heat that,

> Our frontier still presents the anomaly of peace with a small portion of a tribe of Indians, and continual hostility with the balance of the same people, and during the past year very serious depredations have been traced to them, and there have been several encounters between them and the troops on our frontier, in which a number of both soldiers and Indians have been killed. The strangest feature of this state of affairs, and one that demands your serious attention, is the fact that, at the same time that those bands of Comanches, Kioways, &c., are depredating on our citizens, waylaying our roads, destroying our mails to El Paso, &c., an agent of your department is distributing to them a large annuity of goods, arms, and ammunition on the Arkansas river, which is arming them, and giving them the means more effectually to carry on their hostile forays. During the past summer, particularly about the 1st of July, there were several parties of those people with the Kioways, on a visit to the Comanches at the Reserve who did not hesitate to state that the fear of chastisement for past depredations had caused them to seek this frontier, in order to avoid the troops who were in pursuit of them; but upon the call of the agent charged with the distribution of the annuity on the Arkansas, they repaired thither, received their presents, and are again down upon our frontier, are now boasting of the 'presents paid them by the government,' and are prepared to use the arms and ammunition received from the government agent on our troops. Some of the same guns given at the Arkansas river are now on the reserves in Texas, the Indians (Wacoes) who have them having traded for them from the Upper Comanches but a short time since.

The buildings for the school on the Brazos Reserve were nearly completed, and it was expected the school would be in successful operation by November 1, 1857, under a competent teacher. The agent closed his report by attributing the progress of the Brazos Indians mostly to the devoted efforts of Agent Ross. Neighbors read with interest the report of Jonathan Murray, farmer instructor to the Wacos, Tawacanos, and Tonkawas, which stated that besides their other crops, the Chinese sugar cane sent by the department promised a heavy yield. Neighbors thus helped pioneer in introducing the first sorghum crop into West Texas where it has become a highly important staple cash crop.[9]

On the Comanche Reserve, Agent Leeper wrote Major Neighbors,

> Agreeable to the request of Ketemsee I had the crop divided into different lots so as to show each mans share. I think the design is good—they take a much greater interest in it than they did before. Numbers of them are camped in the field with a view to protect their respective interests. They rost green corn and mellons—and then lay down under a shade and sing. I fear it will be rather difficult to obtain hands to work at their buildings for they cannot very well afford to leave their mellons and green corn.

How much better it was to have the Indians lie down under a shade and sing with full bellies from products of their own labor than to subsist by raiding and killing the white settlers. It seemed that at last Major Neighbors's policy was coming to fruition.

The captives held by the Comanches received the attention of Major Neighbors. On June 14, 1857, he had written Lieutenant Colonel Lee at Camp Cooper for assistance in liberating the Mexican captives from the Comanches on the reserve. Lee replied:

> It will give me great pleasure at any time you may designate to furnish them a military escort to Carry them to any lower Military Post, or So far within the line of Settlements as to be beyond the risk of recapture by the Indians;—should you not be able to provide for them out of funds at your disposal, I will issue them provisions for the journey.
>
> I have not the means of transporting them, nor do I Consider myself authorized under the Circumstances to dispatch troops with them out of the Country without orders from the Command genl of the Dept. to whom I will refer your application as you request by tomorrows mail.
>
> I have the honour to be your   Obt Servt

185

The next month Lee rode away to other duties never to return to Camp Cooper.

A rather astonishing turn of events developed out of the Major's painstaking efforts to release the Mexican captives from the Comanches. Out of the group that he returned to Mexico in September, 1857, a sixteen-year old girl, Tomasa, and a twelve-year old boy returned to the Comanche Reservation in February of 1858. These pathetic outcasts stated that they found no relatives in Mexico, and were driven from place to place like dogs. They stole two horses on which they rode until their animals gave out, then the children walked the remainder of the journey. They were nearly starved at the end of their thirty-five day trek. Agent Leeper retained them at his agency until he could learn the pleasure of Major Neighbors in the matter.[11] The captives remained with the Comanches the rest of their lives.

Neighbors did not have the same happy relations with Lee's successor, Captain George Stoneman, the future Union general. After a series of provocations over a period of months, Major Neighbors requested General Twiggs to transfer Captain Stoneman and to place in command of Camp Cooper an officer who would "not either interfere with the proper duties of the agent or circulate *false reports*."

After Captain Stoneman was transferred from Camp Cooper, he reviewed his feud with Major Neighbors, and concluded with asperity that:

> . . . I venture the assertion, that the Indian policy as now being carried out in Texas, will prove a failure, to every party except those charged with the disbursement of the public monies so liberally appropriated by Congress for the support of the Indians; and with the remark, that had I succeeded in eliciting from the tongue or pen of Major Neighbors, any-thing but slander or abuse, I should have accomplished more than has ever been vouchsafed to the efforts of any other officer of the U. S. Army, who may have been brought in contact with that distinguished individual, and should certainly have been very much disappointed at the result.

Then the Indian agents and the military officers on the frontier became involved in a difference of opinion concerning the identity of the perpetrators of a series of serious depredations, the agents asserting that the crimes were committed mostly by Kickapoos with the aid of some Kiowas and northern

Comanches, while the military alleged the offenders were northern Comanches with the connivance of their kinsmen on the reserve.

Acting upon the reports sent him by his agents, Major Neighbors brought the matter to the attention of various officials in positions of authority and called upon them for action. Governor Runnels responded to the information sent him by Major Neighbors by obtaining the authorization from the legislature to call out one hundred mounted volunteers. The governor forwarded a copy of the Major's letter to Senator J. Pinckney Henderson and to the commanding general, who ordered a company of the Second Cavalry to garrison Fort Belknap and to scout the country mentioned in the Major's letter.

Neighbors gave the commissioner of Indian affairs another resume of the deplorable conditions, remarked that the department had received his reports, and demanded to know why nothing had been done. It was notorious, Neighbors averred, that the Indians received arms and ammunition among their presents from their agent at Fort Atkinson. The Major sent a copy of his letter to General Twiggs with the suggestion that a force be sent to occupy the territory of the marauders, or that a campaign be carried out to subject or exterminate them in the early spring, for which the Major offered guides and scouts from the Brazos Reserve Indians.

On Christmas Day of 1857, Major Neighbors set out from the Brazos Agency for San Antonio, where he arrived on January 14, 1858. From that point he faced the new year with all its vicissitudes and uncertainties.

Chapter XI
The Accused

While Major Neighbors was in San Antonio, he called upon General Twiggs to discuss their common frontier problems. The Major was disagreeably astonished at the sight of a report forwarded by Governor Runnels which the general had the courtesy to hand Neighbors. The report was to Governor Runnels from Lieutenant Thomas C. Frost, officer in the state's mounted volunteers, whose idea of the proper tactics of fighting Indians was to watch the bodies of Indians killed by citizens and catch those who came to bury them.[1] In finding something to report, Frost, who owed his opportunity of service to Neighbors's reports, stated without evidence that the reserve Indians were implicated in the raids on the frontier, and declared upon hearsay that "Major Nabors has been petitioned time and again by our citizens to give some attention to the affair—and they have only received curses, threats, insults and renewed outrages . . . ."[2] Frost was following the line laid down by Baylor, Givens, Nelson, and company in an attempt to oust Neighbors and break up the reservations.

Major Neighbors wrote Governor Runnels expressing his surprise and regret that the head of state would circulate a letter "absolutely false in every particular." The Major asked that a copy of his own letter be sent to Frost, whom he castigated thoroughly, and declared that if Frost had spent as much energy in pursuing the Comanche raiders as he had in making his lengthy report, he might have given the frontier the protection that he was employed to give. After warming to the subject, the Major enlightened the governor on his duties as supervising agent:

> It appears from the frequent censures, I, as the Indian agent
> receive from some of the extreme frontier citizens, that they

188

think that, the Genl. Govt. employs me to herd the horses of the citizens generally, when the fact is that I have not a single soldier under my control, and am not charged with the defense of the frontier against Indian depredations: my duties are specific and I can only act as a civil magistrate to execute the Indian Laws & Treaties, and I have no more power to defend the citizens, make war, or defend the frontier than any other citizen, and I must be permitted to protest solemnly against the habit that our citizens and especially the volunteer military force have got into, of legging my name into their report. I hope you in justice to me will send Mr. Frost a copy of this protest, and direct him to leave my name out of his reports, unless he has some specific charge to make against me, when it should be made to Comr. of Indian Affairs, at Washington, as I am not responsible to the military authorities.[3]

When Isaac Mullins, one of Baylor's party, wrote a garbled account to the *Texas Sentinel* of his attempt to obtain scouts from Major Neighbors for a questionable venture into the Indian country, the Major wrote the same paper in an attempt to counteract the erroneous impressions of his duties:

I much regret that after all the sacrifices, hardships and expenses an Indian agent has to under go, that his situation and duties are so little understood by our Citizens—they appear to think that he is merely employed as a genl. Herdsman—for those of our citizens who choose to take a cavayard of Mustangs to the frontier, and that they must be responsible, for every thieving or renegade band of Indians on the frontier—
When the fact is, that he can only act as civil magistrates—and execute specific duties under our instructions from the superior authority—whose instructions we are sworn to obey. We have not a single soldier under our control, have no power to make war, and no force to arrest depredators unless sustained by the Military—so that when we have done so, and report to the proper authorities 'facts' in relation to Indians —whether they be friendly or hostile—our duties are at an end—and I most solemnly protest against the habit of our citizens—and the public journals of the state at all times heaping censure on the agents when ever an Indian depredation is committed—with the same propriety the citizens of Austin might censure their magistrates—because some Loafing scoundrel had stolen a horse or broken up a house. At the same time I make this remark I hold my acts as a public officer open to any investigation that may be deemed necessary Either by our citizens—State authority—or the authorities of the Genl. Govt.

Governor Runnels wrote General Twiggs that the frontier citizens were under arms, that the highest degree of excitement prevailed, and requested Twiggs to call out volunteers. Twiggs replied that he was not authorized to call out volunteers, but made such disposition as he could of his own troops.

Learning that the legislature was in a state of excitement over false reports about the depredations, Major Neighbors set out for Austin City to allay the situation. The Major left San Antonio on January 26, 1858, ate breakfast in New Braunfels the next morning, had dinner in Blanco, and proceeded on his way to the capital. According to Rip Ford, Major Neighbors defended the reserve Indians against the charges of participating in depredations, averred that they were not off the reservations without the permission of an agent, and were amenable to civil process, i.e. "to arrest and punishment as others guilty of criminal offenses." The joint committee of the legislature considering the affair was of the opinion that it would be difficult to identify a warrior in warpaint when seen later in the garb of a reserve Indian.

Because of the raids of the northern Comanches, Kiowas, and Kickapoos, the legislature authorized the governor, as stated above, to call out one hundred and ninety men under Colonel John S. Ford. Major Neighbors ordered the special Indian agents to cooperate with Ford, who was made senior captain in charge of all state forces. Neighbors was optimistic that with Runnels's aid the hostile Indians could be held in check. The Major recalled that his anticipation of trouble had been borne out after the wild Indians were not settled as he recommended, and expressed with prescience the opinion that unless something were done, a conflict would ensue between the reserve Indians and the frontier citizens.

In the meantime the stage was being set for an assault upon Neighbors, the agents and the Indians by reports and charges circulated by Captain Givens and John R. Baylor. Givens reported to department headquarters in San Antonio that before he started scouring the country between the Guadalupe and Fort Belknap in obedience to orders, he was shown by the commanding general a letter from Major Neighbors to Governor Pease stating that the Kickapoos were committing depredations. Givens declared that neither he, Captain J. M. Jones, Lieutenant J. B. Plummer, nor Major G. R. Paul of other detachments found any sign of Kickapoos where Neighbors said they were. Givens said that all on the frontier believed the raiders were Reserve Comanches. The captain said he had seen twenty-five or thirty Indians leave the reservation when Agent Leeper had given permission to only six. Every time the troops killed raiders, Givens said, the Reserve Comanches mourned their dead. Furthermore, Captain Givens declared that the Comanches insulted the settlers' families when the men were away, drove off their cattle, and concealed them in the mountains until paid a reward. The officer also charged that the Indians damaged the settlers' crops. Forays were committed as Major Neighbors reported, said Givens, but the perpetrators were Reserve Comanches.[4]

Major Neighbors and the Reserve Comanches came in for a spurious broadside from a questionable meeting held early in 1858 on the Clear Fork. The charges stated that four Indians were killed in the Leon and Pecan Bayou area who possessed blankets, guns, and other articles like those issued on the Comanche Reserve. (This may well have been for presents for all United States Indians were bought in common in the East.) The charge was made that the reports of Major Neighbors of raids committed by Kickapoos were without foundation and were actually committed by his own Indians. The statement purported to be signed by W. G. Preston, J. B. Dawson, I. W. Curtis, H. McGhee, and F. L. Stockton, and was addressed to Captain N. C. Givens, of Camp Cooper, who certified as to the reliability of Preston.[5]

This was the result of John R. Baylor's calling a mass meeting ostensibly to raise a volunteer force to protect the settlements on the Clear Fork, but it turned out that the purpose was to crystallize public opinion for an attack upon the Reserve Comanches and to petition the authorities for the removal of Major Neighbors as supervising agent. William G. Preston and others rode through the countryside inviting men to attend the meeting on February 1, 1858, at which letters were drawn up addressed to Governor Runnels, Captain Givens, Agent Leeper, and the public prints. James H. Swindells, a gentleman of prominence on the frontier and official surveyor for Young District, stated:

> Prior to the meeting at which the documents referred to were *hatched* (or rather, born), I was but slightly acquainted with Capt Baylor,—I, with a good many others, supposed that from the position which he had held, both as an officer of the U.S. and as a citizen of the State, that he was entitled to full credence,—particularly upon so serious a matter as making the charges against you [Major Neighbors] which he did and in making statements of alledged [sic] facts in regard to the

depredation of Reserve Indians. I could not believe that he would tell a deliberate falsehood upon so grave a subject, and that, too, to a meeting who looked up to him, to verify or deny rumours in relation to the Indians. I as well as other, supposed him to be a *gentleman*, scorning to do a little thing. The gentlemen composing the meeting on the Clear Fork, depended on him for a *true* statement of *facts*, both as to the depredations of Indians, and other *matters*. And then his statements were made with so confident an air, that it carried conviction to all—or nearly all. But when he made statements with regard to you,—what you had said and done, in various parts of the State, I never was more surprised in my life—I did not know what to think—And I here state that the action of the meeting was based almost solely on what Baylor stated to be the truth.

Had I known then what I know now, of Baylor's character for veracity, I should have taken the step which your letter seems to indicate I should have done, and given the lie direct to *all* his statements.

Swindells then contradicted Baylor in several specific instances:

I have since then proven Baylor to have told a deliberate falsehood at the meeting—When he said he was authorized to sign certain men's names to the papers, he lied. When he told the meeting of having a converstion with Kàtemseh, in which Katemseh acknowledged that the Indians killed by Preston's party belonged to the Reserve and that one of his men had come in wounded, and had left the reserve, vowing vengeance against the first white person he met on the Clear Fork, after he got well (and which by the way, was the cause of the threat being made, of breaking up the Reserve) he told a wilful and deliberate falsehood; as is proved by the well known fact, that for some time previous to Baylor's dismissal, Katemseh would not speak to him.

Swindells said, "Since the people have been enlightened as to the real character of Baylor, they are very sorry for what they have done in the premises."[6]

The letter to Captain Givens produced by this assemblage has already been examined, but now becomes more explicable.[7] It was intended of course, for the eyes of General Twiggs and the public. Another letter was drawn up to Agent Leeper in which it was charged that Indians with passes from the agent to hunt also killed cattle and stole horses. The alleged signatories were made to say they they had put up with this state of affairs as long as they could. Henceforth, any Indians found off the reserve without a white man or a Delaware with them were to be killed forthwith. (Baylor as agent had allowed the whole tribe to camp outside.) The threat was made that if a man was killed on the Clear Fork, a force would be raised to break up the reserve. The signatories stated that they had no right on the reserve, while the Indians had no right to be off it.[8] Joseph Chandler, Rufus Olephamt, David Seal, and William Peterson, all of whose names were signed to the document, declared that it was a forgery.[9]

The most significant charge of forgery came from William G. Preston, who had assisted in calling the Clear Fork meeting. He denied writing or signing the letter to Captain Givens, discussed above. Preston declared he knew nothing of the letter until shown a copy at the Clear Fork on August 9, 1858, which he denied "writing or signing and pronounce the same as to signing a base forgery."[10]

It is significant that Captain Givens had signed a statement at the bottom of the letter to him as to the reliability of W. G. Preston.

There were other individuals who dared to take a stand in the face of concerted opposition. John von Hagan declared that he was the outside man on the frontier on the Clear Fork, but had never suffered a depredation from the Reservation Indians. Hagan said there might be bad men among the Reserve Comanches who communicated with the northern Indians, but that the mass were doing well and were content. If it was the aim of the government to break up the reserve, Hagan wanted to know it, as he would feel unsafe in that event. He also denied the correctness of newspaper reports about raids by Reserve Indians.[11]

Others who lit their candles in the darkness were Major Neighbors's old champion, Thomas Lambshead, and J. N. Gibbins, who wrote from Clear Fork Ranch on March 30, 1858:

> We the undersigned are in favour of the Comanche Indians and the Caddos and the other small tribes of Indians for still to remain on the present reservation in Texas[.]
> We the undersigned are in favour of our present Agent Major Neighbors for still to remain in Office.[12]

Shortly before this, identical letters from Lampasas and Williamson counties were sent to Secretary of Interior Jacob Thompson, calling for the removal of Major Neighbors as supervising agent for Texas Indians. The letters alleged that Major Neighbors had not given the frontier the protection he should have; he had been repeatedly informed that the Reserve Indians had committed depredations ever since their settlement on the reserves, yet he persisted, it was alleged, in the face of positive proof, in denying it. The allegation that horses belonging to citizens were found on the Comanche Reserve and that there were few men on the reserve were given as proof of depredations having been committed by Reserve Indians. Furthermore, it was claimed that the complaints of citizens were treated with insult and indignity by Major Neighbors. These chain letters were signed by J. M. Spencer, Isaac Mullins, F. M. Skidmore, W. H. Mullins, Hillary Ryan, and others.

This sudden assault on the agents and Indians by citizens and the caustic attitude of frontier military officers seem inexplicable upon first sight. On closer examination, however, internal evidence in the documents and later events point to John R. Baylor and Captain Newton C. Givens as the guiding influence behind the accusations. Baylor was smarting from his summary dismissal from the Indian service, and sought reprisal. Captain Givens, although opposed to the colonization policy from the beginning, was also a friend of the Baylor family.[13] Isaac Mullins, one of the citizens signing the petition, was from Fayette County, Baylor's former residence. Mullins and some of the signers of the letters attacking Major Neighbors later lent themselves to Baylor's campaign of vituperation against the agents and Indians, while J. M. Spencer may have been the same Spencer whom Major Neighbors had Colonel Johnson evict from Indian fields in 1847.

The main source of opposition to Major Neighbors and the reservation policy was John R. Baylor, the former Comanche agent. Baylor came from a proud family, members of which had been active in the military and legal professions. Baylor was described as being "about six feet two inches high, dark complexion, light hair, dark blue or hazle eyes, raw boned, and very stout."[14] He served with various volunteer military units in the days of the Republic of Texas, and later in the Confederacy. His public works included service in the Texas legislature, to which he was elected in 1851, and later in the Confederate Congress. Judging from the accounts of those who served under him during the frontier troubles, Baylor seems to have been a person of considerable charm and magnetism. He seems also to have been a man of driving energy and reckless ambition, who became the impacable foe of anyone who opposed him. His encounters which ended fatally for at least three other men during his troubled career both before and after the reserve episode are a matter of public record.[15] The former agent apparently blamed Major Neighbors for his dismissal and resented him bitterly. The weapon chosen for reprisal was the arousing of public opinion to oust the Major and the other agents and supplant them with Baylor and this friends. When this failed to come about, the object became that of destroying the reservations and their personnel.

For the next two years, Baylor went to and fro addressing mass meetings, promoting petitions, and carrying on a newspaper campaign of recrimination and vituperation against the Indians and their agents. Baylor and other agitators soon had the frontier citizens bitterly divided into the White Man and the Indian parties. A small newspaper called *The White Man*,[16] published first at Jacksboro and later at Weatherford by Baylor, carried inflammatory articles calculated to keep the public mind agitated.

Galled by the continued Indian raids upon the frontier and upon the Reserve Indians, Agent Ross sent out a scouting party of Indians under the Waco chief, Ah-ha-dot, who left about January 14, 1858, and was gone for thirty days. Major Neighbors learned that the scouting party took about eighty horses and four captives from a camp of northern Comanches on the headwaters of Red and Arkansas rivers. Two of the captives were Mexicans, who made their escape. From the two captive Comanches, Jim Shaw, the interpreter, learned that the depredations on the frontier had been committed by northern Comanches, Kiowas, and Kickapoos under Sanaco's son. A council of chiefs on the Brazos Reserve decreed that the two Comanches be shot, and the executions were carried out outside the reserve by ten men from the different bands on the reserve, since the area inside was considered sacred. One of the horses recovered belonged to the reserve, and upon Agent Ross's notice, white settlers claimed some of their horses from the herd. José María and Campo remained out scouting after Ah-ha-dot's return, and the agent sent out a company of Caddos and Anadarkos to intercept any avenging party of northern Indians who might attempt to retaliate against the Anadarko and Tonkawa chiefs. Ross declared that designing men had stirred up prejudice against the Reserve Indians among new-·comers on the frontier who threatened to attack the reserve, but the agent thought the exploits of the Waco scout had reacted in the favor of the Reserve Indians among the settlers. Major Neighbors learned that the scouting party had brought in the remainder of the Tonkawas, eighty-three in number. These were mostly women and children, destitute and starving, whom Agent Ross clothed and fed.

When Captain Givens's and John R. Baylor's propaganda against Major Neighbors and the Indians reached Washington, Secretary of War John B. Floyd forwarded the documents to Secretary of Interior Thompson. In fairness to everyone concerned, Secretary Thompson ordered the commissioner to cause a thorough investigation to be made into the matter. Nothing was done, however, until Neighbors appeared in Washington to press the issue.

In preparation for his departure, Major Neighbors set his private affiars in order. In one of his few private letters extant, the Major wrote his wife a letter of instructions:

> My Dear Wife
> As to the affiars of life are uncertain—I leave you this book together with my papers—which will show you the state of my affairs—My will is in the hands of Col. Newton.
> Should it be the will of an all wise Providence, that I should not see you again, I hope you will raise our children in the fear of the 'Great Ruler of the universe,' so that they may be honourable not only amongst men—but will [enter] their reward, after Leading an honourable life in that 'house not made with hands Eternal in the Heavens.'
> > With my best love
> > R. S. Neighbors
> To Lizzie A. Neighbors
> > San Antonio
>
> P.S. You will find by [these accounts] that the whole Estate—and all my negroes are included.
> The Patent for the Selma [illegible] Tract of Land, 640 acres of which belong to me, is in the hands of Mr. [illegible] Surveyor.
> > R. S. Neighbors[17]

Major Neighbors may have travelled back to the reservations in the ambulance or carriage which he bought from R. A. Howard in San Antonio. Before leaving for Washington, Neighbors put the reserves in order. When Major Neighbors arrived at the Comanche Agency, he learned that the Reserve Comanches had recovered on the Big Alecheta [Wichita] River six or eight horses bearing the triangle brand of Colonel James Buckner Barry, Esquire, who lived at Flag Pond, in Bosque County. These were part of a herd of fifty-seven horses stolen from Barry in the raid about the last of December of 1857.

Neighbors notified his Masonic brother of the recovery of part of his animals and advised him to claim them as soon as possible, while regretting that more of them were not recovered.

Barry made the loss of his animals a subject of correspondence with the secretary of interior, ascribing his losses to northern Comanches, Kansas, Nebraska, Kickapoo and renegade Indians from the reserves. Reply was made through the commissioner of Indian affairs that Superintendent Rector had been notified to alert Agent A. H. McKisick to attempt to recover the animals from the Indians mentioned north of Red River. Baylor later tried to make capital of this incident.

Major Neighbors not only made every effort to restore stolen animals to frontiersmen, but he also assisted them in making claims on the general government for the loss of animals which could not be recovered from the marauders.[18]

In the meantime Captain Ford's operations on the frontier were fraught with significance for Neighbors and his agents since part of Ford's officers were of the Baylor faction. Ford moved his force to the vicinity of the reserve by four lines, sweeping the country as he went to be certain that no enemy lurked in his rear. Lieutenant Edward Burleson, Jr., moved by way of Camp Colorado road, Lieutenant Allison Nelson from Palo Pinto, Lieutenant James H. Tankersly by Comanche and Buchanan [Stephens] counties, while Ford and Lieutenant W. A. Pitts passed between the "mountains" and Pecan Bayou through Brown, Eastland, and Buchanan counties while examining the valley of Hubbard's Creek.[19] No recent Indian signs were seen by any detachment. Ford ordered Lieutenant Edward Burleson to select a camp site at the mouth of Hubbard's Creek in an area well supplied with water, fuel, and forage.[20]

Ford arrived on March 19, 1858, and went immediately to the Brazos Agency, where Major Neighbors approved of his old associate's mission. Neighbors assembled all the chiefs on the Brazos Reserve who agreed to send as many men with Ford as could be spared from the fields.

Captain Ford, viewing Neighbors's accomplishments, was greatly impressed with the progress of the Brazos Reserve Indians and had the courage to take a strong stand in their favor. He wrote Governor Runnels:

> They have cut loose from the wild Indians for good, and have, so far as they can, identified themselves with the whites, in every way. They say they wish to become Americans. The strides they are making in the way of becoming civilized are

great, and, I might even say, astonishing. They are trying to imitate the whites in manners, in dress, in agriculture, and in all essential particulars. They have large fields of wheat and corn, which they have planted themselves, and are now cultivating. Waggons drawn by oxen and driven by Indians, women and children dropping corn, all give the scenes at the different villages quite an American appearance. There is no disorder, no discontent, and no disposition to give trouble to the Agent or the Government. They are endeavoring to fulfill the treaty stipulations, and to give satisfaction to the Americans. I speak of what I have seen and heard, and believe it is true. I should view any combinations of circumstances which tended towards the breaking up of this Reserve, as a serious misfortune to the State of Texas, and a calamity over which the philanthropist might mourn.[21]

Captain Ford remarked to the governor that there were eleven hundred Indians on the Brazos, under Neighbors's supervision, and he thought that if some of them had not killed somebody's cattle, or stolen someone's horses, then they were better than the same number of white people. Ford was unable to believe, however, that these Indians were preparing to plunder the frontier settlements. On the contrary, Ford stated that the Indians were always ready to assist the whites in war upon the Comanches. Since the beginning of the present hostilities, Ford said the Brazos Indians had recovered stolen horses for their owners, and could show ten scalps they had taken. Ford commended the efficient service of Agent Ross and the superintendency of Major Neighbors.

Captain Ford did not make the same good report of the Comanches and their agent. Without ever having seen Agent Leeper, Ford accepted the report of Baylor's adherents among his officers, and attributed most of the trouble on the frontier to political considerations that had sent incompetent men into the Indian service. Ford declared that Agent Leeper was a cipher, "worth as little on the right, as the left."[22] Ford remarked to the governor that he had orders from the agents to attack the Comanches when found off the reserve.[23]

Captain Ford determined to break up the Comanche Reserve, but before doing so, he required factual reports. He called a conference of his officers and bound them to secrecy concerning his plans which called for the sending out of reconnaissance parties to apprehend the Reserve Comanches in the act of committing depredations. One officer remarked that if a trail from a raid could be traced to the reserve, that would be proof enough. Lieutenant Allison Nelson, a future Confederate general, remarked, "That thing can be managed—the trail can be made." Captain Ford's integrity, and respect for Neighbors, however, would not permit him to engage in making false reports. He rebuked Nelson roundly, declaring: "No, Sir, that will not do, I am responsible to the State, and to public opinion, and I will take no step in the matter, unless I am backed by facts, and of such a character as to justify me before the public. I am willing to punish the Comanches, if they are found guilty; but I am not disposed to do so unjustly and improperly."

Captain Ford then sent Lieutenant Nelson out with a detachment to make a reconnaissance near the Comanche Reserve. Although Nelson was gone for several days, he could find no facts implicating the Comanches. In fact, Lieutenant Nelson reported that the citizens settled around the reserve were opposed to breaking up the Indian colony. The intrigue to break up the reserve was dropped for the time being.[24]

Baylor's party had also high hopes of speedily replacing Major Neighbors with Lieutenant Nelson. Nelson remarked to Captain Ford that Major Neighbors had escaped removal thus far because his accusers had used an improper mode of procedure, but Nelson added, "The men are after him now who will hurt him—he will be removed." Ford was convinced later that Nelson referred to himself and his friends. Notwithstanding that Ford had ordered his officers not to take any part in the controversy between Major Neighbors and the citizens, Lieutenant Nelson continued to consult Baylor and to plot with him against the agents.[25]

For some reason, partly from cupidity perhaps, or possibly to harass the Indian agents further, the military moved Camp Cooper from the land given to the United States government by Texas for the Comanche Reserve to Paint Creek on the private rancho of Captain Givens, the enemy of the reserve program. The location of the Givens rancho was twelve miles west by road from the Comanche Agency, or eight by trail through the wilderness. When Major Neighbors protested to General Twiggs the removal of the post, answer was given that if Agent Leeper felt insecure, he could move the agency nearer the new site of Camp Cooper.[26]

Upon the further representation of Major Neighbors, Colonel Henry Wilson, then in command at departmental headquarters in San Antonio, ordered that one army officer and twenty men be stationed on the Comanche Reserve near the Indian camp or Leeper's agency, as he thought best.

When Agent Leeper requested an escort to protect a burial party who desired to bury a Comanche murdered on the road from the Comanche Reserve to the Brazos Reserve, Captain Nathan George Evans (future Confederate general) replied that he did not feel authorized to protect Indians off the reservations. The old Comanche murdered was on his way to the Brazos Reserve with his family, without permission, Neighbors learned, when he fell in with a party from Lampasas County. All stayed at J. R. King's that night. King heard the whites remarking that if the old man were killed, his horses could be taken. King begged the scoundrels not to jeopardize the white settlers' safety by such a base crime, but to no avail. On the road the next morning, the old Comanche was killed, and his horses taken. His family escaped to the reserve, and an excited burial party of Comanches came down alone after Evans refused an escort.

About this time Neighbors's problems were made more difficult by the shocking murder of the Mason and Cameron families in Jack County. W. A. Ribble remembered with horror the ghastly deed, after ninety years. Apparently as a part of the raid, a clean sweep was made in the Fort Belknap area of all the animals belonging to white settlers, to California emigrants, and to the Waco and Tonkawa Indians. A party of marauders appeared at the double log cabin of the Mason and Cameron families twenty-five miles northeast of Belknap, where the malefactors murdered ten members of both families, including both sets of parents. Mrs. Mason was killed in the cow lot with a babe in her arms. Ribble said that when the infant was found it was sucking the bloody breasts of its dead mother.[27] The bodies of the victims were horribly mutilated. A boy and a girl of the Cameron family escaped. John R. Baylor was foremost in charging the atrocities to the Reserve Comanches. Some weeks after the massacre, a white man by the name of Willis was, with his party, arrested in the area and tried for the crime, but they were cleared of the charge. It was believed by most people on the frontier that the perpetrators were Kickapoos,[28] but Judge Lynch seems to have accounted for at least three white men implicated in the murder.[29]

According to Agent Ross, the murder of the Mason and Cameron families led to great excitement on the frontier, and hundreds of families were said to be leaving, since it was rumored that all the United States troops had withdrawn. Then Agent Ross touched upon the factor which made the frontier populace easily panic-stricken and the prey of demagogues. Ross observed to Major Neighbors:

> Our frontier is settled by citizens from older states who are not accustomed to Indians and cannot judge whether rumors are true or not, consequently stampede on the most frivolous alarms.[30]

Senator Houston took up the attacks upon the reserve system as administered by Major Neighbors, and declared in the Senate that no money had ever been spent so wisely or profitably, in civilizing the Indians and protecting the white settlers. The Senator remarked ironically that he was willing to rebuke Major Neighbors on one matter that was unfashionable and improper:

> Sir, he has been guilty of one heinous outrage, for which he ought to be held amenable to the State. I am willing to arraign and try him on it, and he will be convicted at least of inconsistency with the present rule of the Government, though there is nothing criminal in what he has done, but his conduct is so rare and so extraordinary that it even furnishes some pretext for the suspicion that there is criminality in it. Eighty thousand dollars were appropriated for his agency and he has had the impudence to report to the Department, that out of the $80,000 he has an unexpended balance of $60,000 now on hand. That is an outrageous thing, I insist that such a thing has not been since the establishment of the Government, and therefore he ought to be held responsible for setting such an example. [Laughter] That is the only thing he has done improperly that I have heard of, and it is a rebuke to so many that I think he would not meet with much favor. I will now show the influence that civilization has had upon the Indians under his care.

Senator Houston proceeded to make the floor of the United States Senate a rostrum from which to publicize to the nation the accomplishments of the Texas reserve Indians under the superintendency of Major Neighbors, and declared unequivocably that, "There has not been such an advance made since the settlement of this continent to the present moment, amongst any Indian tribes, as has been made in Texas for an inconsiderable expenditure." Alluding again to Neighbors, Houston stated:

> We have saved you $60,000 through the integrity of a capable man, and I want him to extend his protecting mantle and his sagacious policy over those Indians that are our enemies, and will remain so until they become identified with us as friends, and receive their annuities through our country, and

201

know that we are identical with the other portions of the Union.

While Major Neighbors was at the Comanche Agency in the spring of 1858, he learned from Captain Evans, of Camp Cooper, about the reports made by the military officers on the frontier regarding the perpetrators of depredations there. These reports resulted from General Twiggs's order to investigate the forays reported by Neighbors to Pease in December of 1857. Neighbors declared that since he had not seen the reports, he could not discuss their merits, but that the investigation had been entirely *ex parte*, made without the knowledge of the agents, and that the reports of Givens and Paul had greatly increased the excitement among the white settlers against the reserve Indians. Neighbors then traced the hostility of those two officers to the reservation policy since its inception in 1855, and asked for a full investigation of

> ... the many false charges made against us, which endangers not only our lives but our honors also, and to relieve the Indian service in Texas from the many misstatements made by designing men.

Neighbors said he could not believe for a moment that General Twiggs intended to embarrass the Indian service by a partial investigation, or that the general intended to interfere in the selection of Indian agents, or to encourage the circulation of reports among frontier citizens that were prejudicial to the Indians and the agents. As that had been the result, however, Major Neighbors requested copies of the reports of the military officers on the origin of the depredations and a copy of Captain Stoneman's report on his counting of the Indians, which report had been previously refused the Major. He added, "I shall call on you in person on my arrival for these papers."

Colonel Wilson referred the Major's request to the war department and declined further action. Neighbors was not shown the reports, but it was obvious his civilian critics were familiar with the contents.[31] As has been seen, the reports had already gone forward to Washington. Major Neighbors brought the matter to the attention of the commissioner of Indian affairs and demanded that copies of the reports be obtained for the agents so that they could defend the Indians and themselves from the charges.[32]

In his reckless campaign to injure Major Neighbors, John R. Baylor wrote letters to the public prints charging the Reservation Comanches with committing the depredations on the frontier and charging Neighbors with shielding them for the

202

sake of the salary he received—$2,000 a year. Baylor remarked that if Major Neighbors died a premature death, a stone should be erected inscribed, "Vive la humbug."[33] The Major declined to engage in a newspaper war.

The Major believed that much of the prejudice against the Reserve Indians was created by designing men, among whom he classed John R. Baylor as the principal. The Major obtained certificates from responsible citizens to

> . . . prove that he has even resorted to the criminal practice of forging men's names to some of the numerous petitions for the removal of myself from office, and to create prejudice in the minds of other citizens against the reserve Indians.[34]

After satisfying himself that both reservations were in order, Major Neighbors, notwithstanding threats to waylay him, took his departure in order to prepare for the trip to the national capital. The initial leg of his journey to San Antonio was down the Brazos valley along the military road, which may still be traced by Neighbors's vouchers and by old maps. The Major set out with his interpreter and packman, and had dinner at Keechi Creek on April 9, 1858, at the home of George R. Bevers, east of present Graford.[35] That night Neighbors and his party found lodging on Hullenn's Prairie with Ross C. Betty whose descendents still live in Parker County.[36] Neighbors proceeded on his way and lodged next with Silas Smith, on Red Bear Creek, which heads in the southeast corner of Parker County. Lodging was found next with M. B. Jones, at Towiash Creek, where Fort Graham had formerly been located, fourteen miles west of present Hillsboro. The next stop was at Waco, where Neighbors found lodging for his party and forage for his horses at the Waco House, operated by J. M. Smith and one Herrington. The Major travelled alone from Waco, where for $10.00 on the morning of April 15, 1858, he bought stagefare to Austin City from Stage Agent J. M. Smith. Night found the Major in Belton, where he lodged with John M. Pope. Neighbors travelled without interruption from Belton to San Antonio, via San Marcos and New Braunfels, arriving in San Antonio on April 17, 1858, probably late in the evening. Major Neighbors travelled armed, for he and Agent Ross had been warned that it was unsafe for them to travel the roads, as those on the frontier who had lost the best horses considered Neighbors to be in complicity with the Indians.

Without the express approval of the commissioner, Major Neighbors sometime after April 23, 1858, set out for Washington, where he arrived on May 8, 1858, and remained for thirty-one and one-half days. It has been seen that his purpose in making the trip was to present the side of the Indians and agents and to demand an investigation into the baseless charges against them. One of his first actions was to present to the commissioner the correspondence of Agent Leeper concerning the moving of Camp Cooper and to suggest that the secretary of interior take up the matter of the protection of the agents and Indians with the secretary of war.

Instead of protection from the military, Major Neighbors said some of its officers had conspired to inflame the public mind, especially Major Paul, Captain Stoneman, and Captain Givens. The agents agreed, the Major said, that the reserves could not be maintained unless action were taken by the United States government to protect the Indians and the frontier from depredations. Neighbors was urged, he said, by the agents and frontier citizens to go to Washington to lay the situation before the department and before the Texas delegation in Congress and to ask for immediate action to relieve the frontier.

The Major left everything in order on the reserves, and had no wish to stay longer than necessary, but he asked the usual courtesies due an agent on business in the capital. The Texas delegation in Congress, consisting of Guy M. Bryan, J. Pickney Henderson, John H. Reagan, and Sam Houston, supported Neighbors in his decision to come to the capital.

While Major Neighbors was in Washington, reports reached him of the victory of the Texas Rangers and 100 Reserve Indians over the northern Comanches north of Red River at Antelope Hills where seventy-six scalps, ten prisoners, and about three hundred horses were taken. While the success of the expedition reacted temporarily in favor of the Brazos Reserve Indians, it did not solve the problems of Major Neighbors and the Indian service. While Ford was gone on the expedition, raids continued at various points on the frontier which Ford professed to believe were the acts of the Agency Comanches, and he declared that if "I can fix it upon them I shall give them hell and trust to the people to sustain me."[37] Ford, however, was unable to fix the blame upon the Comanches for with his usual fairness he required evidence,

After the expedition to the Canadian, Captain Ford called upon Lieut William G. Preston of his command to notify citizens who were making charges against the Reserve Comanches, that he desired them to place these allegations in writing and be qualified to them. Not a single man ever came forward to testify against the people they had charged with robbery, theft, and murder. No testimony was procured and the Reserve Comanches were not molested. The consequence of this was, that several of the officers were induced to change opinions, and were led to believe the Reserve Comanches had been misrepresented.[38]

Neighbors's administration was further endorsed by Ford's absolving the Reserve Comanches with the statement that "I have never been able to detect the Reserve Indians in the Commission of a single depredation, or to trace one to their doors."[39] It was noteworthy that those who made the most baseless charges against Major Neighbors and the Reserve Indians feared making statements under oath as much as the devil fears holy water. When given an opportunity to appear before a proper tribunal, the calumniators with one accord began to make excuses.

Major Neighbors attained the object of his visit to Washington: an official investigation of the Indian service, and announced the result to the editor of the Galveston *News*:

I address you this note, for the purpose of warning those who have heretofore unjustly and cruelly slandered the Reserve Indians who can only look to me to defend them, and to state their wrongs, that they must make good their charges, or cease to make them. I detest a newspaper war; it is always personal and ill tempered; but I have copies furnished me by the Department of the Interior, of all the official correspondence of the War Department, on his head, and I now notify the authors of that correspondence that a Tribunal, will be appointed, before which, I shall expect to close this vexatious matter.

The investigation did not get underway until fall.

After Major Neighbors arrived at San Antonio on June 25, 1858, from his trip to Washington, he learned that his experiment in educating academically the Indian youth was making significant progress. The Comanche school had succeeded beyond Agent Leeper's expectations. The attendance was irregular, from four to sixteen a day, but the boys were sprightly, and some learned to read simple sentences, while others learned to spell. Schoolmaster D. Stinson was a competent teacher, but Agent Leeper considered him otherwise undesirable on the reservation and discharged him.[40]

Later in the summer of 1858, Major Neighbors learned from the new teacher employed at the Comanche Reserve that there were good prospects for a successful school at the agency. Schoolmaster Richard Sloan reported:

I have entered upon the labors of an Indian school at this place, and it was truly gratifying, at the opening of the school, to see the interest that the Indians felt in having their children educated to speak the English language. On the day we opened the school there was a full attendance of all the chiefs and all the heads of families. And after Colonel Leeper, the special agent, had addressed them through the interpreter, with regard to the utility of having their children educated, and the intention of the government in so doing, their head chief made a very lengthy speech to his people relative to their future prosperity. I have been in council among the various tribes of Indians, but I never before witnessed so much concern among any other tribe, nor saw such willingness to give the names of their children as students.

The teacher pledged himself earnestly to devote "all my talent, skill, and undivided attention" to the instruction of the Comanche youth, and expressed the expectation that in a short time, as much progress would be shown among the young people in his school as in any in the United States. The curriculum was necessarily simple: reading and spelling. Sloan found nine books in the library: three McGuffey's Eclectic First Readers and six elementary spelling books. He placed a requisition with Major Neighbors for forty-eight more books, and expressed a preference for pictorial spelling books. The schoolmaster found his thirty-seven students very attentive and reported that they spent from six to eight hours studying each day.

Major Neighbors learned that during the summer of 1858, sixty scholars attended the school on the Brazos Agency, with an average daily attendance of thirty-five. The chiefs assured the teacher that after the interference of the harvest, more children would be sent. The Caddos and Tawacanos evinced the most interest in the school. The schoolmaster was Zachariah Ellis Coombes, late of Dallas County, who received $800 a year, the next highest salary at the agency after that of Agent Ross, which was $1500 a year. Coombes reported that his scholars were learning the alphabet, and some were already spelling words of one syllable. It was necessary to issue provisions of beef and flour to the children at school, and the teacher wanted provision made for housing the students near the school. It was a great inconvenience for the parents to send their children to school because of the distance of the villages. The nearest village was one and one-half miles, while most were four miles or more away. Schoolmaster Coombes expressed a need for benches, desks, a bookcase, blackboard, and an

206

interpreter. He confessed he knew not one Indian word, and declared he could not convey the meaning of one word of English to the students. Agent Ross then hired another interpreter, George Williams, a highly competent Delaware.[41] Besides secular education Major Neighbors employed the Reverend Pleasant Tackitt, Methodist circuit rider to preach on the Brazos Reservation.[42]

Since the government employees who assisted Neighbors enter the narrative occasionally, it is well that they be identified as a group. On June 30, 1858, the personnel at the Comanche Agency, besides Agent Leeper, were John Jacobs, interpreter; replaced by John Shirley in that capacity; H. P. Jones, farmer; Thomas Coghill and William Bevans, laborers; and D. Stinson, teacher; replaced by Richard Sloan. On the same date the employees at the Brazos Agency, besides Agent Ross, were H. R. (or R. W.) Moss, farmer; Samuel Church, farmer; Thomas Doane, W. J. Owens, and A. B. Gipson, laborers; A. J. Dysche, blacksmith and armorer; D. Lewars, carpenter; James Shaw and D. A. Bickel, interpreters, as well as George Williams, later employed; and E. Z. Coombes, teacher. Hired to Americanize, ironically some men quickly Indianized, and Ross fired them.

In the summer of 1858, Major Neighbors learned that an amendment to an appropriation bill in Congress had made the Texas Indian Service a regular superintendency, requiring that the agents be appointed by the President and approved by the Senate. Hitherto, the agents in Texas had been special agents appointed solely by the executive branch and paid by riders to other bills. Neighbors wanted to know the effect of the new legislation upon the Texas agents, particularly whether they would have to be immediately reappointed. A year went by before any action was taken by the general government.

When Major Neighbors had called upon General Twiggs in San Antonio after the Major's return from Washington, he offered guides and trailers from the reservations if Twiggs would send an expedition on a campaign against the wild Indians north of Red River. General Twiggs gave his hearty accord and suggested to army headquarters at West Point that the Second Cavalry which had been sent to Utah, after all, be not detached to various posts as formerly, but be sent into the Indian country to "follow them up winter and summer, thus giving the Indians something to do at home and taking care of their families, and they might possibly let Texas alone." Twiggs was recommending that the defensive policy of the last ten years be abandoned. Since a campaign might lead into another department, it was necessary for Twiggs to have the approval of the general in chief of the army. This came to fruition some months later.

Captain Ford believed that there was a ring of white outlaws operating with the Indians to dispose of stolen horses, and proposed to gather data upon the subject. This view was held by many, and still persists in the Belknap area in the twentieth century.[43]

The Dallas *Herald* reported that,

> The present opinion is, that the horse stealing and other depredations on the frontier cannot be attributed to the Indians. The existence of a band of robbers in this State, extending across it and into Mexico, on the one side and the United States Indian territory on the other, is doubted by few,—These scoundrels are in league with the Indians. They find where the horses are, and the Indians, under their guidance and assistance, steal them.

The *Herald* then cited recent events which seemed to give credence to this belief. The Waco *Democrat* voiced the same belief. The existence of such a band of white outlaws was proved by a letter taken from the body of one of them killed by the Second Cavalry on the Clear Fork.[44]

The campaign of vituperation against Major Neighbors, the other agents, and the Reserve Indians was renewed in the summer of 1858. Captain Ford entrusted a report to Lieutenant Nelson, who mailed it to Washington instead of Austin, accompanied by a letter to President Buchanan, in which Nelson grossly slandered Major Neighbors. Nelson acknowledged knowing that a commission had been appointed to investigate the Indian service and declared that he would not burden the President with reports from the frontier. He could not desist, however, from declaring that it was not true that the people were opposed to the reserve policy. He said this report had been circulated by those who wished to close the ears of the government to the charges of "the gross abuse of power on the part of your agents." Nelson demurred that the people had no "powerful & influencial friends at Court," and asserted that they were actually the Indians' best friends, while

> ... those who claim to be their friends 'par Excellence' are their worst enemies. It is they who fleece them of the means that a liberal and humane Government appropriates to elevate & if you could see the degrading vices they are taught

without one redeeming virtue you would be shocked. But I promised not to tax you with this.[45]

In referring to Lieutenant Nelson's activities on this head, Captain Ford observed that he viewed "him as a man who had and is endeavoring to subserve his own ends, and thought it necessary to play a double part to effect his object."

T. C. Alexander of Meridian took notice of the movement to replace Neighbors with Nelson in a letter to President Buchanan, and remarked that,

It is understood that a commission has been appointed to investigate the charges against Major Neighbors. If the case is well prosecuted, I doubt not, enough will be shown to cause his removal, but if he succeeds in getting an ex parte hearing, of course he will be exonerated from all blame or fault.

John R. Baylor, in his campaign against Major Neighbors, kept the public mind agitated on the Indian problem by engaging Agent Leeper in an ill-tempered newspaper duel, in which the alleged complicity of the Reserve Comanches in depredations was the principal topic. Each side produced letters and certificates on the matter. Leeper revealed that Lieutenant Edward Burleson, Jr., reported that Baylor had tried to get a detail of Rangers, stationed at his home for his protection, to help him commit depredations on a neighbor's livestock and make a trail from there to the Comanche Reservation to incriminate the Comanches so that Captain Ford would break up the reserve. Baylor declared that everyone knew he was jesting. Baylor's party made much of Buck Barry's horses (or a part of them) having been found on the Comanche Reserve, but as has been seen, Leeper and Major Neighbors were the first to notify Barry that the Comanches had found his horses.

Baylor wrote Barry more than once, remarking that he was collecting all the evidence he could against Neighbors, the Indians and agents, and indicated that he knew about the commission appointed to investigate the controversy between the citizens and the agents. Baylor declared in a letter to Barry that,

It is important that the citizens should *hang together and unite.* I want Nelson in the place of Neighbors and will do all in my power to aid him . . .[46]

Neighbors's success in settling the Indians, despite opposition, led in part to the continued development of the region in the vicinity of the reserves. Young County attained a population of five hundred souls, while Belknap, the county seat, was thought to be on a nascent boom and was connected with the outside world by various roads and stage lines. The Southern Overland Mail Route from St. Louis to San Francisco was projected through Belknap in the summer of 1858, while a mail and stage line was opened to Dallas via the Brazos Agency, Weatherford, and Fort Worth. The commissioners' court approved the opening of a new road for this purpose from Belknap to the county line via the Brazos Agency.[47] Military traces already connected Belknap with Preston, Waco, Fort Worth, Austin, and San Antonio. The Dallas *Herald* announced the commencement of stage service from Dallas to Belknap, which was made twice a week in comfortable, four-horse hacks, and observed, "Persons having business or desiring to visit the delightful region on the upper Brazos may avail themselves of this mode of traveling at any time." Fort Belknap was designated the headquarters for the Second Cavalry, and a citizen of Belknap, after commenting on the lively times, added, "We will soon have the regimental band here to discourse eloquent music to the good people of this city." With all this prosperity, a concrete court house was built, and lots in the "City of Belknap" rose in value 200 per cent. It was said that nothing could be heard but talk of building contracts. So excited became one citizen that he cried, "Vive la Belknap!"

Despite the threats on his life, Major Neighbors continued to travel the public and military roads unescorted. The Major set out from the Brazos Agency via Fort Mason and Leon Springs for his home in San Antonio, a distance of three hundred miles, where on August 20, 1858, Elizabeth Ann and his children awaited him.

While in San Antonio, Major Neighbors received a letter from Governor Runnels soliciting his good offices in securing relief for the frontier. The governor said that from the *Gazette* extra put out by the versatile John S. Ford and from Barnard's letter, it was clear that the northern Indians had commenced their design to break up the reserve. Governor Runnels concluded his letter to Major Neighbors with the assurance that, "I place great reliance in your own favorable dispositions."

The Major obliged the governor and requested his department to induce the war department to send a sufficient force to protect the frontier. Acting Secretary of War A. M. Dunkard wrote Governor Runnels that he had ordered four companies of cavalry and one of infantry to march from Fort Belknap on September 15, 1858, to Otter Creek, west of the Wichita Mountains, to establish a depot from which to scour the country

210

between Red River and the north fork of the Canadian and between the one hundredth and one hundred and fourth meridians. Two companies of cavalry had been ordered from Kansas to Fort Arbuckle to examine the country near the Wichita Mountains "with a view of placing military posts for the purpose of restraining the Comanches." Twiggs received orders shortly to carry out a campaign according to his desires and along lines which Major Neighbors had long recommended.

Neighbors was shortly apprised of an embarrassing episode involving wild Comanche intruders on the Comanche Reserve and the United States army. When Agent Leeper called upon Lieutenant Cornelius Van Camp to arrest the intruders, a pitched battle appeared imminent, until Van Camp discovered to his astonishment that his men had only one round of ammunition among them. He acceded to the compromise offered by a Reserve Comanche, Toshahua, that the intruders be escorted out of camp by the Reserve Comanches (most of whom had sided with the intruders against Chief Ketumse and Van Camp).

Major Neighbors first conferred with General Twiggs on the debacle. Then in marked contrast to the way military officers had circulated reports to injure the Major, in a private letter to the governor he enclosed a copy of Leeper's report of the affair and asked that the governor not publicize the matter as the Major understood Van Camp was to be court-martialed. The Major concluded,

> I send you this report for your information, and hope that you will not make it public, but use it only officially, as the matter will undergo official investigation, and I can see no good that will result from its publication.

Major Neighbors forwarded to the commissioner of Indian affairs a copy of Leeper's report on the affair of the intruders with the comment that this revealed the influence of the northern Indians upon the reservation. Neighbors said he would investigate the incident in concert with military officers who had been ordered to do so by General Twiggs.

General Twiggs was almost beside himself when he heard of the Van Camp debacle. In transmitting the commanding general's orders to Captain Innis N. Palmer to proceed with Company D to old Camp Cooper until further notice, the adjutant added Twiggs's biting injunction that, "It is especially enjoined that Capt. Palmer shall keep his company liberally supplied with ammunition at all times." Major Neighbors remarked to Governor Runnels that,

> Gen. Twiggs is of course greatly annoyed to think that a company of U. S. Troops should go into a fight with only one round of ammunition . . .

The commanding general declined to be mollified by an explanation.

> From the reports so far received, it only appears that two notorious scoundrels made their appearance at the reserve, and, when ordered off, refused to leave: that the Indian Agent applied to the U. S. officer in command of the troops near the reserve to have these men secured; that the Indians resisted the arrest being made; that the troops when they should have been ready for a fight, if necessary to enforce their commands, were found to be without a sufficient supply of ammunition; and that in consequence of this deficiency, the obnoxious men, instead of being seized by the proper authorities were actually escorted beyond their reach by thirty Indian warriors.[48]

General Twiggs notified the commanding officer at Camp Cooper together with Captain William R. Bradfute, who was to be in the vicinity with forty men, to arrest at all hazards any Indian Major Neighbors desired to have secured.

Agent Leeper stated to Major Neighbors, however, that there were then, on October 9, 1858, no Indians in a state of resistance to him. Any further action would be a violation of the agreement with the Indians whose explanations at the time were considered satisfactory to Lieutenant Van Camp and Lieutenant Phifer. When Major Neighbors arrived at the Comanche Agency, he was convinced that the Comanches were laboring under a misapprehension when Van Camp attempted the arrest, and deemed no further action necessary. Twiggs, who was again almost beside himself, swore that the military would never send any more protection to the frontier.

The department of the interior made no progress toward establishing the Pecos Indian Reserve which Neighbors had secured. When Congressman Bryan forwarded the application of a gentleman for the agency, Secretary Thompson replied that no appointment would be made until the reservation was surveyed. The survey was to be made by John H. Clark, who was also selected to run the lines between the United States and Texas on the west. Thompson added that instructions had been sent to Major Neighbors to proceed as rapidly as possible with the establishment of the reserve.

In October of 1858, Major Neighbors received news of the joint victory of the Second Cavalry under Major Earl Van Dorn and 125 Brazos Indians under Sul Ross over the Comanches in the Indian territory.[49] At the battle of Wichita Village north of Red River, young Sul Ross and Van Dorn both were severely wounded. The casualties were three killed, including Lieutenant Van Camp, ten wounded, and one missing, while the soldiers and Brazos Indians killed fifty-six of the enemy and captured over three hundred animals.[50] Van Dorn continued to operate from Camp Radsminski and next spring with his soldiers and Brazos Indians killed or captured ninety-one Comanches just north of the Kansas line on Crooked Creek, a tributary of the Cimarron River about eighteen miles south of old Fort Atkinson.[51] These victories for a time reacted among the white citizens in the favor of the Brazos Indians.

In their annual reports in September of 1858, the agents detailed the progress of the Indians. Major Neighbors reported there were 371 Comanches on the Upper Reserve, a decrease of 53 souls; by the census of June 30, 1858, there were 1,112 on the Brazos Reserve, an increase of 98 since last year. In spite of their being harrassed, Major Neighbors thought the Comanches had made much more progress than the year before. The Major said the Brazos Reserve Indians had lost considerable numbers of stock animals to the hostile Indians and through their inability to hunt their stray animals because of the hostile attitude of the white settlers. He thought this prejudice had then almost entirely subsided. Neighbors regretted that the northern Indians had not been settled on the new reserve east of North Fork of Red River as he thought that was the only practicable method of halting depredations on the Texas frontier. As for his relations with the military, the Major stated that,

I have endeavored during the year to act fully in concert with the military authorities, and can now state that a good understanding exists between the officers of the army and the agents of Texas, and that the measures now being pursued with our Indians (both those on the reserves and on our borders) have been freely canvassed between the commanding general of Texas and myself, with satisfactory results.[52]

The *Texas Almanac* of 1858 spoke highly of the progress of the Reserve Indians saying,

There is less theft or disturbance, of any kind, among these people, than there is among the same population of Americans. Suffice it that the Feeding or Peace-Policy in Texas is a success. It has demonstrated, beyond doubt, that Indians can be civilized and reclaimed. The Brazos Reserve Indians

213

have tended their own crops, which will compare favorably with any in the State; and have also kept from fifty to one hundred men on ranging service during the season, and have been great protection to the frontier.[53]

At the same time the *Almanac* commended the services of Major Neighbors, the supervising agent, to whom was ascribed the success of the reserves.

While Major Neighbors was absent in San Antonio, his old companion on many hazardous ventures met his untimely end. Jim Shaw on the morning of October 1, while working on his roof, fell from a fence adjoining his house on the Brazos Reserve and broke his neck, death resulting instantly. In reporting Jim Shaw's death, Charles E. Barnard spoke highly of his services to both the state and general governments. He was fifty-eight years of age,[54] having been born in Missouri,[55] probably on the Caw River Delaware Reservation.

Major Neighbors in his capacity as supervising agent, commuted between the two reserves. Once in company with Ketumse and one of his wives, Major Neighbors encountered on the road at the head of Fish Creek a sandstorm so severe that two wagon beds were blown off and several oxen killed.

Along with other agency personnel, Major Neighbors ate at the public mess maintained by young Schoolmaster Coombes and his wife. Coombes gave a human interest item in his diary in which he wrote:

> Major R. S. Neighbors and Chas. E. Barnard made a long chat at the table tonight in the way of advice to me on the subject of education. And finally each wound up with a splendid commendation of his own dear self and actions from boyhood to the present and both talked so much at once both address themselves to me. I was very much puzzled to keep pace with either the fact I was unable to do so consequently lost much that was useful and undoubtedly interesting.[56]

On the morning of October 15, 1858, Coombes went to Neighbors's office for some forms and instead received a sharp reprimand for loose talk. Coming from such a source, this bombshell greatly shocked young Coombes as he confided to his diary:

> The force of the reproof pronounced upon me this morning has cast a gloom and oppression on my feelings which will not easily be eradicated from my memory.

Apparently fear of another reproof from Major Neighbors caused this young self-professed paragon of virtue to be more careful of his tongue, but his pen recorded in his diary his spite thereafter. No one escaped his accusations from the agents down to the lowliest laborers and even the Indians, all of whom he variously accused of gambling, drinking, lewdness, and general licentiousness. He kept his imagination working over time. Young Coombes, nevertheless, confided to his diary his own drinking habits, while reporting Ross and Barnard as being drunk.

By keeping his ear carefully open, the young school teacher gleefully heard Head Farmer Sturm give Major Neighbors an adverse report on the blacksmith whom the young Puritan did not like and characterized as a

> . . . nuisance to the reserve, a needler, a whoremonger, a drunkard, gambler and besides neglects the business entrusted to his care.

Young Coombes averred with satisfaction, "I should rejoice to see him discharged." "Vanity, Vanity, all is vanity," as Coombes noted. Before the day was over, Major Neighbors fell afoul of Coombes instead and "Intimates to me that I am opposed to the Reserves and as a cure for the same he proposed that I become acquainted with the regulations of the department and the act creating them . . . a clue to leave . . . ."

Coombes went to considerable pains to convince his diary that he was innocent of all charges, and to attribute wrong doing to others. His childhood in the aftermath of the Second Great Awakening in Kentucky had not fitted him to be tolerant of the morals and culture of men from the Stone Age nor to understand the problems of administration and personnel on a raw frontier. Indian fertility rites were vulgar to him. To his diary Coombes moralized:

> To show to what a splendid pitch virtue is among some classes of these Indians that some men will bring their wives or sisters and offer them to the stranger or to a known customer for from 50 Cents to $2.50 and still this is making rapid advances to civilization? Well perhaps those in authority do not know these things and if not they will doubtless remain happilay ignorant of them for no employee will trouble himself with obtaining a sound lecture and perhaps a cursing for so doing. And among my acquaintances among the employees I do not know of one singel man who does not confess to enjoying the carresses of Indian Squaw's. [His own dear self excepted.]

By encouraging his students to gossip about the agents,

Coombes was able to get one Caledonia to suppose that she had been tempted by Major Neighbors. On another occasion Coombes gossiped in his diary about his brother Mason to the effect that Coombes suspected Major Neighbors of "civilizing a certain Lipan Squaw today." Had Coombes's gossip with his diary been substantiated, the mortal enemies of the agents would have publicized the incidents. With a United States tribunal under Commissioner Thomas Hawkins sitting at the time on the reserves, it would have been Coombes's duty to report such moral turpitude if it had existed.

Chapter XII
The Vindicated

Meanwhile the tribunal which Major Neighbors had requested to investigate his official conduct had opened. Secretary of Interior J. Thompson apprised Secretary of War J. B. Floyd of the appointment of Thomas T. Hawkins, of Lexington, Kentucky to investigate the official conduct of Major Robert S. Neighbors; and as some of the military officers might be interested, he asked Floyd's approval of the appointment and requested that the officers in Texas extend Hawkins all proper facilities for the investigation. Floyd highly approved the appointment.

Commissioner Mix furnished the investigator, Thomas T. Hawkins, with copies of all correspondence relating to the charges against the agents and Indians and copies of the reports of the agents. Hawkins asked Neighbors to be present at the tribunal to cross examine witnesses, to defend himself against all accusers, and to advise Agents Ross and Leeper. The Major expressed his pleasure with Hawkins's appointment and the intention of offering him every facility.

Captain Givens's reports and the petitions he sponsored for the removal of Neighbors were responsible for the original impetus to investigate the Indian service in Texas. Major Neighbors at San Antonio notified Captain Givens who was stationed at that place that Hawkins was to be at Fort Belknap and Camp Cooper about October 1, 1858, to investigate the charges made by Givens on February 1, and 12, 1858, against Neighbors, the agents, and Reserve Indians. The Major declared he gave Givens this notice so that he could be present if he wished, as Neighbors desired the commissioner to have every facility to investigate. He added, "I shall be pleased to be informed of the course you intend to pursue in this matter, so that I may make my arrangements accordingly." Captain Givens was given every opportunity to attend the hearing, including authorization by General Twiggs, commanding the Seventh Military District, but he declined the offer.

Commissioner Hawkins arrived at old Camp Cooper on September 30, 1858, and requisitioned quarters and other accomodations from Captain Palmer. Hawkins remarked to the commissioner of Indian affairs that with the exception of Agent Leeper, no one appeared interested in his mission. Pending the arrival of affiants, Hawkins proposed to inquire into the conduct of the Indians on the Comanche Reservation, according to his instructions. Then he expected to proceed to the Brazos Reserve.

On September 30, 1858, Major Neighbors returned in his carriage drawn by four government mules and driven by his negro slave Cipio from San Antonio by way of Austin and Waco to the Brazos Agency where he arrived on October 4, 1858. He proceeded to the Comanche Agency on October 8, 1858, where he placed himself and his means at the disposal of Commissioner Hawkins. The Major requested Hawkins to obtain copies of the military orders and reports bearing on the accusations against him as he said he had been refused them. He added, "I am now here and will remain as long as it is necessary with a hope to be enabled to confront my accusers."

Just as Hawkins settled himself to open the investigation at old Camp Cooper, the military ordered the post abandoned again, and it was only with difficulty that he was able to get General Twiggs to order a detail to remain for the duration of the hearing.

There was not a general stampede of citizens to testify before Hawkins against Superintendent Neighbors, the Indians, and agents. The investigator sent notices to all who had preferred charges and published notices of the investigation in four leading journals of north and central Texas, while the agents gave him about twenty names of people who might give evidence. By October 16, 1858, however, only three persons had appeared, and Hawkins declared that they gave only vague accusations about the horse stealing and cow killing "propensities of Indians in general."

Major Neighbors's principal calumniators when summoned to appear before Hawkins began with one accord to make excuses. Allison Nelson, who admitted that he did not even know the man he had accused, demurred that he received the commissioner's letter so late that the hearing would be over before he could gather evidence, although he acknowledged in July that he knew of the investigation. With a flair for sweetness and light, he added,

Besides the charges are too general without specifications either to give Maj. Neighbors that fair opportunity to meet them that justice to him requires & however ready he might be to waive that it would defeat the entire object I had in view in writing the letter—viz—to quiet & put at rest the continued conflict & dissatisfaction of the people among whom I reside toward Maj. N. & the Indians on the Reservations which has threatened serious consequences more than once within the last twelve months & which I have as often used my efforts to turn in a legitimate direction.

Nelson said that as soon as possible, in justice to Neighbors himself and the people, he would gather evidence to support the specifications and furnish Major Neighbors a copy for his rebuttal. This would take time, he said, but unless he, Nelson, were allowed to substantiate his charges, people would say that the investigation was *ex parte*. In other words, when Nelson's allegations were brought to light, they dissolved into mere generalities which had no basis and could not be substantiated.

When John R. Baylor arrived on November 22, 1858, at Belknap after an absence of two months, he said that the notice he received from Hawkins was the first he knew of the court and that he had no opportunity to substantiate his charges.[2] Baylor's letter to Buck Barry on August 2, 1858, however, mentioned the commission appointed to investigate the agents and stated that Baylor was collecting all the evidence he could against them.[3]

At the instance of Major Neighbors, Commissioner Hawkins extended an invitation to James Buckner Barry to attend the tribunal. He demurred that he received notice too late to reach Camp Cooper in time, and suggested that it would save him a tedious ride and two weeks valuable time if the investigation were carried out at his home in Bosque County. In regard to the loss of his horses, Barry admitted that Major Neighbors acted fairly.

Although my testimony might not be worth much for or against him, permit *me* to say in behalf of Major Neighbours that he treated me ver[y] clever [in its obsolete meaning] and gentlemany in the information of some of my horses that was stolen notwithstanding I am satisfied from many circumstances that the Indians on the upper reserve was knowing to the stealing my horses and some of them directly concerned

[in] it though I was not thus satisfied when I made affidavits in presenting a claim to the government for damages done therefore those upper reserve Indians was not included in my affidavit.

Barry, Alexander, and others of Bosque County filed a petition with Hawkins asking the replacement of Neighbors with their fellow citizen, Allison Nelson, but again they presented no evidence of misconduct against the Major. The calumniators could only claim that he took the side of the Indians against the whites. In other words Neighbors was guilty of malfeasance for doing his sworn duty in protecting the Indians against injustice.

Givens, Baylor, Nelson, Barry, and company kept safely out of the way of the commission appointed expressly to investigate the charges they had made against the agents and the Indians.

In winding up the investigation at Camp Cooper in preparation for his removal to the Brazos Reserve, Commissioner Hawkins reported that few of those who had complained had come although his mission was as widely advertised as possible. On the other hand, Hawkins declared that the agents, although laboring under the disadvantage of proving a negative, produced a mass of evidence in favor of them and the Indians. If the lack of investigating business were boring to Hawkins, the excitement on October 22, 1858, was not.

On the evening of October 21, 1858, Commissioner Hawkins learned that a posse of citizens headed by Sheriff R. King of Young County proposed to proceed next day to the Comanche Agency to arrest a Comanche charged with shooting Allen Johnson's young son some months previously. Although Hawkins was ill he went to the agency next day to assist the agents in preventing such an outrage. There he became too ill to mount horse and requested his assistant, J. T. Pickett, to take his place.

That morning Major Neighbors, Agent Leeper, and J. T. Pickett along with Captain Palmer, a sergeant, and forty troopers from D company rode out the road to Belknap to confront the armed posse. After riding four miles, Major Neighbors's party and Sheriff King with fifty well armed men, drew up opposite each other in battle array, the sheriff announced his determination to make the arrest at all hazards, and exhibited a writ from the district court of Wise County. Major Neighbors then drew from his pocket the act of the legislature granting the reserves to the United States and giving the general government exclusive jurisdiction over the Indians settled on the reserves. After reading the act to Sheriff King and his well armed posse, Major Neighbors succeeded after much argument "in convincing King and his party that they were upon an unlawful errand and in persuading them to return peaceably to their homes." Commissioner Hawkins confided to his journal that he thought King was more influenced by the appearance of the troopers than by any legal scruples, and added:

> Will not close these notes without expressing the satisfaction which I, for one, feel at the moderate and judicious manner which characterized the conduct of Agents Neighbors and Leeper—and Captain Palmer as well—on the above trying and unpleasant occasion.[4]

Apparently not a soul appeared at the Brazos Reserve to testify before the tribunal. A council of the Indians was called and a statement was taken from Chief Pockmark describing his investigation of the depredations in Coryell County which showed that the perpetrators were Kickapoos. The Dallas *Herald* declared that after the tribunal was open six weeks, no one appeared to testify.

When Major Neighbors called upon Captain Ford in Austin for an affidavit for the tribunal of Commissioner Hawkins, Ford narrated his failure to prove that the Reserve Indians had committed depredations, the failure of those who had complained to come forward at his invitation to testify against the Indians and agents, the duplicity of Nelson, and other matters already cited in this narrative. Ford praised the progress of the Brazos Reserve Indians, endoresed Agent Ross highly, stated that a visit to the Comanche Reserve removed many of the prejudices he had formerly entertained against Agent Leeper, and declared, "The ordeal through which Major Neighbors has passed endorses him. He needs no commendation from any quarter."[5]

With his official conduct vindicated by the special United States investigator and by responsible public opinion, Major Neighbors, after having just passed his forty-third birthday, set out in his carriage with Cipio at the reins, via Waco and Austin, for his home in San Antonio where he arrived on November 24, 1858.[6] In his comparatively short life, he had already experienced more than is usually vouchsafed to several ordinary mortals. But his ordeal was not over. It had just begun.

Chapter XIII
The Besieged

As Major Neighbors travelled rapidly south toward San Antonio, in his carriage drawn by four government mules, he had no illusions that the troubles for the reservations were at an end. Reports of raids throughout the frontier were coming in to Governor Runnels. Raids and atrocities put the frontier population in a mood for violence against Indians in general. If they could not reach the wild ones, those near at hand on the reservations must suffer the consequences.

Besides the small detachments already operating on the frontier, Governor Runnels called Captain James Bourland and Captain John S. Ford into the field. Bourland was ordered to protect the frontier, to pursue the Indians to their camps, and to cooperate with Van Dorn if practicable, while Ford was ordered to raise a company to "move without delay to a suitable point to protect the exposed settlements, which have recently suffered from Indian depredations." Later the governor ordered Ford to muster in three more companies but forbade him to make any more expeditions into the Indian country, as there was much dissatisfaction in many portions of the country with such excursions.

Major Neighbors was troubled to learn from Captain Ross that statements continued to appear in the *Frontier News* of Weatherford and the *Southern Democrat* of Waco, which were designed to excite and inflame the frontier settlers. The Major found that the authors were the same whose allegations had been proved false by Commissioner Hawkins, and called upon Commissioner of Indian Affairs Denver to publish Hawkins's report to allay the excitement. The Dallas *Herald* remarked that,

Some anonymous writers continue to snap and snarl at Major

Neighbors through the columns of the Waco 'Democrat.' We tell all such that they 'knaw a file,' and had as well betake themselves to the 'Mountains of [Hesperides?].'

A twentieth century observer also suggested that the detractors of Major Neighbors be ignored as one would a pack of cur dogs.

While Neighbors was at home in San Antonio visiting with his wife, and two children, Mary Beatrice and Robert Barnard, the backwash of the Ford-Van Dorn expeditions reached him. Elias Rector, southern Indian superintendent wrote Acting Commissioner Mix objecting to the military attacks upon the Comanches, while they were visiting the Wichitas. The Comanches assumed the Wichitas had betrayed them and had fallen upon their hapless hosts, driving them out of their country upon Fort Arbuckle, hungry and destitute.[1]

In his sympathy for the wild Comanches, Superintendent Rector got little solace, however, from the army officers in the frontier posts. While agreeing to cooperate heartily with Rector, Major W. H. Emory of the First Cavalry and Neighbors's friend at Fort Arbuckle, expressed the opinion that the Comanches would never be settled until after a good beating and thought "they have received nothing more than they deserve."[2]

Meanwhile more colonists were arriving at the Comanche Reserve. In November Agent Leeper apprised Major Neighbors of the arrival of Ketumse's brother who said part of his band numbering eighty souls was approaching the reserve, and that he had sent his son for the remainder on the Arkansas. In December Neighbors learned that the Kotsoteka Comanches (Buffalo Eaters), survivors of Ford's attack, had arrived at the Comanche Reserve on the Clear Fork with the intention of settling. The Major ordered that rations be given them until the will of the department could be learned. Major Emory had conjectured correctly that a good beating would induce the Comanches to settle.

Thus far the reports of difficulties on the frontier were as naught to the bombshell that shattered the peace of Neighbors's home where he was spending the Christmas Season with his family in San Antonio. There he received a message from Captain Ross imploring him to return at once to the Brazos Agency as enemies of the reserve policy had taken the opportunity during the absence of the Major in San Antonio and the absence of Agent Ross at the United States district court in Austin to massacre a party of the reserve

Indians on the bend of the Brazos at the mouth of Keechi Creek. Even those whites in the area friendly to the Indians had embodied for fear of retaliation. J. J. Sturm, the reserve farmer, repaired to the scene of the massacre to investigate and reported to Agent Ross that,

> A more horrible sight I never expect to see. There, on their beds, lay the bodies of seven of the best and most inoffensive Indians on the reserve, their bodies pierced by buck shot and rifle balls, their eyes closed, and their bodies stretched full length, their countenances indicating that they passed from calm sleep to the sleep that knows no waking. One warrior lay outside the camp; he and his wife were both shot. After being shot, he seized his gun and shot the murderer of his wife through the head, and at the same moment another of the murderers shot him through the head. So murderer and murdered both fell dead together.

> The names of the parties who did the fell deed are all known. The most of them were citizens from Erath county. I will give you the names, so far as I have learned them. There were seventeen Indians in all; seven killed, and four severely wounded, and a little boy of the number will probably die.[3]

The Indians were members of Choctaw Tom's party who with the permission of Agent Ross had been hunting several weeks in the area and were upon the point of leaving when men from Golconda (near present Palo Pinto) induced them to remain longer to hunt bear with them. Men from Erath County learned of the presence of the Indians and embodied to attack them. Led by Peter Garland, about twenty men appeared in Golconda on the evening of December 26, 1858, and announced their intention of attacking Choctaw Tom's party. When this met with the disapproval of the community, Garland was understood to say that his party would return home next morning. Instead about daylight Garland and his band attacked the Indian camp. There were twenty-seven Indians in the camp instead of seventeen as first reported. Three of the seven killed were women, while two of the severely wounded were women and three were children. One of the attacking party, Samuel Stephen, son of John M. Stephen of Stephenville, was killed, it was thought by one of his own party, and left on the spot. Citizens of Golconda later retrieved his body and gave him a proper burial.[4] Another of Garland's party, John Barnes, was wounded.

Choctaw Tom had been in Texas for many years and had enjoyed the confidence of the whites. He had served as an interpreter for President Sam Houston at the making of the treaty at Bird's Fort in 1843. Tom married an Anadarko woman and had many children and grandchildren, some of whom had served as nurses among the whites. These descendants along with their relatives were with Tom when his camp was attacked. Tom was not present as he had bought a wagon and had taken it to the reserve. The young men present, two of whom were killed, had just returned from assisting Van Dorn in his notable victory and had permission from Agent Ross to go below the reserve where the grass was good to recruit their horses in preparation for returning to Van Dorn at his request for the spring campaign.

The relatives of the slain were aroused and wanted to take summary vengeance, but José María controlled them with the assurance that Agent Ross would not see them wronged with impunity. Citizens of Palo Pinto (Golconda) in a message to Agents Neighbors and Ross expressed their deep sorrow for the murder of the Indians who had been living among them, hunting, and conducting themselves in a peaceable manner. These citizens expressed their diapprobation of the murder, and called upon agents to protect them from the Indians. When the Indians learned, however, that a body of two hundred men from the frontier counties of Coryell, Bosque, Comanche, Erath, and Palo Pinto had embodied and under Allison Nelson had advanced thirty miles below the reserve to attack and break it up, the colonists fled to the agency buildings for protection. Sturm appealed for troops to Major Thomas who sent Captain Palmer with thirty-four men to take post at the Brazos Agency.

When Major Neighbors received Agent Ross's report of the massacre, he took the stage on January 6, 1859, for the Brazos Agency via Austin, Waco, Dallas, and Weatherford. In Austin the Major called upon the United States Attorney for the Western District of Texas, Richard B. Hubbard, who gave the opinion that the United States courts had no jurisdiction over the case. Governor Runnels assured Major Neighbors, however, that the state would take energetic measures to arrest the murderers and cope with the situation. Thereupon the governor issued a proclamation forbidding the unlawful assembling of armed bands to attack the reserves and calling upon the civil authorities and peace officers to use all legal means to arrest the offenders, as well as calling upon all good and law-abiding citizens to assist the authorities in the execution of their duties.

At Waco Major Neighbors and Joshua R. Carnack made

affidavits for the arrest of Garland's band, and Judge N. W. Battle issued writs to Captain Ford to arrest the offenders. The Major also employed as counsel for the Indians, Attorney Edward J. Gurley of Waco. On the way to the reserve, Major Neighbors said,

> I have used every exertion, since the murder of these Indians, to trace the sources from which it originated. My investigation shows, at Waco, Dallas, Weatherford, and the frontier counties through which I passed on my way up, that the same parties, viz: Mr. Allison Nelson, John R. Baylor, Mr. Alexander, with the addition of their tools, Captain Garland and his party—the same party, in fact, who participated so prominently in the charges against the reserve Indians and agents last summer—are responsible for the whole transaction, and have concocted and carried out the whole of this diabolical murder.

To the Major it was the most cold-blooded murder of women and children that had transpired in Texas since the revolution, and exceeded all the brutality attributed to the Comanches. The history of Texas, he said, did not record that any party of civilized men had murdered the same number of women and children, with or without provocation. He thought that if the state authorities did not arrest and punish the "perpetrators of this most foul murder, that the Indians of this reserve will disband and seek satisfaction." Major Neighbors arrived at the Brazos Agency on January 22, 1859, and instructed Agent Ross to furnish supplies and transportation for the wounded Indians and other witnesses who would travel to Waco to give evidence.[5] According to Coombes:

> The whole agency seems to have forgotten all past differences and have all combined to make the murderers of the Indians suffer for their wanton and cruel outrage upon the Indians.[6]

Major Neighbors learned that on January 8, 1859, three citizens came as commissioners of the assembled citizens to make some amicable arrangements to settle the difficulties. Captain Palmer said they stated that the citizens had no intention of attacking the reserve, but wanted to know the attitude of the Indians. The so-called commissioners of the citizens were George B. Erath, a Vienna Austrian, J. M. Norris, and Dixon Walker, accompanied by twelve men as an escort. Erath arrived back at the camp of the citizens on January 12, 1859, and the group disbanded, after they were told the chiefs had agreed to keep the Indians on the reserve.

In referring to this statement of Erath and company, Major Neighbors said,

As to a settlement of the 'difficulty,' as they call it, no such talk or agreement as that spoken of was made with the chiefs, as Captain Palmer's official report (who was present) clearly shows; and those parties, in order to justify themselves, have resorted to the basest falsehoods to influence public opinion in their favor. José María, the Anahdahko chief, has been here for a week past, and disavows having ever heard of or agreed to any such agreement; and the statement is also contradicted by the head farmer of the reserve, the interpreter, and all others present, except the self-styled commissioners.

Peter Garland and party published a statement attempting to justify their killing of the Indians, and concluded with the statement that, "We have no apology to offer for what we have done." Hubert Howe Bancroft thought the names of these men were doomed to "immortal infamy."[7]

Neighbors's attempts to have Garland's party arrested were fraught with difficulties. When the writs of arrest reached Captain Ford at Camp Leon near Cora in Comanche County on January 22, 1859, that officer declined to serve them as he said no civil authority had the power to give him an order. He offered to assist a sheriff or other civil authority in making the arrest, after such an officer certified that he had exhausted all other means, and then Ford declared he would use force only to repel force.[8] When Major Neighbors, who had left Austin for San Antonio on February 7, 1859, arrived back in the state capital, he called upon Governor Runnels who advised Judge Battle to issue new writs to a civil officer with the assurance that the governor would fully sustain their execution. Local autonomy hampered the governor's efforts.

Neighbors believed that the course pursued by Ford and his men had done much to embarrass the civil authorities in their action. When the Major heard that in place of Leeper, Captain Ford had been recommended as Indian agent, Neighbors wrote Commissioner Denver:

The contemptible pandering of that individual, in the present instance, to the prejudice of a band of lawless men, against the very Indians who had led him to victory last spring over the hostile Comanches, should, in my judgement, forever preclude him from a situation of the kind, or any other where firmness or honesty of purpose is required.[9]

This harsh pronouncement by Major Neighbors was no

doubt prompted in part by the fact that while he was in Austin in early January of 1859, Captain Ford assured him on frequent occasions that he would assist in the arrest of the murderers of Choctaw Tom's party.[10] According to the "gossip box" of the Brazos Reserve, young Schoolmaster E. Z. Coombes, who himself called Ford an ass, the Major poured "thunderous curses upon the Captain very profusedly." Ford said that he stood ready to aid any civil officer in making the arrest, but that "Major Neighbors must be mistaken if he says I ever promised to act as the returning officer in the case." Ford added that it was only as an assistant that he thought of acting.[11] Ford on his part realized the extreme strain under which Neighbors was laboring, and never so far as I have found wrote an unkind word of Neighbors at the time nor in his memoirs written many years after Neighbors's death. Ford had only praise and commendation for him until the end.

Ford believed that if he had attempted to make the arrests, a collision, perhaps a civil war, would have been brought on between his troops and the offenders, and said of himself in his memoirs many years later that,

> It was, no doubt, a fortunate thing for him, and perhaps, for the state too, that, he did not accept the deputation, and attempt to make the arrests.[12]

Ford, having refused to arrest the killers of the Reserve Indians, presently accepted their aid on an expedition. At the Brazos Agency Captain Ross offered him every facility for a scout. Ford's force of forty-five Rangers and thirty of Ross's Indians set out on the morning of February 24, 1859. The same morning Captain Ross received a message, Neighbors learned, from Van Dorn requesting the service of some reserve Indians. Ross sent two of his best scouts and apprised him of the scout by the state troops and reserve Indians, while requesting Van Dorn to lend them assistance should that be necessary. On the trail, Captain Ford decided to march directly for Van Dorn's camp, a distance of about eighty miles from the Brazos Agency, to cooperate with the army on a campaign against the Comanches on the headwaters of Red River.

Early in March of 1859, Major Neighbors in San Antonio, learned from Captain Ross that the plan to attack the reserve had about ripened. After reporting the intended movements of the citizens to Major Neighbors, Captain Ross remarked, "your presence is much needed, as it will require all the influence that can be brought to bear to reconcile the Indians."

Then in the absence of the Major, Ross dispatched an express to Major Thomas at Camp Cooper requisitioning a company of cavalry. Major Thomas replied that he had no troops to spare, but that he would give the letter to Captain John King of the First Infantry, who was expected at the camp near the Comanche Agency.

After waiting in vain at Waco, with the wounded Indians for the trial of Garland and others, Major Neighbors took the stage for San Antonio on February 18, 1859. When he received Captain Ross's communications regarding the projected attack on the Brazos Reserve, the Major hired a carriage in preparation for the trip to the Brazos Agency via Camp Colorado, Camp Cooper, and Fort Belknap. As he was on the point of leaving San Antonio on March 14, 1859, Neighbors forwarded Runnels all the information he had from the frontier, and remarked, "I am now on my way up to meet whatever issue our citizens may deem it proper to make with the Indians." He had not heard from his department regarding the moving the Indians, but had been assured by Guy M. Bryan that the move would be made at an early date. He added:

> It appears to me that it now rests with you as the Executive of the state to see the laws enforced—and to protect the reserves, as Genl Twiggs assured me this morning that he has no more troops to spare for their protection.

Major Neighbors arrived in his carriage at the Brazos Agency on March 23, 1859, at twelve o'clock where Captain Ross brought him up to date on the situation. According to information he had, Baylor and Nelson had gathered armed men at Rock Creek just below the lower line of the reserve with the intention of attacking it. Responding promptly to his call for aid, Captain John King came with one company of infantry, while Captain Bradfute of the Second Cavalry was also present. It is doubtful, however, that Bradfute had any troops with him. During the crisis, forty of the best warriors were with Ford, and five of the best scouts were with Van Dorn.

Major Neighbors wrote Governor Runnels that the reserve war was over for the present, and that,

> The presence of Capt. King's command with one piece of artillery has doubtless been the strongest argument used to disperse this lawless band of marauders.

Captain Ross expressed the opinion to the governor that,

> It is also believed that this move is made for the purpose of screening the parties who committed the late murder from

justice, knowing that writs have been issued for the arrest of all concerned, and placed in the hands of the sheriff of Palo Pinto county.

Besides King's piece of artillery, the hostile citizens may have been deterred by the fact that in spite of their most strenuous efforts the mass of frontier settlers held back from a course of immediate violence. Such a course was called in question by a mass meeting of citizens in Young County at Belknap on March 12, 1859. Resolutions were adopted charging that the breaking up of the reserves and the forcible expulsion of the Indians would expose the frontier to imminent danger, and threaten the lives of white families and their property. It was recommended instead that the Indians be removed by petitioning the war and interior departments. If these petitions were ignored, then Young County would join the others in expelling the Indians, the resolutions said.

During March of 1859, Major Neighbors became involved in an issue far removed from the reserve troubles which made Austin a scene of commotion and excitement. A contemporary referred to it as the Public Printing Controversy which he said had elicited the interest of nearly every citizen. The principals involved were I. A. Paschal *versus* John Marshall, W. S. Oldham, and Dr. Josephus Murray Steiner, or roughly Houston and anti-Houston factions. Paschal was a business associate of Major Neighbors in the railroad business and a fellow San Antonian, while Steiner was in the opposite political camp and on the other side of the Indian controversy from the Major.

The people in the Houston camp appear to have accused John Marshall, editor of the *Texas State Gazette* and Oldham of having charged the state for printing "rule and figure work, two for one." Dr. J. M. Steiner and George T. Moore became involved by publishing a statement refuting the charge, while former Governor E. M. Pease became involved by sustaining the Paschal version of counting Marshall's work.[13]

Pease's Connecticut origin was legged into the picture by Oldham who said, "In both these instances I see the cunning hand of the Yankee pettifogger." Oldham claimed Pease as governor had allowed claims similar to the ones in question.

The Marshall-Oldham or Anti-Houston crowd became abusive and bombastic in purported invitations to pseudo duels. One challenger wished to avoid a formal duel, allegedly because of constitutional disabilities, and suggested firing on sight at a chance meeting in a public place. The Anti-Houston faction had its chance on March 15, 1859. About one o'clock Paschal, his son, and clerk, appeared on Congress Avenue armed with double-barreled shotguns and proceeded to Jacob DeCordova's office where Steiner and Marshall were standing in conversation. As Paschal and his associates crossed the street, Steiner and Marshall withdrew inside De Cordova's office, whereupon Paschal cursed them and called in vain for them to come out.

It seems that Neighbors became involved by a letter of his said to have been published in the *Southern Intelligencer* of March 9, 1859. A contemporary reported

> You have, doubtless, ere this, seen the action of Paschal's *special* committee of reference [Paschal was a member of the legislature] to whom this 'Pamphlet' was submitted, also the letter of Maj. Neighors'. Up to the appearance of these extraordinary documents, the difficulty was generally considered settled, so far as Marshall and Paschal were concerned, by all parties. Neighbors' letter is a direct attack upon Dr. Steiner, and coming from an unexpected source, and at an unexpected time, it received such a signal rebuke from Steiner, that the friends of both parties are involved in the vowed and much deprecated controversy.

Steiner's rebuke took the form of a bombastic notice in the public prints:

> Actuated by a low instinctive bullism that has characterized you through life, you have voluntarily to espouse the quarrel of a wretched poltroon, whose cowardice has compelled him to dishonor himself and in your eager haste to do so, you have forgotten every truthful instinct that your maker has implanted in your bosom—Your antecedents however embolden me to indulge in the hope that in seeking redress, (if you desire it) for what I have said, you will not permit either the constitution or your conscience to intervene between your rights and your valor.

Neighbors had met men before on the field of *mort combat*, but E. J. Gurley reported that Neighbors and Steiner had been reconciled by friends.

Sam Houston, in his gubernatorial campaign of 1857 had paid his compliments to these worthies as follows:

> William S. Oldham—though he stole and sunk those bank books in the river and ran away to Texas, he is not yet in the penitentiary, J. M. Steiner—a murderer. John Marshall —a vegetarian—he won't eat meat and one drop of his blood would freeze a dog . . . .[14]

At Fort Graham on September 6, 1853, Steiner had killed Major

Ripley A. Arnold with whom Major Neighbors was on friendly terms.

While Neighbors was enroute from San Antonio, Captain Ford, after a fruitless scout to Camp Radziminski, where a blizzard halted operations, returned to the Comanche Agency on March 10, 1859, with the Reserve Indians. He then proceeded to the Brazos Agency and thence to Camp Leon in Comanche County. Ford apprised Governor Runnels that excitement still prevailed on the frontier, and that families were said to be "forted up." Reports of robberies from Red River to the Colorado gave a feeling of insecurity, although Ford said he had seen no Indian sign. Ford informed the governor, however, that,

> The threatened combination of frontier settlers against the Reserves has not passed over, and indeed, I may say there are many causes to render the apprehension of coming difficulties, dangers and troubles, not only reasonable, but alarming.[15]

George Barnard also informed Governor Runnels of a deep-laid scheme to destroy the Indians, Major Neighbors, and agents of the Brazos Reserve. The leaders were Baylor, Nelson, Garland, and Motherell who Barnard's informant George B. Erath, said, were particularly determined to kill Major Neighbors and Captain Ross and had offered rewards for their scalps.[16]

Writing of the activities of Baylor and his associates, Attorney Gurley of Waco wrote Governor Runnels that,

> These leaders make it their business to watch closely the public sentiment from one extent of the frontier to the other, and immediately following any pacific demonstration, they take steps to counteract it, and to increase the excitement and animosity against the Reservations. George B. Erath has just returned from a tour upon the frontier. Wherever he went he addressed the people, and in some of the counties he succeeded in restoring reason and judgment. But he no sooner left than his influence was counteracted by firebrands of some kind from these designing men. Col. M. T. Johnson has also been amongst them, and advised pacific policy. He succeeded in one or two counties, but in others they threatened to stake him to a limb, and compelled him to desist.

Meanwhile Major Neighbors travelled from the Brazos Agency via Camp Cooper and Camp Colorado to San Antonio where he arrived on April 7, 1859, with the determination to remain until the commissioner replied to his previous inquiries on the policy to be pursued in case the reserves were attacked again. He declared to the commissioner of Indian affairs that,

> It is but justice to the agents of Texas who have maintained their ground to the present time to be relieved from a portion of their responsibilities by direct instructions from the department for their government, and the Indians will not be content with any thing less than a 'talk from their Great Father.'

Major Neighbors had been recommending for more than a year that the reserves be abandoned and the Indians moved to the new reserve east of the North Fork of Red river. On February 22, 1859, Neighbors again forcibly urged upon the commissioner the propriety of moving the Indians.

It took Neighbors almost as long to persuade the government to abandon the reservations as it had for him to get them established, but finally on April 19, 1859, he received authority to abandon them. Acting Commissioner Charles Mix wrote him on March 30, 1859, that in view of his several reports, it was painfully manifest that the colonization of the Indians in Texas must be discontinued, "the reservations abandoned, the Indians removed where they can be protected from lawless violence, and effective measures adopted for their domestication and improvement." Mix was of the opinion that the removal of the Indians could not be commenced before fall or winter.

Neighbors communicated the change of policy to Governor Runnels and leading journals which published the news. The Major indicated that he would proceed to the reservations as soon as he received the funds estimated for the last quarter. He had been urging the department for some time to forward the funds for the Texas service for the previous quarter. He had frankly told Mix on April 12, 1859, that:

> In no case have I ever overdrawn the appropriation, and it is unjust to those who furnish supplies to the Indians, and extremely embarrassing to the agents to have the funds for the Indian department of Texas withheld so long, or until the quarter expires.

The difficulty over funds grew out of a change in the Indian service in Texas. Ironically, after thirteen years and when the general government was on the point of moving the Indians out of Texas, Major Neighbors received news that the Indian service had been put upon a permanent footing and that he had been appointed superintendent. On May 13, 1859, the Major acknowledged receipt of President Buchanan's commission appointing him superintendent of Indian affairs in Texas, along with the commissions of Ross and Leeper as agents. The President on March 3, 1859, signed the letters patent making Neighbors's term of office four years effective on March 1, 1859.

The news of the appointments was too much for Baylor. He drew up a petition reading,

> Gentlemen: Your course and conduct for the last eighteen months having utterly failed to give satisfaction to the citizens of the frontier of Texas, and for the reason that the opinion prevails generally in all the frontier counties that you have acted in bad faith to the Indians and white man, and having been disappointed in the long cherished hope that you would be removed from office, but, on the contrary, having learned that you have lately been reappointed, we take this our only method to make known to you our unqualified disapprobation of your course as agents, and to demand your immediate resignation.[17]

In regard to the troubles on the frontier, Neighbors read with interest the appraisal of Captain Ford, who with grim foreboding and rare prescience wrote:

> The frontier is in a bad way. The feeling of insecurity, of hostility to the Reserve Indians, and many imaginary and dreadful evils they persuade themselves are near, render the frontier people violent and, in many respects unreasonable. It has been a difficult matter for the last several years to sustain the frontier settlements *in status quo*. We have had the assistance and co-operation of the Reserve Indians, place them on the opposite side, throw into the scale some four hundred of the best warriors in the United States, imbued with a belief that we have been unfaithful to our pledges, and thirsting for revenge, then tell me where you think the line of frontier settlements will be within five years and when the war will end. This, in my opinion, is exactly the state of affairs which threatens us. Once let an infuriated mass of men attack the Reserves, break them up, interfere with the United States Government in the consummation of a settled Indian policy, and we may apprehend danger, trouble and bloodshed from Red River to the Rio Grande.

> The Federal authorities can, if they choose, view it as a war between the frontier people and the Indians with whom they are at peace. They may say they wantonly attacked a people with whom they had made treaties, that they have violated treaty obligations—the Supreme law of the Land—and they may decline any interference in the matter. We should then

have worse than a Florida war saddled upon us. I do not take it upon myself to sit in judgment upon the border settlers —they may be right—but I have never been able to detect the Reserve Indians in the commission of a single depredation or to trace one to their doors, and I do think the measures instituted by the people have been impolitic and precipitate. I have said this much because I know you are feelingly alive to the interests and the welfare of the frontier.[18]

Major Neighbors enclosed the above extract from his old friend to the commissioner, remarking that Captain Ford had expressed the same views to the governor, yet he, Runnels, had taken no measures to prevent the conflict.

It was widely believed on the frontier that Governor Runnels was trying to decide the most popular step to take on the eve of the coming election. A letter from J. G. Thomas, a purported friend of Runnels, was forwarded from Jack County to the Birdville *Union* in which, upon widespread demand, it was published. The editor observed quizzically that he thought some irony could be detected in the letter.

Jack County,
April 15th 1859.

To His Excellency, 'Dick Runnels,'—

You wished me to ascertain the '*facts* in the case'—and if the Indians under 'Ross and Neighbors,' *should show* out to be *guilty*, (of which you entertained no doubt) to report the same to your 'Excellency' by the first mail, that you might take *popular steps* by the 'sitting of the Houston Convention.' You wished me also to ascertain the *feelings* of the people along the frontier, as to the *popularity* of our *mutual friends* Maj. Neighbors, Capt. Ross, Charley Barnard, Jo. Walker and others of like reputation;—whether they are considered *real actors* behind the scene or *merely accomplices* in the Indian depredations along the frontier! Whether Neighbors and Ross are *longer* able to keep the public in the *dark*, as to the guilt of '*their Indians*'—(which we both held they could not do.) And . . . to ascertain if the frontier would instruct their delegates at the Houston Convention to favor the renomination of your Excellency for Gov. &c, &c! All of which, I have been *intensely* anxious to 'ascertain,'—I have spared 'neither time nor expense' (as you requested) to get the 'facts in the case.' I *now* with an *amalgam* of feeling of 'sorrow and joy,' give your 'Excellency' the result of my labors. In the first place, in regard to the guilt of the Reserve Indians, *the facts like Cactus prickles jut out all around*! The Reserve Indians (or as Col. A. G. Walker would say the 'Red, rougish rascals!')

have committed ALL the depredations in the counties of
'Erath, Jack, Palo Pinto, Comanche, and other counties adjoining the Reservation,' to the citizens of which, you addressed
your late Circular, (or Bull, as the people out here call it!)
of the 12th March, (last month.) There has been a meeting
of delegates, just come off at Col. Loving's in Palo Pinto
county, the object of which was 'to ascertain the facts in the
case'—that is, to get the *proof,* showing that the *'pet* Indians'
are the aggressors.

At the convention, I am informed in a letter from my friend-
--------at-----, that the testimony, riveting guilt on the 'red rougish rascals,' (as Colonel Walker would say) was as *numerous*
as 'grass hoppers' or, as Pigeons at 'roosting time.'[19] . . .

Runnels's behavior gave some substance to the allegations.

In accordance with his instructions, Major Neighbors
informed Superintendencnt Rector of the numbers and condition of the Indians to be moved to his district. According to
the census rolls of Agents Ross and Leeper, there were 258
Tonkawas, 204 Tawacanos, 171 Wacos, 380 Comanches, 244 Caddos, including the Shawnees and Delawares intermarried with
them, and 235 Anadarkos, making a total of 1,492 souls. The
Major then indicated which bands would readily associate with
each other. The Caddos, Anadarkos, Delawares, and Shawnees
could be settled together and might be affiliated with the bands
of these people already settled in the Choctaw lands. The Wacos
and Tawacanos would readily affiliate with the Wichitas as
they spoke each other's language and were old associates by
intermarriage and past experiences. The Tonkawas were a
separate and distinct tribe who would need a separate location
but one near enough to be influenced by the more civilized
bands. The Indians had with them a good blacksmith, school
teacher, and farmers, and Major Neighbors recommended that
these employees be retained for the present as the Indians
were accustomed to them and would like them better than
strangers.[20] He offered to send a party of the principal chiefs
to any point Rector named and to come himself.

Those hostile to the reserve system in Texas were not content to wait for Neighbors to remove the Indians. In San
Antonio Neighbors learned from Agent Ross that Baylor and
others were still making exciting speeches in the surrounding
counties. Only a few days earlier, Baylor had made a speech
in Golconda in which he used extremely threatening language
against the agents and Indians. Ross added, "I also heard that
he is now prowling around the reserve with a body of armed

men with the avowed object of taking scalps."

In the midst of this extremity, Neighbors learned that during the past month fifty Indians from the reserve had joined Van Dorn in his campaign in the north, and five had gone to join Captain Albert Gallatin Brackett as guides for the Second Cavalry with the promise that Ross would protect their women and children. Four days later Agent Ross informed Superintendent Neighbors that according to Parson Tackitt who had been to Golconda, John R. Baylor had left there with a band of armed men with the avowed intention of taking scalps. Captain Ross immediately informed Captain Plummer who sent to Camp Cooper for reinforcements. The chiefs were notified and immediately assembled their people near the agency buildings for protection, which entirely suspended farming operations. When Lieutenant William E. Burnet arrived from Camp Cooper with reinforcements, Captain Ross learned that Baylor had made an attack upon the Comanche Reserve Indians and that a detachment of cavalry was in pursuit of him and his party. Ross remarked to Neighbors with acerbity that,

> I had hoped that when it was made known that the government intended to remove the Indians from Texas as soon as practicable, that the agitators would become quiet; but they are now more clamorous than ever, It seems that ponies, and not protection, is the groundwork of this move. Some of these exasperated men have succeeded very well in the pony move.

Agent Leeper was of the opinion that the announcement of the coming removal of the Indians emboldened the leaders of the disturbances ten-fold.

Reports of the projected attack upon the Reserve Indians led Major Neighbors to express the opinion to the commissioner that the reserves could not be maintained in peace for any length of time. Therefore Superintendent Neighbors recommended that the Indians be removed immediately. The superintendent informed the commissioner that he would proceed at once to the reserves, and he had no doubt but that the Indians would be happy to leave.

Before Major Neighbors announced his intention to leave for the frontier, an incident full of fateful portent for him had already occurred. On May 7, 1859, Fox, a faithful Caddo expressman, returning from Agent Blain to Agent Ross was captured just before he reached the reserve line. Fox with six others had gone as expressmen for Agent Ross to Agent Blain at

Fort Arbuckle and to look for horses stolen from the reserve. When they had returned to a point within ten miles of the agency and were near the reserve line, they were charged and fired upon by fifteen men from Patrick Murphy's house, that served as the stage stand of the Southern Overland Mail. The Indians did not attempt to defend themselves, but Fox ordered his men to head for the timber. An Indian called Half American John had his mule shot from under him, and Fox who was poorly mounted was captured. He was taken to Patrick Murphy's house about one-half mile distant where he showed his assailants his pass from Ross. The gang took from Fox the papers from Agent Blain to Agent Ross, read and kept them, and started with Fox along the stage road toward Jacksboro. The Indians who escaped reached the agency and gave the alarm. Agent Ross immediately gave orders to Dr. Sturm with thirty-seven Indians and two Mexicans to accompany Lieutenant Burnet of the First Infantry with a company of soldiers in pursuit of the abductors of Fox. So hot was the pursuit that ten miles from Murphy's house, the party from the agency came upon the lifeless body of Fox, scalped, warm, and still bleeding, a few yards from the road. The Indians quickly covered Fox's body with a blanket and some brush and the pursuit continued, upon Lieutenant Burnet's orders, to Jacksboro where they got no information.[21]

While at his home in San Antonio, Major Neighbors learned that Bishop George Foster Pierce of the Methodist Episcopal Church, South, with his family had arrived in the city, and although the bishop and his family lodged at the newest hotel, The Menger, it was so crowded that they had to sleep on the floor of the billiard room. The next morning the Major's pastor, Dr. Jesse Boring, reported to the bishop that, "Major Neighbors expected and desired us to remove to his house. We availed ourselves of this kindness, and soon transferred to more comfortable quarters" Bishop Pierce and his family apparently arrived at the Major's house on Thursday, May 12, 1859, and took their departure on Monday, May 16, before the Major left for the frontier on May 17.[22]

Disregarding Colonel Leeper's warning that hostile parties were waylaying the roads to murder the Major, he embraced his wife and children, said farewell for what was to be the last time and set out from San Antonio for the Comanche Agency. It was a particular hardship for Neighbors to leave home at this time. Elizabeth Ann, who was always frail, was then unwell and expecting their fourth child to be born any day. From Leon Springs, twenty-six miles north of San Antonio the Major wrote:

My Dear Wife —

I hope you are reconciled to my leaving. We are in the hands of an all ruling Providence and we cannot disobey his mandates. It is my destiny to sacrifice myself for others—as soon as I can control, I will devote myself to you—I cannot say much—

I send you a ham and a piece of Beef by my friend [Mr. Ward] from Leon Springs —

Don't expect me to say much my first day out—feel assured that I am yours —

Kiss the children and may the Great Ruler of the Universe Bless and Guard you —

Make Dr. [Ferdinand von] Herff visit you every day—I will return to you as soon as possible.

Your Husband truly
R. S. Neighbors[23]

Duty led him on to his last fateful tour of the frontier.

Unknown to Neighbors as he rode up the trail to the reserves, they were under attack by 500 men who had gathered in Jacksboro under John R. Baylor and Peter Garland. Women presented them a banner inscribed "Necessity knows no law," while preacher Noah T. Byars blessed the venture as a righteous crusade. Byars had been fired as government blacksmith for the Republic of Texas and rejected as missionary to the Brazos Reserve.

Baylor sent Garland with 250 men in an unsuccessful attempt to capture the artillery at Camp Cooper since traitors among the troops at the Brazos Reserve apprised them of the strength of the fortifications at that place. When Baylor and his 250 men advanced on the Brazos Agency, with the avowed intention of destroying the Indians, he declined to attack after a confrontation with Captain J. B. Plummer. In leaving, Baylor's party killed two elderly Indians. The attack was timed to take advantage of the absence of seventy warriors with Van Dorn. Chief José María with 50 warriors accompanied by Lieutenant Burnet pursued Baylor's 250 men eight miles to William Marlin's rancho where they took possession of his buildings after shooting at him and making him take to the timber.

José María and his men killed seven of the raiders while being careful not to fire into Marlin's house for fear of killing his family. The Indians lost three killed. Baylor's men later retreated to their camp on Dillingham Prairie near Rock Creek,

239

organized into minute companies and dispersed.

This bare account gives little of the excitement and drama of events as they became known piecemeal in dispatches to Neighbors. When Major Neighbors rode up to the Comanche Agency on May 25, 1859, he was handed a copy of the official report of Captain Plummer, describing the fight:

> Sir; I have the honor to inform you that information was brought to me this morning, at about half past ten o'clock, that Captain Baylor, with about two hundred and fifty men, had marched upon the reservation to attack the Indians, and was then about one mile distant and approaching the agency where my command and the Indians were encamped. I immediately dispatched Captain Gilbert with his company to meet Captain Baylor, and to demand of him "for what purpose he had come upon the reservation with an armed body of men?" To that demand he replied, that "he had come to assail certain Indians of this reserve, but not to attack any whites, but should the troops fire upon his men during the fight, he would attack them also, or any other whites who did the same thing, and treat all alike." He desired my reply, and would wait for it three quarters of an hour.

> As soon as I received the above message, I sent Lieutenant Burnet to Captain Baylor, with instructions to say to him that "my orders were to protect the Indians on this reserve from the attacks of armed bands of citizens, and that I would do.so to the best of my ability, and with the arms in my possession; and that I warned him in the name of the government of the United States to leave this reservation.

> Captain Baylor rejoined, that this message did not alter his determination of attacking the Indians on the reserve, and that he would attend to leaving it himself; that he regretted the necessity of coming in collision with the United States troops, but that he had determined to destroy the Indians on this and the upper reserve, if it cost the life of every man in his command.

> The Indians, in the meantime, as well as the troops, prepared for action, and some of the former, who were mounted, were hovering near Captain Baylor and his men, watching their movements. By friendly signs, they induced a very old Indian to approach them, when they tied a rope around his neck, and then moved off in a westerly direction, but before going far, killed and scalped their prisoner. They were followed by fifty or sixty Indians, constantly exchanging shots with them; and eight miles from the agency, and about one and a half miles from the limits of the reserve, they came to a stand, taking possession of a farmer's house and out buildings; there

the Indians fought them until dark, when they returned to their reservation. They killed, they state, five of Captain Baylor's men, and had one of their own number killed, besided the one I have already mentioned, and several wounded.

I am, very respectfully, your obedient servant,

J. B. Plummer
Captain 1st Infantry,
comanding.[24]

Major Neighbors then addressed Captain Ross a message, saying:

Dear Captain

I arrived here yesterday—and expected to come to your agency today but owing to the news of your victory over the enemy and they, threatening this reserve next—I have concluded to wait here until I hear from you so please write me all the particulars of your fight by return express—and give me such other information as you have in regard to matters generally.

The Major would do all he could to sustain Ross and as soon as practicable he would concentrate all the Indians and troops at the Comanche Agency and prepare for the worst. Neighbors said he hoped Ross would keep on the defensive,

but if those desperadoes again come on the reserve "*Try and wipe them out.*" All intelligent citizens below sustain us—and as long as we can claim the defensive for the Indians we will be sustained—

He declared the Comanches were ready to fight, and expressed the determination to "try and give as good an account of ourselves as you have done, if we are attacked."[25]

Major Neighbors wrote his brother-in-law, Joe L. Evans, that the official military report of the attack was being sent to headquarters in San Antonio by that mail, and requested him to see Captain John Withers to have it published. Baylor was then on the Clear Fork, Neighbors said, with an undetermined number of men, and added, "We are preparing to give him a warm reception if he attacks us." The Major called upon his brother-in-law to arouse their mutual friends "and tell them not to let the lies so freely circulated by Baylor and his Crowd Create a false impression." Baylor's party, Neighbors observed, had abused the citizens who would not join them as much as they had the Indians. Neighbors wondered what Governor Runnels was doing, and declared, "It is a disgrace both to him and the state, that such outrages should be allowed."[26]

Next day Major Neighbors wrote his brother-in-law again that "last night I sent to Baylor's Ranch and found that he was not at home or I should have brought him up to the agency and made him account for his sins." Neighbors wondered that the executive of Texas should permit a lawless band to attack United States posts and bring on such grave issues; observed that the troops, defending their own posts, would not go outside the limits of the reserve; and added,

> Baylor and his party has thus been badly whipped and all the Citizens are opposed to his proceedings. Numbers who came with him are now leaving—and are concerned that he has led them into Error and are not willing to make the issue that he proposes.
>
> I shall have writs taken out as soon as I can reach a U.S. Commissioner, and Endeavor to have some of the leaders arrested and brought before the U.S. Court at Austin. You can show this to the papers for Publication as we have nothing to hide.
>
> Give my love to my wife and family, and for God's sake attend to my affairs—Especially my wife in her present condition.[27]

Neighbors reported to the commissioner of Indian affairs that,

> At present there are about three or four hundred men in the neighborhood of the two reserves. They are lawless, and, as far as I can learn, are not sustained by any respectable or law abiding citizens, but exist as a mob of the worst portion of the new emigrants to this newly-settled frontier, and will compare favorably with the celebrated band of Montgomery, in Kansas Territory, and it is believed that they are the same class.

Until he had finished his letter, Major Neighbors had only the official report of Captain Plummer of the fight upon which to draw. Before sealing his letter to the commissioner, the Major added in a postscript that he was also enclosing the official report of Special Agent S. P. Ross.[28]

Ross began:

> Dear Major: I received your communication by Lieutenant James H. Holman. I am truly glad to hear of your arrival among us. Your presence will have much influence with the Indians. They express great satisfaction at your arrival, as they began to think you were not coming. They are not satisfied with Barnard's absence. He has not yet arrived.
>
> You requested the particulars of the fight. Sir, on the 23d

instant, J. R. Baylor, with his band of marauders, drew up in line of battle between the Waco village and the agency buildings, and within six hundred yards of the latter place, where Captain Plummer had an interview with him through the proper medium: for particulars, I refer you to Captain Plummer's report, forwarded by this express. Soon after the last communication was delivered to Baylor, he commenced retreating; came upon an old man eighty years of age, killed him; also an old woman, working her little garden, and killed her. This was done on Salt Creek, (near the crossing), and a short distance from the agency buildings, and here the fight commenced. Only a few Indians at first, but increased to fifty by the time they arrived at William Marlin's house. It was a running fight all the way. At the house the sharpest contest ensued.

Baylor's men took the house and fought from the cracks. During the engagement, five Indians were wounded, and old Sergeant (Caddo John) killed. The Indians were cautious during the fight not to fire at Marlin's house, fearing lest some of his family might be accidentally injured, and soon withdrew, failing to induce Baylor's men to come out and make an open fight. Captain Bradfute has just returned from Belknap; saw Baylor and his party, and reports that two of his men were killed, three severely wounded, and several slightly, that have gone home. During the contest Jim Pock Mark, second chief of the Anahdahkoes, rode up to the house, called for Baylor to come out and give him single combat, which Baylor respectfully declined. I have also been informed that Baylor has dispatched one company of his men to intercept the return of the seventy-five Indians who accompanied Major Van Dorn in his late expedition. However, I hope that my express will meet the Indians, which will place them on their guard, and prevent them from being intercepted or surprised by Baylor's party.

Ross added that his agency was well-prepared to receive company. Good picket defensive works had been prepared of poles and beef hides with flanking bastion and traverses, large enough to hold all the women, children, and a thousand soldiers and warriors. Captain Ross thought it would be better not to move the Indians to the Comanche Reserve as they had a great deal of property which could not be moved without great loss, and that with the natural advantages of defense at the Brazos Agency and the additional preparations made by Captain Plummer, he believed a good defense could be made there. Ross concluded by stating that the different tribes had been united by him and were determined to defend themselves to the death.[29]

Other details came out about Baylor's attack on the Brazos Reserve. "A GOOD CITIZEN" writing to the editors of the Waco *Southerner* from the Brazos Agency on the day of the fight brought out that Baylor had tried to intimidate the Army officers by threatening them with civil trials and hanging if any of the attacking party were killed.[30] Baylor's party, the correspondent, said had intercepted government supplies[31] for the Indians, killed their cattle, and stolen their horses. He concluded:

> Baylor has publicly threatened to hang Capt. S. P. Ross, Mr. Chas. Barnard, and Maj. Neighbors, also threatens James Duff, U.S. Deputy Marshal, Harvey Mathews, Wm. Marlin, Mr. Bandy the Sheriff of Young county, and others, all of whom are among the best citizens in the county—We think it is now time that the State and General Government take notice of this offender against the law and rights of the good people of the frontier of Texas.

Concerning the arrival of Baylor's band at Marlin's ranch, one account told that the leaders requested Mrs. Marlin to prepare dinner, which she reluctantly did,[32] while Baylor's son said, however, that she told Baylor that he and his men were worse than the Indians and ordered them off.[33] Mrs. Marlin said Baylor's men were so badly frightened that some prayed, and one took up the boards and got under the floor. They were still so afraid next day they buried their dead in the yard instead of in a nearby cemetery.[34]

According to Baylor's men, they exchanged fire with the Indians. Charles Goodnight said Baylor fired at a distant Indian, knocking feathers from his headdress. Whereupon Baylor exlcaimed, "Damn you! If I can't kill you, I can pick you!"[35]

Neighbors wrote his brother-in-law from the Comanche Agency that,

> We have been on the alert but have not been molested. I hear the filibusters are now on Rock Creek below Brazos Agency, and still threatened the lower reserve, but many dissensions exist in their camp, and it is believed by many that they will finally break up and go home without doing us any more serious damage. It appears now that Baylor with his small band of *desperadoes* and *horse thieves* led the attacking party on the reserve without knowledge of many who are really good Citizens, and who joined the party because they believed the Base Lies that had been put in Circulation by

himself, Nelson, Garland, the Murderer of the Caddos, etc., and as soon as they found the Position into which they had been led, they refused to continue with him. It is said that he was so badly scared when they reached Bill Marlin's house[36] that he hid under Mrs. Marlin's bed where herself and the little children had got for safety. [According to Baylor's party he was among the skirmishers.] The Indians would have destroyed the house if it had not been for Marlin's family being in it. This is the most disgraceful transaction that I have ever known. 250 White men Guilty of It is bad Enough to run from about 50 Indians, but to take shelter in the house of a Private family of women and children after shooting at Her Husband and making him take to the timber for Safety is disgraceful beyond measure. They in leaving rode off his horses. They have sent out a huge party to cut off the 70 Warriors from the reserves who have been with Major Van Dorn now returning home after a Glorious Victory Over the Enemy in which many of them Distinguished themselves.

The Major then gave his opinion of the other offenses committed by the hostile parties:

The whole transaction has been the most disgraceful affair that has ever been Witnessed in our State. I have not detailed now all the charges that can be made. They have stopped the mails for the last 3 trips from Dallas to Belknap, Robbed Waggons, etc., etc. . . It is shameful that the Govt should permit this state of affairs. All the Courts in the neighborhood of this Lawless band have been suspended and almost every other enormity committed when it all might have been avoided If we had an Executive who would do anything to prevent It except to promulgate fresh Proclamations for Popularity—which he never intends to carry out.[37]

On June 5, 1859, Major Neighbors received intelligence that a band of five hundred men had left the camp on Rock Creek to attack the Comanche Reserve. Major Neighbors and Lieutenant Robert N. Eagle proceeded at once to that reserve with sixty cavalrymen, but the report was a feint on the part of Baylor's party "to enable them to scatter for fear of an attack from the cavalry." Neighbors found that two more companies of cavalry had arrived at the Comanche Reserve. Those with the eighty men who had come earlier to the Brazos Reserve with Lieutenant Eagle and George B. Crosby gave ample force to defend the reserves against the lawless mob even if there were the one thousand men reported. It was a sad commentary on conditions on the frontier that troops, who were fighting the real enemy to the north who had devastated Texas for years, had to be recalled to protect their Reserve Indian allies from the assaults directed by hostile white men.

Neighbors believed the whole party had been disbanded, after stealing horses from the reserves and from citizens around it, waylaying roads, stopping travellers, robbing wagons, and stopping the mails. He added to the commissioner of Indian affairs:

It is unfortunate at this time that we have in the State of Texas a governor who appears to be afraid to enforce the laws of the State, to arrest criminals, or to endeavor to put down a mob, although it is apparent that almost every property holder, or those who may be classed as good and responsible citizens, are not in any way engaged in this foray, and do not sympathize with it, and, if sustained by the executive of the State, would in a very short time, arrest this band of lawless marauders. They acknowledged, in the town of Belknap, after the attack on the reserve on the 23rd, that there were about fifty horse-thieves and notorious desperadoes in their party.[38]

Neighbors described the fight to his wife in one sentence. He then expressed his anxiety for his expectant wife and concluded:

So with my best love to yourself and our dear children and hopes for your safe recovery and hoping that [you will not] permit yourself to feel any uneasiness on my account, as I shall endeavor to discharge my duties so as to return to you honorably.

After learning of the birth of a son christened Ross Simpson Neighbors, the Major wrote his wife:

My Dear Wife

I received by yesterdays express a note from Joe also one from Mr. Birdsall. They inform me of your safe delivery of a 'fine fat handsome Boy.'

Permit me My Sweet Wife to congratulate you and to Express a hope that the pleasure he may afford you in after life may nicely compensate you for all the pain he has cost you, and to hope that you will soon recover and enjoy better health than ever heretofore. I have been through many trials—but none that has given me more pain than my separation from you during your trials. But I have Evidence that I have done my duty—and saved a poor and ignorant race from death by being here—and I am satisfied that you will approve the course that I have pursued.

Our difficulties are gradually assuming a manageable shape and I hope soon to report them over and that I shall soon be able to 'Pay respects' to the 'small stranger.' I saw the 'Little Cherub' last night in a Dream. He was as beautiful [as an] angel and smiled sweetly on me when I kissed him. I am happy to learn that you secured all necessary attention from our kind friends. Thank them for me. I go to the lower agency today and will write you and Joe and Birdsall from that Point. I saw Mr. and Mrs. Duff yesterday—they come to San Antonio today to reside. Dick Howard was also here. I had many congratulations and cracked several Balls of Champagne to your and the Strangers health. Give my love to all. Kiss our 3 children and remember me to all our friends. Having no news of importance and with my best love and wishes for your health and happiness.

I remain as Ever

Your very true and Devoted

Husband

R. S. Neighbors

Later Neighbors wrote his wife:

I am happy to have received your kind letter of the 8th inst by which I learn that you have safely recovered and that the *new baby* is well and fat—this is indeed gratifying—and as you say he is like his Brother and sister, I hope he will be as healthy, and as good a child.

We certainly, so far, are blessed in our children for beauty and health—and we should be thankful to a Divine Providence—Then My Dear Wife, as we really have but little else to live for, let us Endeavor to be grateful to Providence and try to raise them to be a living honour and monument, to us—after we pass away.

He added, "I cannot yet say when I will be home. I am extremely anxious to make this my last visit to the frontier on Indian matters . . ."

While defending Baylor in the state courts for enforcing prohibition while Indian agent, Neighbors was preparing to prosecute him and others for killing Indians on the reserve and other charges. Neighbors requested United States Commissioner Chesley Dobbs to gather evidence to forward to the United States District Attorney R. B. Hubbard at Austin.

The superintendent declared that it was unfortunate that the general government did not take action after his recommendations in March either to move the Indians, or to provide for their defense. The reserves were virtually broken up. Forty died during an epidemic while confined during the seige. All work had ceased, and the Indians declined even to cultivate their small gardens. The chiefs made no serious objection to moving, although they "think themselves badly treated."

Before Superintendent Neighbors's latest communication could reach Washington, the department of the interior had already drafted orders for the immediate removal of the Indians based upon the superintendent's letter of May 12, 1859. The secretary of war had prepared orders for the military to escort the Indians during the removal to the leased district east of the North Fork of Red River between the 98th and 100th meridians where Superintendents Neighbors and Rector were to act jointly in locating the Texas Indians at proper sites.

Neighbors had already appealed to Rector for aid, concluding,

> Then sir, as an officer of the Indian Department, as a good citizen and one upon whose large philanthropic views in favor of the much abused Indian, I would for myself and the agents who co-operate with me, appeal for all the aid you can give us in our present strait, so that we may place these poor people out of the hands of an infuriated mob.[39]

Superintendent Rector, in view of Superintendent Neighbors's communication, had decided to take action. He invited Neighbors to meet him at Fort Arbuckle to confer on the removal of the Texas Indians. Neighbors replied that he would be at the appointed place with twenty-five of the principal men between the first and fifth of July.

On June 26, 1859, Superintendent Neighbors, with the head men of the Comanches, Wacos, Tonkawas, Tawacanos, Caddos, and Anadarkos, set out from the Brazos Agency for Fort Arbuckle in the Chickasaw Nation, 160 miles distant, where he arrived on June 30. Superintendent Rector arrived at Fort Arbuckle later in the day, from an exploration of the leased district, and the two superintendents conferred. Each then made a separate report to the commissioner in which they agreed on the policy to be pursued in moving and settling the Texas Indians in the Indian territory.

Based upon his observations during an exploration of the leased district, Superintendent Rector pronounced most of it to be "utterly worthless, and unsuitable for human habitation." The 98th meridian was found to lie much farther west than supposed, hence beyond the Cross Timbers, good streams, and arable valleys. The region he chose for the Texas Indians was on the main False Washita, whose valley he said was one of great fertility and covered with the "thickest and finest grass," and on the Canadian whose valley Rector's guides assured him was similar to that of the False Washita.

Superintendent Rector was surprised at the wide latitude of action the department had accorded Major Neighbors, and reminded the commissioner of the very little discretion allowed Rector, which embarrassed him in carrying out policy in the present emergency. Rector referred to this matter a number of times, requesting that he be given the same powers that Neighbors enjoyed. Superintendent Neighbors concurred fully with Rector's report and in this application for more power, remarking that the utmost harmony had prevailed between himself and Superintendent Rector during the interviews.[23] On July 1, 1859, the two superintendents held a council of the chiefs of the Indians from Texas and those north of Red River who were to be settled also on the new reserve. The chiefs were told that as they must live together thereafter, it behooved them to become acquainted, which recommendation was heartily followed. Speeches of eloquence followed from chiefs of both groups, including José María, Ketumse, and the council and meal ended amicably.

Neighbors returned to Texas to face the issues raised by Governor Runnels in his political campaign of 1859. For some months anarchy had reigned supreme on the frontier in the jurisdictional no man's land between the Texas and the United States governments. The governor and the commanding officer of the Eighth Military District each contended that the other was responsible for maintaining law and order.

When Runnels explained that the reason for his delay in replying was his absence from Austin, others explained his absence thusly:

> The *Intelligencer* says it is generally believed at Austin that one reason why Runnels and Lubbock [the lieutenant governor] are absent from the post of duty while blood is flowing on the frontier, is because they don't know what to do—are not equal to the emergency.

Meanwhile on June 13, 1859, an express arrived at the Brazos Agency from Governor Runnels bearing a letter addressed to Allison Nelson and others. As Major Neighbors unfolded the political document, he perceived that the Indians could expect no protection from the state. In an election year, the governor had appointed a partisan committee whose report hopefully would garner as many votes as possible. Of the personnel of the committee, Runnels remarked:

> You may be assured that the board will be composed of men

whose interest or sympathies are identified with the frontier, and whose high standing and character will afford a sure guarantee to the citizens that all their rights will be safe in their hands.

On June 16, 1859, the five commissioners appointed by Runnels presented themselves before Neighbors at the Brazos Agency. They were George B. Erath; J. M. Smith; Richard Coke, the future governor; John Henry Brown; and J. M. Steiner. Coke's attitude is unknown, but the others were in varying degrees adverse to the reserve policy and the Indians. Neighbors had very positive answers to the commissioners' queries.

The Major said the charges against the Indians had been disproved by Hawkins's court. The charges against the agents, Neighbors said, had been treated with contempt by them as no one who had known him since he entered Texas in 1836 would be misled by "designing men, without clear antecedents." He then reviewed his record with that gift for succinctness which marked all his writing:

> I have been in Texas since 1836; served my country in responsible stations until 1842, and, after two years imprisonment in Mexico, entered the service again as Indian agent under the old republic, and served to the end of Mr. Polk's administration in that capacity; then as a commissioner of the State to New Mexico; two years in the Legislature as representative of Bexar county; as the elector of the western district during Mr. Pierce's canvass; and for the last six years as the supervising Indian agent, without ever having a single charge brought against me, until they were placed in the present shape before the people by the parties heretofore alluded to. Captain S. P. Ross, the resident agent of this reserve, came to Texas at an early period, and served his country with equal honor and integrity up to the present day. We both have families, and all our interests are identified with Texas. If this is not a sufficient guarantee, with the confidence expressed by having our appointments renewed by the President of the United States this spring, and our nominations unanimously approved by the United States Senate, then I fear that we shall be unable to convince the people of Texas, unless they will grant us, what we have demanded from the first, 'an investigation by any legal tribunal, either in the State or out of it.'

The superintendent declared that the charges against the Indians were equally false. This was proved, he said, by the three victories they had participated in over the Comanches under Captain Ford and Major Van Dorn. Secondly, he said, good citizens always appeal to the laws.

There is not on file any legal affidavit, or other testimony, to show that *any Indian on either reserve has committed a single one of the many* depredations *charged to them*, although the parties making these charges have been called on frequently to produce the evidence; and it must appear preposterous to attempt to impose such falsehoods upon the people of the frontier, "as the agents shielding the Indians in crime." When the parties making the charges are afraid to come before the courts of the country with even one single affidavit to 'make' a charge valid; and I assert, without fear of contradition from any source whatever, that there has not been, within my knowledge; a single violation of the treaty between the Indians of the reserves and the United States. There are no provisions in that treaty by which those Indians are to be kept within the limits of the reserves; nor is there any law or rule that would compel the Indians to submit to it, as they all have the right to claim protection under the State laws, should they choose to do so. It is consequently only a police regulation between the chiefs, the United States military, and the agents, by which the Indians are confined as strictly to the reserves as possible, and for the last six or eight months they have not been permitted to go out, even to hunt their own stock, except in company with some responsible white man; and the United States troops have been equally vigilant, in order to protect the Indians from being shot down by some lawless person, or of bringing about a collision with citizens, which both agents and military officers have been determined to prevent, if possible.

The commissioners had solicited the Major's opinion on the causes of the late disturbances and the measures he had taken to allay them. He had a very decided opinion on the cause:

In regard to the fourth paragraph of your letter, I can only give it as my opinion that the causes are, first, the unbounded ambition of Messrs. Nelson, Baylor, &c., to obtain the offices held by Captain Ross, Colonel Leeper, and myself, and to get control of the money appropriated by the general government for the support of the Indians on the reserves, they have frequently said, in their publications "that they [the agents] have a good time of it,' and J. R. Baylor was considered, I have no doubt, a good judge, because he was dismissed from the service by the general government for 'having a good time of it' during the eighteen months that he was in service. This his own accounts will show whenever any one chooses to investigate.

251

Neighbors said he had adopted the usual means of a disbursing officer and had asked and obtained a hearing before a legal tribunal which acquitted all parties accused of all charges and whose findings were certified to by the Texas delegation in Congress, the executive of the state, and were published generally in the newspapers of the day.

Regarding the moving of the Indians at the "earliest practicable moment," the Major declared the intention of the government to move the Indians had been published throughout the state, and he had urged the government to move them as early as possible. He would move them when the orders came. As to the disposition of the Indians, they had assured Neighbors that they "are willing to bury the past if let alone," and were willing to rely upon the laws of the land for a redress of their grievances. This was more than Baylor's party had been willing to do, the Major said, for Baylor had "endeavored to massacre their wives and children while they were yet with Major Van Dorn in the service of their country."

Neighbors then fell upon the governor's insinuating paragraph:

> This movement is the result of many difficulties and continued quarrels and disturbances between the citizens on that frontier and the Indians at the agency, which has been unceasing for months past.

Neighbors declared that the governor appeared to entertain the belief that the Indians and agents were parties to the quarrels and disturbances.

> Had this language been used by any private individual, I should simply denounce it as false; but knowing the desire of his excellency to preserve quiet on the frontier, I can only attribute it to the many rumors put in circulation to prejudice the people of the State against the Indians. I therefore most solemnly protest on the part of the United States, against the application of that paragraph or sentiment of his excellency to the Indians of this reserve; and will assert, without fear of contradiction, that no single instance has any Indian quarreled with a frontier citizen on this reserve, or off of it, to my knowledge; and, further, that neither the Indians nor agents have ever had any lot or part in this matter, but have in every case acted in self-defense.

Neighbors assured the commissioners and those beyond them that he should continue to use all his means to prevent any further collision between the Indians and those in hostile array against them, and wished the gentlemen success in their mission to restore peace and quiet to the frontier.[42]

The appointment and activities of the commissioners were even more reprehensible to John R. Baylor, for different reasons. He rallied a meeting in Weatherford on June 20, 1859, in which resolutions were adopted by the body expressing approval of the recent activities of embodied citizens; expressing the intention to resist the arrest of any members of the recent expedition by any source whatever; recommending the organization of a militia to remove the Indians or destroy them altogether; and

> 5. *Resolved*, That we regard the recommendation of the so-called peace commissioners, in the calling out of one hundred (disinterested) troops for our frontier protection, as a gross insult to our frontier citizens.

Neighbors expressed the opinion to the commissioner of Indian affairs that Baylor and Nelson were organizing to attack the reserves again and were stirring up the people with speeches in which they reiterated the old charges that had been brought against the Reserve Indians. The Major impressed upon the commissioner the need to move the Indians as quickly as possible.

When the semi-weekly mail hack from Dallas ploughed to a halt before the Brazos Agency the evening of Saturday, June 18, 1859, about 3:00 p.m., the sack contained, among other mail, the Dallas *Herald* of June 15, 1859. After the rumble of the wheels, the drumming of the horses' hooves, and the crack of the coachman's whip had died away, Major Neighbors sat in his office scanning the news of the last week. As his eyes ran over a letter from "Dr." J. R. Worrall of Jacksboro the Major's temper rose higher and hotter than the warm summer day outside. In a letter to the editor, Worrall gave his version of the attack on the reserve and the murder of the Indian Fox, whom Worrall characterized as a horse thief. Worral was, no doubt, a good judge of matters on the frontier, as he had only moved from Gainesville to Jacksboro after January 17, 1859. In spite of the Major's repugnance to newspaper wars, as he and Captain Ross discussed Worrall's piece, they decided not to let it go unnoticed. After mature reflection, they sat down in the office on June 20, 1859, and wrote the editor of the Dallas *Herald*.

> Dear Sir:—I notice in your paper of the 16th inst., a long communication signed by J. R. Worrall, of Jacksborough, giving what he calls a true statement of facts, in regard to the

recent attack on this Reserve by Baylor's party. Mr. Worrall, as you say, 'writes with dignity.' But a more complete [tissue] of misrepresentations in part or in whole, has never been written for a newspaper in this State, and we would be doing the whole country an injustice, as well as ourselves and the Indians on the Reserves, if we fail to give his whole view of our Indian troubles, a plain contradiction under our own proper signatures, and to request Mr. Worrall to show upon what authority, he makes such grave charges against the Indians and the agents. Mr. Worrall knows as well as we do, that no such appeals as he speaks of, were ever made to the agents or any other constituted authority. That no agreements were made by the agents to keep the Indians on the Reserves, and that the "Many depredations" complained of in Jack county, by him, if committed at all, has never been brought before the proper legal authorities of the country; we defy him to prove one single case complained of, has ever been legally investigated, and his whole dignified letter, is a mere assertion in keeping with numerous others of the same sort, promulgated by Baylor, Nelson, & Co., to mislead our citizens, and to excuse the lawless acts committed by that party, while in the neighborhood of the Reserves, and to excuse those who killed the Caddo Indian, and broke open official letters, which he was carrying from Agent Blain to Agent Ross.

We have known the Indian Fox for 15 years, or since he was a boy, and can prove that his character was as good as Mr. Worrall's or any other citizen of Jack County. He was born on the Brazos river, and has never lived out of Texas, done good service in Ford's fight and with Maj Van Dorn, was civilized and trusty in every respect, and deserving of a different fate. If Mr. Worrall is so law abiding, why did he not see that this man was held a prisoner, until some proof was brought against him. For a true statement of the attack on the Reserve, I refer you and the country, to the published report of Capt. Plummer, U.S.A., as the only true statement of that whole affair. When facts are published, I can fully rely upon the judgment of an intelligent people, but they would be outraged was Mr. Worrall's letter suffered to pass without contradition, which must be our apology for troubling you with this letter. There is now an intelligent Commission from the Governor investigating this movement of our citizens, we are willing to rely upon their investigation for a vindication of the Reserves. [He had not yet received the notes from Smith and Erath written that day.] We are willing and anxious to meet any legal issue with our citizens on this subject, but protest against either a newspaper controversy or with a mob, such as Baylor's company, who attack this Reserve.

> Very truly yours, & c.,
>
> Robt. S. Neighbors
> Supt. Indian Affairs for Texas
>
> S. P. Ross
> Special Indian Agent, Texas.

This letter was used as the pretext for sinister repercussions some months later by the Major's adversaries.

Neighbors's confidence in the governor's peace commissioners was shattered when he received notes from two of them revealing the *ex parte* nature of their proceedings. Commissioner J. M. Smith addressed a hurried note to Neighbors and Ross, which read:

> I would beg leave to inform you, as a friend, that much complaint and proof of depredations, of a circumstantial character, strongly implicating your Indians, have been furnished, and both dating back before the settling of the United States commissioner's court, and since. The evidence was furnished by [Patrick] Murphy and Hamon, as well as Captain Hamner, and others. There is no doubt, also, but that still another movement is on foot to attack the agency again, as soon as the troops leave and you can be caught off your guard. I am fully satisfied the destruction of the reserves is determined on, and they had rather kill you two than the Indians. I have heard that sentiment from almost all. I make this statement to you as a friend. I fear the commission will not make as favorable a report as I had hoped they would. In great haste. . .[43]

The Major no doubt frowned as he read a note from Erath who stated that to prevent another rising, the commissioners had decided to call out a hundred men, not to repulse the aggressors, but to herd the Indians within the reserves. The men were to come from McLennan and Bell counties and were to be commanded by Brown or Smith, or both.[44]

After reflecting upon the activities and instructions of the state commissioners, Major Neighbors remarked to the head of his bureau that,

> By a careful perusal of these papers, you will see that the reserve Indians can expect no protection from the State authorities. In fact, they have no disposition to investigate the facts.[45]

After a hurried tour of the frontier, the commissioners

reported unfavorably about the Reserve Indians and indirectly damned the agents with faint praise. In keeping with the governor's instructions, the commission called out 90 men to herd the Indians on the reserves until they should be removed. In view of John Henry Brown's partisan activities, Major Neighbors was not in his most gracious and hospitable mood when Brown appeared at the Brazos Agency to announce his mission to police the reserves. As Runnels's electioneering tool, his reception was such that he retired to his camp at Caddo Spring on the east line of the reserve.

An acrimonious correspondence ensued between the two men as Brown undertook to keep the reserves under surveillance and the Indians herded on them. In a collision at the Comanche Reserve, one Indian was killed, one wounded, and two of Brown's men wounded. In his correspondence and actions, Brown bore out Neighbors's assertion that Brown was Runnels's electioneering tool. The volatile episode succinctly summarized above unfolded as follows:

Brown said he had arrived at Caddo Spring on the night of July 11, 1859, at the head of nearly one hundred volunteer troops (ninety was the actual number) placed under his command by the state of Texas.[46] His commissioned officers, he said, were Lieutenants J. W. Nowlin, Wilson W. White, James D. Bell, and J. Y. Carmack. Brown declared that his leading object was to prevent another collision between the citizens and Indians under Neighbors's superintendency. Brown quoted the instructions to himself:

> As you are fully apprised of the existing difficulties, and the complicated state of affairs demanding the exercise of prudence, impartiality, and firmness, it is unnecessary to impress them upon you further than to say that the object is to prevent any further collision between the citizens on the one side, and the Indians, their agents, and the federal army, on the other, and for this purpose, you are instructed forthwith to repair with said force [100 men] to the vicinity of the reserves, and act as a police guard around them, to prevent Indians from leaving them until they shall be finally removed; and while treating all Indians found off the reserves, unaccompanied by an agent, or some responsible white man, as hostile, at the same time preventing hostile assaults upon the reserves.

Brown stated that from his headquarters near the Caddo Spring on the Brazos on the east line of the reserve, scouts would be kept around the reserve as well as between the two reserves, and added,

It is not my wish or province to discuss the unfortunate state of affairs existing on this frontier. I can only say that the State has adopted this course as the only means within its power of restoring quiet and tranquility to the frontier.[47]

Major Neighbors submitted Brown's letter to Captain Plummer for his consideration and informed Brown that

I can assure you that I have no desire to discuss with you the subject of our frontier difficulties. When I did so before, when you were here as commissioner, I was under the impression that you would act *"impartially"* in your investigations; but am sorry to see from the newspaper publications made by yourself and others, that you had already prejudged the Indians on the reserves, and accused them of having "committed most, if not all, of the late depredations of this frontier." As I am not prepared to admit any such assertions, I, of course, as the superintendent of Indian affairs, do not feel authorized or justified in aiding you in the exercise of a surveillance over them.

After quoting Captain Plummer's observations, Neighbors added,

I, the same as Captain Plummer, have my duties defined by orders from the general government. They are specified. I shall endeavor to execute them, but shall carefully avoid coming into collision with any portion of our frontier citizens. Should the "police" you propose to exercise around the United States reserves lead to a colision with the Indians who will be sent out to gather their stock, you alone must be responsible for the consequences, and the State will have to settle with the general govegnment whatever losses she may sustain by your operations, if any.[48]

Captain Plummer stated that his orders were to protect the Indians at the Brazos Agency from attacks from armed bands of citizens, and further he would be pleased to assist Major Neighbors and Captain Ross in the execution of their duties.[49]

Brown reacting to Neighbors's remarks concerning Brown's partisan activities replied:

Now, Sir, as an individual, I might view your remarks quoted as seeking a personal issue. I neither seek nor will accept such an issue. But for myself and the commissioners who acted with me, I deny in toto your assertion. Without exception, the commissioners, previous to their appointment, had been opposed to the assaults on the Reserves, and had believed the charges against the Indians, were mainly unfounded, though they were not familiar with facts on either side. Their Report, now published, speaks for itself.[50]

In reporting to Governor Runnels, Brown thought that the frontier people were satisfied with his course and that not enough disaffected could be collected to attack the Indians on their march north. He added:

But for the excitement pending the election and the consequent desire of reckless demagogues to fan the flames until that event shall have passed, I think quiet would in the main prevail.

Brown recapitulated to Runnels the political activities of himself and the other volunteer military officers on behalf of Runnels in the race for governor against Houston. Bearing out Major Neighbors's charge, that Brown was Runnels's electioneering tool, Brown wrote:

Mr. McFarlane arrived at noon yesterday & remained till this morning. He reports a few important changes in your favor below, among them Pearce tavern keeper at Meridian. I think I stuck Dr. Joliner & 5 others near there & a few along the route. Were the election one or two months off you would easily carry the frontier. As it is all that can be done is to reduce Houston's majority. This will be considerably done by changes to you, but more by causing many not to vote who intended to vote for H. I tremble for the result—hope for the best & fear the worst. I gave McF a letter to Dr. Worral at Jacksboro. From there on the pamphlets will tell. I have been exceedingly guarded; but as an individual, wherever the door opened have detailed facts from 1836 on & often with good effect. The truth, alas, has come too near the election, to do its work on the immediate frontier, but it is sown in good ground & will grow, success or defeat. None but a witness can realize the work the Waco & Birdville traitors have done to lead the frontier to ruin.

Nowlin has worked for you & so has Lieut Bell—

In haste
Your friend come weal, come woe.[51]

Woe came.

The first collision as noted above between Reserve Indians and the state troops, Neighbors learned, occurred near the Comanche Reserve on July 24, 1859, when Lieutenant J. W. Nowlin unsuccessfully attempted to arrest Chief Kaharaway. As others continued to join the Indian scouts, Leeper became apprehensive and rode toward the point. He heard firing before he reached Tryall Jackson's place and galloped his horse in

258

between the contestants. Leeper succeeded in stopping the fight, but one Indian had been killed, another severely wounded, while two of the volunteers were severely wounded, but not mortally.[52]

Back at the Brazos Reserve, Captain Plummer took John Henry Brown to task for allowing his men to scout on the reserve after Brown had avowed his intention of attacking the Indians. It was proper, Plummer said, for the men to come on the reserve provided they reported to the authorities and stated their intentions. Otherwise he thought Brown himself could see that men coming indiscriminately on the reserve would excite the Indians, especially since the fight at the Upper Reserve and that he had

> no doubt you will unite with me in the hope that these Indians many of whom have but recently returned from an expedition against the Comanches in which they fought in defence of the lives and property of the frontier settlers, may soon be permitted to leave the State unmolested.[53]

Brown denied that the men seen skulking south of the agency were his, and speculated that they were citizens who had complained to him that they had been to the agency to learn about their cattle but could get no satisfaction and prayed his intercession.[54]

Major Neighbors informed Brown that the parties alluded to by him had misrepresented, "if *nothing* worse and I should like to know their names," and added:

> I shall return to the State in a short time and reserve my duties as a citizen. Then those who appear determined to force unjust issues on me, will have to meet them.[55]

Major Neighbors dispatched young Peter Ross with his rejoinder to Brown at Caddo Spring. Brown demurred that he did not know the names of those who claimed they had been refused permission to search for their cattle. He was able to remember that James Anderson, who lived two miles below Belknap, seemed to be the leader of a party of seven.[56]

When Neighbors received Brown's note, it happened that quite a number of citizens were present at the agency for the purpose of seeking their cattle among those of the Indians. It should be said that the Reserve was not fenced, neither were the ranges of the citizens. Cattle roamed at large and were rounded up periodically for the purpose of determining ownership, branding, and marking. It did not necessarily indicate theft when another's cattle were found among someone else's herd. Major Neighbors took a statement from the citizens concerning their treatment while hunting their cattle and forwarded it to Brown, with this note:

> I have received your note of yesterday. In order that you may not have an excuse without *reporting* testimony to make any more "false publications" I send you a copy of statements made by responsible citizens [stock raisers] in regard to the Indian Cattle, and the privileges they have had on the reservations.
>
> You appear to be equally as fortunate now in your sources of information (having taken the Statement of a man [James Anderson] who was presented at the last Grand Jury of this county for cattle stealing) as you were when you were here as a disinterested Commissioner."[57]
>
> P.S. I have reserved the original of the paper sent you for further use.

The certificate of Robert Shaw concurred in by many other citizens followed.

> I hereby certify that I have been on the Reserve some three or four days hunting stock and have no hesitation in saying that I have met with no hindrance whatever in any way, from the Government officials or anyone in looking and examining for myself or those with me and I also have seen citizens on the reserve undisturbed hunting cattle.
>
> I also state that I have heard Maj. R. S. Neighbors Supt. Indian Affairs request that any and all citizens who wished could visit the "pen" where the Indian Cattle were kept and satisfy themselves, and should they find any belonging to them to drive them off—

This statement was concurred with and amplified by G. Cravens, James Duff, C. S. Carter, Isaac R. Vannoy, John Murray, U. A. Whitten, J. D. Young, F. M. Harris, and M. S. Dalton. The last two said they had raised stock near the reserve for the last three years.

When Captain Brown received Major Neighbors's note at the hands of S. J. Billingsly on the night of July 30, 1859, Brown writhed under the barbs, but managed to write with a show of restraint:

> Your note of yesterday, enclosing a copy of what purports to be a copy of the statement of several persons in regard to hunting cattle on the Reserve was received by Mr. S. J. Billingsly last night. In reply I have to say that I regret to see an old citizen of Texas who has filled many offices under the Republic & State and now holds a commission from

260

the Federal government in communications that should be strictly official and couched in courteous terms, descend to personalities which I regard with contempt.[58]

While Neighbors would never admit to Brown the legality of his demand that the Indians be accompanied by a white man when searching for the cattle off the reserve, as a matter of practice, according to his own statement, Neighbors had not for months previously sent them out without a white man, nor did he after Brown established his police of the reserves.

After a hard day's work preparing to move the Indians, Major Neighbors, on the night of July 20, 1859, set out for the Comanche Agency via Fort Belknap. At Belknap the Major wrote his brother-in-law a letter of thanks for giving some supervision to the Major's ranch where the corn had been completely pastured because of the dry weather. Neighbors then commented on conditions on the frontier.

> Some excitement—and Baylor is making his arrangements, we are informed, to attack us on the Road. We do not fear him. The worst Enemy we have is John Henry Brown, the Electioneering tool of Gov. Runnels. He arrived at the Reserves a few days ago with about 100 men under Runnel's orders—for the purpose of *herding the Indians and U.S. Troops until we Cross Red River.* It appears that John Henry's orders—that Runnels is determined to give us a practical demonstration of his disunion principles by making war *on the U.S. authorities,* Endorsing Baylor and Nelsons Treason and complicating matters on our frontier ten times worse than Baylor has, even when under the orders of the genl govt. We have every preparation made to move the Indians out of the State, and we who are citizens have to be taxed to Enable him to carry out his treasonable violations of the Laws of the State—This is the true state of affiars here—as shown by Brown's own letters which I have. They are official—or I would send copies. But I can show that this is the result of Runnel's orders and Brown's actions.[59]

Two companies of troops were recalled to the Brazos Reserve, and two more would arrive in a day or two. Hence Runnels's acts, instead of protecting the citizens, Neighbors averred, had rendered it necessary for the United States to send in all of Major Van Dorn's cavalry to prevent difficulties and to protect the state's interests until the Indians could be moved out of Texas. Neighbors predicted that Runnels's actions "will in 3 months break up this whole frontier."

> This is an unhappy state of affairs which I shall credit duly

to Runnels—I have but one consolation which is that Sam Houston will get almost a unanimous vote on the frontier—& will beat him at least 20000 votes. [*The margin was 9,000.*] There is no two parties here and [I] do not believe he, R—will get 3 votes in this County [Runnels got 30 to Houston's 93], and Houston's stock is still on the rise. I have no news. I am well but very busy. Tell Lizzie that I received her letter but can't write her tonight as I have just arrived and very tired and shall start at 2 oclock—is now 10 o.c.—The thermometer has been at 107 for two days and I have marks of perspiration all over this letter.

Give my love to all. I will write to Lizzie from Cooper. Hoping Old Sam will be elected and wishing success to yourself and family and all friends I am
                    Very truly yours
                    R. S. Neighbors[60]

As Neighbors correctly regarded Brown as the electioneering tool of Runnels, so Brown had a very decided opinion of Neighbors. In a private letter to Runnels, Brown said after the election:

The conduct of Maj. Neighbors towards me as the head of the company, has convinced me that he is a bad & base man——corrupt in the extreme—your bitter enemy & the warm friend of Gen. Houston. My report will throw light on this subject, but not by any means all within my knowledge as officials papers must be couched in certain words. Only in person could I explain fully.

Consider this confidential to yourself & friends only.[61]

Already the escort and transportation for removing the Indians were arriving. Neighbors thought that the caravan would be on the road by July 30, 1859, and that the trip would be made in fifteen days. In the meantime, however, countless details and much hard work had to be done to dismantle and say requiem over Neighbors's dream and years of planning.

Shapley Prince Ross, (1811-1889) United States Indian Agent.
Date of picture unknown. Courtesy of the Texas Collection,
Baylor University, Waco, Texas.

Lawrence Sullivan Ross (1838-1898). Courtesy, The Texas Collection, Baylor University, Waco, Texas.

John Robert Baylor (1822-1894). Courtesy, The Texas Collection, Baylor University, Waco, Texas.

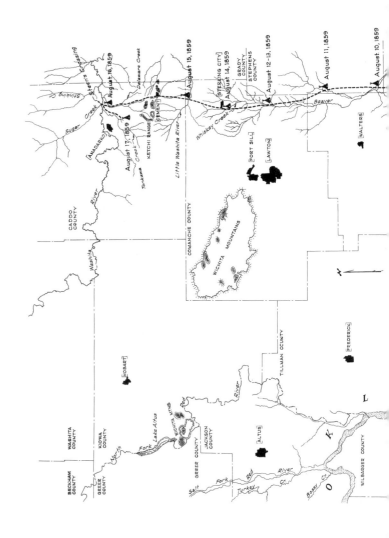

266

Map of Indian Exodus Route of 1859.

Texas State Marker for Brazos Indian Reservation School.

BRAZOS INDIAN
RESERVATION SCHOOL (1858-1859)

Operated for Indian children living on Brazos Reservation, a 37,000-acre refuge created by state in 1854. Here over 1,000 Anadarko, Caddo, Delaware, Ioni, Shawnee, Tawakoni, and Tonkawa people lived, farming and acting as U. S. Army Scouts.

Despite racial strife outside reserve, teacher Z. E. Coombes (1833-1893) reported unusual good will and harmony in classroom. Subjects taught were English, spelling, writing, and arithmetic. From 34 to 60 students were enrolled.

School closed when Indians were moved North in 1859.

(1972)

The school was founded by Major Neighbors in 1857. The date on the marker is wrong.

Ross O. Scull, great grandson of Major R. S. Neighbors; Ross Simpson Neighbors, Jr., grandson of Major R. S. Neighbors; and the author at the Texas State Marker, Fort Belknap, for the dedication October 21, 1967.

MAJOR
ROBERT SIMPSON
NEIGHBORS

who served in the army of Texas 1839. Captured by General Woll 1842. U. S. Indian Agent 1845. Born in Virginia November 3, 1815. Died September 14, 1859.

Texas State Centennial Marker, 1936, honoring Major R. S. Neighbors. United States flag was placed by Caddo Indians from near Anadarko, Oklahoma, who on Memorial Day place wreaths and perform tribal ceremonials around the grave site which by tradition is that of Major Robert Simpson Neighbors.

Chapter XIV
A Gallant Knight

"I have this day crossed all the Indians out of the heathen land of 'Texas' and am now 'out of the land of the philistines'."

Thus wrote Major Robert S. Neighbors of the Indian exodus out of Texas.

Under the direction of Major Neighbors, preparations for the exodus of the tribes had gone on apace on both reservations. Appraisals were made of the value of property which could not be removed, such as agency buildings, Indian houses made of logs or grass, and estrayed animals which could not be recovered because of hostilities. The value of animals lost by the Reserve Comanches alone amounted to $14,922.50.[1] One Tawacano was killed by someone unknown to the agents, while trying to recover his animals outside the reserve. Patrick Murphy, stock raiser and former sheriff of Young County whose father operated the Southern Overland Mail stage stand northeast of the reserve, later admitted to John Henry Brown that he had committed the deed. Neighbors sold the hogs and made arrangements for Ashley Marlin and John F. Buttorff to collect all estrays possible. Captain J. B. Plummer also left a small detail at the agency to guard a quantity of military supplies.

Food stuff such as flour, of which the Indians were especially fond, beef, salt, and corn, were purchased by Major Neighbors for the march north. Charles Edward Barnard, agency sutler, drove beeves to be slaughtered enroute. Transportation was furnished by the principal contractor, James Duff, in concert with Peter F. Ross of McLennan County, the agent's son, and C. Dejoux of Bexar County. Their contract called for furnishing eighty wagons and Mexican carts drawn by oxen and driven by white, Mexican or negro teamsters. United States Army Surgeon J. W. de Waldegg was employed to accompany the expedition. Superintendent Neighbors was hampered and embarrassed throughout the whole operation because no funds had been placed at his disposal by his department for months. Neighbors, feeling that it was unjust to make the contractors and employees wait for their funds, again raked the commissioner of Indian affairs over the coals. The entire operation was carried out on faith in Neighbors's word.

It was Neighbors's plan to move the Texas Indians to the locality of the proposed Wichita Agency on the Washita River near the mouth of Sugar Creek—named for maple trees—in present Caddo County, Oklahoma, some four miles east of present Anadarko. He intended to follow, as far as the Washita River, Major Enoch Steen's Road from Fort Belknap to Fort Riley. Neighbors directed Agent Leeper to lead the Comanches by Van Dorn's new road from Camp Cooper to the Little Wichita River, and thence to a rendezvous with the Brazos Reserve Indians at the crossing of Red River. As there was the threat of an attack on the Indians enroute by Baylor's band, Neighbors requested a military escort from Major General David E. Twiggs, commanding general of the Department of Texas. As in months past, there was the novel spectacle of United States troops protecting peaceful Indians from violent whites.

Orders arrived at Camp Cooper near the Comanche Agency in Throckmorton County authorizing Major George H. Thomas, future Rock of Chickamauga, to accompany Major Neighbors with two companies of the Second Cavalry and two companies of the First Infantry.[2] Major Neighbors sent Colonel Leeper, Comanche agent, his quota of transportation and supplies, and instructed him to notify the commanding officer of his escort when ready to move.[3]

Neighbors notified Thomas at Camp Cooper that the assembly point or camp for the personnel from the Brazos Agency would be on Salt Creek, six miles from the agency and just above the road from Fort Worth to Fort Belknap.[4] When Thomas demurred that this location would divide the command and invite attack, Neighbors explained that scarcity of water elsewhere had determined the choice, but changed the site to within three miles of the agency, near the Belknap Crossing on Salt Creek. Neighbors added that he was gratified to have Thomas as the commander of the escort, and would cooperate with him as closely as possible.[5]

At last all was in readiness. Since Major Neighbors had come to Texas in 1836, he had witnessed the Indian tribes driven across Texas from one field after another. This was his last opportunity to remove them from danger. In preparation for the movement, the cumbrous cavalcade of wagons, Mexican carts, ambulances, cattle, horses, dogs, and 1,051 Indians from the Brazos Reserve assembled at the camp on Salt Creek near the Belknap Crossing three miles from the agency. After Neighbors closed the door of his log office for the last time on the afternoon of Sunday, July 31, 1859, he rode his mount through a heavy downpour of·rain to the temporary Indian camp on Salt Creek.[6]

John R. Baylor's desire to break up the reserves had been realized.

About eight o'clock on the morning of Monday, August 1, 1859, Major Neighbors gave orders for the cavalcade to take up the line of march under escort of G and H companies of the Second Cavalry Regiment and one company of the First Infantry Regiment under the command of Major George H. Thomas.

After travelling about ten miles on the first day, Major Neighbors ordered a halt near the rancho of Judge Peter Harmonson on Salt Creek where Neighbors opened the polls for the agency personnel to vote in the state election.[7] In the gubernatorial contest, the incumbent, Governor Hardin R. Runnels, was making the fight of his life against Sam Houston, whom he had defeated two years before. The issues on the surface were the Indian problem and defense of the frontier; underlying was the issue of union or secession. The chief justice of Young County refused authority for holding the election, but James H. Swindells, practicing physician, former district surveyor and Neighbors's friend, sent the Major the necessary forms for the poll book and returns, as well as Harvey Matthew's copy of the *Digest*. Swindells indicated that the originals should go to the Texas secretary of state and the duplicates to the chief justice of Young County, Alexander McRae Dechman, native of Nova Scotia.[8]

On the morning of Tuesday, August 2, 1859, the line of march began at about seven o'clock toward Cottonwood Spring, one mile west of present Jean,[9] which was dry. The cavalcade was compelled to proceed to the West Fork of the Trinity, a distance of twenty-one miles from Harmonson's rancho, before a sufficient quantity of tolerably good water was found for all the animals. At the West Fork, beeves were killed, and sacks of flour issued the emigrants. From Cottonwood Spring to a point well inside Clay County, Van Dorn's Road, which Neighbors was following coincided with Preston Road and in part with Marcy's California Trail of 1849 as well as Steen's Road.[10] A trek of twenty-one miles on Wednesday, August 3, 1859, took the weary refugees to the Little Wichita River in Clay County five miles east of present Windthorst, where they arrived through a heavy rain that brought welcome relief from the torrid summer heat. The expedition lay over on the Little Wichita on Thursday August 4, where rations of beef and flour were issued. Six miles' travel on August 5, took the expedition to Frogpond, a hole of very good water.[11]

Neighbors travelled northeasterly until he crossed the Little Wichita at Van Dorn's Crossing six miles south of present Jolly. At an early hour on August 6, Neighbors set the cavalcade in motion, and after twelve miles came to an unnamed creek of good water, presumably present Turkey Creek. Eighteen or twenty miles of travel and thirteen hours in the saddle on Sunday, August 7, 1859, brought the expedition to Red River where camp was made on the Texas side at a very good spring of water two miles below the mouth of the Big Wichita River. (The site of later Confederate Camp Jackson.) Here Agent Leeper with his family and negro slaves came on with 370 Comanches and an escort of one company of the First Infantry under Captain Charles C. Gilbert. Of the start from the Comanche Agency, Joseph B. Thoburn,—who interviewed participants according to Muriel H. Wright—heard from Agent Leeper's daughter that:

> The departure was accompanied by a perfect babel of noise, Indians galloping hither and thither calling to each other; hosts of pappooses shrieking and wailing from fright at seeing so many strange faces and such undue excitement; dogs howling, barking and fighting the intruding canine contingent — Mules having dire presentment of arduous labors in store for them, brayed out dismal protests. The blasts of the cavalry trumpet, shrill notes of the fife, and the roll of the Infantry drum all contributing to the din, and pandemonium of the exodus.

Since the march was across open prairie, the caravan moved in line rather than in column. With the military occupying the center, the front extended about three miles. When game such as deer was startled from hiding, at least a thousand dogs, Thoburn supposed, took up the chase, accompanied by scores of yelling Indians, mounted and on foot. The heat and fatigue decimated the packs of dogs. One big cur finished the trip carried like a papoose on the back of an old squaw.

According to Thoburn, quoting Leeper's daughter again

> Sometimes the camps were extremely picturesque, being pleasantly shaded and cool after a long day's march through

274

dust and heat. With the timber which fringed the creek channel as a background, there stood out in bold relief the long line of white tents of the military escort and the hooded wagons of the commissary and sutler, and then up and down the valley, on either flank, the hundreds of Indian tepees and campfires, which sent up their flickering flames as night closed down on the scene, making it seem like a vision of enchantment. As darkness thickened, the thumping of the Indian tom-toms, accompanied by the droning, monotonous songs of the Indians, the barking of an army of dogs and the weird howling of hungry coyotes, constituted a peculiar medley which lulled tired travelers into restful slumber.[12]

Because of the threats of attack by the enemy enroute, secrecy had been kept so well that even John Henry Brown "with all diligence could not learn when the Indians would leave the Reserve." On August 2, he tardily took up the pursuit and was at Cottonwood Spring on the night of August 3, when Patrick Murphy arrived and alleged that the Reserve Indians had stolen five horses from him as they were leaving.[13] Brown established Camp Nowlin on the flat north of Van Dorn's Crossing of the Little Wichita River,[14] from which he scoured the country forty miles to the east, forty miles to the west, and north to Red River, he said. Brown tried to corroborate his statement that he had taken thirteen horses from a party of Reserve Indians rather than from wild Indians by the specious logic that he had found dog tracks on the trail.[15] Wild Indians, too, had dogs from time immemorial.

On Monday, August 8, 1859, Major Neighbors committed the long column of 1,420 Indians, four companies of troops, agency personnel, and teamsters to the treacherous waters and quicksands of Red River at Major Enoch Steen's Crossing two miles below the mouth of the Big Wichita.[16] After several hours of strenuous exertion, the last soul was landed safely on the other side. Neighbors wrote his wife:

> If you want to hear a full description of our Exodus out of Texas read the 'Bible' where the children of Israel crossed the Red Sea. We have had about the same show, only our enemies did not follow us to Red River. If they had—the Indians would have in all probability sent them back without the interposition of Divine Providence.[17]
>
> Yesterday was Sunday but I did not know it until 8:00 o c[lock] at night after being on horseback 13 hours. But I am still in excellent health and hope that when I do get home that you will yet be satisfied with your old husband in place of 'taking the chances for a new one.' I feel assured as you say

that your two boys are superior to any others in San Antonio—You should give me at least a portion of the credit for their 'good looks.' [He had no idea that a historian would poke around in his letters.]

I am glad you received the draft. It is all right. I hope you will do as you best can until I get home and I will try then to do my part. Give my regards to all and remember [me] to my friends. I will attend to the newspapers when I have nothing more important. But don't trouble yourself for I am 'all right' and I shall keep myself so for the benefit of 'my wife and children'—and I have no favors to [ask] of my enemies.

Give my love to Joe and Kate. I can't discuss the Brandy question with you at present but must say that I should be sorry if Joe should yield to that influence.[18]

I will write you again as soon as I get off the Road which I think will be five days and I will write you as soon as I can after that time. Keep up your spirits—and do the best you can. I have no control over my own time. Col. Leeper and family are now with us—they joined us this morning—with the Comanches—all are well. [Joe Mays?] has gone to the States. They [Brown's party] sent their agents but as I am not yet settled in camp for the night I have had no talk—they crossed Red River while I was crossing the plains [one hundred wagons] and about 1500 Indians.

I will be with you as soon as I can. Give my love and kisses to the children. Kindest regards to Dr. [Jesse] Boring [Methodist preacher] and to my lady friends. I am as ever truly your affectionate

Hubsand

R. S. Neighbors[19]

The expedition travelled three miles to Copperas Creek, present Whiskey Creek, in present Cotton County, Oklahoma, where camp was made by its tolerably good water. Expressmen from John Henry Brown arrived charging the Reserve Indians with having stolen Patrick Murphy's horses on leaving. Brown's dissatisfaction was also expressed at his alleged inability to relay the citizens' request to examine the Indian livestock because he had been unable to learn the time of departure. Major Thomas gave answer that the utmost diligence had been used to prevent the Indians from leaving the line of march and that Major Neighbors had given the citizens every opportunity to search the herd for cattle not belonging to the Indians. The citizens were perfectly satisfied, Thomas said, that "none of their cattle were being carried away."[20]

From Neighbors's camp, Beaver Creek lay like a willow limb on the prairie with its branches pointing northerly to his destination on the Washita River. Neighbors's journal is too terse to allow tracing his itinerary in detail, but fortunately the map of Major Enoch Steen's route which Neighbors was following has been preserved.[21] Enroute Neighbors sent an Indian express to Agent Samuel A. Blain of the Wichita Agency apprising him of his approach.[22]

An express arrived one day from Camp Cooper with orders from General Twiggs in San Antonio directing Major Thomas with the two companies of cavalry to return at once to Camp Cooper. The two companies of infantry were also to return as soon as the destination was reached. Neighbors dryly observed that the Indians would be left without a troop for their protection. That night the Indian express returned from Agent Blain's camp with news of a fight with a band of Kiowas in which one Kiowa had been killed and a Reserve Caddo wounded at the head of Beaver Creek.[23] The Kiowas stole all the horses of the expressmen for good measure. Agent Blain, enroute to the proposed agency site, had been invested so tightly by northern Comanches that he was cut off from contact with Superintendent Rector. This was not a very propitious beginning for the colonization of the Texas Indians. On August 15, Major Thomas with the cavalry turned back for Camp Cooper.

Neighbors passed through the Keechi (Ketchi) range of hills at present Cement, which was skirted slightly to the west, and thence up the right bank of Delaware Creek.[24] After seventeen and one-half miles of travel, Neighbors halted the cavalcade at Major Steen's Crossing of the False Washita River where a poor camp site was found at the mouth of Sugar Creek.[25] Next morning Neighbors moved the camp some four miles up the Washita to a beautiful, high valley on the right bank of Tonkawa Creek in present Section 36,[26] where the grazing was good and excellent springs furnished water. Neighbors remained at this point awaiting the arrival of Superintendent Rector or his deputy to whom the Major could officially deliver up the Indians and government property. Agent Blain arrived from Fort Arbuckle and was present when Neighbors held a council at which some of the principal Indians were present. Captain J. B. Plummer and his command of infantry left for Camp Cooper on Saturday, August 20, 1859.

At this point Neighbors learned why for months no funds had been placed at his disposal. During the hostilities in Texas, his inability to take a new oath and execute a new bond as superintendent instead of as supervising agent caused his funds to be withheld. His strong protests led to a change of orders, but too late to assist in the removal.[27]

When weather permitted, Neighbors, with the assistance of Captain Ross, Colonel Leeper and the Indians, explored the surrounding country for sites for the Texas tribes. Neighbors became almost ecstatic about the country.

> This is, in my judgment, truly a splendid country. The valleys are from one to five miles wide on alternate sides of the Washita. The soil, to judge from the heavy coat of grass and weeds, is very rich, and similar in appearance to the valley lands of Red River, and will, in my judgment, prove a superior farming country. The adjacent hills are covered with post oak of the best quality for building and fencing, and the timbered bottoms of the river and creeks afford a good supply of black walnut, over-cup or burr oak, and red cedar. I also noticed in the hills good quarries of stone, but had no means of testing its qualities. The whole country also abounds in good springs of the coldest freestone water and to judge from the unusual height of the timber, and the luxuriant growth of grass it must be sufficiently seasonable to produce good crops.

The sites selected for the Indian tribes were from three to seven miles from Blain's agency, and were approved by him. Blain had moved his agency to a site on the south side of the False Washita four miles above Major Steen's Crossing.[28] The agency seems to have been located at Neighbors's camp. Blain explained that the water in the Washita at his former camp was hot and continuously contaminated by his Indians and their stock. At the new spot were several springs of good water, pure and cold, and so situated "that the wildest and filthiest Indian in this Agency cannot render it unfit for use."[29]

While encamped, Major Neighbors heard by express from an old friend, Major William Hemsley Emory, First United States Cavalry, commanding Post Antelope Hills. Neighbors expressed his pleasure at hearing from him and invited Emory to join him with his command. Neighbors had heard that Emory had bad water and bad grass, while Neighbors had plenty of both of good quality at his camp. "This is proving a much better country than I expected," Neighbors exclaimed, and added, "Old Sam Houston is elected govr. of Texas by an overwhelming majority. I have no other news—cant you come down!"[30]

278

Even the frontier people, who knew that Houston advocated peace with the Indians had voted overwhelmingly for him. That they were not unaware of the underlying issue is shown by the fact that the frontier voted by a heavy majority against secession.[31]

In preparation for closing out his career as superintendent of Indian affairs for Texas, Major Neighbors requested the reports of Agents Ross and Leeper for the last few months. Ross recited the course of the hostilities, and added:

> I have reported the state of Affairs from time to time to the Executive of the State but he has given us no protection, on the contrary, he has organized Rangers for the purpose of confining the Indians within the Reserve at the time that their cattle and horses were stolen publicly and sold at Jacksboro at auction by the people of that county, knowing them to belong to Indians of the Brazos Reserve.[32]

Agent Leeper remarked that if he described the past difficulties it would be but to repeat a twice told tale. He placed the blame on the impotence of the general government and the action of the governor in sending state troops to police the Indians. The agent averred that if the Indians had wanted to fight, the state troops would have had to apply to the United States Army for protection.[33]

After receiving word from Superintendent Rector that Agent Blain was to act as his deputy, Superintendent Neighbors on September 1, 1859, delivered over to Blain 1,420 Indian souls—six having died enroute and one having been born—along with all government and Indian property. Neighbors then requested to be ordered on to Washington to tender his final settlement and resignation since he had moved his Indians into another jurisdiction of Indian affairs.[34]

At first Neighbors was greatly relieved to be free of his responsibilities. Only forty-three years of age, he had become hoary-headed on the trek from Texas, so great had been his anxiety for the safety and welfare of the Indians in his charge. But the beauty of the country and the resurgence of his great natural powers turned his mind again to the Indian service, and he is said to have considered asking for the appointment of agricultural instructor for his former Indian charges. In that event he intended to move his family, negro slaves, and property to the Washita region and to "go to work in real earnest and make these people a self sustaining people.[35]

In the meantime he was anxious about his wife and children

from whom he had been long absent. In conclusion he wrote his wife,

> So you must kiss the children for me, the new Baby and all.... my best love to Kate and Joe.... Remember me kindly to your mother and family.

Neighbors's departure from the Indians was a heart rending one. In past years when he was in their camp, they felt that his protecting mantle would shield them from all harm. For years they had eagerly watched for his coming and had ridden out to meet him. Some times he had come to give presents, some times to chastise them for wrong doing, some times to chide, but always to counsel, advise, and to encourage them. Through the years that he had been with them, babies had become sturdy youths, young boys had become stalwart warriors, warriors had become middle-aged men, and middle-aged men had become patriarchs. As late as 1929, his memory was still alive among those remaining few who knew him.[36] Of his parting with the Indians Neighbors wrote his wife:

> My dear wife, the most painful task I have had to perform since I kissed you and the dear children goodbye was to separate from the Indians.
>
> I made my last talk yesterday—Old Placedo [Tonkawa chief] cried like a child at the thought of my leaving, and if it was put to a vote there is not one that would agree for me to leave ...
>
> There were a thousand warriors present, and I shook hands with each of them. Some of the old warriors, whom I have known ever since I have been Agent among them, clung to me, and refused to let me go. When I rode off from them, they threw themselves upon the ground, yelling, in the wildest grief, so that it required all my fortitude to leave them. I have labored hard for them, trying to discharge my duty, in the sight of God and man.[37]

Thus the Major departed from their lodges to return no more.

The troops that escorted the Indians on the removal had long since returned to Texas according to their orders. Major Neighbors had recommended and Rector had approved retaining the government employees from the reserves in Texas. The Major's return party consisted of twenty civilians, including Captain Ross, his sons Peter F. and Robert S.,[38] and Colonel Leeper. Thirteen of the party were civilian employees of the agencies. A wagon and two ambulances accompanied the cavalcade.[39] Major Neighbors was said to have returned to Texas in his carriage or ambulance driven by his negro servant or slave.[40] The Indians had become greatly attached to Captain Ross, and his departure also saddened them. It seems to have been expected that Colonel Leeper would return as agent to the Comanches.

The return march was begun on September 6, 1859. The journey was fraught with danger. The northern Comanches and Kiowas, whose chastisement Major Neighbors had directed on numerous occasions, were lurking near. The Kickapoos with whom Major Neighbors had trouble throughout his career in the Indian service and whom he had ordered out of Texas more than once were not far away. Besides the hostile Indians, there was the worse ring of renegade white horse thieves and murderers in league with them along the frontier from Mexico to Kansas, and it was said to Utah. Moreover Baylor's men who had been robbed of their Indian prey might seek vengeance upon the small returning party. John Henry Brown and his state troops had fortunately disbanded and gone home. Several days before the Major left camp, his friends implored him not to return by way of Belknap. While he agreed to their entreaties, he expressed the belief that there was no danger to be apprehended in Belknap.[41]

On the second day out, Major Neighbors and his colleagues were attacked by a large band of wild Indians and white renegades.[42] The ensuing fight occurred just after Neighbors's party had halted for the noonday meal.

Captain Ross, who was the most experienced Indian fighter with the party did not like the signs, so he directed that the mules be tied to the wagons and fed and that the horses be picketed with short ropes, with guards posted. Even with these precautions, several Indians crept stealthily up through the tall grass to the horses and began to untie them before they were discovered. Colonel Leeper grasped a shotgun and started for the marauders. They opened fire on him, wounding him in the abdomen, in the leg and in the wrist. Indeed, it is more than probable that he would have been killed had not a despised Mexican (who had been regarded as a coward by the other men of the party) rushed to his relief. The Indians who had attempted to steal the horses were then reinforced by a large band which came on the gallop. As the engagement became general, Peter Ross, George Christopher and several others, availing themselves of the sheltering bank of a ravine, passed around the Indians and charged them from the rear with Colt's revolvers, whereupon the Indians fled, leaving several of their number dead on the field. After the fight was over and the party was preparing to resume its journey, Frank Harris (who was afterward captain of the gunboat 'Simon

Sugg' in the Confederate service) took a canteen of water and said to Captain Ross, 'That Indian I shot had short hair. I am going to wash the paint off of his face and see if he is not some old acquaintance of ours.' Suiting the action to the word, he found that the body of the supposed dead Indian was in reality that of a red headed white man. No one in the party was able to identify the body, however, and thus the fate of another renegade was found in a justly deserved oblivion.[34]

Nevertheless, the Indians and renegades got away with three animals, including Colonel Leeper's fine horse. Major Neighbors was well armed for any fight. He was bearing a Sharp's rifle, a Colt six shooter, a Bowie knife, a Derringer pistol, and a pocket knife.[44]

After binding up Colonel Leeper's wounds, the party resumed its journey down the trail, with Leeper suffering intensely. To elude any hostile pursuing party, Major Neighbors turned off the trail after dark and camped in a small ravine. A cold rain began to fall, but a fire was not lit for fear of revealing the camp to marauders. When Red River was reached the next day, it was found to be at flood stage, and it was necessary to construct a raft on which the group was ferried over to the opposite shore amid great danger. The Little Wichita River and other streams were found to be at flood stage also and were crossed with great difficulty.[45]

Neighbors's intention was to proceed to Camp Cooper, but the Brazos was found at high stage when he and his associates reached it near Belknap late in the evening on September 13, 1859. The party was compelled to make camp and spend the night.[46]

Next morning Major Neighbors insisted upon going into the village of Belknap, one-half mile east of the fort, although warned that his life was in danger. Major George H. Thomas, the future "Rock of Chickamauga," offered Neighbors an escort but this he declined. Neighbors spent about two hours in the office of County and District Clerk William Burkett writing reports to wind up his accounts as superintendent of Indian affairs. About eleven o'clock Neighbors remarked to Burkett:

I am now free from all responsibility to the government. I will now return to my dear wife [in San Antonio] and sweet children, never to leave them again, until separated from them by death; and, at this moment I would give all I possess in the world, to see them.[47]

Major Neighbors and a Mr. McKay[48] then left Burkett's office to see Colonel Leeper in the post hospital. They had scarcely left when Burkett heard the report of a gun, but thought nothing of it. In an instant McKay stepped back into Burkett's office and said, "Major Neighbors is killed."

Major Neighbors and McKay had proceeded not more than fifty paces when Neighbors walked into a carefully laid ambuscade which had been prepared while he was in Burkett's office. Patrick Murphy, gun in hand, with a certain Williams met Major Neighbors and accosted him:

"Neighbors, I understand that you have said that I am a horse-thief. Is it so?"

"No, Sir, I never did," answered Neighbors, placing his hand on his own gun, it was said. As he was explaining, Edward Cornett, Murphy's brother-in-law, stepped out from behind a chimney, put his double barrelled shot gun at the Major's back, and shot him with twelve buckshot at such close range a hole was burned in his coat.[49] Eight or ten buckshot took effect. Neighbors exclaimed, "Oh, Lord," and fell mortally wounded. Sheriff Edward Wolfforth ran up to Major Neighbors as he lay dying and spoke to him. Neighbors attempted to speak but could not. In ten or twelve minutes he breathed his last. William Burkett came out immediately upon learning that Major Neighbors was shot and directed the sheriff to summon a jury and hold an inquest.

A jury assembled, witnesses testified before Burkett, and after hearing the evidence, the jury gave the verdict that Major Robert S. Neighbors met his death at the hands of Edward Cornett. The sheriff was said to be on the alert to seize him, but it seems he never was arrested. Burkett returned to his office and wrote Neighbors's wife the tragic news.[50]

Burkett took from the Major's person his effects, including his fire arms, his gold watch, his spectacles and case, $116. a silver pencil case, a bunch of keys, one cartridge box, and a gum overcoat. Burkett said he had been instructed by the agents and Frank Harris, Agent Ross's son-in-law, to keep these in his custody until directed where to send them.[51] Colonel Leeper took into his keeping such government property as was in the Major's possession, including an ambulance, four mules, two pairs of harness, stationery, and other articles.[52]

Various versions were immediately woven around the death of Major Neighbors. One told that an Indian, "a poor, decrepit, old warrior, fast tottering down the declivity of life," witnessed the scene. "As soon as Major N. fell, the old savage began to yell, and scream, in most piteous tones of lamentation; and refused to be comforted, continued his wailing the entire day."[53]

Another account told that fear of the ring of assassins, who threatened with instant death anyone who approached the fallen agent, so gripped the area that,

> Although it is probable that death was instantaneous, the body of Major Neighbors lay untouched in the sandy street from morning until late in the afternoon, when it was taken up by Colonel Leeper's negro servant, who digged a grave and buried it.[54]

An authentic reference to his burial was by William Burkett who wrote Neighbors's widow that "The body will be interred tomorrow morning, accompanied by the [coroner's] jury."[55] While the body of Major Neighbors lay in state, a Masonic brother placed upon it the emblematic white apron, the symbol of the fraternal order to which the Major had given faithful allegiance.[56] It is believed by the Major's family that he was buried in the civilian cemetery about one-half mile east of Belknap. Nevertheless, the state of Texas in the centennial year of 1936 erected a monument at the site of the military cemetery one-half mile northwest of Fort Belknap in honor of the memory of Robert S. Neighbors. However, L. W. Kemp, chairman of the agency representing the state, told the writer at a later date, that it had been his intention to erect the monument in the civilian cemetery. The records in the National Archives as well as in the Office of Indian Affairs do not disclose where Neighbors was buried.[57] The remains of all persons buried in the military cemetery were removed to a national cemetery in San Antonio on February 16, 1907. Only two were definitely identified.[58] The weight of evidence seems to indicate then that Neighbors was not buried in the military cemetery.

Henry Williams, an aged settler, in 1936 pointed out to Charles Harold Atkinson a rock vault in the Belknap civilian cemetery which he said enclosed the grave of Major Neighbors.[59] This vault is twenty-one feet north of the vaults of Charles and Conrad Newhouse. Unsettled conditions, the Civil War, and the death of his widow in 1863 precluded the further marking of the Major's grave by her[60]. The remains of Colonel Jesse Stemm, Indian agent murdered by Kickapoos, were removed from Fort Belknap military cemetery in 1910 and reinterred with high honors in Washington, D.C.[61] But Neighbors in an unknown grave, "now lies [as a friend said]—a mangled corse, beneath the perpetual green of the north-western prairies."[62]

"Cut off in the full vigor of life and health," as William Burkett declared, Neighbors's death was mourned by his friends throughout the nation. Some eulogies were couched in phrases reminiscent of the romantic and chivalrous language of William Shakespeare and Sir Walter Scott whose literature was esteemed in the South of that period. The editor of the San Antonio *Herald* observed:

> Though he won not a chieftan's death, as he had striven to do upon the battle field; yet, his end was noble, as the plumed Knight's could be; for he died at the post of duty—the noblest, and bravest of earth could have done no more.

And--------

> After life's fitful fever, in his grave, he sleeps well.[63]

After speaking of the dastardly conduct of those who assassinated Major Neighbors, another later remarked:

> Thus had the spirit of human envy and hatred found its fruition, not alone in the woes of unoffending Indians, but also in the untimely taking off of as gallant a knight as any who ever balanced a lance or drew a broadsword in behalf of the oppressed . . . .

> Man's inhumanity to man is found in many a chapter of the history of the American frontier, but in none do the deeds of true heroism and fidelity shine brighter by reason of such a dark background than do those of Major Robert S. Neighbors, Capt. Shapley P. Ross and Col. Matthew Leeper and their associates of the Indian service and of Major George H. Thomas, of the army, who joined in protecting the helpless Indians and conveying them to an asylum far from danger. Were it not for such nobility of character amid scenes of tumult and disorder, one might well question the rightfulness of the claim of his race to supremacy among the sons of men. It is hoped that the story of these men, who risked not only their personal standing by reason of their championship of an unpopular cause, but even life itself, may not be forgotten, while men would inspire their children with the example of unselfish service. If other men acquired fame in war, let it be remembered also that these wrought mightily for peace.[64]

After noticing the account of Major Neighbors's death in the *Daily Missouri Republican,* the editor of a paper in Belleville, Illinois, observed that grief would be carried to many a household.

> Most sincerely do we mourn his death, and we extend our sympathies to his brother ASA NEIGHBORS, and Mrs. HUGHES, of our city. Brave and generous to a fault, he will be lamented by his many friends in this region of country. The reader will be struck by the cowardly manner of his death.

When the news of the death of Major Neighbors reached San Antonio, the district court was in session. Upon the motion of John A. Wilcox, seconded by S. G. Newton, the court with the Honorable Edmond J. Davis presiding declared that in recognition of the Major's public services and social worth which had

> so endeared him to all who knew him that 'to name him was to praise,' it would be a mark of respect to his memory, grateful to this community and acceptable to the family and friends of the deceased that this court should now adjourn, and the Court fully concurring with the sentiments expressed by the Bar, on consideration thereof.
>
> It is ordered that as a token of respect for the public services and private character of the deceased and of sympathy and condolence with his afflicted and bereaved family, this Court do now adjourn till Monday morning next at 9 o'clock A.M. and that a copy of these proceedings be furnished by the Clerk of this Court to the papers of this City and to the widow of the deceased.[65]

One who had known him twenty-five years observed that:

> Major Neighbors was a member of the Masonic order, an honorable man, a warm and devoted friend, and a citizen of liberal public spirit. Whatever his faults (and who had them not?) they will be forgotten with his death, which has cast a gloom over this community and brought sadness to many a hearth.[66]

After commenting on the Major's great yearning to be with his wife and children once more, a personal friend and Masonic brother reflected that,

> Little did he think, that his next meeting with her, and them, would be in the great hereafter: He dreamed not that in ten minutes more, he would have passed to 'that undiscovered country, from whose bourne, no traveler returns.'

The brother of the "mystic tie" declared that he seldom had seen the truth more forcibly illustrated that "In the midst of life, we are in death." He remarked that the Major had hoped to reach home on September 15, his wife's birthday, but upon being detained, he had written that she might look for him on the twentieth of September. Instead she received the messengers of his death.[67]

The editor of one of the San Antonio papers commented that:

> Major Neighbors is an old Texian, and has long been identified with her frontier history, a high toned honorable gentleman, ardently beloved by all who knew him and his sudden and unexpected death, in this horrid manner is a dreadful shock to his numerous personal friends, but what a pang of bitter grief, to the heart of his bosom companion, his dear wife and little ones, all may truly sympathize and condole with the severely bereaved one, but no words can

express the grief that calamity of this kind, brings upon the heart of the widow, and orphan children. We trust in this their hour of affliction they may find consolation in that hope, which looks forward to a union in the bright spirit land, where deeds of horror are unknown.[68]

Charles Goodnight observed that a brave man has no chance against a gang of lawless men since a law abiding man shoots only when he must, the lawless without cause.[69] The manner in which Major Neighbors met his death was roundly damned throughout the nation. His killing was called a "cold-blooded and cowardly assassination"; J. M. Smith called it a "horrid murder." One editor declared that Major Neighbors was "most cruelly and wantonly assassinated." Another charged that the Major was "brutally, basely, and most cowardly murdered," and that he apparently "could not realize that he was in the midst of cowardly assassins, murderers, and horse thieves." Secretary of Interior Jacob Thompson wrote Governor Sam Houston with indignant detestation of the murder of Superintendent Neighbors. Old Sam in reply bitterly damned the "lawless and base assassination of Major Neighbors," adding, "The recollection of these things is too painful to dwell upon, and had a competent Executive ruled Texas, they would not have occurred, in my opinion."[70]

Lieutenant William E. Burnet wrote his father, ex-president David G. Burnet,

The 'Baylor Party' have murdered Major Neighbors and, I suppose would like to get others. The assassination of Major Neighbors was a most foul and cowardly murder; but in good keeping with the other acts of the same party . . . . I have been sometimes sorry for the part I took against these people but this to my mind puts the matter beyond all question: and I only regret that I did not push things against them at *Marlins* as I might have done.[71]

It is not easy to determine the motives for the assassination of Robert S. Neighbors. He never realized who killed him, and his assassin was an entire stranger to him, Neighbors never having seen him before nor at the time of the assassination.[72] J. M. Smith, a prominent citizen, called Edward Cornett a "drinking, blustering, dissolute desperado, and has before murdered his man."[73] He continued on his career of violence after assassinating Major Neighbors.[74] Cornett and Murphy were natives of the United Kingdom—Murphy, and probably Cornett, was from Ireland.

Some of the purported motives for the assassination of Major Neighbors follow. Colonel Leeper reported to Washington that, "This tragical affair was said to have been occasioned by pretty free conversations on the part of Major Neighbors on account of the killing of a reserve Indian [Fox] not long since."[75] Murphy feigned to believe that Neighbors had accused him and others of stealing horses,[76] which Neighbors denied as he was killed. Murphy may have feared prosecution in the courts by Neighbors for the role Murphy played in the killing of at least two reserve Indians outside the reservation.[77] Some part of the motive was probably contained in the statement of Commissioner Greenwood that Superintendent Neighbors

> was murdered by some person or persons, whose vengeful animosity it is supposed, he had incurred by his zealous and uncompromising efforts to protect the Indians and their property from wrong.[78]

The *Daily National Intelligencer* of Washington, D.C., repeated that the Major was killed because of "his severe animadversion upon the murder of a reserve Indian [Fox] which occurred recently."[79] In referring to the motive for the murder of his friend Neighbors, Captain Randolph B. Marcy spoke of the foul massacre of the Reserve Indians and remarked:

> Major Neighbors, who subsequently commented severely upon the turpitude of the act, was shortly afterward shot in the back by one of the cowardly assassins, and died in a short time.[80]

An unlikely story was given expression in the middle of the twentieth century by one who should have known to the effect that the assassin of Major Neighbors was an employee of George T. Howard, former Indian agent, who had differred with Major Neighbors over policy.[81]

Walker K. Baylor, son of John R. Baylor who led the attacks on the reservations, said he had been asked many times why Ed Cornett killed Major Neighbors and replied:

> Of course, I do not know why. I only know a few facts which tend to soften Cornett's act which I briefly give:
>
> It is a fact that a few months before the trouble at the reservation before described, the Indians invaded the premises of Ed Cornett in his absence and carried Mrs. Cornett away captive and she was never again heard of. It is also true that Major Neighbors had caused the United States troops to defend the Indians against the Texans when they attempted to drive them out of the state. It is also true that Major Neighbors accompanied the Indians when they left Texas for their home across Red River. It is also true that Major Neighbors was strictly in sympathy with the Indians and minimized what they had done along our frontier and was bitterly opposed to the course pursued by the Texans.

288

Ed Cornett disagreed with Major Neighbors on all these questions, as did nearly all the citizens in that section. Those facts, coupled with the fact of the captivity of his wife, which in itself was enough to render his mind incapable of cool reflection and, perhaps, the bitter feeling which existed between the two factions—Indian men and White men [both groups white men] was the cause of the killing.[82]

The flaw in the first motive given by Walker K. Baylor is the fact that Cornett's wife, according to her own brother, Patrick Murphy, disappeared on November 7, 1859, *after the murder of Major Neighbors*,[83] and it is highly doubtful that she was abducted by the Indians at all. In the other circumstances cited by Baylor, Major Neighbors was performing the duties which he was sworn to perform and which humanity itself dictated.

Parker Johnson, Texas Ranger and contemporary of Neighbors, stated that Neighbors was killed because the leaders of the late disturbances feared he would bring them to justice for their crimes.[84] Neighbors had initiated proceedings to have the ring leaders tried in the federal courts since the state courts had proved impotent.

Anarchy ensued on the frontier after the assassination of Major Neighbors. According to Agent Ross the friends of law and order were disorganized by the Major's death, as he had been their bulwark. After his violent removal, the leaders of violence were emboldened and in a mass meeting in Belknap threatened with assassination the remaining reservation personnel.[85] Edward Cornett remained at large.[86] He was finally indicted for the murder of Major Neighbors by the Young County grand jury on May 24, 1860, but he failed to appear for trial.[87] According to one account, the trial court was broken up by the false report of the abduction of Cornett's wife. When the pursuing party followed the false trail to Red River, it was so high that only a crow could have crossed.[88] Indian Agent Samuel Blain had information that Cornett's wife had actually gone to friends in the Chickasaw Nation,[89] while another report said Cornett's friends had taken his wife to his mother in Collin County the day before the trial and then reported the alleged abduction by the Indians.[90] Cornett hid out in the hills around Belknap.

When the Reserve Indians heard of Neighbors's death, they wept, moaned, and wailed for many days. and threatened to avenge his death. They were robbed of that satisfaction by Sheriff Wolfforth's *posse comitatus* who killed Edward Cornett in the Belknap hills on May 25, 1860, while attempting to arrest him for trying to kill Dennis Murphy, his wife's father or brother of the same name.[91]

When James Vance, the executor of Major Neighbors's estate, along with the Major's wife, according to his will, confirmed the death of the Major on September 25, 1859, he wrote Major D. C. Buell in Washington, D.C., to request that Captain Ross be retained to settle the accounts of Major Neighbors. Vance said Ross had the entire confidence of the Major's family and had a full knowledge of his business.[92]

When Special Agent E. B. Grayson was sent from Washington to settle the Major's accounts, he invited Agents Ross and Leeper to San Antonio to assist him and at the same time settle their own accounts.[93] Grayson found that Major Neighbors had established a reputation for extreme rigidity in following contracts and allowing claims, even unto the last,[94] and there was a balance to his credit of $37,985.02.[95] A few minor claims turned up later. John S. Ford, faithful to the memory of his friend to the last, declared that the fact that the United States was indebted to Major Neighbors was, "An incontrovertible proof of his honesty in the administration of financial affairs."[96]

After certifying to the correctness of Major Neighbors's accounts, Special Agent Grayson felt constrained to remark to Commissioner Greenwood:

> The prosperous and flourishing condition of the reserves as shown by these returns the comfortable condition of the Indians, the great accumulation of their stock from an investment for them in 1855, their having arrived at a point in improvement and certain means of support almost to be independent of farther support from the Department makes it a source of regret indeed that they could not have been left unmolested in their fortunate condition. Reckless and unprincipled, and hard of heart must have been the men who coveting the possessions of these inoffensive people, were determined on breaking up their homes, and driving them from the land of their Fathers, and that too when there was not the common excuse of depriving the red man of his lands—for here is an empire of country that will take a century to fill up entirely.[97]

All was not lost, however, for the Major had proved that it was possible to colonize the Texas Indians and introduce them to the settled arts of civilization. After he removed them to the fertile region north of Red River, he did all he could to insure that the experiment to make them an agrarian people would continue. Their descendants live in the same region today in the Washita Valley where Major Neighbors left them.[98]

The settlers on the frontier, by the removal of the Indians

and the assassination of Major Neighbors, did not gain that repose which reckless men had so heartlessly promised them. Instead they were harrassed as never before. The dire forebodings of J. M. Smith after the murder of the Major were too well borne out when he exclaimed:

And woe to the frontier now, it will have less sympathy and protection than ever from the Genl. Government, as Neighbors was one of the few officials that was known to be strictly honest, and always had the entire confidence of the authorities at Washington.[99]

Next year after the Major's death, John Salmon of Erath County wrote Governor Houston that, "We have the worst times that I ever saw in Texas and I have bin in it twenty one years[100] John Elkins who had helped to break up the reserves admitted that conditions in Texas were far worse after the removal, and declared that counties a hundred miles to the east of the frontier became a prey to the depredators.[101] John R. Baylor's son declared,

Personally, I think the killing of Major Neighbors was about the greatest misfortune that could have befallen our northern frontier. I think he could have, by his influence over the Indians, prevented largely the horrible murders of men, women and children along our northern frontier for many years after his untimely death.[102]

The Texas Reserve Indians after their removal were charged with returning to Texas to raid, but those Indians, Agent Blain, and the military officers proved to the satisfaction of a commission sent by Governor Houston that they were not involved.

If the Texas frontier had been chastised as with whips before, it was then scourged as with scorpions and receded a hundred miles. During the Civil War when the much complained-of-arms of the United States were withdrawn, the wild, northern Indians fell upon the hapless Texas frontier with such violence that a whole tier of frontier counties was disbanded, including Young County. The few families who remained in the county were huddled in the abandoned buildings of Fort Belknap and in isolated stockades. The frontier reverted so far to a wilderness that during snow storms buffalo sought shelter in the abandoned buildings of Fort Belknap. A hundred years and more after the death of Major Neighbors, the town whose sandy street soaked up the blood of the martyred agent is no more. The former town east of the restored fort has been erased from the face of the earth, and the site is at present a ploughed field. The raids in north Texas did not cease until 1876 when the northern Comanches were settled on reservations as Neighbors had recommended so long ago.

History cannot be written in the subjunctive. It is idle and futile to speculate what Major Neighbors might have done had he been vouchsafed three score and ten years, in which to serve his country. According to his executor, he left but little property.[103] Nevertheless, he left a heritage of honesty and integrity in the administration of public offices of trust which will bear emulation in any age. Although he knew there was a settled purpose on the frontier to take his life, he would not be driven from his post nor shrink from danger. He showed how to defend a trust unto the death. The end was approached with firm resignation as he said, "We are in the hands of an all ruling Providence and we cannot disobey his mandates. It is my destiny to sacrifice myself for others."

History has been kind to him. Rupert Norval Richardson gave this appraisal of the Major's career.

> Although he was struck down in his [forty-fourth] year, Neighbors succeeded in leaving behind him a record of constructive public service that entitles him to a place in the annals of great American pioneers. The courage manifested by the supervising agent and his resident agents, Ross and Leeper, in protecting their Indian wards against the onslaughts of the unreasonable citizens is an inspiring example of selfless devotion to duty.

While Walter Prescott Webb said, "Some sort of providence was to put an end to the life of the man who had given that life in the service of the Indians."

W. W. Newcomb, Jr., thinks Robert S. Neighbors was:

> . . . an idealistic youth who suddenly appeared from nowhere to embrace the Texas Revolution and the cause of Texas. Perhaps unconsciously on his part, though, the subject of his lifelong fervent pursuit was not Texas but was the elusive maiden, humanity. He espoused her cause, as well as that of her sister, decency, for 21 years as a soldier, Indian agent, elected official, and in other capacities. He gained not in wealth from his positions or because of them, in an age when it was accepted that one do so. But that he strove for her was a gain for all men, not only Texas; it made him a Texan to remember.[104]

The world may form its own conclusions. As John S. Ford remarked, "The ordeal through which Major Neighbors has passed endorses him. He needs no commendation from any quarter."

Footnotes

Chapter I

[1]Livingstone Porter, Capitola, California, to K.F.N., October 20, 1953, Notes and Letter Files of K. F. Neighbours, Wichita Falls, Texas.

[2]Senate Committee on Indian Affairs of the Republic of Texas, October 12, 1836, Indian Affairs Papers, Texas State Archives, Austin, Texas. The tribe designated above as the Tawacano had its named spelled in various ways: Touacara, Tah-wah-carro, Tawakaro, To-wac-co-ni, Tehuacana, Tah-wah-ca-roos, and Tawakoni. The spelling Tawacano has been adopted in this work as bearing some resemblance to the original as found by the writer in the Archivo General de la Nacion in Mexico City.

[3]Houston to Burnet, April 25, 1836, Army Papers, Texas State Archives, Austin, Texas.

[4]Neighbors to Peace Commissioners, June 16, 1859, *Senate Executive Documents*, 36 Cong., 1 Sess., Doc. No. 2, 660.

[5]Mrs. Catherine N. (S.H.) Darden, Dallas, Texas, September 20, 1910. Neighbors Letters, Private Collection, Texas Memorial Museum, Austin, Texas, hereafter referred to as Neighbors Let. Pvt. Coll.

[6]Muster Roll Book, MS, 126, General Land Office, Austin, Texas; Bounty File Number 843, Certificate No. 1197, General Land Office, Austin, Texas.

[7]Alice Atkinson Neighbors, Life and Public Works of Robert S. Neighbors, MS. M.A. Thesis. The University of Texas, 1936; Amelia W. Williams and Eugene C. Barker (eds.), *The Writings of Sam Houston*, V, 165.

[8]Williams and Barker cite Muster Roll Book, MS, 127, General Land Office, which shows one Robert Nabors to have served in Company C. Colonel Coleman's Regiment, from December 1 to December 31, 1836. A certificate of Lieutenant Nicholas Lynch on August 24, 1837, however, shows that this was Robert W. Neighbors. Comptroller Military Service Records, Texas State Archives. The bounty claimed for said service was by Robert W. Neighbors, Bounty Certificate No. 1198, Rusk County File No. 68, General Land Office.

[9]Certificate No. 293, Milam Third Class, File 668, General Land Office. The certificate was issued to Robert S. Neighbors in Harris County, but he assigned the certificate to Morgan C. Hamilton on November 9, 1844, who located the land in Williamson County.

[10]Frederick Adams Virkus, *The Compendium of American Genealogy*, Vol. 7, 397; *Virginia Magazine of History and Biography*, Vol. 18, pp. 40-43; Dauphin County, Pennsylvania Deed Book Z-1-576; Ralph Beaver Strassburger, *Pennsylvania German Pioneers*, Vol. 3, p. 237f; Anna Mary Charles, church secretary, First Reformed Church, Lancaster, Pennsylvania, to K.F.N., December 9, 1966, notes and Letter Files of Kenneth F. Neighbours; J. B. Riestap, *General Illustrated Armorial*, by Victor and Henri Rolland, Vol. 5, plates CXXII & CXXIII. Newell E. Neighbours to K.F.N. August 14, 1935.

[11]Alice Atkinson (Mrs. R.S.) Neighbors, Life and Public Works of Robert S Neighbors, MS, M.A. Thesis, University of Texas, 1936, p. 1. United States census of 1880 for Belleville, Illinois shows Mary Hughes nee Neighbours's father born in Maryland.

[12]Records in County Clerk's Office, Charlotte Court House, Virginia.

[13]Records of the War Department. National Archives, Washington, D.C.. photostatic copies loaned the writer by Alice Atkinson (Mrs. R.S.) Neighbors.

[14]He was christened Samuel Robertson Neighbours. The names of the other children are Mary, Nancy, Joel, Asa, William and John.

[15]Homer Spellman Thrall, *History of Methodism in Texas*, 109.

[16]Alice Atkinson Neighbors to K.F.N., July 16, 1948.

[17]H. B. Chermside, County Clerk, to K.F.N., December 7, 1953. Notes and Letter Files of K.F. Neighbours, Wichita Falls, Texas.

[18]Records of Charlotte County Court, Order Book No. 24, p. 47; Order Book No. 21, p. 169; United States Census, 1 30, Vol. 9; Charlotte County, Virginia, p. 60ff; Order Book No. 22, p. 60ff and p. 224.

[19]Alice Atkinson (Mrs. R.S.) Neighbors to K.F.N., January 2, 1954.

[20]Property Books, 1820-1828, Charlotte County Virginia.

[21]Guardian Book No. 5, p. 5, September 6, 1822, Charlotte County, Virginia.

[22]Neighbors left a large locker full of personal papers which were kept in the family for many years. His daughter-in-law offered them to The University of Texas through Professor George Pierce Garrison. When Garrison died, the offer was found among his effects, but when a representative of the University went for the papers, they had been burned, since it was felt there was no interest in them. Alice Atkinson Neighbors to K.F.N., August 16, 1953. The records of the Methodist Church of Jackson, Louisiana, which might have thrown some light on his early life, were burned. The Reverend John B. Shearer to K.F.N., November 21, 1953. Fire likewise destroyed the Texas Adjutant General's Office.

[23]William B. Parker, *Notes Taken During the Expedition Through Unexplored Texas*, 116.

[24]Darden, September 20, 1910, Neighbors Let. Pvt. Coll.

[25]Neighbors's petition to St. Albans Lodge, No. 28, Jackson, Louisiana; Minutes in the Archives of St. Albans Lodge, photographic copies furnished Kenneth F. Neighbours by F. A. Jenkins on December 24, 1953, Notes and Letter Files of Kenneth F. Neighbours, Wichita Falls, Texas. F. A. Jenkins, P. M., St. Albans Lodge, to K.F.N., December 24, 1953, Notes amd Letter Files of Kenneth F. Neighbours, Wichita Falls, Texas. For R. S. Neighbors's Masonic

career, see Kenneth F. Neighbours, "Robert S. Neighbors, Texan," *Texas Grand Lodge Magazine*, 1956.

[26]Minutes of Holland Lodge No. 1, Scottish Rite Temple, Houston, Texas; microfilm copies made available by James D. Carter, Austin, Texas, now librarian, Scottish Rite Council, Washington, D. C.

[27]Macum Phelan, *History of Methodism*, 95.

[28]C. C. Cox, "Reminiscences of C. C. Cox," *The Quarterly of the Texas State Historical Association*, VI, 18.

[29]Comptroller Military Service Records, Texas State Archives, Austin, Texas; E. W. Winkler, *Secret Journals of the Senate, Republic of Texas, 1836-1845*, p. 136.

[29a]Neighbors to Clendennin, August 4, 1840; Clendennin to Neighbors, August 5, 1840, Army Papers, Texas State Archives, Austin, Texas.

[30]Neighbors, Quartermaster Accounts and Vouchers, Texas State Archives, Austin, Texas.

[31]Lamar, *The Papers of Mirabeau Buonaparte Lamar*, VI, 135; Joseph Milton Nance, *After San Jacinto: The Texas-Mexican Frontier, 1836-1841*, p. 235.

[32]Cazneau to Neighbors, April 8, 1841, Quartermaster Papers, Texas State Archives, Austin, Texas.

[33]Neighbors Let. Pvt. Coll.

[34]Comptroller Military Service Records, Texas State Archives, Austin, Texas.

[35]Certificate of H. L. Upshur, August 19, 1851, Public Debt Papers, Texas State Archives, Austin, Texas.

[36]Certificate of John C. Hays, San Antonio, June 6, 1849, Public Debt Papers, Texas State Archives, Austin, Texas.

[37]According to General Adrian Woll, his scouts brought in four of the commissioners who implored him not to attack the city as the Texans would force the citizens to resist. The commissioners were made prisoners for their pains. Joseph Milton Nance, "Brigadier General Adrian Woll's Report of His Expedition into Texas in 1842," *The Southwestern Historical Quarterly*, LVIII, 529.

[38]Frederick C. Chabot, *Perote Prisoners*, 91.

[39]Alice Atkinson Neighbors, Life of R. S. Neighbors, MS, M.A. Thesis, The University of Texas, 1936, p. 11.

[40]Chabot, *Perote Prisoners*, 96.

[41]Joseph Milton Nance, "Brigadier General Adrian Woll's Report of His Expedition into Texas in 1842, *The Southwestern Historical Quarterly*, LVIII 533.

[42]Certificate of James L. Trueheart and R. S. Neighbors, November 1, 1849, Public Debt Papers, Texas State Archives, Austin, Texas.

[43]James L. Trueheart's Diary, quoted in Chabot, *Perote Prisoners*, 96. Trueheart's great great grandson, Marion Hair, was the writer's room mate

at Southern Methodist University in the spring of 1949.

[44]Richard A. Burleson (ed.), *The Life and Writings of Rufus Burleson*, pp. 572, 687f, and 841.
Judge Hutchinson's diary may be found in E. W. Winkler, "The Bexar and Dawson Prisoners," *Texas Historical Association Quarterly*, XIII, 292-324. Herbert Gambrell, *Anson Jones*, 259.

[45]Certificate of James L. Trueheart and R. S. Neighbors, Public Debt Papers, Texas State Archives, Austin, Texas.

[46]Chabot, *Perote Prisoners*, 122.

[47]Chabot, *Perote Prisoners*; Smithwick, *Evolution of a State*, 274.

[48]Marcy, *Thirty Years of Army Life*, 393ff.

[49]Edward T. Manton to his uncle Edward Manton January 1, 1843. Letter file of Edward T. Manton, copies of which are in possession of his great grandson William A. Cooper of Wichita Falls. By coincidence Cooper, long time friend, his wife Nancy, his brother Robert and I visited Presidio San Carlos de Perote during Christmas week of 1974. We could not enter because it is still a prison with 5,000 felons inside. Robert supposed his ancestor missed the clams and oysters of New England.

[50]Thomas Jefferson Green, *Journal of the Texian Expedition Against Mier*, 266f.

[51]R. A. Brakley to S. A. Maverick, Perote, April 15, 1843; Rena Maverick Green, Samuel Maverick, *Texan: 1803-1870*, p. 246.

Chapter II

[1]Minutes of the Treaty of Bird's Fort, September 28, 1843, Record Book, Bureau of Indian Affairs, 1842-1843, hereafter referred to as Rec. Bk. Ind. Aff. The treaty with the Comanches is in the treaty casket in the vault of the Texas State Archives, Austin, Texas.

[2]Western to Neighbors, February 12, 1845, Rec. Bk. Ind. Aff.

[3]Western to Neighbors, March 2, 1845, Rec. Bk. Ind. Aff.

[4]Marcy, *Thirty Years*, 174ff.

[5]Parker, *Unexplored Texas*, 237f; Marcy told the same story.

[6]Neighbors to Western, February 4, 1846, Indian Affairs Papers, Texas State Archives, Austin, Texas.

[7]Butler to Medill, January 12, 1846, Indian Office Letters Received, now deposited in the National Archives, photostatic copies in the Library of The University of Texas, Archives Division, hereafter referred to as Ind. Off. Let. Recd.

[8]Grant Foreman, "The Texas Comanche Treaty of 1846," *Southwestern Historical Quarterly*, LI, 321.

[9]*United States Statutes at Large, 1846-1851*, IX, 844-849.

[10]Williams and Barker (eds.), *Writings of Sam Houston*, V, 352.

[11]Rupert Norval Richardson, *The Comanche Barrier to South Plains Settlement*, 145; Torrey Brothers to Medill, November 28, 1846, Ind. Off. Let. Recd.; Williams and Barker (eds.),*Writings of Sam Houston*, VIII, 41; Torrey & Co. to Houston January 9, 1847, Ind. Off. Let. Recd.

[12]Horton to Polk, October 21, 1846, Indian Affairs Papers, Texas State Archives, Austin, Texas.

[13]Henderson to Marcy, January 12, 1847, Ind. Aff. Papers.

[14]Carl, Prince of Solms-Braunfels, *Texas, 1844-1845*, pp. 1ff; Thomas W. Streeter, *Bibliography of Texas, 1795-1845: Part III United States and European Imprints Relating to Texas, Volume II, 1838-1845*, p. 571. Rosa Kleberg remembered Prince Carl as a "conceited fool." Rosa Kleberg, "Early Experiences in Texas," *Texas Historical Association Quarterly*, II, 172.

[15]Ferdinand Roemer, *Texas, Mit besonderer Rucksicht auf deutsche Auswanderung und die physischen Verhaltnisse des Landes*, 283ff.

[16]Neighbors to Medill, April 24, 1847, Ind. Off. Let. Recd. For Meusebach's role in the treaty making, see Rudolph Leopold B. Riesele, *The History of the German Settlements in Texas, 1831-1861*, p. 185.
For a less flattering account of Meusebach, see Armin O. Huber, "Frederic Armand Strubberg, Alias Dr. Shubbert, Town-Builder, Physician and Adventurer, 1806-1889," *West Texas Historical Association Year Book*, XXXVII, 37-71; see also a sympathetic account in Irene Marschall King, *John O. Meusebach: German Colonizer in Texas*.

[17]Copies of the treaty are in the Solms-Braunfels Archives, the Library of The University of Texas, Archives Division, Austin, Texas. Mrs. Irene Marschall King obtained the original manuscript of the treaty.

[18]Neighbors to Medill, April 13, 1847, Ind. Off. Let. Recd.

[19]Henry R. Schoolcraft, *Information Respecting the History, Condition and Prospects of the Indian Tribes of the United States*, 125ff. For use made of Neighbors's report by scholars see, Rupert Norval Richardson, *The Comanche Barrier to South Plains Settlement*, and Ernest Wallace and E. Adamson Hoebel, *The Comanches: Lords of the South Plains*. Kenneth F. Neighbours, "Letters and Documents about the Old Town of Fort Belknap," *West Texas Historical Association Year Book*, XXXV, 158.

[20]F. Schubert to Cappes, March 13, 1847, Solms-Braunfels Archive, Vol. 43, p. 131. According to Armin O. Huber, Schubert's real name was Frederic Armand Strubberg. Armin O. Huber, "Frederic Armand Strubberg, Alias Dr. Schubert, Town-Builder, Physician and Adventurer, 1806-1889, *West Texas Historical Association Year Book*, XXXVIII, 37.

[21]Hays to Neighbors, July 15, 1847, Ind. Off. Let. Recd.

[22]Neighbors to Medill, Austin, August 5, 1847, *House Executive Documents*, 30th Congress, 1st Session, Doc. No. 8, p. 897f.

[23]Neighbors to Medill, September 14, 1847, *House Executive Documents*, 30th Congress, 1st Session, Doc. No. 8, p. 902.

[24]Neighbors to Medill, August 6, 1847, Ind. Off. Let. Recd.

[25]Neighbors to Medill, March 2, 1848, *House Executive Documents*, 30th Congress, 2d Session, Doc. No. 1, p. 584f.

²⁶Neighbors to Medill, November 18, 1847, Ind. Off. Let. Recd.

²⁷Mrs. L. R. Clark, unpublished manuscript, L. S. Ross Papers, Baylor University; *A Memorial and Biographical History of McLennan, Falls, Bell, and Coryell Counties, Texas*, pp. 88-102; R. Henderson Shuffler, "Christmas in the Cross Timbers," *Texas Parade*, December, 1964, pp. 10-13.

²⁸Neighbors to Medill, February 16, 1848, Ind. Off. Let. Recd.

²⁹Neighbors to Medill, March 2, 1848, *House Executive Documents*, 30th Congress, 2d Session, Doc. No. 1, p. 579.

³⁰Neighbors to Medill, March 2, 1848, *Ibid.* 581. A Kickapoo village still exists in Coahuila near Muzquiz. Frank X. Tolbert, "Wisconsin Tribe Lives in Mexico," The Dallas *Morning News*, April 9, 1961. On board a troop ship in the Southwest Pacific the present writer once addressed a trooper from Mexico in Spanish only to be told he spoke none. He was a descendant of Indians from the United States. See also Alfonso Fabila, *La Tribu Kickapoo de Coahuila*.

³¹J. Martin, Map of Palo Pinto County, 1856, copy given writer by Mr. George Terrell, Newcastle, Texas.

³²See J. De Cordovas, *Map of the State of Texas*, compiled by Robert Creuzbaur, 1849. For landmarks mentioned on Neighbors's itinerary see also the excellent annotations of E. B. Ritchie, "Copy of Report of Colonel Samuel Cooper, Assistant Adjutant General of the United States, of Inspection Trip from Fort Graham to the Indian Villages on the Upper Brazos Made in June 1851," *Southwestern Historical Quarterly*, XLII, 327 ff. According to Ritchie the Caddo, Keechi, Waco, and Tawacano villages are submerged beneath the waters of Possom Kingdom Lake.

³³Ford, Memoirs (MS), IV, 725.

³⁴Ross Papers, File No. 2, Baylor University, typescript by Mrs. L. R. Clark, p. 34. José Maria, chief of the Anadarkos, was said to have been raised to a Master Mason, in a French Lodge in Canada. George W. Tyler, "Capture and Release of Colonel Norris' Surveying Party by Chief Jose Maria—A Masonic Incident—1838," Sue Watkins (ed.), *One League to Each Wind: Accounts of Early Surveying in Texas*, 203.

³⁵Neighbors to Medill, February 15, 1849, Ind. Off. Let. Recd.

³⁶John D. Affleck, *History of John C. Hays*, Part I, Library of The University of Texas, Archives Division, p. 737f.; Howard Lackman, "The Howard-Neighbors Controversy: A Cross-Section in West Texas Indian Affairs," *Panhandle-Plains Historical Review*, XXV, 8.

³⁷See Edward S. Wallace, *General William Jenkins Worth*.

³⁸Worth to Medill, December 27, 1848, Ind. Off. Let. Recd.

³⁹Marcy to Worth, December 10, 1848, *House Executive Documents*, 31st Congress, First Session, Vol. 5, Serial No. 573, Document 17, p. 271 f.

Chapter III

¹Hays to P. H. Bell, quoted in *Northern Standard*, February 10, 1849.

²Deas to Bryan, June 9, 1849, *Senate Executive Documents*, 31st Congress,

1st Session, Doc. No. 64, p. 25.

³Ford, Memoirs (MS), III, 504; IV, 719. Ford twice wrote that Torrey's was "north" of Waco. Pierce M. Butler's map of 1846 (courtesy of Fred R. Cotton) shows a trading house on the North Bosque *north* of Waco, designated as Warren's Trading House, but which doubtless belonged to Torrey Brothers in 1849, as they had one there in 1842. See Winfrey, *Texas Indian Papers, 1825-1843*, p. 125.

⁴See R. N. Richardson, "Jim Shaw the Delaware," *West Texas Historical Association Year Book*, III, 3-12. Neighbors to Harney, June 4, 1849, Records of the War Department Letters Received, National Archives, Washington, D.C. Hereafter referred to as Rec. War Dept. Let. Recd.

⁵Ford, Memoirs, (MS), III, 504f. According to Ford these boon companions both met tragic ends. Sullivan was killed and mutilated by the Comanches. Neal was killed in Texas by a negro soldier during Reconstruction.

⁶Idem.

⁷Idem.

⁸Ibid., 507.

⁹Noah Smithwick, *The Evolution of a State: or Recollections of Old Texas Days* (Austin, 1900), 181.

¹⁰Ford, *Memoirs* (MS), III, 507.

¹¹Ibid., 507-508.

¹²Ibid., 510.

¹³Ibid.

¹⁴In signing death certificates as adjutant during the Mexican War, Ford appended to the bottom, "Rest in Peace." As the casualties mounted this was shortened to R.I.P., which became his sobriquet. Walter Prescott Webb, *The Texas Rangers: A Century of Frontier Defense* (New York, 1955), 124.

¹⁵Ford, *Memoirs* (MS), III, 527.

¹⁶Ibid.

¹⁷Ibid., 511-512.

¹⁸Snake Spring was located on the John W. Dancy grant of land; Records of the General Land Office, File Number 2-310. Correspondence with Emsy H. Swaim of Eden was of assistance in locating the actual site of the spring. While the writer was in Eden on December 1, 1953, Swaim referred him to R. G. Armor, his cousin, who held the land upon which Snake Spring was located. Armor drove the writer to the vicinity. Since 1901 silt has filled the stream to a depth of four or five feet, and the only water present is in pools formed by seepage. Armor stated that when he came to the region in 1901, the watercourse was a bold, running stream, deep enough to swim a horse and full of bass and trout. He thought Snake Spring itself flowed out from under a ledge of limestone, and ran by the spot where later a horse rancher had his dwelling. On the edge of the dry rivulet grows a huge live oak tree. Just north of the limestone ledge, is a modern dwelling.
Armor died on December 26, 1963, E. H. Swaim to K. F. Neighbours and J. W. Williams, Eden, December 30, 1963.

299

[19]Dr. Henry Connelley of Missouri opened the trail to Chihuahua in 1839-1840. It was abandoned because of the caprice of Mexican duties. Joseph Carroll McConnell, *The West Texas Frontier*, I, 43f.

[19a]Clayton W. Williams, "That Topographical Ghost—Horsehead Crossing!", *Old West*, Winter, 1974, p. 51. Williams locates Horsehead Crossing in Survey No. 44, Block 9, H & G N Survey in Pecos County.

[20]Mr. Loyal Humphries of Balmorhea pointed out the location of these land marks to Mr. J. W. Williams and the writer on September 1, 1959. An acequia from Sandia Spring wound around the base of the boulder to irrigate the fields of the Mexican settlement of San José at a later date. Draining the tule lake lowered the water table so that the acequia no longer runs. The actual foundations of the fort were located by Loyal Humphries and shown to the writer as well as J. Dale Terry, Thomas Thompson, and Dennis Lynch on November 21, 1961. The fort is in Houston and Great Northern Railroad Company Survey, Block 13, Section 56. Humphries to K.F.N., March 28, 1964, interview and observation. The present writer pooled his knowledge of history with Mr. and Mrs. Humphries's knowledge of the terrain to locate this historic site.

[21]Ford, Memoirs (MS), III, 516f

[22]Ibid.

[23]*Texas Democrats*, June 23, 1849. There are stone ruins and other evidence at the Cherry Canyon Spring which slightly favor it as the site.

[24]Jo Ellis's Water Hole has not been identified. It could have been any one of the characteristic surface holes of water that form in the region during the periods of rainfall. Loyal Humphries to K.F.N., November 21, 1961.

[25]Ford, Memoirs (MS), III, 517. Loyal Humphries believes this was sotol, not mescal.

[26]Ibid.

[27]*Texas Democrat*, June 23, 1849. Carrizo Pass could not have been Bass Canyon, since Eagle Mountain is on one's left when seen from Bass Canyon and Eagle Spring is invisible. From B Bar Canyon Neighbors could have passed between Beach and Tumble Down mountains, and thence through Bean Canyon and out into the valley where the present railroad emerges; or he could have gone from B Bar Canyon down Sulphur Creek and out by present Alamore where Eagle Spring is definitely on the right. On November 24, 1961, Mrs. R. B. Durrill was kind enough to point out these land marks to the present writer. Our observations were borne out by the report and maps of Captain S. H. Carpenter, Company H, Tenth Cavalry, dated October 8, 1878, which I found in the National Archives, Washington, D. C.

[28]Ford, Memoirs (MS), III, 518.

[29]Whiting to Totten, June 10, 1849, *House Executive Documents*, 31st Congress, 1st Session, Doc. No. 5, p. 281.

[30]George Washington Trahern (A. Russell Buchanan, ed.), "Texas Cowboy from Mier to Buena Vista," *Southwestern Historical Quarterly*, LVIII, 85.

[31]Alvino Zambrano was a sergeant in the Spanish army stationed at the Presidio de San Elceario in 1816. Lista de los Destinos militares, "Provinicias Internas, Relaciones Despachadas, Licencias absolutas de soldados de las pro-

vincias Internas de Oriente y Occidente Tomo 188, Archivo General de la Nacion, Palacio Nacional, Mexico City.

³²Cuervo or Cuerbo Spring, according to Conkling, is one mile south of the Texas-New Mexico line in the northeast corner of Hudspeth County in township 1, block 68, section 1.

³³Richard H. Dillon, (ed.), *The Gila Trail: The Texas Argonauts and the California Gold Rush*, by Benjamin Butler Harris, p. 45ff.

³⁴Neighbors to Worth, March 7, 1849, Ind. Off. Let. Recd.

³⁵Neighbors to Brown, August 13, 1849, *ibid.*

³⁶Richardson, *Comanche Barrier*, 157.

³⁷For the significance of this attack, see Llerena Friend, *Sam Houston: The Great Designer*, 198.

Chapter IV

¹Bell to Senate, January 3, 1850, Governors Letters, *Texas State Archives*; H.P.N. Gammel (comp.), *The Laws of Texas*, 1822-1897, III, 773.

²Neighbors to Munroe, February 23, 1850, *House Executive Documents*, 31st Cong., 1st Sess. (Serial No. 577), Document No. 66, p. 2.

³*Northern Standard*, June 1, 1850.

⁴Neighbors to Bell, Doña Ana, March 23, 1850, MS.; Governors Letters.

⁵For the evidence substantiating Neighbors' charges, see Arie W. Poldervaart, *Black-Robed Justice: A History of the Administration of Justice in New Mexico*, 21-35; and Twitchell, *The Military Occupation of New Mexico*, 160-175.

⁶Antonio José Otero and Charles Beaubien.

⁷Neighbors to Bell, Santa Fe, April 14, 1850, Santa Fe Papers, Part II. United States Indian Agent James S. Calhoun also wrote his superior of the expected use of the Pueblo Indians in the power struggle between the military junta and its opposition in New Mexico. Calhoun was one of Taylor's secret agents sent to foment sentiment for a state government in New Mexico.

⁸Neighbors to Munroe, April 14, 1850, *ibid.*; Neighbors to Munroe, April 15, 1850, with enclosed documents; Munroe to Jones, April 16, 1850, *Senate Executive Documents*, 31st Cong., 1st Sess. (Serial No. 561), Document No. 56, pp. 10-15.

⁹Amelia Williams and Eugene C. Barker (eds.), *Writings of Sam Houston*, V, 187ff.

¹⁰Webster to Bell, August 5, 1850, Santa Fe Papers, Part II.

¹¹Holman Hamilton, *Zachary Taylor: Soldier of the Republic*, 155; Archives of St. Alban's Lodge No. 28, Jackson, West Feliciana Parish, Louisiana; Taylor to Senate, June 17, 1850, *Senate Executive Documents*, 31st Cong., 1st Sess. (Serial No. 561), Document No. 56, p. 1. Taylor replied to the Senate, "I state that no such orders have been given."

¹²Hamilton. *Zachary Taylor: Soldier in the White House*, 379.

[13]*Northern Standard*, July 20, 1850; Ernest Wallace, "Charles DeMorse: Pioneer Editor and Statesman" (Lubbock, 1943), 111.

[14]Neighbors to Bell, Santa Fe, April 14, 1850, Governors Letters.

[15]Calhoun to Brown, June 19, 1850, July 31, 1850, and August 13, 1850, in Annie Heloise Abel (ed.), *Official Correspondence of James S. Calhoun*, 212-253. According to Abel, James S. Calhoun was said variously to have been the brother, half-brother, or first cousin of John C. Calhoun. He was later the first territorial governor of New Mexico.

[16]Twitchell, *Military Occupation of New Mexico*, 197.

[17]*Northern Standard*, July 13, 1850.

[18]The first name of Judge Rabb was furnished by Walter P. Freytag, president of the Fayette County Historical Society, and by microfilm copies of the United States census for 1850 on file in the Eugene C. Barker Texas History Center.

[19]LaGrange Resolutions, July 6, 1850, Governors Letters.

[20]Hamilton, *Zachary Taylor: Soldier in the White House*, 375.

[21]Original letters are in Santa Fe Papers, Part II, Texas State Archives.

[22]*Northern Standard*, September 7, 1850.

[23]Bell to legislature, August 13, 1850, *Senate Journal, Third Legislature, Extra Session*, 5-17, and appendix.

[24]*Northern Standard*, September 7, 1850.

[25]Binkley, "The Question of Texas Jurisdiction in New Mexico under the United States," *Southwestern Historical Quarterly*, XXIV, 38.

[26]See also Emil Frederick Wurzbach, *Life and Memoirs of Emil Frederick Wurzbach: to which is appended some papers of John Meusebach*, translated by Frantz J. Dohmen, p. 14.

[27]*Texas State Gazette*, August 2, 1851; Frank Schmidt, County Clerk, Guadalupe County, Texas, to K. F. Neighbours, February 3, 1964, Notes and Letters Files of Kenneth F. Neighbours, Wichita Falls, Texas.

[28]Darden, Sketch of Neighbors (MS), Neighbors Letters, Private Collection.

[29]Alice A. Neighbors to K.F.N., San Antonio, July 29, 1948.

Chapter V

[1]*Texas State Gazette*, May 3, 1851.

[2]*House Journal Texas*, Fourth Legislature, Regular Session, 1851-1852, hereafter referred to as *House Journal*, 1851-1852.

[3]Gammel, *Laws of Texas*, III, 141.

[4]Lea to Lea, February 17, 1852, Ind. Off. Let. Recd.

[5]*House Journal*, 1851-1852, p. 873.

[6]James Irby to K.F.N., June 18, 1953.

[7]Connor owned land in Young County, but this league was in Haskell County. R. N. Richardson to K.F.N., March 2, 1964.

[8]Howard Lackman, "The Howard-Neighbors Controversy; A Cross-Section in West Texas Indian Affairs," *Panhandle Plains Historical Review*, XXV, 6.

[9]Neighbors to Maypenny, May 8, 1854, Ind. Off. Let. Recd.

Chapter VI

[1]Williams and Barker (eds.); *Writings of Sam Houston*, V, 353. Houston was not referring to Hays's expedition to Chihuahua as supposed by Howard's biographer, Howard Lackman, "The Howard-Neighbors Controversy: A Cross-Section in West Texas Indian Affairs," *Panhandle-Plains Historical Review*, XXV, 8. The reference was to United States Army officers.

[2]Rupert N. Richardson, "Removal of Indians from Texas in 1853: A Fiasco," *West Texas Historical Association Year Book*, XX, 89.

[3]Neighbors to Manypenny, August 6, 1853, Ind. Off. Let. Recd.; Howard to Manypenny, September 17, 1853, *ibid*.

[4]Hill to Neighbors, August 10, 1853, *ibid*.

[5]Neighbors to Manypenny, August 6, 1853, Ind. Off. Let. Recd.

[6]Report to Pease from Waco, probably forwarded by George B. Erath, April 16, 1854, Ind. Off. Let. Recd.

[7]Neighbors to Manypenny, May 2, 1854 to September 10, 1854, *ibid*.
A detailed account of this disagreeable issue is given in Kenneth F. Neighbours, Robert S. Neighbors in Texas, 1836-1859: A Quarter Century of Frontier Problems, MS, doctoral dissertation, The University of Texas, 1955, pp. 267-279.

Chapter VII

[1]Davis to Bell, September 19, 1853, Governors Letters, Texas State Archives, Austin, Texas.

[2]Bell to legislature, October of 1853, Indian Affairs Papers, Texas State Archives, Austin, Texas.

[3]Parker, *Unexplored Texas*, 116, 210.

[4]*Ibid.*, p. 218. See also Rupert N. Richardson, "Jim Shaw, The Delaware," *West Texas Historical Association Year Book*, III, 11.

[5]Abstract 541, Texas Emigration and Land Survey No. 294, General Land Office, Austin, Texas; Elihu Lewis Baldwin to K.F.N., Jean, Texas, April 9, 1955. The spring runs only in wet weather at present. In the great drought of 1886, Rancher Eichelberger watered 500 head of cattle there. The spring was a favorite camping place of emigrants and the military. It can easily be confused

with a spring presently also called Cottonwood Spring which is one mile north of Jean but two miles east of Preston road.

[6]This site is on the B. C. North Survey just east of the Sweeney Survey. J. M. Graham to K.F.N., November 13, 1962.

[7]Marcy to Cooper, January 15, 1855, Senate Executive Documents, 34th Cong., 1st Sess., Doc. No. 60, p. 4. Booker Bowen flew the present writer over the route of Neighbors and Marcy. Monte R. Lewis was with us.

[8]For a careful tracing of the route, see J. W. Williams and Ernest Lee, "Marcy's Exploration to Locate the Texas Indian Reservation in 1854," *West Texas Historical Association Year Book*, XXIII, 107-132. The present narrative differs in a few places.

[9]José Mares enroute to explore a route from Santa Fe to San Antonio camped at the same area on September 9, 1787.

[10]The present owners are Jerry and Louis Hodge. John Kay to K.F.N., May 8, 1962.

[11]File No. 1-1124, Wichita County, General Land Office, Austin, Texas, surveyed September 29, 1858, by James H. Swindells, District Surveyor; Conrad Neuhaus and Isaac Langston, Chain Carriers.

[12]Parker, *Unexplored Texas*, 135. Parker's account of the escort is difficult to reconcile with the terrain. He states that after the horse party left, the escort proceeded ten miles north to a tributary of the Big Wichita where they repaired the wagon wheels with pecan laths. This could only be the Holiday Creek. Several days later, the escort traveled north for several hours where they met Neighbors as stated. One could not travel north to strike the Little Wichita, but southwest—from the Big Wichita.

[13]Reuben Crenshaw to K.F.N., December 27, 1954.

[14]Marcy to Cooper, January 15, 1855, *Senate Executive Documents*, 34th Cong., 1st Sess., Doc. No. 60, p. 8.

[15]Reuben Dave Crenshaw to K.F.N., December 27, 1954. This alert fifteen-year-old high school boy took a specimen to his high school laboratory in Seymour where analysis proved it to be copper. Professor C. L. Bristol of Allen Military Academy, Bryan, Texas, found the same result. From samples of other ores picked up near Table Top by the writer, Bristol found traces of iron, nickel, potassium, arsenic, lead, and strontium. Bristol to K.F.N. January 12, 1955.

[16]Marcy to Cooper, January 15, 1855, *Senate Executive Documents*, 34th Cong., 1st Session, Doc. No. 60, p. 8f. Quannah Parker was also authority for this being a favorite camp site.

[17]W. A. Springer to K.F.N., Aspermont, Texas, December 31, 1954.

[18]Marcy to Cooper, January 15, 1855, *Senate Executive Documents*, 34th Cong., 1st Sess., Doc. 1, No. 60, p. 10f. R. Ernest Lee, his son, R. Ernest Lee, Junior, and the writer located Marcy's observatory point on Panther Canyon

[19]*The Missouri Republican*, Saint Louis, October 4, 1854; The New Orleans *Picayne*, October 9, 1854.

[20]W. A. Springer to K.F.N., Aspermont, Texas, December 31, 1954.

[21]Marcy to Cooper, January 15, 1855, *Senate Executive Documents*, 34th Cong., 1st Sess., Doc. No. 60, p. 11.

[22]W. A. Springer to K.F.N., Aspermont, Texas, December 31, 1954; Reuben Crenshaw to K.F.N., December 27, 1954.

[23]Reuben Crenshaw to K.F.N., Lake Kemp, Texas, December 27, 1954. On the spot observation by R. Ernest Lee, Dick Gore and the writer confirmed these facts.

[24]According to Colonel M. L. Crimmins, gentlemen of the Major's period were a small class whose training gave them the bravery and other qualities for leadership. The middle class survived by avoiding danger, the lower by running away from it. M. L. Crimmins, "Major Van Dorn in Texas," *West Texas Historical Association Year Book*, XVI, 127.

[25]Marcy to Cooper, January 15, 1855, *Senate Executive Documents*, 34th Cong., 1st Sess., Doc. No. 60, p. 12.

[26]Double Mountain is situated on rangeland presently owned by Sam A. "Slinging Sammy" Baugh, the football star.

[27]*The Missouri Republican*, Saint Louis, October 4, 1854.

[28]Marcy's observation post is two miles north of the present road which runs past the abandoned school house and about one mile west of the present ranch road from Kiowa Peak.
Double Mountain appears as one, two, or three peaks depending upon the direction from which it is seen.

[29]W. A. Springer to K.F.N., December 31, 1954.

[30]Marcy to Cooper, January 15, 1855, *Senate Executive Documente*, 34th Cong., 1st Sess., Doc. No. 60, p. 14.

[31]Ray Scurlock, who lived on Swenson Ranch at the foot of Flat Top Mountain, obligingly took a stick and on the damp earth drew the outline of the mountain for the writer.

[32]J. C. Yeary, Jr., Work Unit Conservationist, United States Department of Agriculture, Soil Conservation Service, Haskell, Texas, to K.F.N., January 27, 1965, Notes and Letter Files of Kenneth F. Neighbours, Wichita Falls, Texas. On March 27, 1965, R. E. Lee, Sr., W. B. Neighbours and I found these lakes described.

[33]Parker, *Unexplored Texas*, 168.

[34]Tiny Malone and Mrs. Jeffie Parsons, Parsons Grocery, to K.F.N., December 31, 1954.

[35]Parker, *Unexplored Texas*, 180.

[36]Stemm's farm embraced Survey MD-1002, Abstract 234; Survey 3-1038, Abstract 228, and Abstract 229; Survey 3-1036, Abstracts 188 and 190. His house was on Survey 3-1036, Abstract 190. Records of General Land Office, Austin, Texas.

[37]Ford, Memoirs (MS), IV, 535; John C. Duval, *Big Foot Wallace*, 110-118.
[38]Pease to Neighbors, March 16, 1855, Ind. Aff. Papers.

Chapter VIII

[1]Neighbors to Manypenny, September 16, 1854, *Annual Report of the Commissioner of Indian Affairs*, 1854, p. 158f.

[2]Alice Atkinson Neighbors to K.F.N., July 29, 1948, Notes and Letter Files of K. F. Neighbours, Wichita Falls, Texas.

[3]Steen to Calhoun, January 10, 1855, Ind. Off. Let. Recd. For Lyendecker's first name see, the United States census of 1850 for Bexar County; *Texas Indian Papers*, III, 154; and V. H. Torrance, "Simplicity Lost: Government Complicated," Fort Worth *Star Telegram*, May 12, 1963, p. 9. Calhoun was the son of John C. Calhoun.

[4]Hill to Neighbors, March 31, and April 3, 1855, Ind. Off. Let. Recd. According to one source, feeble remnants of Adaes, Keechies, Nacogdoches, Towiash, Enguisacoes and Tejas were included among the East Texas tribes on the reserve. Fannie McAlpine Clarke, "A chapter in the History of Young Territory," *Texas Historical Association Quarterly*, IX, 53.

[5]Hill to Neighbors, March 31, and April 3, 1855, Ind. Off. Let. Recd. The site was a beautiful location near the bluffs of Dry Creek. The springs still flow and scattered stones mark the site of the buildings. Carrie J. Crouch, *Young County: History and Biography*, 15f.

[6]Frank van der Stucken, Fredericksburg, to Conrad Neuhaus, Fort Belknap, June 22, 1855, Neuhaus Papers, private collection, restricted.

[7]Frank van der Stucken to Conrad Neuhaus, June 22, and August 30, 1855, Neuhaus Papers, private collection, restricted.

[8]Fan to Baylor, San Antonio, September 30, 1855, Baylor Family Letters, 1838-1858, photostatic copies in the Library of The University of Texas, Archives Division.

[9]Fan to Baylor, December 9, 1855, *ibid.*

Chapter IX

[1]Thomas B. Van Horne, *The Life of Major-General George H. Thomas*, 12f.

[2]Carl Coke Rister, *Robert E. Lee in Texas*, 23; George F. Price, *Across the Continent with the Fifth Cavalry*, 25.

[3]Douglas Southall Freeman, *R. E. Lee*, I, 360f.

[4]Shirley to Barnard, January 6, 1854, Ind. Off. Let. Recd.; Baylor to Neighbors, January 17, 1856, *ibid.*; Charles P. Roland and Richard C. Robbins, "The Diary of Eliza (Mrs. Albert Sidney) Johnston: The Second Cavalry Comes to Texas," *Southwestern Historical Quarterly*, LX, 485f; William Preston Johnston, *The Life of Gen. Albert Sidney Johnston*, p. 188.

[5]Baylor to Sister Fan, March 10, 1856, Baylor Family Letters, 1838-1858, Library of The University of Texas, Archives Division.

[6]Mrs. R. S. Neighbors to K.F.N., July 29, 1948.

[7]Neighbors to his wife, February 4, 1856, Neighbors Let. Pvt. Coll.

[8]Lambshead to Manypenny, May 1, 1856, Ind. Off. Let. Recd. Lambshead was born in Devon, England in 1805. Seymour V. Connor, *The Peters Colony of Texas*, 307; *West Texas Historical Association Year Book*, XXXIII, 14-16.

[9]Neighbors to Manypenny, Comanche Agency, May 14, 1856, Ind. Off. Let. Recd.

[10]Elm Fork and Clear Fork west of Phantom Hill have since switched names.

[11]Lee to Neighbors, May 22, 1856, Neighbors Let. Pvt. Coll.

[12]Lee to Neighbors, May 24, 1856, *ibid.*

[13]Rister, *R. E. Lee in Texas*, 40.

[14]*Ibid.*, 42.

[15]Ross to Neighbors, June 30, 1856, Ind. Off. Let. Recd.

[16]Mrs. Horace Ledbetter to K.F.N., April 3, 1963, Notes and Letter Files of K. F. Neighbors, Wichita Falls, Texas.

[17]Dallas *Herald*, July 6, 1856.

[18]Colonel M. L. Crimmins (ed.), "Colonel J. K. F. Mansfield's Report of the Inspection of the Department of Texas in 1856," *Southwestern Historical Quarterly*, XLII, 127.

[19]Comanche Sam, christened Sam Houston by his captors, was captured as an eight or ten year old boy when Colonel John H. Moore destroyed the Comanche Village on the Colorado in 1840. He was reared by Judge William N. Eastland and returned to his people by treaty. John Holmes Jenkins, III (ed.) *Recollections of Early Texas: The Memoirs of John Holland Jenkins*, p. 175 f.

Chapter X

[1]Petition signed by thirty-seven citizens including Peter Harmonson, J. R. King, L. L. Williams, W. R. Peveler, Jesse Sutton, James Duff, William Burkett, W. N. P. Marlin, and Edward J. Gurley, Ind. Off. Let. Recd.

[2]One of the cards was sent to the writer by Mrs. R. S. Neighbors, Jr., Christmas of 1950.

[3]Baylor applied for a leave through Major James Belger, U.S.A., Baylor's brother-in-law, but Commissioner Manypenny informed Belger that the application must come through Major Neighbors. Manypenny to Neighbors, January 21, 1857, Ind. Off. Let. Sent.

[4]Baylor to Fan, April 5, 1856, Baylor Family Letters, 1838-1858, Library of The University of Texas, Archives Division.

[5]Neighbors to Denver, July 15, and September 3, 1857, Ind. Off. Let. Recd.

[6]Neighbors to Peace Commissioners, June 16, 1859, *Senate Executive Documents*, 36th Cong., 1st Sess., Vol. 1, Doc. No. 2, p. 661.
Lieutenant William E. Burnet stated that Baylor's discharge involved public money. Burnet to Burnet, July 13, 1859, Raymond Estep, "Lieutenant William E. Burnet Letters: Removal of the Texas Indians and the Founding of Fort Cobb," *The Chronicles of Oklahoma*, XXXVIII, 373, and 381.

[7]Baylor to Mix, Cactus Hill, Wise County, July 6, 1859, Ind. Off. Let. Recd. No evidence was found in the National Archives that Baylor's accounts were ever paid.

[8]George Wythe Baylor to O. W. Baylor, January, 1900, photostatic copy in the Texas Collection of Baylor University.

[9]Kenneth F. Neighbours, "Chapters from the History of Texas Indian Reservations," *West Texas Historical Association Year Book*, XXXIII, 3ff; J. R. Quinby, *et al*, *Grain Sorgum Production in Texas*, Bulletin 912, College Station, Texas, Texas Agricultural Experiment Station, July, 1958, p. 17.

[10]Lee to Neighbors, Camp Cooper, June 16, 1857, Neighbors Let. Prt. Coll.

[11]Leeper to Neighbors, February 12, 1858, *ibid*. For the remarkable career of the girl captive, Tomasa, who later married Joel Chandler, himself part Cherokee, see George W. Conover, *Sixty Years in Southwest Oklahoma: or The Autobiography of George W. Conover*, Anadarko, N. T. Plummer, 1927; and Hugh D. Corwin, *The Kiowa Indians: Their History and Life Stories*. Tomasa married secondly George W. Conover.

Chapter XI

[1]Frost to Runnels, February 8, 1858, Cora, Comanche County, Indian Affairs Papers, 1845-1859, Texas State Archives, Austin, Texas.

[2]Frost to Runnels, January 8, 1858, Governors Letters, Texas State Archives, Austin, Texas.

[3]Neighbors to Runnels, January 20, 1858, *ibid*.

[4]Givens to John Withers, assistant adjutant general, February 12, 1858, *ibid*.

[5]Citizens to Givens, February 1, 1858, *ibid*.

[6]Swindells to Neighbors, June 10, 1858, Ind. Off. Let. Recd.

[7]See page 467f.

[8]Baylor *et al* to Leeper, February 1, 1858, Ind. Off. Let. Recd.

[9]Certificate of Chandler *et al*, July 7, 1858, *ibid*.

[10]Statement of W. G. Preston, August 9, 1858, *ibid*.

[11]Von Hagan to Major [Neighbors?], March 27, 1858, Ind. Off. Let. Recd.

[12]Statement of Lambshead *et ux*, Clear Fork Camp, March 30, 1858, *ibid*.

[13]Mother to Baylor, June 4, 1858, Baylor Family Letters, 1838-1858, Library of The University of Texas, Archives Division.

[14]Proclamation of President Sam Houston, Washington-on-the Brazos, October 19, 1844, Proclamations & Colony Contracts No. 48 IV/57, 1842-1844, pp. 95-97, Texas State Archives, Austin, Texas; *Telegraph and Texas Register*, January 8, 1845. A portrait of Baylor hangs in the Alamo Annex.

[15]*Ibid*.; Fan to Baylor, December 30, n.d., John R. Baylor, Miscellaneous Personal Papers, Library of The University of Texas, Archives Division; George Wythe Baylor to O. W. Baylor, editor of *Baylor Magazine*, a photostatic copy,

Texas Collection, Baylor University, January, n.d., 1900; J. C. Eldridge, Department of State, to Benjamin F. Hill, February 15, 1845; Domestic Correspondence, Texas State Archives, Austin, Texas. For biographical sketches and references to John R. Baylor, see O. M. Roberts, Texas, 292; the *Handbook of Texas*; John L. Waller, "Colonel George Wythe Baylor," *Southwestern Social Science Quarterly*, XXIV, 24-28; and Charles Summerfield Walker, A History of the Confederate Territory of Arizona (MS) M.A. Thesis, Southern Methodist University, 1933. For a sketch and picture of John R. Baylor, see J. Evvetts Haley, *Men of Fiber*, p. 5f.

[16]Fred R. Cotten placed a copy of *The White Man* in the Eugene C. Barker Texas History Center of The University of Texas.

[17]Neighbors to his wife, San Antonio, March 12, 1858, Neighbors Let. Pvt. Coll.

[18]Charles Mullins to G. M. Bryan, Lampasas, March 19, 1858, Ind. Off. Let. Recd.

[19]Named for John R. Hubbard, T. E. & L. surveyor.

[20]Ford to Runnels, Camp Runnels, March 31, 1858, Indian Affairs Papers, 1845-1859, Texas State Archives, Austin, Texas; Ford, Memoirs (MS), IV, 684f, Library of The University of Texas, Archives Division.

[21]Ford to Runnels, Brazos Agency, April 7, 1858, Governors Letters, Texas State Archives, Austin, Texas.

[22]*Ibid.*

[23]Ford to Runnels, Camp Runnels, April 14, 1858, *ibid.*

[24]Ford's affidavit to Hawkins, Austin, November 22, 1858, Ind. Off. Let. Recd.

[25]Burleson to Hawkins, Austin, November 22, 1858, *ibid.*

[26]As Givens was evacuating Fort Phantom Hill, it burned, it was said. C. C. Rister, "The Border Post of Phantom Hill," *The West Texas Historical Association Year Book*, XIV, 9f.

[27]Ribble to K.F.N., interview, Graham, September 10, 1848.

[28]C. E. Barnard to G. Barnard, May 25, 1858, Ind. Off. Let. Recd.

[29]James K. Greer, (ed.) *A Texas Ranger and Frontiersman: The Days of Buck Barry in Texas, 1845-1906*, p. 123; Joseph Carroll McConnell, *The West Texas Frontier: or A Descriptive History of Early Times in Western Texas*, I, 295.

[30]Ross to Neighbors, May 31, 1858, Ind. Off. Let. Recd.

[31]Baylor to *Dallas Herald*, April 1, 1858.

[32]Neighbors to Mix, San Antonio, April 22, 1858, Ind. Off. Let. Recd. Copies of these reports went to Governor Runnels which probably accounts for Neighbors's detractors being familiar with their contents.

[33]Baylor to Dallas *Herald*, April 1, 1858.

[34]Neighbors to Mix, Brazos Agency, April 2, 1858, Ind. Off. Let.

[35]Joseph Carroll McConnell, *The West Texas Frontier*, p. 167.

[36]Fred R. Cotten to K.F.N., August 5, 1954. J. Evetts Haley, *Charles Good-*

night: Cowman and Plainsman, p. 104.

[37]Ford to Runnels, Camp Runnels, May 23, 1858, Governors Letters, Texas State Archives, Austin, Texas.

[38]Ford's affidavit to Hawkins, November 22, 1858, Ind. Off. Let. Recd.

[39]Frank Brown, Annals of Travis County and of the City of Austin (MS), Chapter XIX, 17, Texas State Archives, Austin, Texas.

[40]Census by Agent Ross, July 5, 1858; Leeper to Neighbors, June 30, 1858, Ind. Off. Let. Recd.

[41]For a study of the Reserve Indian schools. see Kenneth F. Neighbours, "Masons and Texas Indian Schools," *Texas Grand Lodge Magazine*, No. 10, XXVI, pp. 313-317.

[42]Thrall, *History of Methodism in Texas*, 128.

[43]Henry Williams, Junior, to K.F.N., Newcastle, September 8, 1948.

[44]Richardson, *Comanche Barrier to South Plains Settlement*, 250.

[45]Nelson to Buchanan, Waco, July 15, 1858, Ind. Off. Let. Recd. Nelson was later a Confederate general.

[46]Baylor to Barry, Buchanan County, August 2, 1858, James Buckner Barry Papers, 1848-1912, Library of The University of Texas, Archives Division.

[47]See the Texas Emigration and Land map of 1859, and the General Land Office Map of 1859 of Young County. General Land Office, Austin.

[48]Withers to commanding officer at Fort Belknap, October 6, 1858, Ind. Off. Let. Recd. Expecting to be relieved next day, Van Camp's men had about shot up their ammunition.

[49]Neighbors to Mix, October 19, 1858, Ind. Off. Let. Recd.

[50]Van Dorn to Withers, October 5, 1858, Dallas *Herald*, October 10, 1858.

[51]Joseph B. Thoburn and Isaac M. Holcomb, *A History of Oklahoma*, 71; George F. Price, *Across the Continent With the Fifth Cavalry*, p. 80.
Camp Van Camp at present Newcastle was named in honor of the Lieutenant. Van Camp was a protege of Thaddeus Stevens. Typescript of Mrs. L. R. Clark, Ross Papers, Letter File No. 2, Texas Collection Baylor University, Waco, Texas.

[52]Neighbors to Mix, San Antonio, September 16, 1858, *Senate Executive Documents*, 35th Cong. 2d Sess., Vol. 1, Doc. No. 1, p. 526.

[53]Quoted in Homer Thrall, *Pictorial History of Texas*, 468.

[54]Barnard to Cook, October 1, 1858, Brazos Agency, Dallas *Herald*, September 20, 1858.

[55]List of employees at Brazos Agency, March 31, 1858, Ind. Off. Let. Recd.

[56]Barbara Neal Ledbetter (ed.), *The Diary of a Frontiersman, 1858-1859*, p. 8f.

Chapter XII

[1]Nelson to Hawkins, Palo Pinto, Bell County, October 26, 1858, Ind. Off. Let. Recd.

[2]Baylor to Thompson, Belknap, November 22, 1858, *ibid.*

[3]Baylor to Barry, August 2, 1858, James Buckner Barry Papers, 1848-1912, Library of The University of Texas, Archives Division.

[4]Alexander, *et al,* to Thompson, October 29, 1858, *ibid.*

[5]Ford's Affidavit to Hawkins, November 22, 1858, Ind. Off. Let. Recd.

[6]Voucher No. 10, *ibid.*

Chapter XIII

[1]Rector to Mix, Fort Smith, October 22, 1858, and October 23, 1858, *Senate Executive Documents*, 36th Cong., 1st Sess., Vol. 1, Doc. No. 2, p. 583-586.
The baseless myth that the Comanches were on a peaceful mission under United States auspices is still perpetuated in the twentieth century.
Rector to Thompson (confidential), November n.d., 1858, Ind. Off. Let. Recd. Albert Pike referred to Elias Rector as the Fine Arkansas Gentleman who got drunk on whiskey once a week and sobered up on wine. James, *The Raven,* 186.

[2]Emory to Rector, Fort Arbuckle, December 14, 1858, Ind. Off. Let. Recd.

[3]Sturm to Ross, December 28 and 30, 1858, *Senate Executive Documents,* 36th Cong., 1st Sess., Vol. 1, Doc. No. 2, pp. 588-590.
Joseph Carroll McConnell locates Choctaw Tom's camp at "Indian Hole on Elm Creek about six miles north and a little east of Palo Pinto." Joseph Carroll McConnell, *The West Texas Frontier: Or a Descriptive History of Early Times in Western Texas.*

[4]George Ely was present when John M. Stephen stepped upon the wagon to look at his dead son. When the sheet was lifted, Stephen staggered and nearly fell. J. W. Williams, Ely's grandson, to K.F.N., January 24, 1961. See also Ely's own story in Emanuel Dubbs (ed.), *Pioneer Days in the Southwest from 1850 to 1879,* p. 261.

[5]Neighbors to Denver, Brazos Agency, January 30, 1859, Ind. Off. Let. Recd. The Major left for Waco on February 1, 1859.

[6]Coombes, *The Diary' of a Frontiersman,* 38.

[7]Hubert Howe Bancroft, *The North Mexican States and Texas,* II, 410. The names of the men were Daniel Thornton, J. Hightower, E. Fireash, T. Willie, W. E. Motheral, W. W. McNeal, Robert Duval, J. P. Harris, W. Fitzgerald, A. L. Braw, R. Dupuy, W. J. F. Lowder, W. Wood, J. Barnes, H. Highsaw, J. R. Waller, George Hardin, Samuel Stephens, and one Dalton. According to Mrs. Barbara Ledbetter, one Fonderberg was in on the killing.

[8]Ford to E. J. Gurley, January 22, 1859, *Senate Executive Documents,* 36th Cong., 1st Sess., Vol. 1, Doc. No. 2, p. 606.

[9]Neighbors to Denver, Waco, February 14, 1859, *ibid.,* 604.

[10]Ford, Memoirs (MS), IV, 765.

[11]Ford to Runnels, Camp Leon, February 16, 1859, Governor's Letters.

[12]Ford, Memoirs (MS), IV, 765.

[13]W. S. Oldham to Messrs. E. M. Pease, John L. Haynes, James F. Johnson, James H. Raymond, Jno. M. Swisher and William Alexander, *Texas State Gazette*, March 12, 1859.

[14]A. W. Terrell, "Recollections of General Sam Houston," *The Southwestern Historical Quarterly*, XVI, 120.

[15]Ford to Runnels, Camp Leon, April 12, 1859, Governors Letters, Texas State Archives, Austin, Texas.

[16]Barnard to Runnels, Waco, May 4, 1859, *ibid.*

[17]Baylor, Nelson, Oliver Loving, *et al* to the agents, April 25, 1859, Ind. Off. Let. Recd.

[18]Ford to Wilcox, April 12, 1859, *ibid.*

[19]Clipping in Neighbors Let. Pvt. Coll., signed by J. G. Thomas.

[20]Neighbors's wise provision for his associates assured them of a future competence. Several later married Indian women. Some of these agency employees were partly Indian themselves, such as Joseph Chandler and J. J. Sturm. Hugh D. Corwin, *The Kiowa Indians: Their History and Life Stories*; George W. Conover, *Sixty Years in Southwest Oklahoma; Carter, On the Border with Mackenzie*, 527.

[21]Sturm to Ross, May 8, 1859; Coombes to Neighbors, May 8, 1859, Ind. Off. Let. Recd. According to Burnet he had with him one hundred Indians and only two soldiers. Burnet to Burnet, May 9, 1859, Raymond Estep, "Lieutenant W. E. Burnett [sic]: Notes on Removal of Indians from Texas to Indian Territory," *The Chronicles of Oklahoma*, XXXVIII, pp. 298-301.

[23]Robert Birdsall to Neighbors, San Antonio, Ma- 23, 1859, Neighbors Let. Pvt. Coll; George F. Pierce, "Foot Prints Across the Continent," *Texas Christian Advocate*, quoted in *Northern Standard*, September 3, 1859.

[23]Neighbors to his wife, May 17, 1859, Neighbors Let. Pvt. Coll. Ferdinand von Herf had been a member of the German idealistic and intellectual community of young bachelors of Bettina.

[24]Plummer to Assistant General, May 23, 1859, *Senate Executive Documents*, 36th Cong., 1st Sess., Vol. 1, Doc. No. 2, p. 644f. Baylor lost seven men; four killed in the battle; three mortally wounded who died that night. Ida Lasater Huckaby, *Ninety-Four Years in Jack County, 1854-1948*, p. 57f.
Lieutenant William E. Burnet stated that he and Ross's son led the Indians. He believed Baylor's band was impressed by the range and accuracy of the two Minie rifles used by the Indians. Raymond Estep, (ed.), "Lieutenant William E. Burnet Letters: Removal of the Texas Indians and the founding of Fort Cobb," *The Chronicles of Oklahoma*, XXXVIII, 372. In 1848 Claude Etienne Minie a Captain in the French Army perfected a new conoidal bullet, hollow at the base, which expanded to engage the rifles in the bore of the piece thereby allowing greater range, velocity and accuracy. This revolutionary principle was adopted by the United States Army in 1855. John K. Mahon, "Civil War Infantry Assault Tactics," *Military Affairs*, XXV, 59.

[25]Neighbors to Ross, Comanche Agency, May 26, 1859, Ind. Off. Let. Recd.

[26]Neighbors to Evans, May 26, 1859, Comanche Agency, Neighbors Let. Pvt. Coll.

[27]Neighbors to Evans, Comanche Agency, May 27, 1859, Neighbors Let. Pvt. Coll.

[28]Neighbors to Mix, Comanche Agency, May 27, 1859, *Senate Executive Documents*, 36th Cong., 2d Sess., Vol. 1, Doc. No. 2, p. 643f.

[29]Ross to Neighbors, May 26, 1859, *Senate Executive Documents*, 35th Cong., 2d Sess., Vol. 1, Doc. No. 1, p. 643f.
H. A. Hamner shot the Indian. In Jacksboro during the Civil War, Hamner was "swung to a cottonwood limb" under undisclosed circumstances. Huckaby, *Ninety-Four Years in Jack County*, 96. Hamner also killed a man in South Texas. See Ben E. Pengenot, *Paso del Aguila*, p. 84.

[30]*Senate Executive Documents*, 35th Cong. 2d Sess., Vol. 1, Doc. No. 1, p. 643f.

[31]The seizure of government supply trains was admitted by one of the band, James Buckner Barry, James K. Greer (ed.), *A Texas Ranger and Frontiersman: The Days of Buck Barry in Texas*, 1845-1906, p. 115.

[32]Carrie J. Crouch, *Young County: History and Biography*, 22.

[33]W. K. Baylor, "The Old Frontier: Events of Long Ago," *The Bloody Trail*, 51f. The Baylor side of the fight has been well publicized. See John M. Elkins, *Indian Fighting on the Texas Frontier*, and Charles Goodnight's account in J. Evetts Haley, *Charles Goodnight*, 26ff.

[34]Raymond Estep, "Lieutenant William E. Burnet Letters: Removal of the Texas Indians and the founding of Fort Cobb," *The Chronicles of Oklahoma*, XXXVIII, 373.

[35]J. Evetts Haley, *Charles Goodnight: Cowman and Plainsman*, 30.

[36]William N. P. Marlin owned land which touched the Brazos River one and one-half miles beyond the west line of the reserve, Map of Young County, General Land Office, Austin, Texas, December 7, 1941. According to W. A. Ribble, however, the fight took place seven miles west of Graham, which agrees with Plummer's report.

[37]Neighbors to Evans, Comanche Agency, May 30, 1859, Neighbors Let. Pvt. Coll.

[38]Neighbors to Greenwood, Brazos Agency, June 10, 1859, *Senate Executive Documents*, 36th Cong., 1st Sess., Vol. 1, Doc. No. 2, p. 648ff.

[39]Neighbors to Rector, May 28, 1859, Ind. Off. Let. Recd.

[40]Neighbors to Greenwood, July 4, 1859, *Senate Executive Documents*, 36th Cong., 1st Sess., Vol. 1, Doc. No. 2, p. 683f.

[41]Runnels to Nelson et al, June 6, 1859, *ibid.*, p. 655.

[42]Neighbors to commissioners, June 16, 1859, *ibid.*, 662.

[43]Smith to Neighbors and Ross, n.d., *Senate Executive Documents*, 36th Cong., 1st Sess., Vol. 1, Doc. No. 2, p. 663.

[44]Erath to Neighbors and Ross, Russell's Store, June 20, 1859, *ibid.*, 663.

[45]Neighbors to Greenwood, Brazos Agency, June 25, 1859, *ibid.*, 665.

[46]For a fanciful account of Brown's entry, see James Pike, *Scout and Ranger: Being the personal Adventures of James Pike of the Texas Rangers in 1859-60*, p. 24, 30, 34.

[47]Brown to Neighbors, July 14, 1859, *Senate Executive Documents* 36th Cong., 1st Sess., Doc. No. 2, p. 689.

[48]Neighbors to Brown, July 17, 1859, *ibid.*, 690f.

[49]Plummer to Neighbors, Brazos Agency, July 16, 1859, *ibid.*, 691.

[50]Brown to Neighbors, July 22, 1859, Governors Letters, Texas State Archives, Austin, Texas.

[51]Brown to Runnels, July 22, 1859, *ibid.* For the political ramifications, see John Henry Brown, *Indians Wars and Pioneers of War*, p. 121.

[52]Leeper to Neighbors, Comanche Agency, July 24, 2859, *Senate Executive Documents*, 36th Cong., 1st Sess., Doc. No. 2, p. 692f.

[53]Plummer to Brown, July 26 (Brown thought July 28), 1859, Governors Letters.

[54]Brown to Plummer, July 28, 1859, *ibid.*

[55]Neighbors to Brown, July 29, 1859, *ibid.*

[56]Brown to Neighbors, July 29, 1859, *ibid.*

[57]The grand jury returned a true bill against James Anderson. Minutes of the District Court of Young County, I, November 27, 1958, p. 8.

[58]Brown to Neighbors, July 31, 1859, Governors Letters.

[59]It is interesting to note thus early the sharp cleavage into Union and extreme state rights parties. Neighbors correctly divined that Runnels was a secessionist. It is interesting to note also that the issue, at least on the frontier, was not slavery but the defense of the frontier.

[60]Neighbors to Evans, Belknap, July 20, 1859, Neighbors Let. Pvt. Coll.

[61]Brown to Runnels, Belton, September 5, 1859, Governors Letters, Texas State Archives, Austin, Texas.

Chapter XIV

[1]Richardson, *Comanche Barrier*, 257; and Indian Office Letters Received. Marlin gathered 200 head of estrays; 500 horses and cattle remained at large belonging to Brazos Reserve Indians. Ross to Greenwood, May 30, 1860, *ibid.*

[2]Special Order No. 57, July 18, 1859, Ind. Off. Let. Recd.

[3]Neighbors to Leeper, July 25, 1859, *ibid.*

[4]Neighbors to Thomas, July 25, 1859, *ibid.*

[5]Thomas to Neighbors, July 26, 1859; Neighbors to Thomas, July 27, 1859, *ibid.*

[6]R. S. Neighbors, "Memorandum of Travel from Brazos Agency, Texas, to False Ouachita Agency, C.N.," Indian Office Letters Received.

[7]Neighbors, "Memorandum of Travel," Indian Office Letters Received. The rancho was a quarter mile above the intersection of present Highway 380 and Salt Creek in Survey 431, Abstract 638. George A. Terrell to K.F.N., Fort Belknap, October 24, 1959.

[8]Swindells to Neighbors, Belknap, July 23, 1859, *ibid.* In an interesting aside at present obscure, Swindells added, "P.S. If you will look in the last *"Herald,"* you will find Dick Pryor's 'Sphincter Arm' muscle, and the orifice encircled thereby, distinctly shown—In close proximity too, you will find his brains, or what designates as such." Pryor had just become editor of the *Herald*. It does not appear how he had aroused the ire of Swindells and Neighbors.

[9]Abstract 541, Texas Emigration and Land Company Survey No. 294, General Land Office, Austin, Texas.

[10]J. W. Williams, "The Van Dorn Trials," *The Southwestern Historical Quarterly*, XLIV (January, 1941), map on p. 334.

[11]Neighbors, "Memorandum of Travel," Indian Office Letters Received.

[12]Jeanne V. Harrison, "Matthew Leeper Confederate Agent at the Wichita Agency, Indian Terrtory," *The Chronicles of Oklahoma*, XLVII, 246.

[13]Brown to Thomas, Camp Nowlin, August 6, 1859; Runnels to Brown, August 4, 1859; Murphy to Brown, Cottonwood Spring, August 4, 1859; Governors Letters, MS, Texas State Library, Archives Division, Austin, Texas. Brown acted before receiving the Governor's order to trail the Indians.

[14]Williams, "The Van Dorn Trials," *The Southwestern Historical Quarterly*, XLIV (January, 1941), 333. Williams's grandfather, George B. Ely, one of Brown's party, identified the site of Camp Nowlin for Williams. Here Ely and Smith Estes fell ill of dysentery. Ely probably saved his life by cooling his fever in the river's water, contrary to doctor's orders. Estes followed orders and died. See also Ely's account in Emanual Dubs (ed.) *Pioneer Days in the Southwest from 1850 to 1879*, p. 262.

[15]Brown to Runnels, August 19, 1859, Governors Letters.

[16]C. D. Patterson, Map of Clay County, c. 1882. One of the army officers, William E. Burnet, son of President David G. Burnet, wrote his father that four companies of cavalry and two of infantry would accompany the expedition. He estimated the total number involved in the emigration at 2500 with a like amount of livestock. Burnet to Burnet, Camp Cooper, July 28, 1859, "Lieutenant William E. Burnet Letters: Removal of the Texas Indians and the Founding of Fort Cobb," Raymond Estep (ed.), *The Chronicles of Oklahoma*, XXXVIII, 377. Also see H. Bailey Carroll, "Stewart A. Miller and the Snively Expedition of 1843," *Southwestern Historical Quarterly*, LIV, 269, Andy Hardy took the writer and Troy Kelly to the mouth of the Big Wichita which is about two miles below where it debouches into the bed of the Red River—the two rivers use the same bed for this distance before merging.

[17]Neighbors to his wife, August 8, 1859, Neighbors Letters, Private Collection.

[18]Major Neighbors was a delegate to the temperance convention in Austin at an earlier date. Mrs. R. S. Neighbors to K.F.N., August 30, 1948.

[19]Neighbors to his wife, Camp on Red River, C.N., August 8, 1859, Neighbors Let. Pvt. Coll.

20Brown to Thomas, Camp Nowlin, August 6, 1859; Thomas to Brown, Copperas Creek, August 8, 1859, Governors Letters. Because of the rough terrain on the left bank of Whiskey Creek at its mouth, the early road ran up the right bank about three miles before crossing. O. D. Worsham to K.F.N., Henrietta interview, August 25, 1859.

21*Supreme Court of the United States, October Term, 1894, No. 4, Original, The United States, Complainant, vs. The State of Texas, In Equity* (Washington, 1894), I, 172. Steen's map was pointed out to me by Mr. J. W. Williams, and the National Archives confirmed it. Victor Gondos, Jr., Archivist in Charge of Old Army Branch, to K.F.N., May 8, 1958, Notes and Letter Files of K. F. Neighbours, Wichita Falls, Texas.

· 22Neighbors, "Memorandum of Travel," Indian Office Letters Received; Neighbors to Blain, August 9, 1859, *ibid.*

23Neighbors, "Memorandum of Travel," *ibid.*; T. A. Washington to Thomas, August 1, 1859, *ibid.*; Neighbors to Greenwood, August 18, 1859, *Senate Executive Documents*, 36th Congress, 1st Session, Document No. 2, p. 697.

24Steen's map indicated that his route skirted to the west around the Ketchi range. A reconnaisance by the writer and Mr. J. W. Williams indicated that the most practical route from the Ketchi range to the Washita would have been up the right bank of the Delaware Creek. The deep sand and scrub oaks of the crests of the rolling hills on each side of Delaware Creek would have been too rough to have been travelled conveniently by the wagons and carts of the expedition. An old map in the office of Mr. Fred Harrison and son, abstractors, Anadarko, shows an old road along the right bank of Delaware Creek which indicates the practicability of the conjecture. Map of Survey of Township 6, Range 9 West, dated 1873. William E. Burnet, however, stated that, "this was scrub black jack—and the sand so deep that the teams could hardly drag the wagons through it: This lasted until we came within about a mile of the river; then there is a flat, in many places liable to overflow, and a fringe of Cotton Woods just on the bank of the River," Burnet to Burnet September 5, 1859, Camp Cooper, "Lieutenant William E. Burnet Letters: Removal of the Texas Indians and the Founding of Fort Cobb," Raymond Estep (ed.), *The Chronicles of Oklahoma*, XXXVIII, p. 378.

25Neighbors, "Memorandum of Travel," Ind. Off. Let. Recd. This side was corroborated by a composite map of a portion of Caddo County prepared by Edward F. Moran, Jr., County Surveyor, who had his information from two aged Kiowas, Tom Dietrich and Enoch Smokey, whose knowledge is heresay, but considered reliable as both men are highly respected by both races. Moran also found an Indian trail crossing just below Sugar Creek on survey notes of Township 7, North 9 West, by H. C. L. Hackbust, October 10-21, 1873, which doubtless marks the site of Steen's Crossing, one sixteenth of a mile below the mouth of Sugar Creek on the False Washita River.

26Neighbors, "Memorandum of Travel," Ind. Off. Let. Recd.; Edward F. Moran, Jr., to K.F.N., March 28, 1959. The camp site was on the branch of Tonkawa Creek in the first big canyon east of present Indian City.

27Mix to Neighbors, July 22, 1859; Neighbors to Mix, August 20, 1859; Cutts to Greenwood, July 28, 1859; Mix to Neighbors, August 5, 1859; Neighbors to Greenwood, September 2, 1859; Greenwood to Neighbors, August 11, 1859, Ind. Off. Let. Recd.

28Neighbors to Greenwood, September 3, 1859, *Senate Executive Documents*, 36th Congress, 1st Session, Document No. 2, p. 700.

29Blain to Rector, August 20, 1859, Ind. Off. Let. Recd. According to Edward

F. Moran, Jr., a two storied agency building was later erected at this site. This proved to be a temporary location.

[30]Neighbors to Emory, August 26, 1859; Ind. Off. Let. Recd.

[31]Ida Lasater Huckaby, *Ninety-four Years in Jack County*, p. 76f.

[32]Ross to Neighbors, August 25, 1859, Ind. Off. Let. Recd.

[33]Leeper to Neighbors, August 31, 1859, *ibid.*

[34]Neighbors to Greenwood, September 2, 1859; Neighbors to Rector September 2, 1859; Neighbors to Greenwood, September 3, 1859, Senate Executive Documents, 36th Congress, 1st Session, Document No. 2, p. 700.

[35]Neighbors to his wife, n.d., clipping from the *Union Democrat*, Seguin, n.d.; Neighbors to his wife, September 4, 1859; Bickel to Mrs. R. S. Neighbors, June 8, 1860, Neighbors Letters, Private Collection.

[36]Deposition of an aged Caddo woman, Mary Inkanish, to Ross Hume, August 25, 1929, Fort Cobb, Indian Affairs Papers, Texas State Archives, Austin, Texas.

[37]Neighbors to his wife, September 4, 1859; Neighbors to his wife, n.d., *The Union Democrat*, n.d., Neighbors Letters, Private Collection. The 1,000 warriors included Blain's Indians.

[38]Captain Ross named the boy for his friend Neighbors. Mrs. R. S. Neighbors to K.F.N., August 30, 1948, on note appended to bottom of Evans to Neighbors, May 23, 1859.

[39]Unidentified newspaper clipping, n.d., Neighbors Letters Pvt. Coll.

[40]Catherine Darden, "Sketch of Major Neighbors," *ibid.*

[41]Bickel to Mrs. R. S. Neighbors, June 8, 1860, *ibid.*

[42]Leeper to Greenwood, September 15, 1859, Records of the Bureau of Indian Affairs, Letters Received, General Services Administration, National Archives and Records Service, Washington 25, D.C.

[43]Joseph B. Thoburn, "The Coming of the Caddos," *Sturm's Oklahoma Magazine*, XI, 1910.

[44]Burkett to Mrs. R. S. Neighbors, September 14, 1859, *ibid.*

[45]Unidentified clipping, n.d., *ibid.*; Leeper to Greenwood, September 15, 1859, *Senate Executive Documents*, 36th Cong., 1st Sess., Doc. No. 2, p. 701f. Thoburn states that the Wichita River was crossed on a raft, but the time indicates that it was the Red and another source agrees that it was Red River.

[46]*Ibid.*

[47]*Union Democrat*, n.d., Neighbors Letters, Private Collection.

[48]This was probably A. J. MacKay, listed in the 1860 census of Throckmorton County as a speculator from New York worth $28,000.

[49]Raymond Estep, "Lieutenant William E. Burnet Letters: Removal of the Texas Indians and the Founding of Fort Cobb," *The Chronicles of Oklahoma*, XXVIII, 384.

[50]Burkett to Mrs. R. S. Neighbors, September 14, 1859; newspaper clipping, Neighbors Letters, Private Collection; Dallas *Herald*, September 21, 1859.

[51]Burkett to Mrs. R. S. Neighbors, September 14, 1859, Neighbors Letters, Private Collection. The account of the assassination is from Burkett and various newspaper clippings in Neighbors Letters Private Collection, and from Dallas *Herald*, September 21, 1859.

[52]Leeper to Greenwood, September 15, 1859, Ind. Off. Let. Recd.

[53]*Union Democrat*, clipping, n.d., Neighbors Letters, Private Collection.

[54]Thoburn, "The Coming of the Caddos," *Sturm's Oklahoma Magazine*, XI.

[55]Burkett to Mrs. R. S. Neighbors, September 14, 1859, Neighbors Letters, Private Collection.

[56]Alice Atkinson (Mrs. R. S.), Neighbors to Kenneth F. Neighbours, August 21, 1948.

[57]Henry Kahn, Director of Natural Resources Records Division, National Archives, Washington, D. C., to Kenneth F. Neighbours, July 13, 1948; John Collier, Commissioner of Indian Affairs, to Mrs. R. S. Neighbors, Jr., October 14, 1935; L. W. Kemp to K.F.N., November 27, 1948.

[58]Captain Audrey W. Priebe, Memorial Division, Office of the Quartermaster General, Washington 25, D.C., to Kenneth F. Neighbours, August 3, 1948.

[59]Charles Atkinson to Alice Atkinson (Mrs. R.S.) Neighbors, Jr., March 25, 1935. Atkinson later pointed out the vault to the present writer.

[60]Mrs. R. S. Neighbors, Jr., to Kenneth F. Neighbours, July 29, 1948.

[61]Joseph Carroll McConnell, *The West Texas Frontier*, I, 280f.

[62]*San Antonio Herald*, n.d., Neighbors Letters, Private Collection. On August 9, 1962, the writer and others on the recommendation of R. N. Richardson and George Hill of the Texas State Historical Survey Committee and the Young County Historical Survey Committee moved the state marker to the vault in the civilian cemetery.

[63]*Union Democrat*, n.d., Neighbors Letters, Private Collection.

[64]Thoburn, "The Coming of the Caddos," *Sturm's Oklahoma Magazine*, XI, 1910.

[65]Order of Bexar County District Court, September 25, 1859, *ibid.*

[66]Unidentified newspaper clipping, n.d., *ibid.*

[67]*Union Democrat*, n.d., Neighbors Letters, private collection.

[68]Clipping from an unidentified San Antonio paper, *ibid.*

[69]J. Evetts Haley, *Charles Goodnight: Cowman and Plainsman*, p. 223.

[70]Houston to Thompson, Austin, May 1, 1860, Amelia Williams and Eugene C. Barker (eds.), *The Writings of Sam Houston* (Austin, University of Texas Press, 1938), VIII, 38.

[71]Burnet to Burnet, Camp on Red River, n.d. Raymond Estep (ed.),

"Lieutenant William E. Burnet Letters: Removal of the Texas Indians and the Founding of Fort Cobb," Part II, *The Chronicles of Oklahoma*, XXXVIII, 384.

[72]Leeper to Greenwood. September 15, 1859, *Senate Executive Documents*, 36th Congress, 1st Session, Document No. 2, p. 702.

[73]J. M. Smith to editor of unidentified paper, Neighbors Letters, Private Collection.

[74]Minutes of District Court of Young County, Friday, May 25, 1860, I, 58.

[75]Leeper to Greenwood, September 15, 1859, *Senate Executive Documents*, 36th Congress, 1st Session, Document No. 2, p. 702.

[76]J. M. Smith to editor of unidentified paper, Neighbors Letters, Private Collection.

[77]Murphy to Brown, August 4, 1859, Governors Letters, MS, Archives Division of the Texas State Library, Austin, Texas; Sturm to Ross, May 8, 1859, Indian Office Letters Received.

[78]Greenwood to Thompson, *Senate Executive Documents*, 36th Congress, 1st Session, Document No. 2, p. 383.

[79]*Daily National Intelligencer*, Washington, D.C., September 30, 1850.

[80]Randolph B. Marcy, *Thirty Years of Army Life on the Border*, p. 223.

[81]Quoted in Howard Lackman, "The Howard-Neighbors Controversy: A Cross-Section in West Texas Indian Affairs," *Panhandle-Plains Historical Review*, XXV, 16. H. Bailey Carroll to K.F.N.

[82]W. K. Baylor, "The Old Frontier: Events of Long Ago," *The Bloody Trail in Texas*, after 1924.

[83]Murphy to Secretary of War, November 15, 1859, Indian Office Letters Received.

[84]Parker Johnson to Earl Veal, Fort Belknap. Veal to Kenneth F. Neighbours, March 12, 1948.

[85]Ross to Greenwood, May 5, 1860, Indian Office Letters Received; J. S. (John Shirley) to Bickel, December 10, 1859, Indian Affairs Papers, 1845-1859, Archives Division, Texas State Library, Austin, Texas.

[86]Minutes of Young County District Court, I, 58.

[87]*Ibid.*, 57.

[88]Carrie J. Crouch, *Young County: History and Biography*, p. 157.

[89]Blain to Greenwood, February 3, 1860, Indian Office Letters Received.

[90]McConnell, *West Texas Frontier*, I, 333f.

[91]The Dallas *Herald*, June 6, 1860.
Tradition says M. T. Johnson's Texas Rangers were in on the kill. James Pike, *Scout and Ranger: Being the personal adventures of James Pike of the Texas Rangers in 1859-1860*, xvi; Webb, *The Texas Rangers: A Century of Frontier Defense*.

[92]Vance and Brother to Buell, September 25, 1859, Ind. Off. Let. Recd.

[93]Grayson to Leeper, December 13, 1859, San Antonio, *ibid.*

[94]Grayson to Greenwood, San Antonio, January 9, 1860, *ibid.*

[95]John J. Cisco to Greenwood, February 2, 1860, *ibid.*

[96]Ford, Memoirs (MS), IV, 741.

[97]Grayson to Greenwood, January 7, 1860, Ind. Off. Let. Recd.

[98]For the location and condition of the Texas Indians in Oklahoma, see Muriel H. Wright, *A Guide to the Indian Tribes of Oklahoma.*

[99]Clipping in unidentified paper, n.d., Neighbors Let. Pvt. Coll.

[100]Salmon to Houston, June 25, 1860, Ranger Papers, Texas State Archives, Austin, Texas.

[101]Elkins, *Indian Fighting on the Texas Frontier*, 28.

[102]Baylor, "The Old Frontier: Events of Long Ago," *The Bloody Trail in Texas.*

[103]The 1860 census indicated his widow had real estate valued at $25,000 and personal estate of $5,000.

[104]W. W. Newcomb, Jr., "Major Robert S. Neighbors," *The Mustang*, Vol. 2, p. 64.

Bibliography
Primary Sources

Manuscripts

Army Papers, Texas State Archives, Austin, Texas.

Barry, James Buckner, James Buckner Barry Papers, 1848-1912, Library of the University of Texas, Archives Division.

Baylor Family Letters, 1838-1858, photostatic copies in the Library of The University of Texas, Archives Division.

Baylor, John R., Miscellaneous Personal Letters, originals in possession of Mildred Burrows Garrett, San Antonio, Texas, photostatic copies in the Library of The University of Texas, Archives Division.

Caperton, John C., Sketch of Colonel John C. Hays, MS, Library of The University of Texas, Archives Division.

Cartographic Records, National Archives, Washington, D.C.

Comptroller Military Service Records, Texas State Archives, Austin, Texas.

Dashiell Letters, Library of The University of Texas, Archives Division.

Domestic Correspondence, Texas State Archives, Austin, Texas.

Enlistment Papers, Texas State Archives, Austin, Texas.

Erath, George Bernard, Memoirs of Major George Bernard Erath, MS, Library of The University of Texas, Archives Division.

Executive Record Book No. 39 (III/24), Texas State Archives, Austin, Texas.

Executive Record Book No. 40 (III/26), Texas State Archives, Austin, Texas.

Files of Land Grant Records, General Land Office, Austin, Texas.

Ford, John S., Ford's Correspondence, 1860-1865, Texas State Archives, Austin, Texas.

Ford, John S., John C. Hays in Texas, MS, Library of The University of Texas, Archives Division.

Ford, John S., Memoirs of John Salmon Ford, MS, Library of The University of Texas, Archives Division.

Governors Letters, 1846-1860, Texas State Archives, Austin, Texas.

Hamrick, Edward, Edward Hamrick Papers, Library of The University of Texas, Archives Division.

Indian Affairs Papers, 1835-1860, Texas State Archives, Austin, Texas.

Indian Office Letters Received, National Archives, Washington, D.C., photostatic copies in the Library of The University of Texas, Archives Division.

Indian Office Letters Sent, National Archives, Washington, D.C., photostatic copies in the Library of The University of Texas, Archives Division.

Johnston, Albert Sidney, Albert Sidney Johnston Papers, Tulane University Archives.

Lackman Papers, Howard Lackman's Private Collection, The University of Texas at Arlington.

Letter File, General Land Office, Austin, Texas.

"Lista de los Destinos militares," Provincias Internas Relaciones de Oriente y Occidente Tomo 188, Archivo General de la Nación, Palacio Nacional, Mexico.

Maverick, Mary A., Memoirs of Mary A. Maverick, MS, Library of The University of Texas, Archives Division.

Maverick, Samuel A., Journal of the Chihuahua Expedition, MS, Library of The University of Texas, Archives Division.

Maverick, Samuel A., Diary of Samuel Augustus Maverick, MS, Library of The University of Texas, Archives Division.

Maverick, Samuel A., Sam Maverick Papers, 1850-1859, Library of The University of Texas, Archives Division.

Military Papers, Texas State Archives, Austin, Texas.

Minutes of the Bexar County District Court, San Antonio, Texas, 1859.

Minutes of the District Court of Young County, Graham, Texas, I, 1856-1860.

Minutes of Harmony Lodge, No. 6, Scottish Rite Temple, Galveston, Texas, microfilm copies in possession of James D. Carter, Austin, Texas.

Minutes of Holland Lodge, No. 1, Scottish Rite Temple, Houston, Texas.

Minutes of St. Albans Lodge, No. 28, Archives of St. Albans Lodge No. 28, Jackson, Louisiana.

Muster Roll Book, MS, General Land Office, Austin, Texas.

Neighbors Letters, Private Collection, Texas Memorial Museum, Austin, Texas, photostatic copies of a few of the documents in Library of The University of Texas, Archives Division.

Neighbors, R. S., Quartermaster Accounts and Vouchers, 1839-1841, Texas State Archives, Austin, Texas.

Probate Minutes of Bexar County, San Antonio, Texas.

Proclamations and Colony Contracts No. 48 (IV/57), Texas State Archives, Austin, Texas.

Public Debt Papers, Texas State Archives, Austin, Texas.

Quartermaster Papers, Texas State Archives, Austin, Texas.

Ranger Papers, Texas State Archives, Austin, Texas.

Records of the Bureau of Census, Seventh Census, National Archives, microfilm copy in the Library of The University of Texas, Eugene C. Barker Texas History Center.

Record Book, Bureau of Indian Affairs, 1842-1843, MS, Texas State Archives, Austin, Texas.

Records of the Memorial Division, Office of the Quartermaster General, Washington, D.C.

Records of the Natural Resources Records Division, National Archives, Washington, D.C.

Records of the War Department, Letters Received, National Archives, Washington, D.C.

Records of the War Department, National Archives, Washington, D.C.

Santa Fe Expedition Papers, Parts I and II, Texas State Archives, Austin, Texas.

Solms-Braunfels Archive, Library of The University of Texas, Archives Division. Seventy volumes, Typed by Mrs. Bertha Brandt.

Treasury Letters, Military, Texas State Archives, Austin, Texas.

Will Books, Nos. 4 and 5, Charlotte County Court House, Charlotte, Virginia, Young County Court Records, I, 1856-1860.

Printed

Abel, Annie Heloise, (ed.), *Official Correspondence of James S. Calhoun*, Washington, Government Printing Office, 1915.

Annual Report of the Commissioner of Indian Affairs, 1854, Washington, A.O.P. Nicholson, Printer, 1855.

Armstrong, Robert, *Proceedings of the Democratic National Convention Held at Baltimore, June 1-5, 1852*, Washington, Robert Armstrong, 1852.

Barry, James Buckner (James K. Greer, ed.), *A Texas Ranger and Frontiersman: The Days of Buck Barry in Texas, 1845-1906*, Dallas Southwest Press, 1932.

Baylor, W. K., "The Old Frontier: Events of Long Ago," *The Bloody Trail in Texas*, Bandera, Marvin Hunter, n.d., after 1924.

Brown, John Henry, *History of Texas*, St. Louis, Becktold & Co., 1893.

Brown, John Henry, *Indian Wars and Pioneers of Texas*, Austin, L. E. Daniel, 1896.

Burleson, Richard A. (Ed.), *The Life and Writings of Rufus Burleson*, n.p., n.d., Georgia J. Burleson, Publisher, 1901.

Carl, Prince of Salme-Braunfels, *Texas, 1844-1845*, Houston, The Anson Jones Press, 1936.

Chabot, Frederick C., *The Perote Prisoners*, San Antonio, The Naylor Company, 1934.

Congressional Globe, 32 Congress, 1st Session, Part III.

Conover, George W., *Sixty Years in Southwest Oklahoma: or The Autobiography of George W. Conover*, Anadarko, N. T. Plummer, 1927.

De Cordova, Jacob, *Texas: Her Resources and Her Public Men*, Philadelphia, JJ. B. Lippincott & Co., 1858.

Dillon, Richard H. (ed.), *The Gila Trail: The Texan Argonauts and the California Gold Rush,* by Benjamin Butler Harris, Norman, University of Oklahoma Press, 1960.

Dubbs, Emanual, *et al, Pioneer Days in the Southwest from 1850-1879,* Gutherie, Oklahoma, The State Capitol Company, 1909.

Duval, J. C., *The Adventures of Bigfoot Wallace,* Austin, The Steck Company, reprint, 1936.

Elkins, John M., *Indian Fighting on the Texas Frontier,* Amarillo, Russell & Cockrell, 1935.

Executive Documents, 31st Congress, 1st Session.

Falconer, Thomas, *Texas Santa Fe Expedition, 1841-1842,* New York, Dauber & Pine Bookshops, Inc., reprint, 1930.

Gammel, H. P. N., *The Laws of Texas,* Austin, 1898, Ten volumes.

General Regulations for the Government of the Army of the Republic of Texas, Houston, Intelligencer Office, Sam Whiting, Printer, 1839.

Green, Thomas Jefferson, *Journal of the Texian Expedition Against Mier,* New York, Harper & Brothers, 1845.

Green, Rena Maverick (ed.), *Samuel Maverick: Texan 1803-1870, A Collection of Letters, Journals and San Antonio,* privately printed, 1952.

House Executive Documents, 30th Congress, 1st Session; 31st Congress, 1st. Session; 31st Congress, 2d Session.

House Journal Texas, Fourth Legislature, Regular Session, 1851-1852, Austin, State Gazette, 1852.

Journal of the House of Representatives of the State of Texas, Fourth Legislature, Extra Session, Published by authority, Austin, J. W. Hampton, State Printer, 1853.

Ledbetter, Barbara Neal, (ed.), *The Diary of a Frontiersman, 1858-1859,* Newcastle (Author), 1962.

Marcy, Randolph Barnes, *The Prairie Traveler: A Hand-Book for Overland Expeditions,* New York, Harper & Brothers, 1859.

Marcy, Randolph Barnes, *Thirty Years of Army Life on the Border,* New York, Harper & Brothers, 1866.

Parker, William B., *Notes Taken During the Expedition Through Unexplored Texas,* Philadelphia, Hays & Zell, 1856.

Pike, James, *Scout and Ranger: Being the Personal Adventures of*

James Pike of the Texas Rangers in 1859-60, Princeton, Princeton University Press, 1932.

Pratt, Willie W. (ed.), *Galveston Island: The Journal of Francis C. Sheridan*, Austin, University of Texas Press, 1954.

Proceedings of the Grand Royal Arch Chapter of the Republic of Texas, 1841-1849, Houston, Dealy and Baker, 1897.

Roemer, Ferdinand, *Texas, Mit besonderer Rucksicht auf deutsche Auswanderung und die physischen Verhaltnisse des Landes*, Bonn, bei Adolph Marcus, 1849.

Roemer, Ferdinand, *Texas, with particular reference to German immigration and the physical appearance of the country*, Translated from the German by Oswald Mueller, San Antonio, Standard Printing Company, 1935.

Report of the Commissioner of Indian Affairs, 1856, Washington, A. O. P. Nicholson, Printer, 1857.

Roberts, O. M., *Texas*, Atlanta, Confederate Publishing Company, 1899.

Schoolcraft, Henry R., *Information Respecting the History, Condition and Prospects of the Indian Tribes of the United States*, Part II, Philadelphia.

Senate Executive Documents, 31st Congress, 1st Session; 33d Congress, 2d Session; 34th Congress, 1st Session; 35th Congress, 1st Session; 35th Congress, 2nd Session; 36th Congress, 1st Session.

Senate Journal, Third Legislature, Extra Session, Austin, 1850.

Smithwick, Noah, *Evolution of a State: Or Recollections of Old Texas Days*, Austin, The Steck Company, reprint, 1935.

Sorgel, Alwin H., *Neueste Nachrichten aus Texas. Zugleich ein Hülferuf an den Mainzer Verein zum Schutze deutscher Einwanderer in Texas*, Eisleben, G. Reichardt, 1847.

Sowell, A. J., *Rangers and Pioneers of Texas*, San Antonio, Shepard Brothers & Co., 1885.

Stapp, William P., *The Prisoners of Perote*, Philadelphia, G. B. Zieber and Company, 1845.

Supreme Court of the United States, October term, 1894, No. 4, Original, The United States, Complainant, vs. The State of Texas, in Equity, Washington, 1894, I.

Thrall, Homer Spellman, *History of Methodism in Texas*, Houston, E. H. Cushing, 1872.

Treaties Between the United States and Indian Tribes, Richard Peters (ed.), Boston, Little, Brown, and Company, 1861.

United States Statutes at Large, 1845-1851, IX, Boston, Little, Brown, and Company, 1855.

Williams, Amelia W., and Eugene C. Barker (eds.). *The Writings of Sam Houston*, Austin, University of Texas Press, 1938-1943, Eight volumes.

Winkler, E. W., *Secret Journals of the Senate, Republic of Texas, 1836-1845*, Austin, Austin Printing Company, 1911.

Wurzbach, Emil Frederick, *Life and Memoirs of Emil Frederick Wurzbach: To which is appended some papers of John Meusebach*, Translated by Frantz J. Dolmen.

Newspapers

Austin City *Gazette*, Austin, 1841-1842.

Daily National Intelligencer, Washington, 1859.

Daily Texian, Austin, 1842.

Dallas *Herald*, Dallas, 1856-1859.

Graham *Leader*, Graham, Texas, 1876-1878.

Mercantile Advertiser, Houston, December 29, 1849, original in Library of Congress.

Northern Standard, Clarkesville, Texas, 1842-1859.

The *Missouri Republican*, Saint Louis, October 4, 1854.

The New Orleans *Picayune*, October 9, 1854.

San Antonio *Herald*, San Antonio, 1854.

San Antonio *Ledger*, San Antonio, 1858.

Telegraph and Texas Register, Houston, 1842-1852.

Texas Democrat, Austin, 1849.

Texas National Register, Washington-on-the Brazos, 1844-1845.

Texas Sentenel, Austin, 1840-1858.

Texas State Gazette, Austin, 1849-1855.

Tri Weekly Star, San Antonio, 1854.

Periodicals

Cox, C. C., "Reminiscences of C. C. Cox," *The Quarterly of the Texas Historical Association*, VI

Crimmins, M. L., (ed.), "Colonel J.K.F. Mansfields Report of the Inspection of the Department of Texas in 1856," *Southwestern Historical Quarterly*, XLII.

Crimmins, M. L., "Freeman's Report of the Eighth Military Department," *Southwestern Historical Quarterly*, LI-LIV, 1947-1951.

Estep, Raymond, "Lieutenant William E. Burnet, "Letters: Removal of the Texas Indians and the Founding of Fort Cobb," *The Chronicles of Oklahoma*, XXXVIII.

Estep, Raymond, "Lieutenant W. E. Burnett [sic]: Notes on Removal of Indians from Texas to Indian Territory," *The Chronicles of Oklahoma*, XXXVIII.

Harrison, Jeanne V., "Matthew Leeper Condeferate Agent at the Wichita Agency, Indian Territory," *The Chronicles of Oklahoma*, XLVII.

Kleberg, Rosa, "Early Experiences in Texas," *Texas Historical Association Quarterly*, II, 172.

Ritchie, E. B., "Copy of Report of Colonel Samuel Cooper, Assistant Adjutant General of the United States, of Inspection Trip from Fort Graham to the Indian villages on the Upper Brazos made in June, 1851," *Southwestern Historical Quarterly*, XLII, 327, ff.

Roland, Charles P., and Richard C. Robbins, "The Diary of Eliza (Mrs. Albert Sidney) Johnson: The Second Cavalry Comes to Texas," *Southwestern Historical Quarterly*, LX.

Trahern, George Washington, A Russell Buchanan (ed.), "Texan Cowboy from Mier to Buena Vista," *Southwestern Historical Quarterly*, LVIII.

Secondary Sources

Books

Allen, J. Taylor, *Early Pioneer Days in Texas*, Dallas, Wilkinson Printing Co., 1918.

Bancroft, Hubert Howe, *The North Mexican States and Texas*, II, San Francisco, History Company, 1889.

Barker, Eugene C., Charles Shirley Potts, and Charles W. Ransdell, *A School History of Texas*, Chicago and New York, Row, Peterson, and Company, 1913.

Barker, Eugene C., *Stephen F. Austin: The Father of Texas*, Austin.

Biesele, Rudolph Leopold, *History of the German Settlements in Texas*, Austin, Von Boeckmann-Jones Company, 1930.

Biggers, Don H., *German Pioneers in Texas*, Fredericksburg, Publishing Company, 1925.

Binkley, W. C., *The Expansionist Movement in Texas*, Berkeley, University of California Press, 1915.

Biographical Directory of the Texan Conventions and Congresses, 1832-1845, Austin, 1941.

Carroll, H. Bailey, *The Texan Santa Fe Expedition*, Canyon, Texas, Panhandle-Plains Historical Society, 1951.

Conkling, Roscoe P. and Margaret B., *The Butterfield Mail, 1857-1869*, Glendale, California, The Arthur H. Clark Company, 1947.

Corwin, Hugh D., *The Kiowa Indians: Their History and Life Stories*, Lawton (author), 1958.

Crouch, Carrie J., *Young County: History and Biography*, Dallas, Dealey and Lowe, 1937.

DeShields, James T., *Border Wars of Texas*, Tioga, Herald Company, 1912.

DeShields, James T., *Cynthia Ann Parker*, San Antonio, Texas, The Naylor Company, 1934.

Dictionary of American History, James Truslow Adams, (ed.), III, New York, Charles Scribner's Sons, 1940.

Fabila, Alfonso, *La Tribu Kikapoo de Coahuila*, Mexico, Secretaria de Educacion Publica, 1945.

Ford, Fred Hugo and J. L. Brown, *Larissa*, N. p., McFarland Publishing Company, 1951.

Foreman, Carolyn Thomas, *The Cross Timbers*, Muskogee, Oklahoma, The Star Printery, 1947.

Freeman, Douglas Southall, *R. E. Lee: A Biography*, New York, Charles Scribner's Sons, 1948, Four volumes.

Friend, Llerena, *Sam Houston: The Great Designer*, Austin, University of Texas Press, 1954.

Gambrell, Herbert, *Anson Jones: The Last President of Texas*, Garden City, New York, Doubleday and Company, Inc., 1948.

Ganoe, William Addleman, *The History of the United States Army*, New York, D. Appleton-Century Company, 1943.

Haley, J. Evetts, *Charles Goodnight: Cowman and Plainsman*, Norman, University of Oklahoma Press, second printing 1949.

Haley, J. Evetts, *Ford Concho and The Texas Frontier*, San Angelo, San Angelo *Standard-Times*, 1952.

Haley, J. Evetts, *The XIT Ranch in Texas*, Chicago, The Lakeside Press, 1929.

Hawkins, Walace, *The Case of John C. Watrous: United States Judge for Texas*, Dallas, University Press in Dallas, 1950.

Hodge, Frederick Webb, *Handbook of American Indians North of Mexico*, I, Washington, D.C., Government Printing Office, 1907.

Hollon, W. Eugene, *Beyond the Cross Timbers: The Travels of Randolph B. Marcy*, Norman, University of Oklahoma Press, 1955.

Huckabay, Ida Lasater, *Ninety-Four Years in Jack County, 1854-1948*, Austin, The Steck Company, 1949.

Kemp, L. W., and S. H. Dixon, *The Heroes of San Jacinto*, Houston, The Anson Jones Press, 1932.

King, Irene Marschall, *John O. Meusebach: German Colonizer in Texas*, Austin, University of Texas Press, 19.

Knight, Oliver, *Fort Worth: Outpost on the Trinity*, Norman, University of Oklahoma Press, 1953.

Members of the Legislature of the State of Texas from 1846 to 1939, n.p., n.d.

Nance, Joseph Milton, *After San Jacinto: The Texas-Mexican Frontier, 1836-1841*, Austin, Texas, University of Texas Press, 1963.

Phelan, Macum, *A History of Early Methodism in Texas, 1817-1866*, Dallas, Cokesbury Press, 1924.

Poldervoar, Arie W., *Black-Robed Justice: A History of the Administration of Justice in New Mexico*, Santa Fe, 1940.

Post Register, Lockhart, Texas, July 29, 1937.

Quinby, J. R., *et al*, *Grain Sorghum Production in Texas*, Bulletin 912, College Station, Texas, Texas Agricultural Experiment Station, July, 1958.

Richardson, Rupert Norval, *The Comanche Barrier to South Plains Settlement: A Century and a Half of Savage Resistance to the Advancing White Frontier*, Glendale, California, The Arthur H. Clark Company, 1933.

Richardson, Rupert Norval, *Texas: The Lone Star State*, New York, Prentice-Hall, Inc., 1943.

Rister, Carl Coke, *Border Captives: The Traffic in Prisoners by Southern Plains Indians, 1835-1875*, Norman, University of Oklahoma Press, 1940.

Rister, Carl Coke, *Robert E. Lee in Texas*, Norman, University of Oklahoma Press, 1946.

Simmons, Frank E., *History of Coryell County*, Gatesville, Coryell County News, 1936.

Streeter, Thomas B., *Bibliography of Texas, 1795-1845: Part III, United States and European Imprints Relating to Texas, Volume II, 1838-1845*, Cambridge, Harvard University Press, 1960.

Thoburn, Joseph B., and Isaac M. Hoscomb, *A History of Oklahoma*, San Francisco, Doub & Company, 1934.

Thrall, Homer Spellman, *A Pictorial History of Texas*, St. Louis, N. D. Thomas & Company, 1879.

Twitchell, Ralph Emerson, *The History of the Military Occupation of New Mexico from 1846 to 1851*, Denver, Colorado, The Smith-Brooks Company, 1909.

Van Horne, Thomas B., *The Life of Major-General George H. Thomas*, New York, Charles Scribner's Sons, 1882.

Vestal, Stanley, *Bigfoot Wallace*, Boston, Houghton Mifflin Company, 1942.

Wade, Houston, *Notes and Fragments of the Mier Expedition*, LaGrange Journal, Second Edition, 1937.

Wallace, Edward S., *General William Jenkins Worth*, Dallas, Southern Methodist University Press, 1953.

Wallace, Ernest and E. Adamson Hoebel, *The Comanches: Lords of the South Plains*, Norman, University of Oklahoma Press, 1952.

Webb, Walter Prescott, and H. Bailey Carroll (eds.), *Handbook of Texas*, Austin, The Texas State Historical Association, 1952.

Webb, Walter Prescott, *The Great Plains*, New York, Ginn and Company, 1931.

Webb, Walter Prescott, *The Texas Rangers: A Century of Frontier Defense*, New York, Houghton Mifflin Company, 1935.

Wharton, Clarence, *What Became of Judge Baird*, Houston, The Anson Jones Press, 1940.

Wilbarger, J. W., *Indian Depredations in Texas*, Austin, Hutchings Printing House, 1890.

Winkler, Ernest William, *Platforms of Political Parties in Texas*, Austin, University of Texas Press, 1916.

Wooten, Dudley G., *A Comprehensive History of Texas*, Dallas, William G. Scarff, 1898.

Wright, Muriel H., *A Guide to the Indian Tribes of Oklahoma*, Norman, University of Oklahoma Press, 1951.

Wright, Muriel H., *Story of Oklahoma*, Oklahoma City, Webb Publishing Company, 1929-30.

Yoakum, Henderson, *History of Texas*, New York, Redfield, 1856.

Periodicals

Banks, C. S., "Mormon Migration into Texas," *Southwestern Historical Quarterly*, XXIV.

Bender, A. B., "Opening Routes Across West Texas, 1848-1856," *Southwestern Historical Quarterly*, XXXVII, 1934.

Binkley, W. C., "Activities of the Texas Army after San Jacinto," *Journal of Southern History*, VI, 1940.

Binkley, W. C., "Question of Texas Jurisdiction in New Mexico Under the United States, 1845-1850," *Southwestern Historical Quarterly*, XXIV.

Clarke, Fannie McAlpine, "A Chapter in the History of Young Territory," *Texas Historical Association Quarterly*, IX.

Crimmins, M. L., "Major Van Dorn in Texas," *West Texas Historical Association Year Book*, XVI.

Foreman, Grant, "The Texas Comanche Treaty of 1846," *Southwestern Historical Quarterly*, LI, 1938.

Geiser, S. W., "List of Masonic Lodges Founded in Texas, Chartered 1838-1880, which later demised," *Southwestern Historical Quarterly*, XL.

Greenwood, "Opening Routes to El Paso in 1849," *Southwestern Historical Quarterly*, XLVIII.

Huber, Armin O., "Frederick Armand Strubberg, Alias Dr. Shubbert, Town-Builder, physician and adventurer, 1806-1899," *West Texas Historical Association Year Book*, XXXVIII.

Koch, Lena Clara, "The Federal Indian Policy in Texas, 1845-1860," *Southwestern Historical Quarterly*, XXVIII, XXIX, 1925-1926.

Lackman, Howard, "The Howard-Neighbors Controversy: A Cross-Section in West Texas Indian Affairs," *Panhandle-Plains Historical Review*, XXV.

McGrath, J. J., and Wallace Hawkins, "Perote Fort—Where Texans Were Imprisoned," *Southwestern Historical Quarterly*, XLVIII.

Mahon, John K., "Civil War Infantry Assault Tactics," *Military Affairs*, XXV.

Muckelroy, Anna, "The Indian Policy of the Republic of Texas," *Southwestern Historical Quarterly*, XXV, XXVI, 1922-1923.

Nance, James Milton, "Brigadier General Adrian Woll's Report of His Expedition into Texas in 1842," *The Southwestern Historical Quarterly*, LVIII.

Neighbours, Kenneth F., "The Expedition of Major Robert S. Neighbors to El Paso in 1849," *Southwestern Historical Quarterly*, LVIII.

Neighbours, Kenneth Franklin, "The Marcy-Neighbors Exploration of the Headwaters of the Brazos and Wichita Rivers in 1854," *Panhandle-Plains Historical Review*, XVII.

Neighbours, Kenneth F., "Masons and Texas Indian Schools," *Texas Grand Lodge Magazine*, XXVI.

Neighbours, Kenneth F., "Robert S. Neighbors, Texan," *Texas Grand Lodge Magazine*, 1952.

Newcomb, Jr., W. W., "Major Robert S. Neighbors," *The Mustang*, vol. 2.

Richardson, Rupert Norval, "Jim Shaw the Delaware," *West Texas Historical Association Year Book*, III.

Richardson, Rupert Norval, "Removal of Indians from Texas in 1853: A Fiasco," *West Texas Historical Association Year Book*, XX, 1944.

Shuffler, R. Henderson, "Christmas in the Cross Timbers," *Texas Parade*, December, 1964, 10-13.

Strecker, John K., "Chronicles of George Barnard," *The Baylor Bulletin*, Waco, Baylor University Press, 1928.

Tolbert, Frank X., "Wisconsin Tribe Lives in Mexico," The Dallas *Morning News*, April 9, 1961.

Tyler, George W., "Capture and Release of Colonel Norris's Party by Chief Jose Maria—A Masonic Incident—1838," Sue Watkins (ed.), *One League to Each Wind: Accounts of Early Surveying in Texas*, [1964].

Williams, J. W., and Ernest Lee, "Marcy's Exploration to Locate the Texas Indian Reservations in 1854," *West Texas Historical Association Year Book*, XXIII.

Williams, J. W., "Military Roads of the 1850's in Central West Texas," *West Texas Historical Association Year Book*, XVIII, 1942.

Williams, O. W., "From Dallas to the Site of Lubbock in 1877," *West Texas Historical Association Year Book*, XV, 1939.

Winkler, S. W., "The Bexar and Dawson Prisoners," *Texas Historical Association Quarterly*, XIII, 292-324.

Unpublished Theses, etc.

Affleck, John D., History of John C. Hays, MS, Library of the University of Texas, Archives Division.

Barrett, Arrie, Federal Military Outposts, Texas, 1846-1861, MS, M. A. Thesis, University of Texas, Archives Division.

Brown, Frank, Annals of Travis County and of the City of Austin, MS, Texas State Archives, Austin, Texas.

Clark, Mrs. L. R., unpublished manuscript, L. S. Ross Papers, Baylor University.

Havins, T. R., Noah T. Byers, MS, Ph. D. Dissertation, The University of Texas, 1941.

Mayhall, Mildred Pickle, Indians of Texas: The Atakapa, the Karankawa, the Tonkawa, MS, Ph. D. Dissertation, The University of Texas, 1939.

Neighbors, Alice Atkinson, Life and Public Works of Robert S. Neighbors, MS, M. A. Thesis, The University of Texas, 1936.

Neighbours, Kenneth F., Robert S. Neighbors in Texas, 1836-1859: A Quarter Century of Frontier Problems, MS, doctoral dissertation, The University of Texas, 1955.

Noel, Virginia P., The United States Indian Reservations in Texas, 1845-1849, MS, M. A. Thesis, The University of Texas, 1924.

Ogier, W. C., Settlement of the Texas-New Mexico Boundary Dispute, MS, M. A. Thesis, University of Texas, 1929.

Walker, Charles Summerfield, A History of the Confederate Territory of Arizona, MS, M. A. Thesis, Southern Methodist University, 1933.

Winkler, Ernest William, History of the Cherokee Indians in Texas, MS, M. A. Thesis, The University of Texas, 1901.

Maps

A New Map of Texas, E. Yeager, Galveston, 1840, Letters from Collectors of Customs to the Secretary of Treasury (RG 56), The National Archives, Washington, D.C.

Captain Marcy's Map of Red River, Records of the Office of the Chief of Engineers, Map Q74, The National Archives, Washington, D.C.

Colton's New Map of the State of Texas, compiled from J. De Cordova's large Map (date illegible, but after 1858), Library of The University of Texas, Archives Division.

General Highway Maps of Oklahoma Counties, prepared by the Oklahoma Department of Highways in cooperation with the U. S. Department of Commerce, Bureau of Public Roads, N.D.

General Highway Maps of Texas Counties prepared by the Texas State Highway Department in cooperation with the U. S. Department of Commerce, Bureau of Public Roads, 1951-1955.

General Land Office Maps of Texas Counties Showing the Location of Land Grants, General Land Office, Austin, Texas.

General Land Office Map of Texas, Austin, 1951.

J. De Cordova's Map of the State of Texas, Compiled from the records of the General Land Office of the State by Robert Creuzbaur, Houston, 1849, Library of The University of Texas, Archives Division.

Map of the Country upon the Brazos and Big Witchita River Explored by Captain R. B. Marcy 5th U.S. Infy. Embracing the Lands appropriated by the State of Texas for the Use of the Indians, The National Archives, Washington, D.C.

Map of the Frontier of the 8th Mil. Dept., Topl. Office, 8th Mil. Dept. (signed) J. E. Johnston, Lt. Col. by Bvt., Records of the Office of the Chief of Engineers, Headquarters Map Fil, Map No. Q 50 (RG77), The National Archives, Washington, D.C.

Map of a Route from Austin-City to Paso Del Norte &c Compiled mostly from the journal & notes taken by Dr. John S. Ford of his exploring expedition in company with Mjr. Robert S. Neighbors in March, April & May, 1849, Robert Creuzebaur, Fecit, Library of The University of Texas, Archives Division.

Map of the Route Pursued by Governor Butler from Fort Gibson to Waco Village in 1846. Photostatic copy furnished by Fred R. Cotton, Weatherford, Texas.

Map of Texas and Part of New Mexico, compiled in the Bureau of Topographl. Engrs. chiefly for military purposes, 1857, Map Q65 (RG77), The National Archives, Washington, D.C.

Map of Texas from the most recent authorities, Philadelphia, C. S. Williams, 1845, Library of The University of Texas, Archives Division.

Map of the Route to the Indian Villages on the Upper Brasos [sic], made in June 1851 by Col. Cooper & Major Sibley 2d Dragons. Drawn by Major Sibley, Library of The University of Texas, Archives Division.

No. 1 A Map to illustrate the most advantageous communication from the Gulf of Mexico and The Mississippi Valley to California and the Pacific Ocean, compiled by Robert Crewzbaur, 1849, Library of The University of Texas, Archives Division.

Plot of Itinerary Map from Fort Griffin to Bryan, Texas, March 20-April 10, 1869, Library of The University of Texas, Archives Division.

Plot of Itinerary Map from Fort Concho to Austin, March 23-April 13, 1869, Library of The University of Texas, Archives Division.

Plot of Itinerary Map from Austin to Fort Griffin, Texas, November 28-December 24, 1868, Map Files, Department Engineer, Southern Department, Fort Sam Houston, Texas, Library of The University of Texas, Archives Division.

Plot of Itinerary Map from Fort Richardson, Texas, to Waco, Texas, February 15-23, 1869, Library of the University of Texas, Archives Division.

Plot of Itinerary from Fort Concho, Texas, to Fort Sill, Indian Territory, December 8, 1873, to January 11, 1974, Map Files, Department Engineer, Southern Department, Fort Sam Houston, Texas, Library of The University of Texas, Archives Division.

Map of Central Texas Military Trails, Records of the Office of the Chief of Engineers, Headquarters Map File, Map No. Q52 (RG77), The National Archives, Washington, D.C.

Reconnoissances from San Antonio de Bexar to el Paso del Norte by Bvt. Col. [J. E.] Johnston, and of the Frontier of Texas from the False Washita to Eagle Pass, by Lieut. W. H. C. Whiting, Records of the Office of the Chief of Engineers, Headquarters Map File, Map No. U. S. 144 (RG77), The National Archives, Washington, D.C.

Sketch of the Route Taken by a Scouting Party from Phantom Hill to Double Mountain, Texas, 1852, General Land Office, Austin, Texas.

United States Department of the Interior, Geological Survey Maps of sections of Texas.

Index

Bryan, Francis T., 83.
Bryan, Guy B., 105,
   204, 212, 229.
Buchanan, James, 179, 208, 209.
Buell, D. C., 290.
Buffalo Hump, 29, 34, 36,
   39, 41, 46, 70-71, 73-74,
   112, 154, 174.
Bureau of Indian Affairs,
   Texas, 26, 28.
Bureau of Indian Affairs of the
   United States, 36, 82, 222.
Burkett, William, 175, 282,
   283, 284.
Burleson, Edward, 14, 15.
Burleson, Edward, Junior, 197.
Burnet, David G., 36.
Burnet, William E., 237-240, 287.
Buqurr, P. L., 106.
Butler, Pierce M., 28, 29,
   30, 31.
Buttorff, John F., 271.
Byars, Noah T., 239.

Caddo, 6, 30, 39, 41, 44,
   47, 111, 133, 158,
   164, 236.
Caddo, John, 243.
Caddo Village, 44.
Caldwell, Mathew, 17.
Caledonia, 216.
Calhoun, James S., 95.
Cameron family, 200.
Camp Cooper, 169, 171,
   185, 199, 204, 211,
   229, 237-238.
Camp Jackson, 274.
Camp Leon, 227, 232.
Camp Nowlin, 275.
Camp Radziminski, 213, 232.
Campo, Tonkawa Chief, 47, 195.
Canutson, Canute, 113.
Capron, Horace, 108.
Carmack, J. Y., 256.
Carnack, Joshua R., 225.
Carroll, H. Bailey,
   acknowledgements to 1.
Carrizo Mountains, 77.
Carter, C. S., 260.
Carter, De James D.,
   acknowledgements to 2, 295.
Casey Draw, 76.
Casey Spring, 77.
Castle Mountain, 75, 81.
   Picture of, 60.
Castro, Lipan leader, 114.
Cozneau, William L, 13.

Chambliss, William P., 165.
Chandler, Joseph, 193.
Cherokee, 6, 39, 45.
Cherry Canyon, 76.
Cheyenne, 144.
Chihuahua, State of,
   68-69, 74-75.
China Waterhole, 82.
Chinese Sugar Cane, 185.
Chiquito, Lipan chief,
   43, 46, 47, 114.
Choctaw, 6, 69, 80, 179.
Choctow Tom, 224, 227.
   Massacre, 223-226.
Christopher, George, 281.
Church, Samuel, 207.
Cimarron River, 213.
Cipio, Negro slave,
   218, 221, 280.
Clark, John H., 212.
Clark, Ted, 1.
Clay, Henry, 83, 89.
Clear Fork, 223.
Coffee's Trading House, 29.
Coghill, Thomas, 207.
Cola del Aguila, see
   Puerto de la.
Colquhoun, L., 22.
Comal County, 114.
Comanche, 6, 25, 26, 27,
   30, 34, 37, 41, 46,
   70-76, 80, 85, 223.
   Kotsoteka, 42, 204, 223.
   Nocona, 42, 159, 184,
      195, 197, 213.
   Peneteka, (also Hois),
      42, 34, 36, 46,
      149, 154, 163.
   Tenawish, 42, 159,
      168, 172, 204.
   Yamparico, 162.
Comanche County, 225, 227.
Comanche Peak, 29, 47, 111.
Comanche Reserve, 150, 164,
   198, 229, 232, 237-238,
   241, 245, 256.
Compromise of 1850, 83.
Conger, Roger, 2.
Congress of the Republic of
   Texas, 13, 14, 87.
   Indian land policy, 111.
Congress of the
   United States, 31, 88.
Connelley Trail, 75.
Connor, John, 30, 36,
   38, 107, 133, 137.
Connor, Dr. Seymour V., 2.
Cooke, Lewis P., 15.

343

345

347